ARINACCHI GALLERY

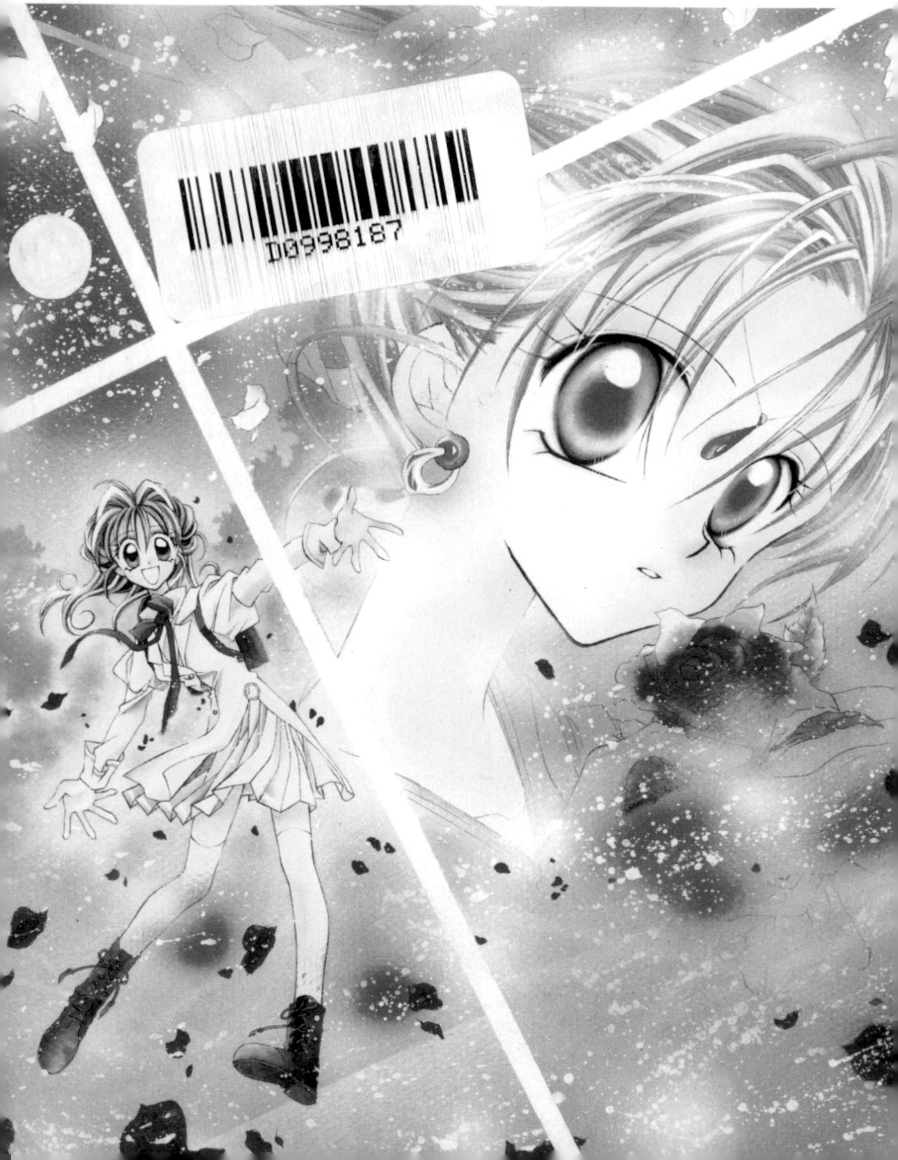

COMMENT FROM **CURATOR ARINACCHI**

This was an illustration drawn for a shikishi, so it's square. I drew it thinking of Maron walking home with her head filled with girly dreams... The background was done with pink and purple color spray. The spray has gone out of production now, so this illustration is even dearer to me because I will never be able to recreate this color.

PHANTOM THIEF
Jeanne

2

STORY AND ART BY
Arina Tanemura

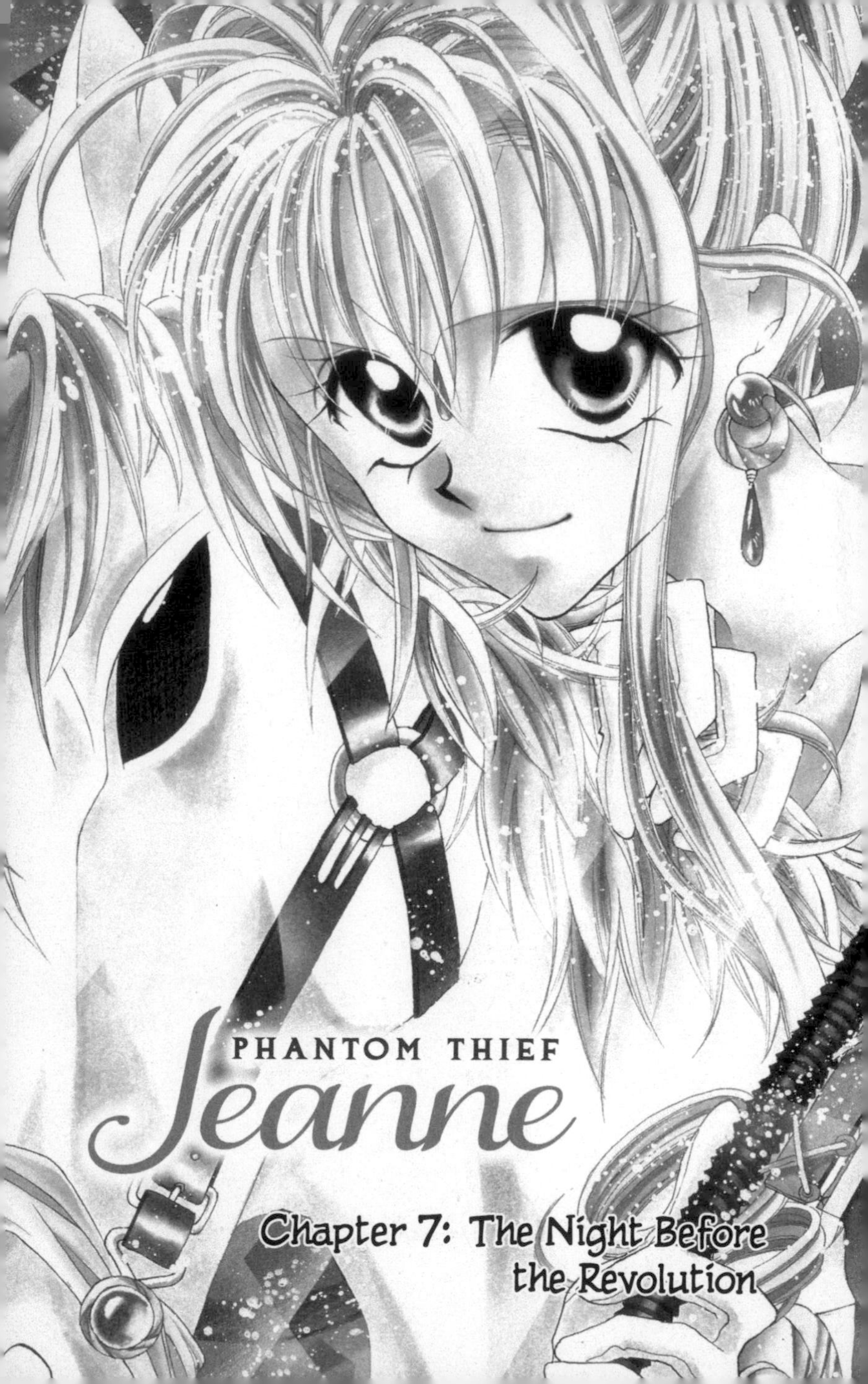
PHANTOM THIEF
Jeanne
Chapter 7: The Night Before the Revolution

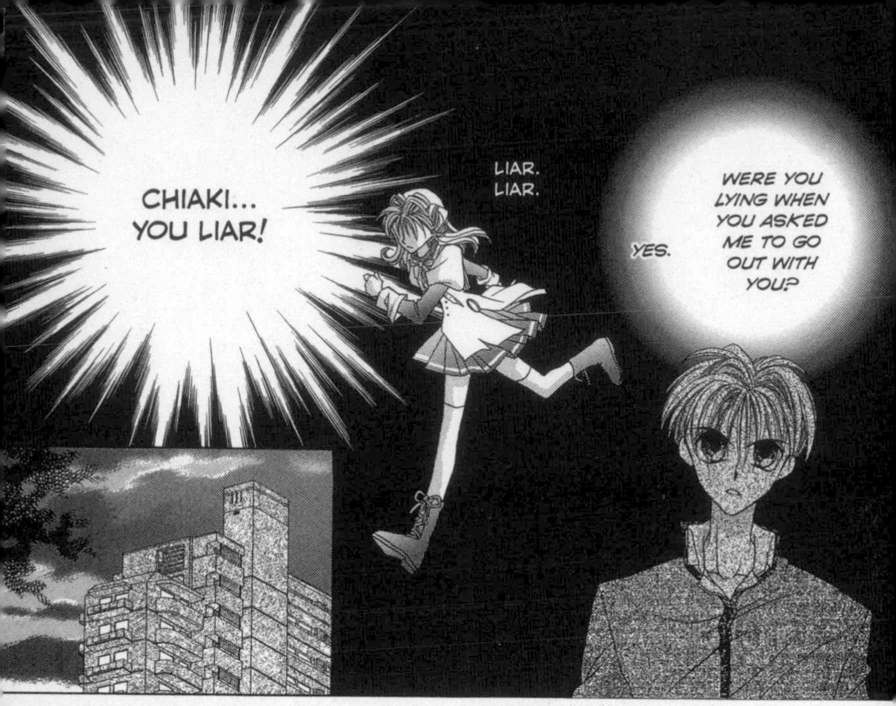
WERE YOU LYING WHEN YOU ASKED ME TO GO OUT WITH YOU?
YES.
LIAR. LIAR.
CHIAKI... YOU LIAR!

PHANTOM
THIEF
JEANNE

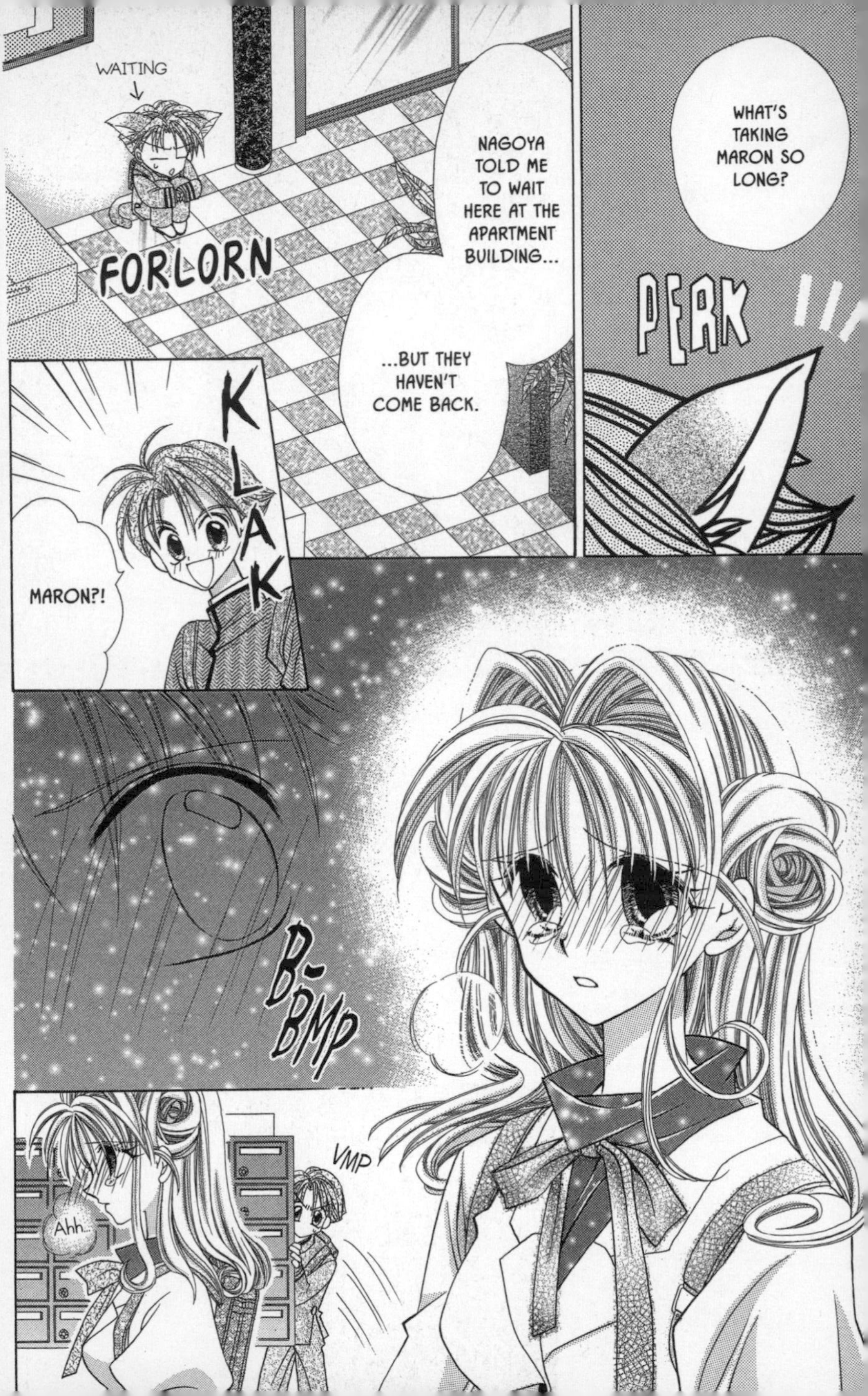
WHAT'S TAKING MARON SO LONG?
PERK
WAITING
FORLORN
NAGOYA TOLD ME TO WAIT HERE AT THE APARTMENT BUILDING...
...BUT THEY HAVEN'T COME BACK.
KLAK
MARON?!
B-BMP
VMP
Ahh...

...THIS FEELING BEFORE.

I'VE HAD...

EACH TIME I OPENED MY MAILBOX HOPING TO SEE A LETTER FROM MY PARENTS...

...I ALWAYS FELT SO BETRAYED.

PHANTOM THIEF JEANNE

I FINALLY FOUND SOME HAPPINESS...

...FROM THE LITTLE NOTES CHIAKI KEPT LEAVING ME...

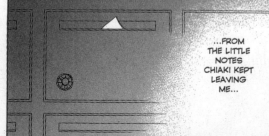

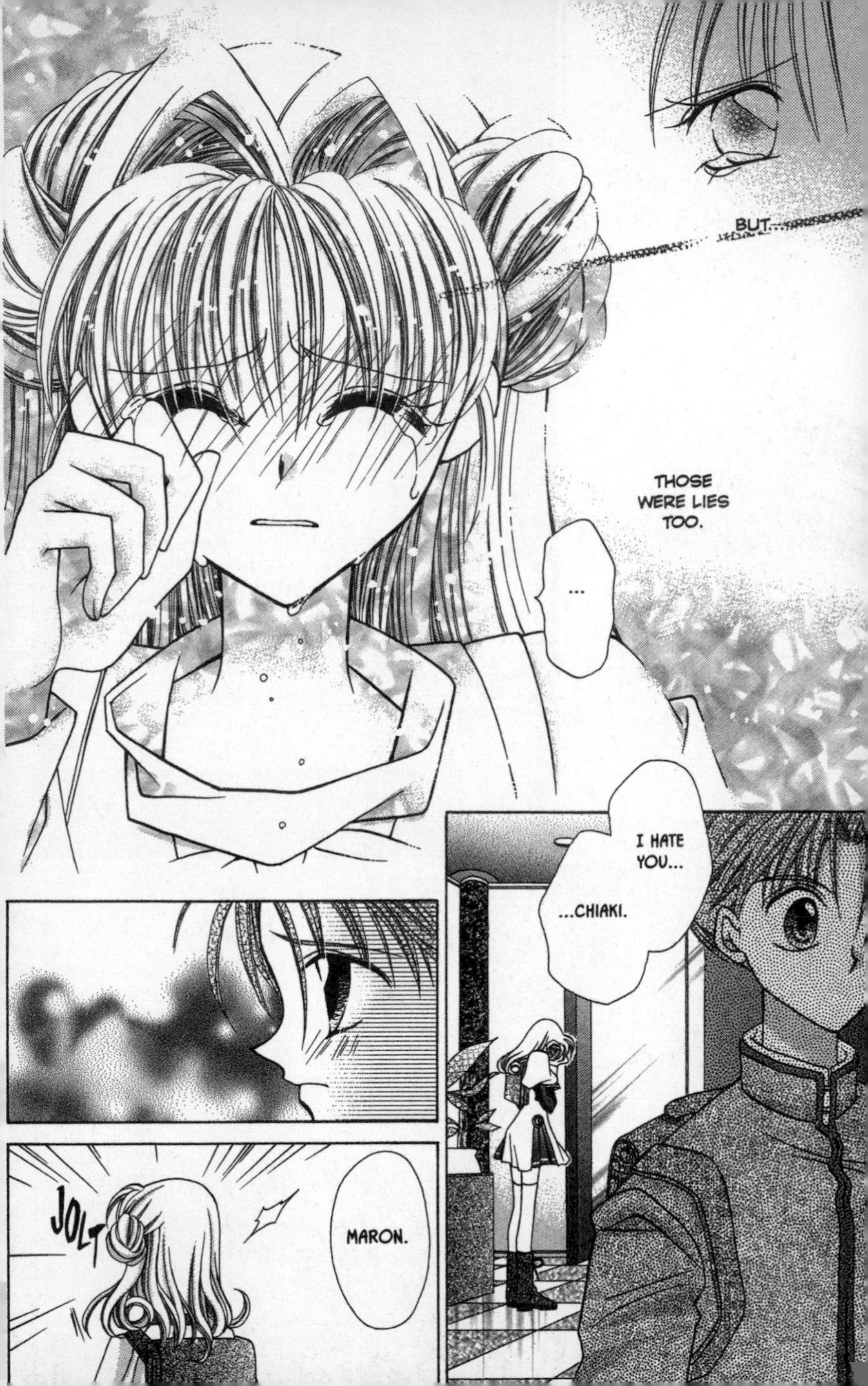
BUT...
THOSE WERE LIES TOO.
...
I HATE YOU... ...CHIAKI.
JOLT
MARON.

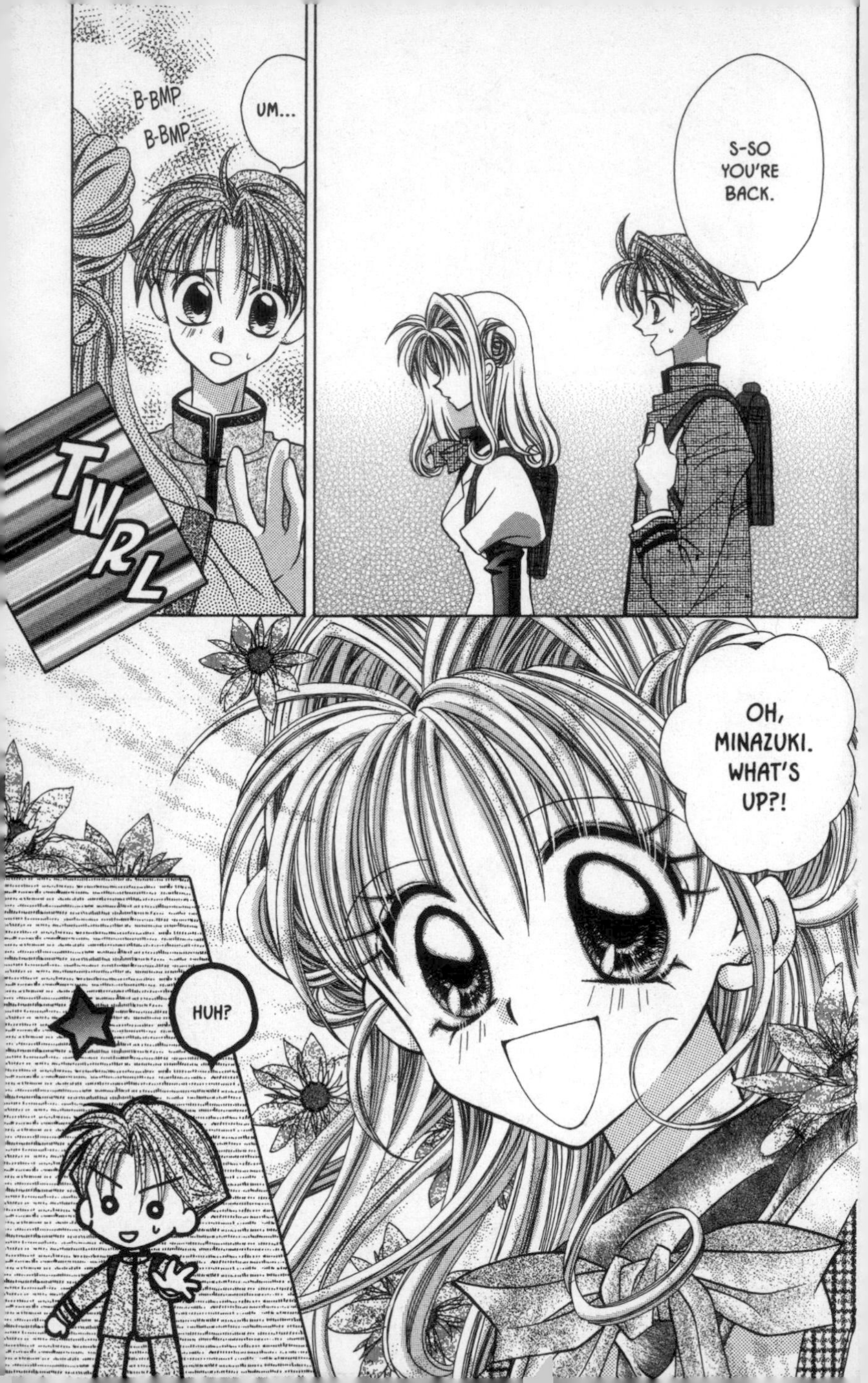
S-SO YOU'RE BACK.
UM...
B-BMP
B-BMP
TWRL
OH, MINAZUKI. WHAT'S UP?!
HUH?

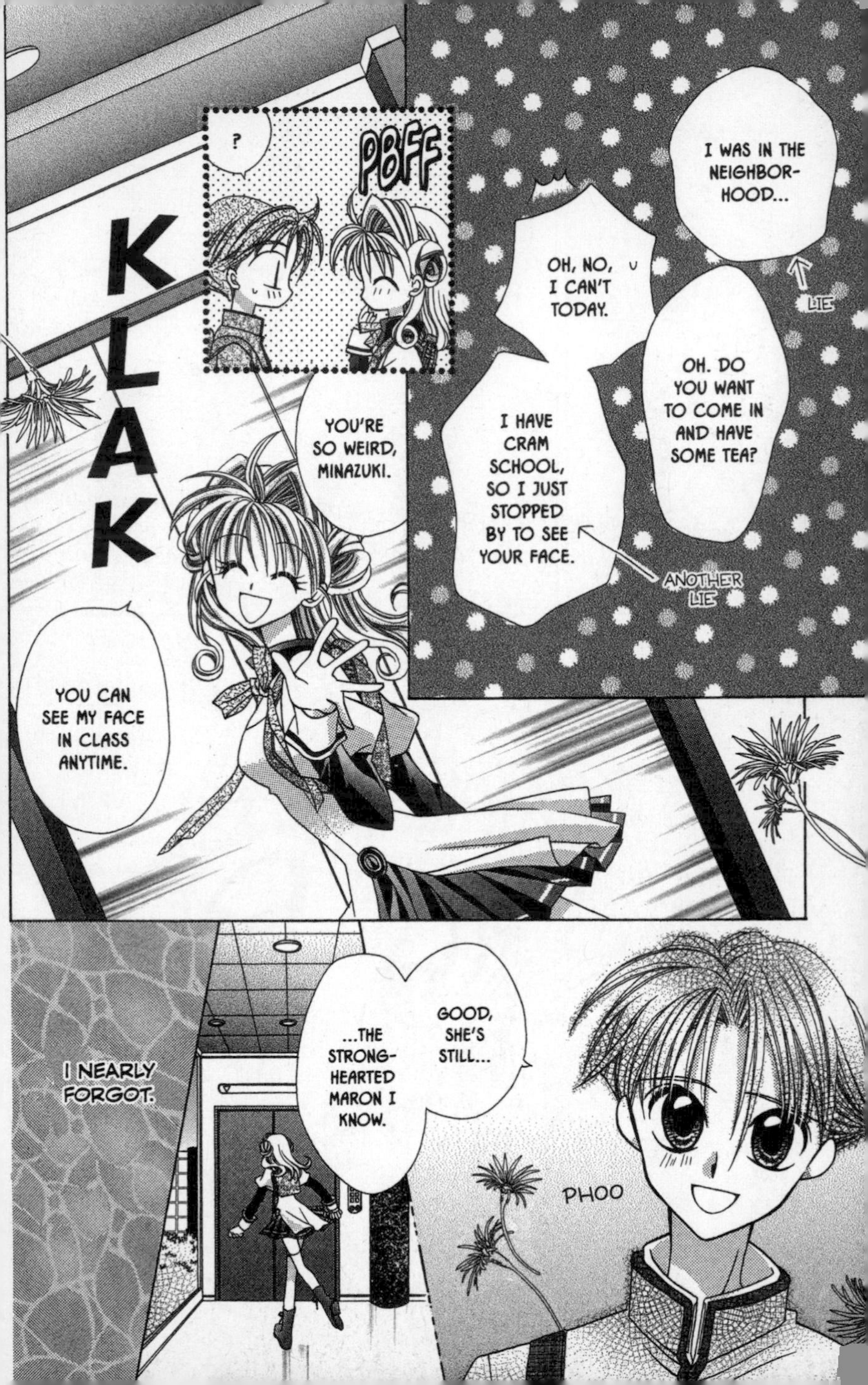
I WAS IN THE NEIGHBOR-HOOD...
LIE
OH. DO YOU WANT TO COME IN AND HAVE SOME TEA?
OH, NO, I CAN'T TODAY.
I HAVE CRAM SCHOOL, SO I JUST STOPPED BY TO SEE YOUR FACE.
ANOTHER LIE
PBFF
?
YOU'RE SO WEIRD, MINAZUKI.
KLAK
YOU CAN SEE MY FACE IN CLASS ANYTIME.
GOOD, SHE'S STILL...
...THE STRONG-HEARTED MARON I KNOW.
PHOO
I NEARLY FORGOT.

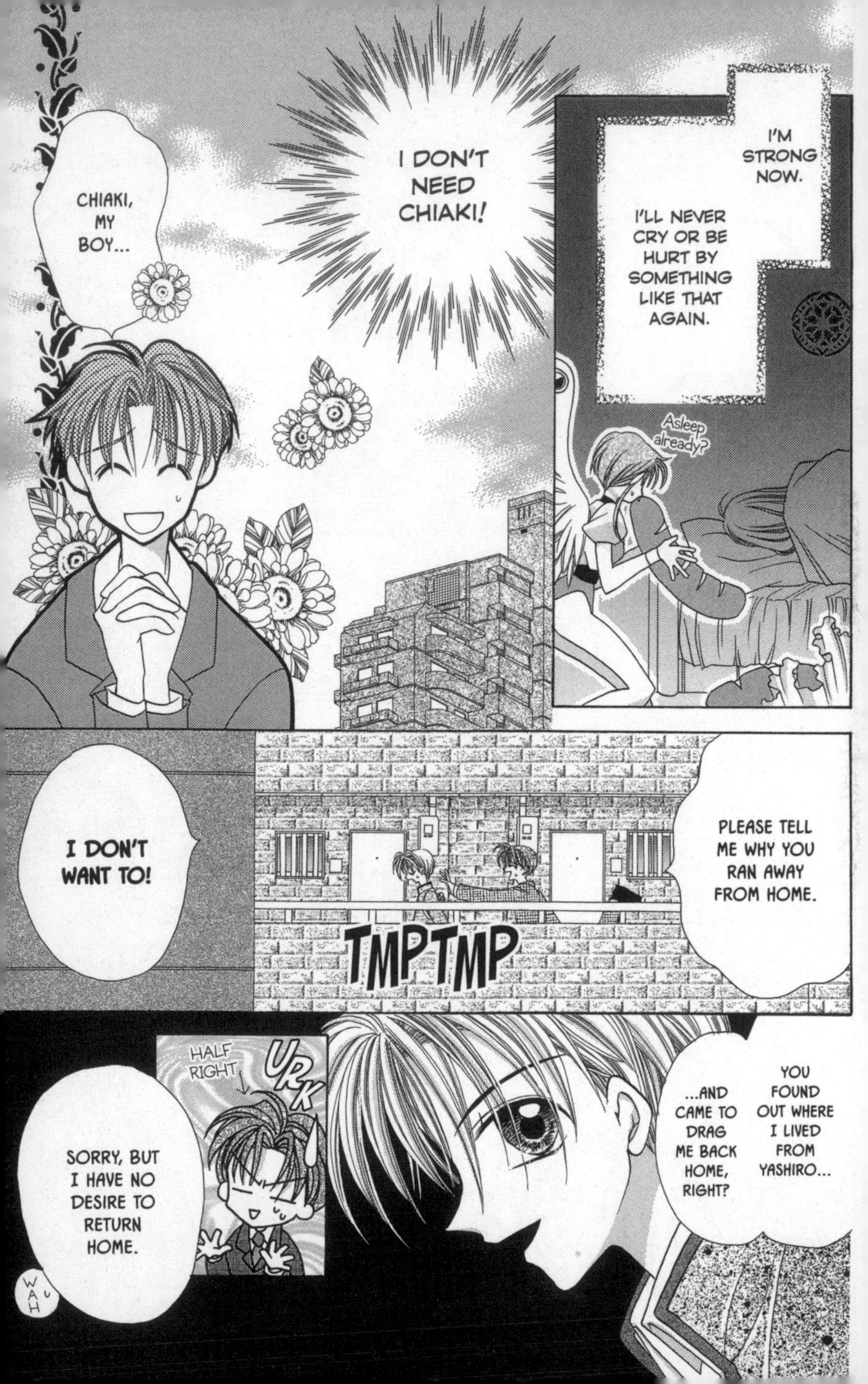
I'M STRONG NOW.
I'LL NEVER CRY OR BE HURT BY SOMETHING LIKE THAT AGAIN.
Asleep already?
I DON'T NEED CHIAKI!
CHIAKI, MY BOY...
PLEASE TELL ME WHY YOU RAN AWAY FROM HOME.
TMPTMP
I DON'T WANT TO!
YOU FOUND OUT WHERE I LIVED FROM YASHIRO...
...AND CAME TO DRAG ME BACK HOME, RIGHT?
HALF RIGHT
URK
SORRY, BUT I HAVE NO DESIRE TO RETURN HOME.
WAH

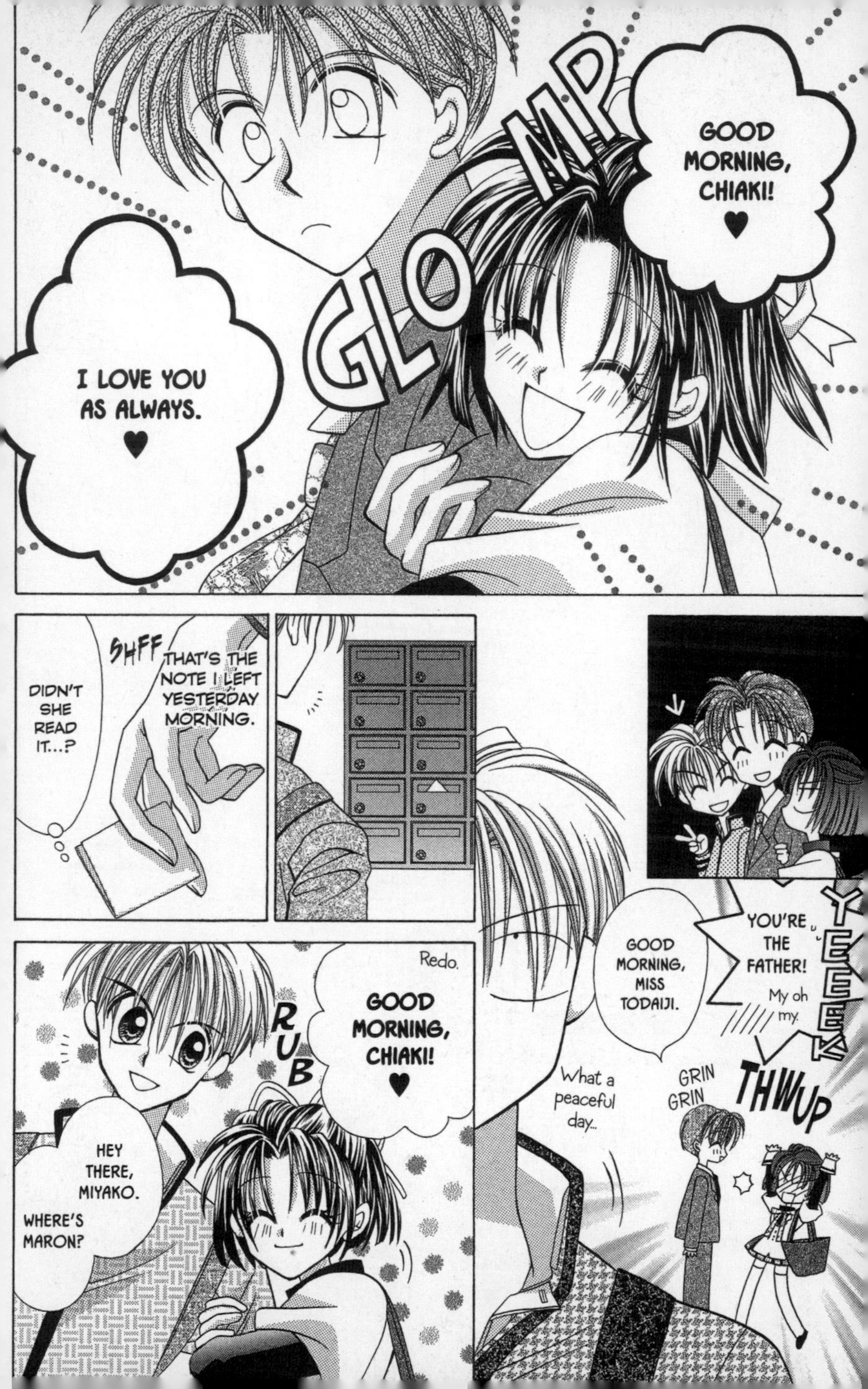
GLOMP
GOOD MORNING, CHIAKI! ♥
I LOVE YOU AS ALWAYS. ♥
SHFF
THAT'S THE NOTE I LEFT YESTERDAY MORNING.
DIDN'T SHE READ IT...?
YEEEK
YOU'RE THE FATHER!
My oh my.
GOOD MORNING, MISS TODAIJI.
THWUP
GRIN GRIN
What a peaceful day...
Redo.
GOOD MORNING, CHIAKI! ♥
RUB
HEY THERE, MIYAKO.
WHERE'S MARON?

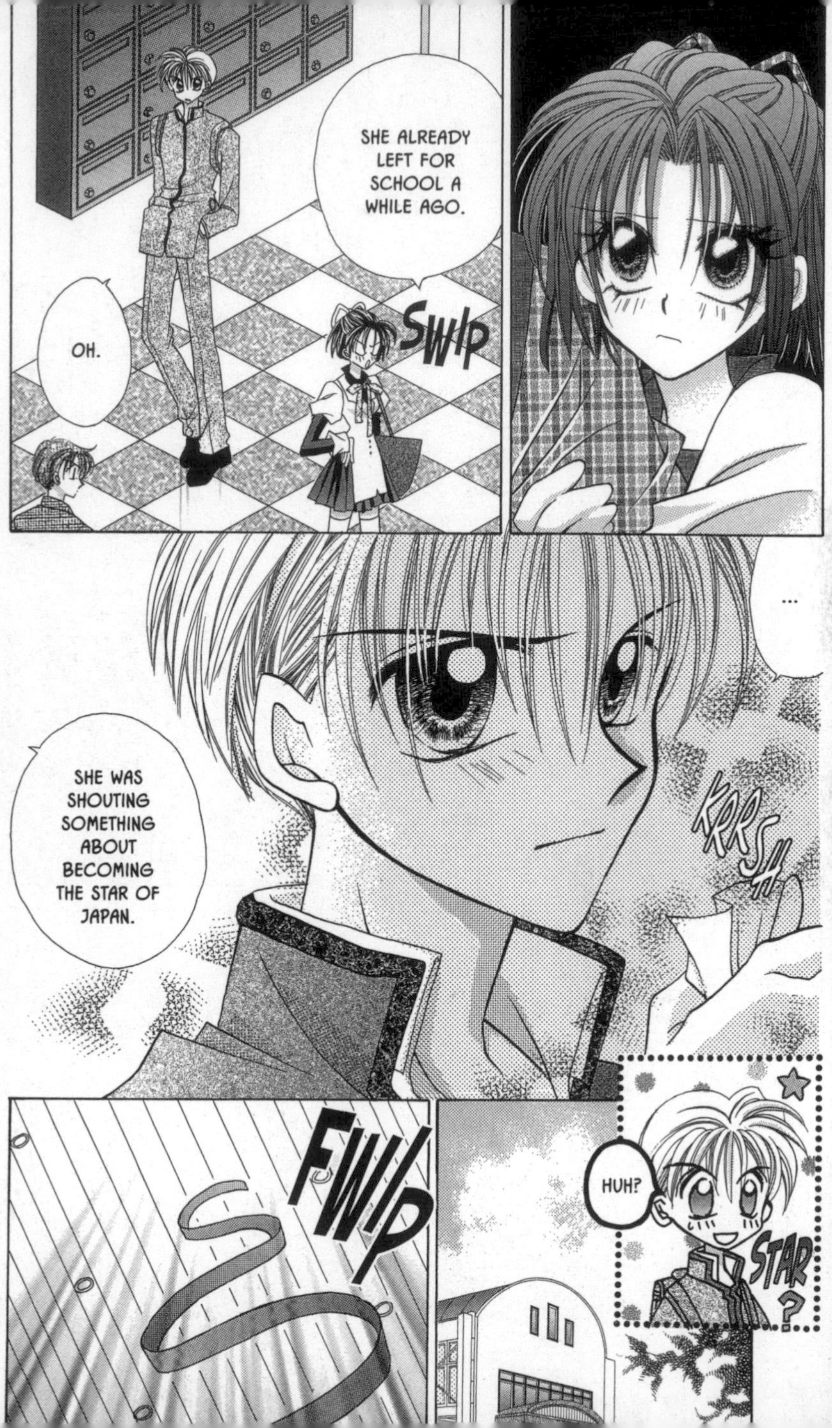
SHE ALREADY LEFT FOR SCHOOL A WHILE AGO.
SWIP
OH.
...
SHE WAS SHOUTING SOMETHING ABOUT BECOMING THE STAR OF JAPAN.
KRRSH
HUH?
STAR?
FWIP

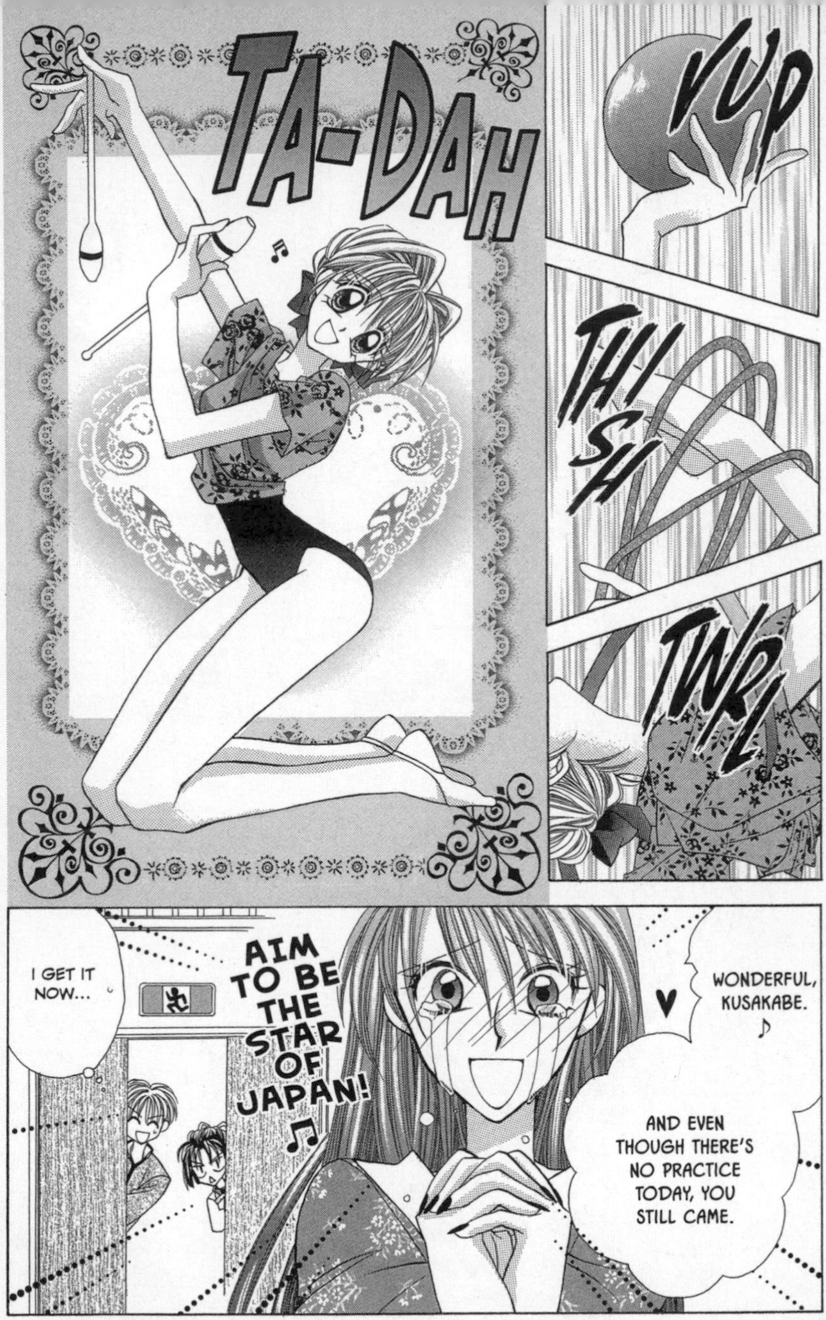
VUP
THISH
TWRL
TA-DAH
WONDERFUL, KUSAKABE. ♪
AND EVEN THOUGH THERE'S NO PRACTICE TODAY, YOU STILL CAME.
AIM TO BE THE STAR OF JAPAN! ♫
I GET IT NOW...

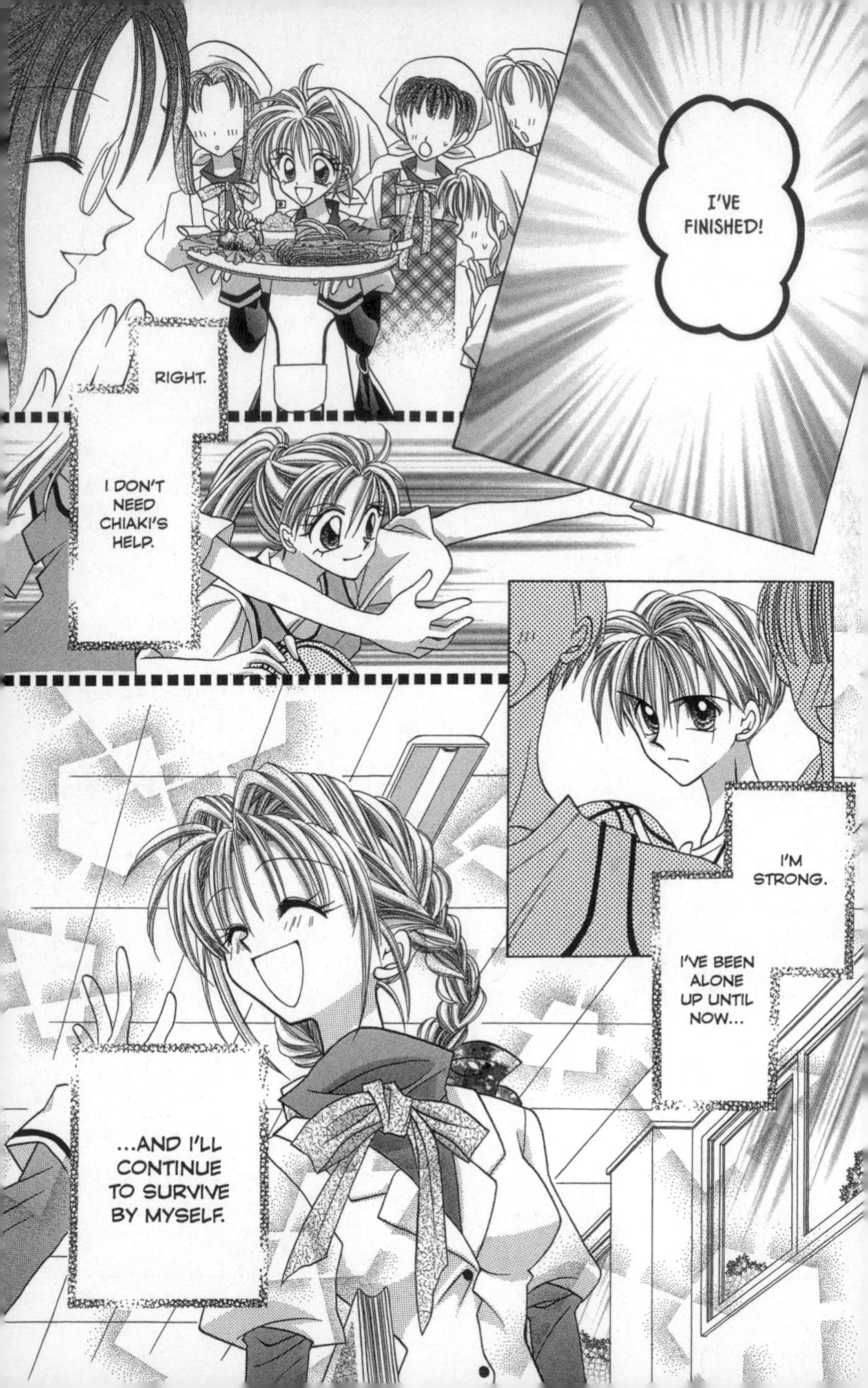
I'VE FINISHED!
RIGHT.
I DON'T NEED CHIAKI'S HELP.
I'M STRONG.
I'VE BEEN ALONE UP UNTIL NOW...
...AND I'LL CONTINUE TO SURVIVE BY MYSELF.

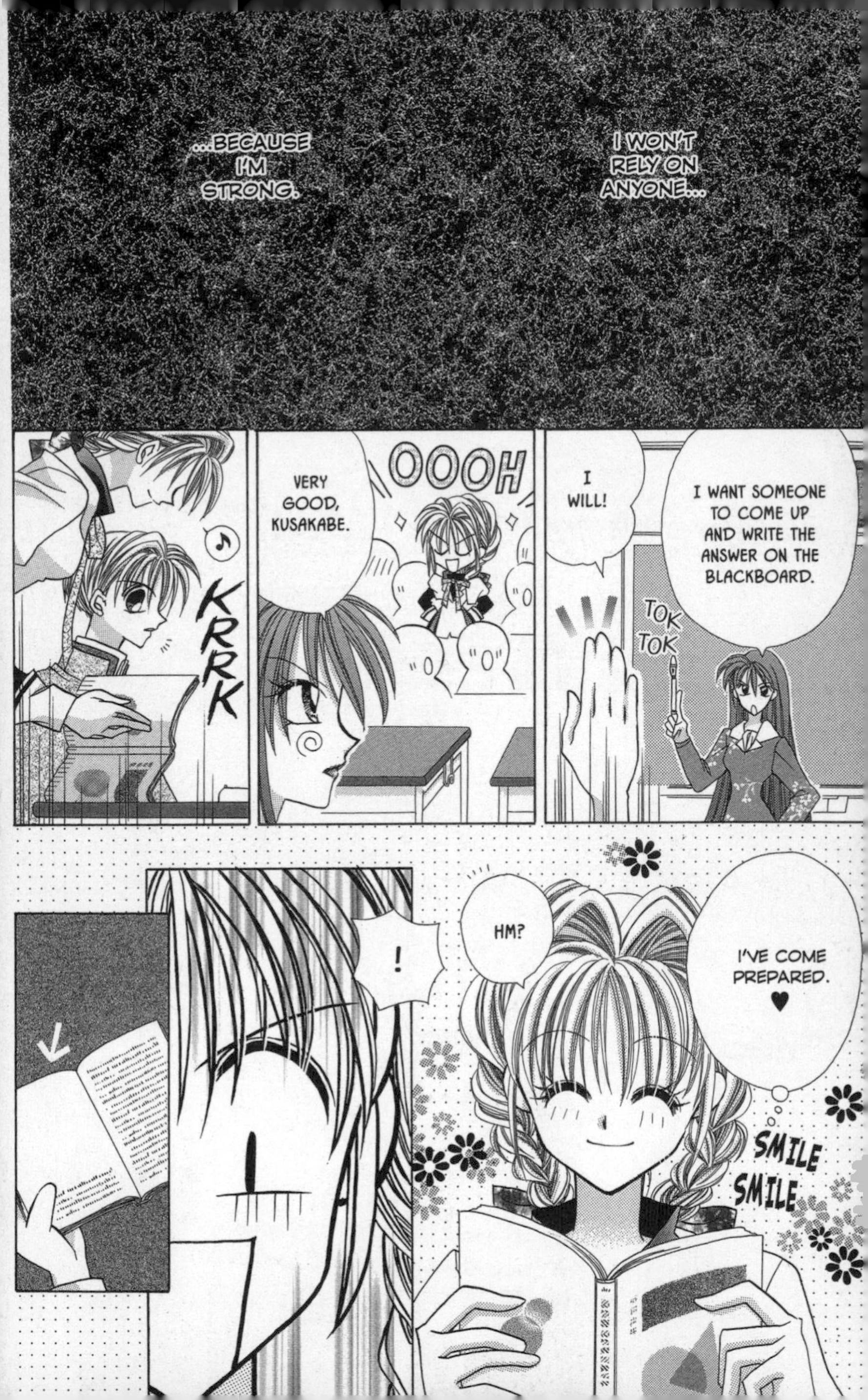
I WON'T RELY ON ANYONE...
...BECAUSE I'M STRONG.
I WANT SOMEONE TO COME UP AND WRITE THE ANSWER ON THE BLACKBOARD.
TOK TOK
I WILL!
OOOH
VERY GOOD, KUSAKABE.
KRRK
I'VE COME PREPARED. ♥
HM?
SMILE SMILE
!

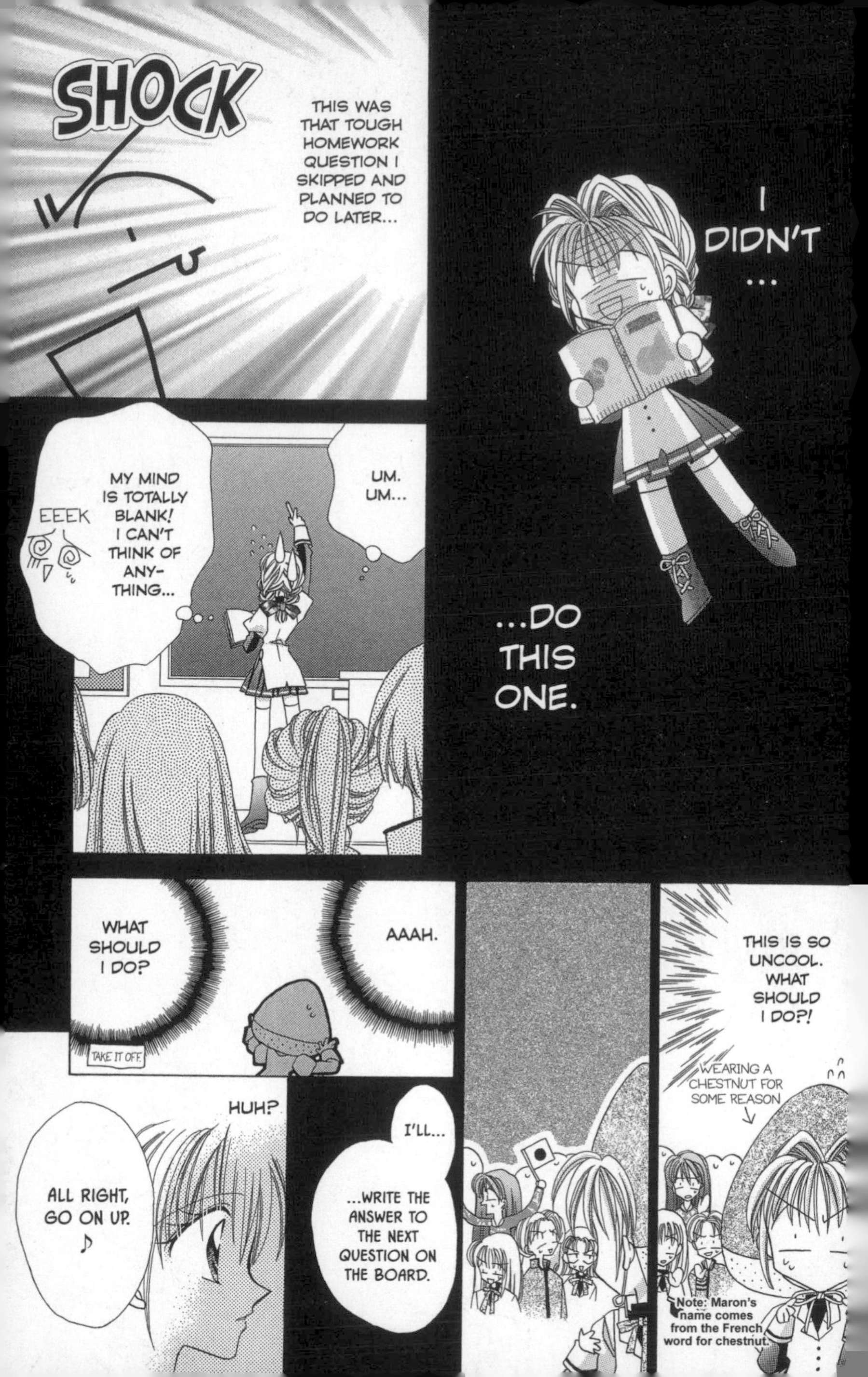
I DIDN'T ...
...DO THIS ONE.
THIS WAS THAT TOUGH HOMEWORK QUESTION I SKIPPED AND PLANNED TO DO LATER...
SHOCK
UM. UM...
EEEK
MY MIND IS TOTALLY BLANK! I CAN'T THINK OF ANY-THING...
THIS IS SO UNCOOL. WHAT SHOULD I DO?!
WEARING A CHESTNUT FOR SOME REASON
Note: Maron's name comes from the French word for chestnut.
AAAH.
WHAT SHOULD I DO?
TAKE IT OFF.
I'LL...
...WRITE THE ANSWER TO THE NEXT QUESTION ON THE BOARD.
HUH?
ALL RIGHT, GO ON UP. ♪

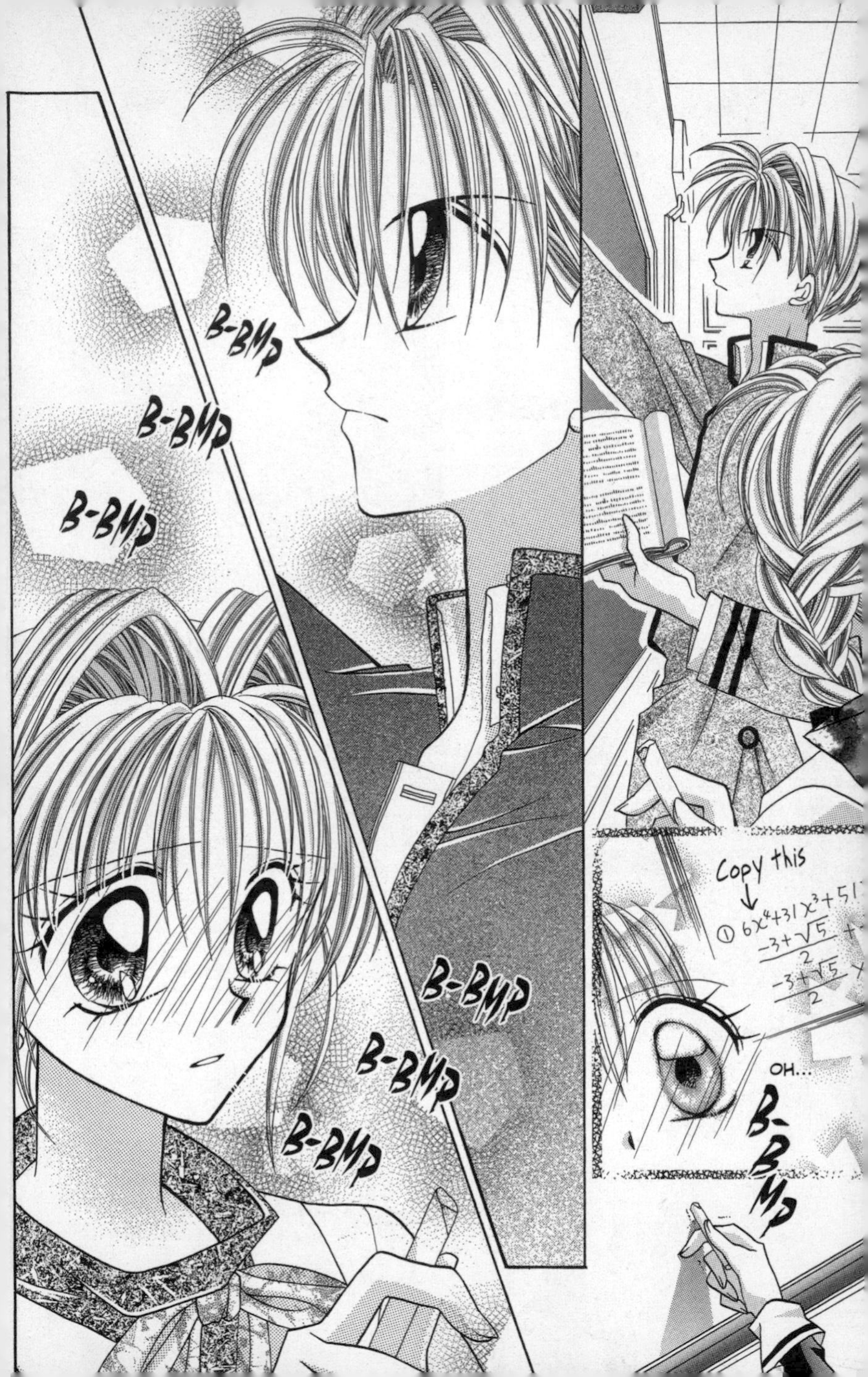
Copy this
OH...
B-BMP
B-BMP
B-BMP
B-BMP
B-BMP
B-BMP
B-BMP

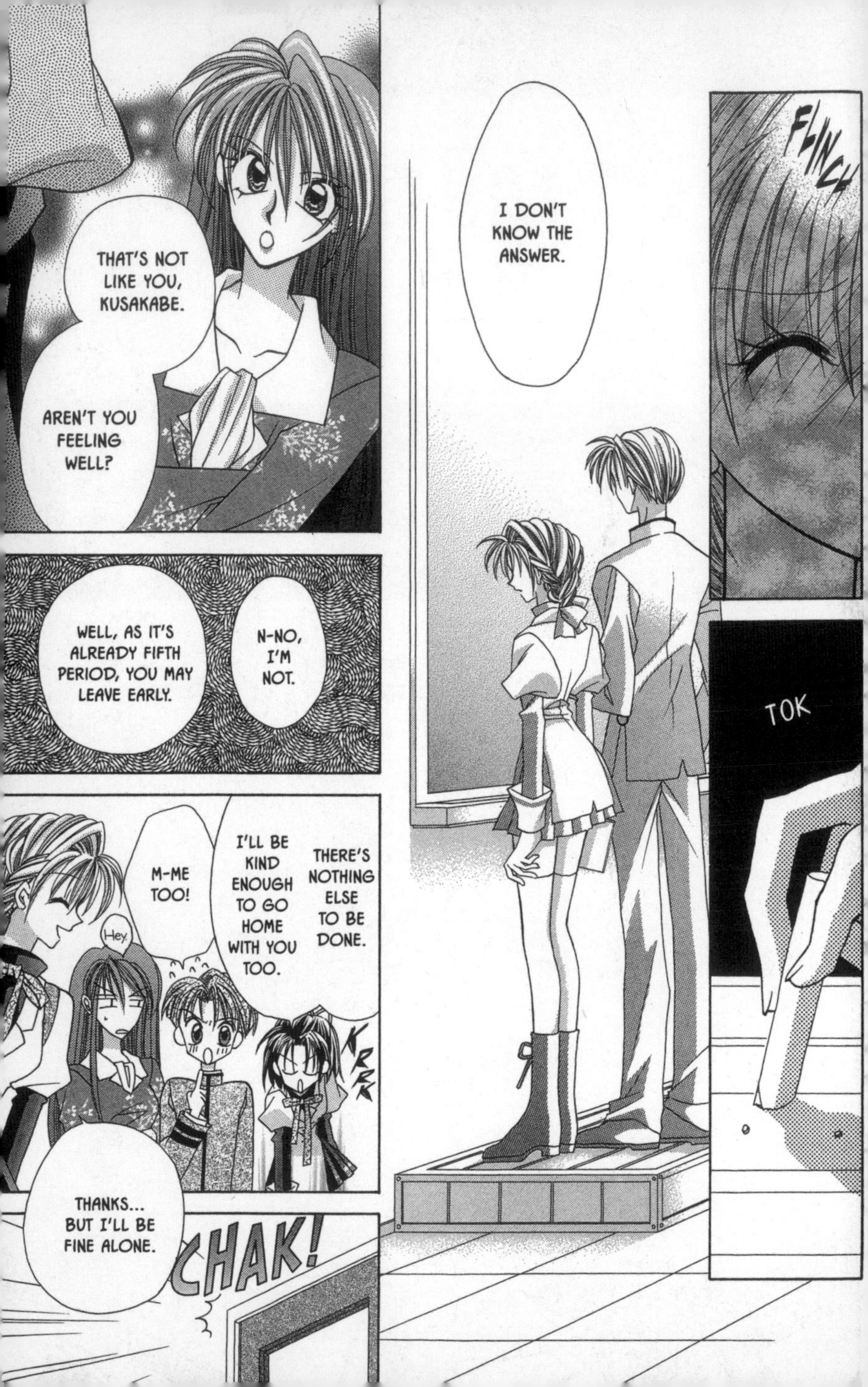
FLINCH
TOK
I DON'T KNOW THE ANSWER.
THAT'S NOT LIKE YOU, KUSAKABE.
AREN'T YOU FEELING WELL?
N-NO, I'M NOT.
WELL, AS IT'S ALREADY FIFTH PERIOD, YOU MAY LEAVE EARLY.
THERE'S NOTHING ELSE TO BE DONE.
I'LL BE KIND ENOUGH TO GO HOME WITH YOU TOO.
M-ME TOO!
Hey.
KRRK
THANKS... BUT I'LL BE FINE ALONE.
CHAK!

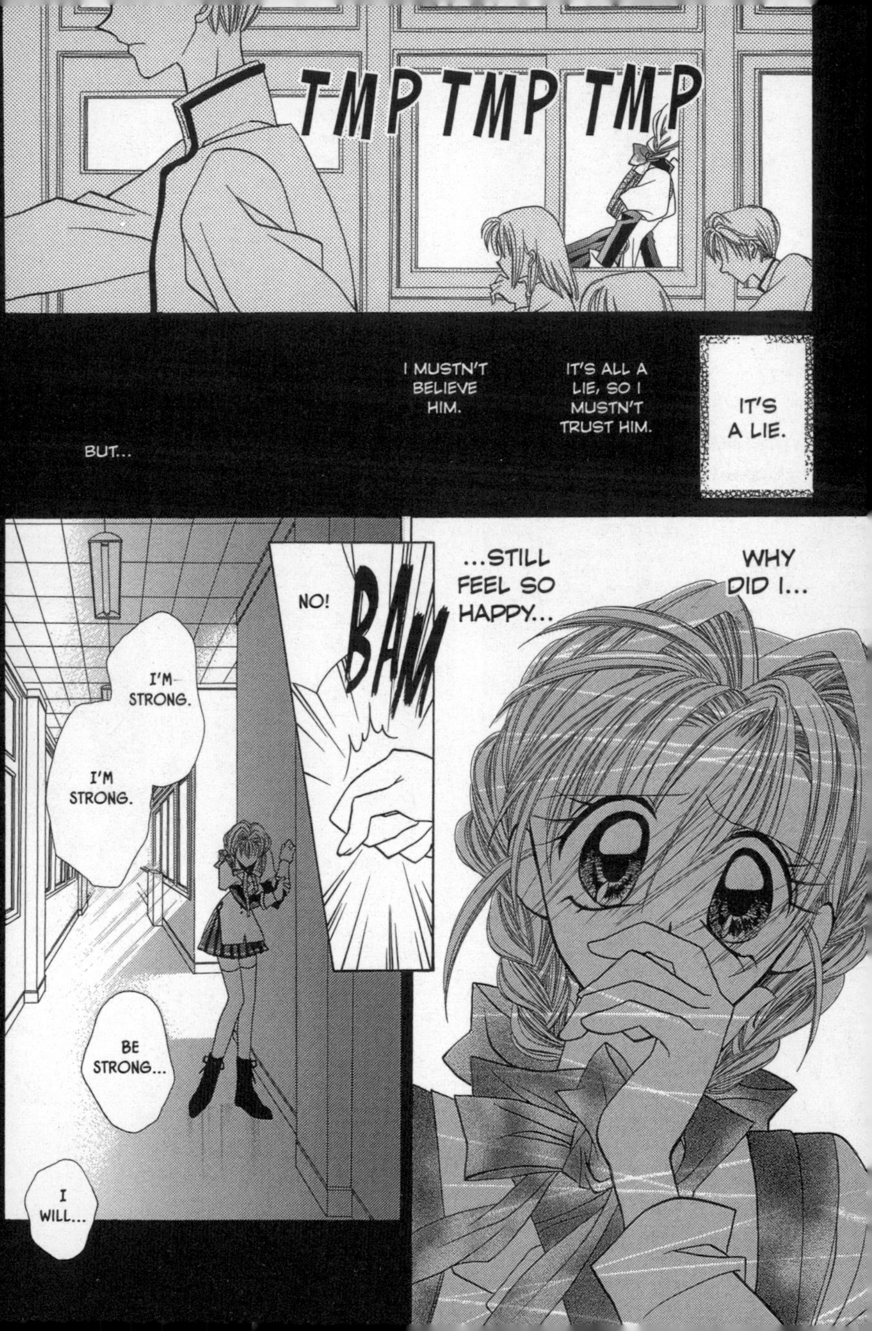

TMP TMP TMP
IT'S A LIE.
IT'S ALL A LIE, SO I MUSTN'T TRUST HIM.
I MUSTN'T BELIEVE HIM.
BUT...
WHY DID I...
...STILL FEEL SO HAPPY...
BAM
NO!
I'M STRONG.
I'M STRONG.
BE STRONG...
I WILL...

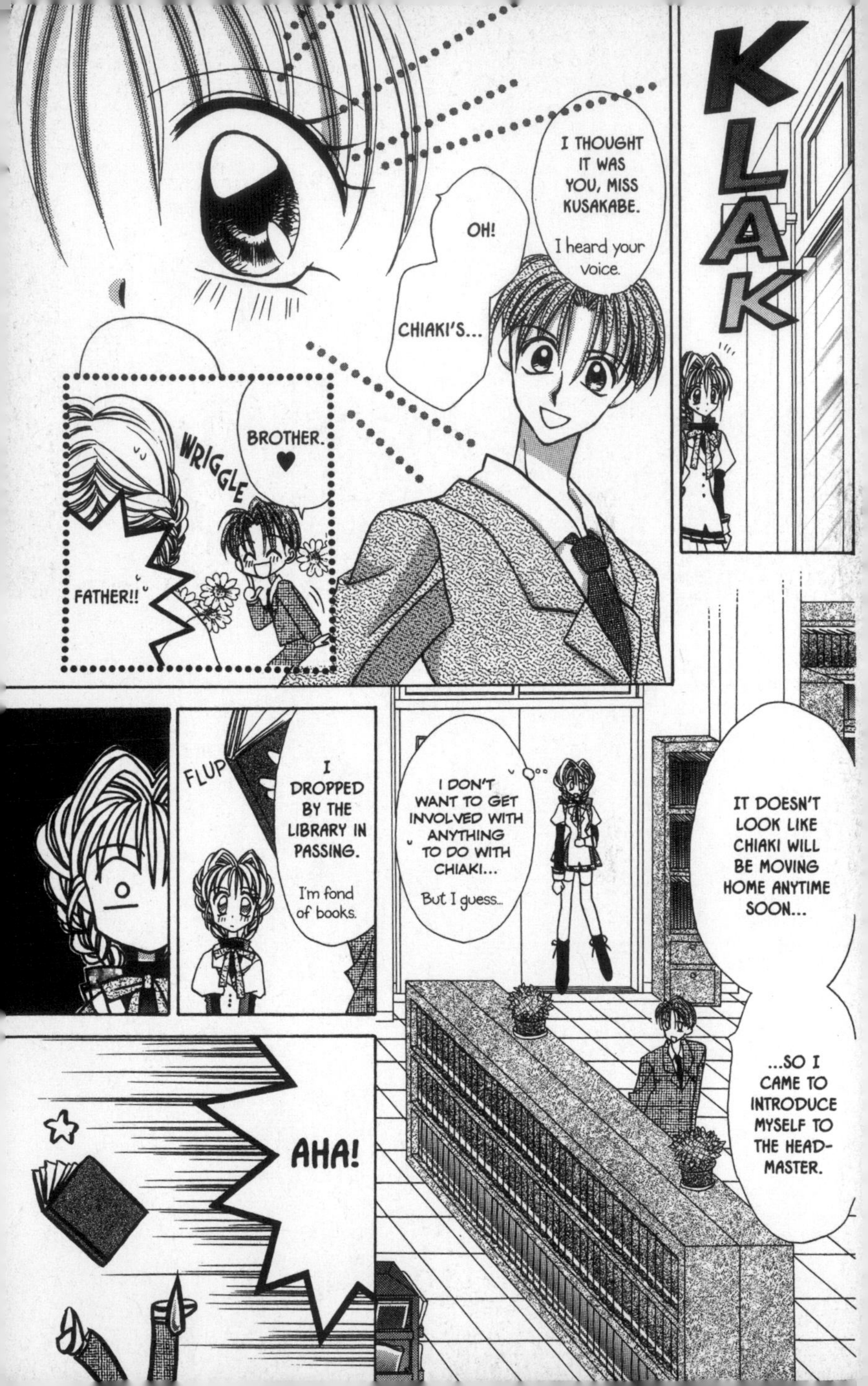

KLAK
I THOUGHT IT WAS YOU, MISS KUSAKABE.
I heard your voice.
OH!
CHIAKI'S...
BROTHER. ♥
WRIGGLE
FATHER!!
IT DOESN'T LOOK LIKE CHIAKI WILL BE MOVING HOME ANYTIME SOON...
...SO I CAME TO INTRODUCE MYSELF TO THE HEAD-MASTER.
I DON'T WANT TO GET INVOLVED WITH ANYTHING TO DO WITH CHIAKI...
But I guess...
I DROPPED BY THE LIBRARY IN PASSING.
I'm fond of books.
FLUP
AHA!

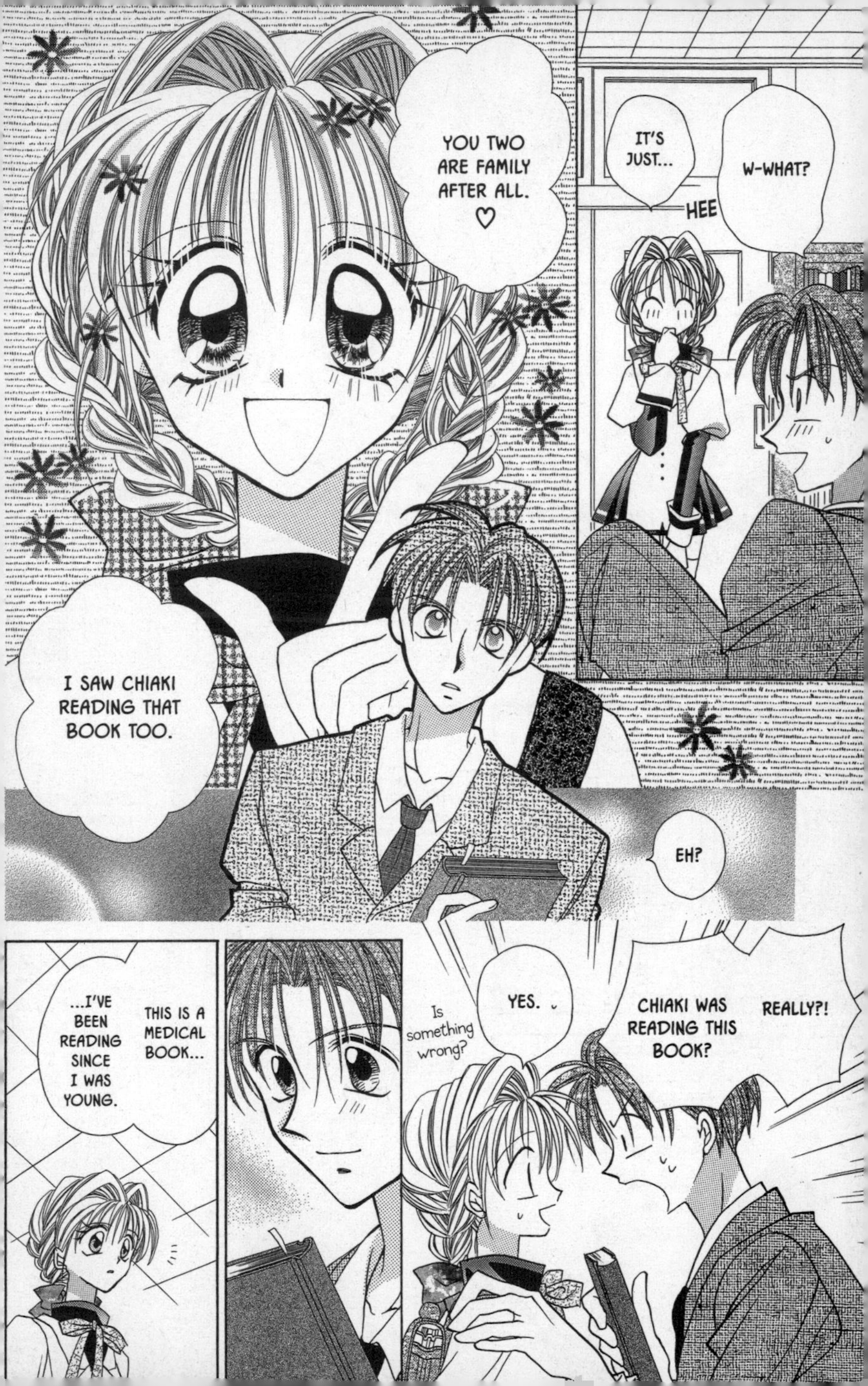
W-WHAT?
IT'S JUST...
HEE
YOU TWO ARE FAMILY AFTER ALL. ♡
I SAW CHIAKI READING THAT BOOK TOO.
EH?
REALLY?!
CHIAKI WAS READING THIS BOOK?
YES.
Is something wrong?
THIS IS A MEDICAL BOOK...
...I'VE BEEN READING SINCE I WAS YOUNG.

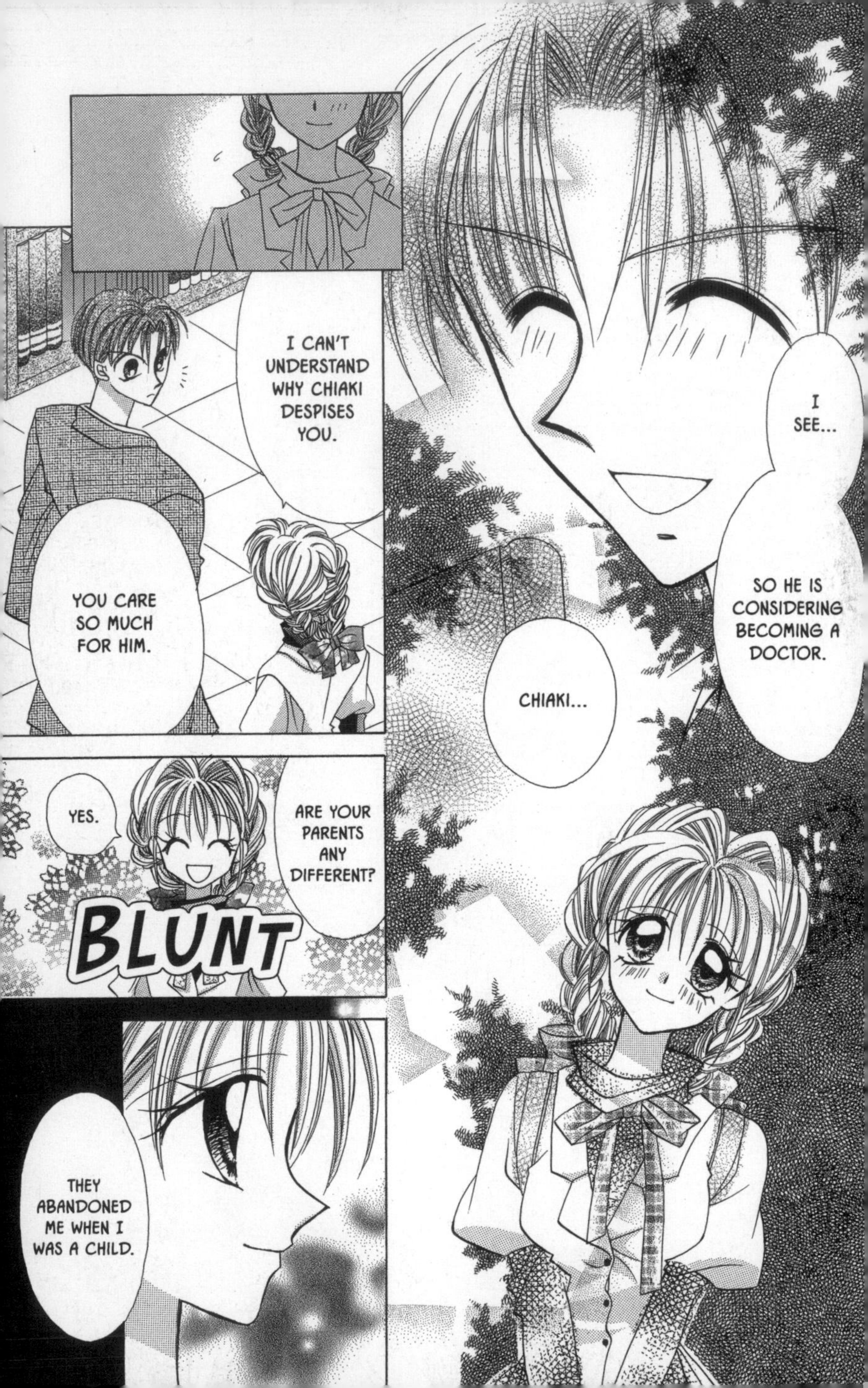
I SEE...
SO HE IS CONSIDERING BECOMING A DOCTOR.
CHIAKI...
I CAN'T UNDERSTAND WHY CHIAKI DESPISES YOU.
YOU CARE SO MUCH FOR HIM.
ARE YOUR PARENTS ANY DIFFERENT?
YES.
BLUNT
THEY ABANDONED ME WHEN I WAS A CHILD.

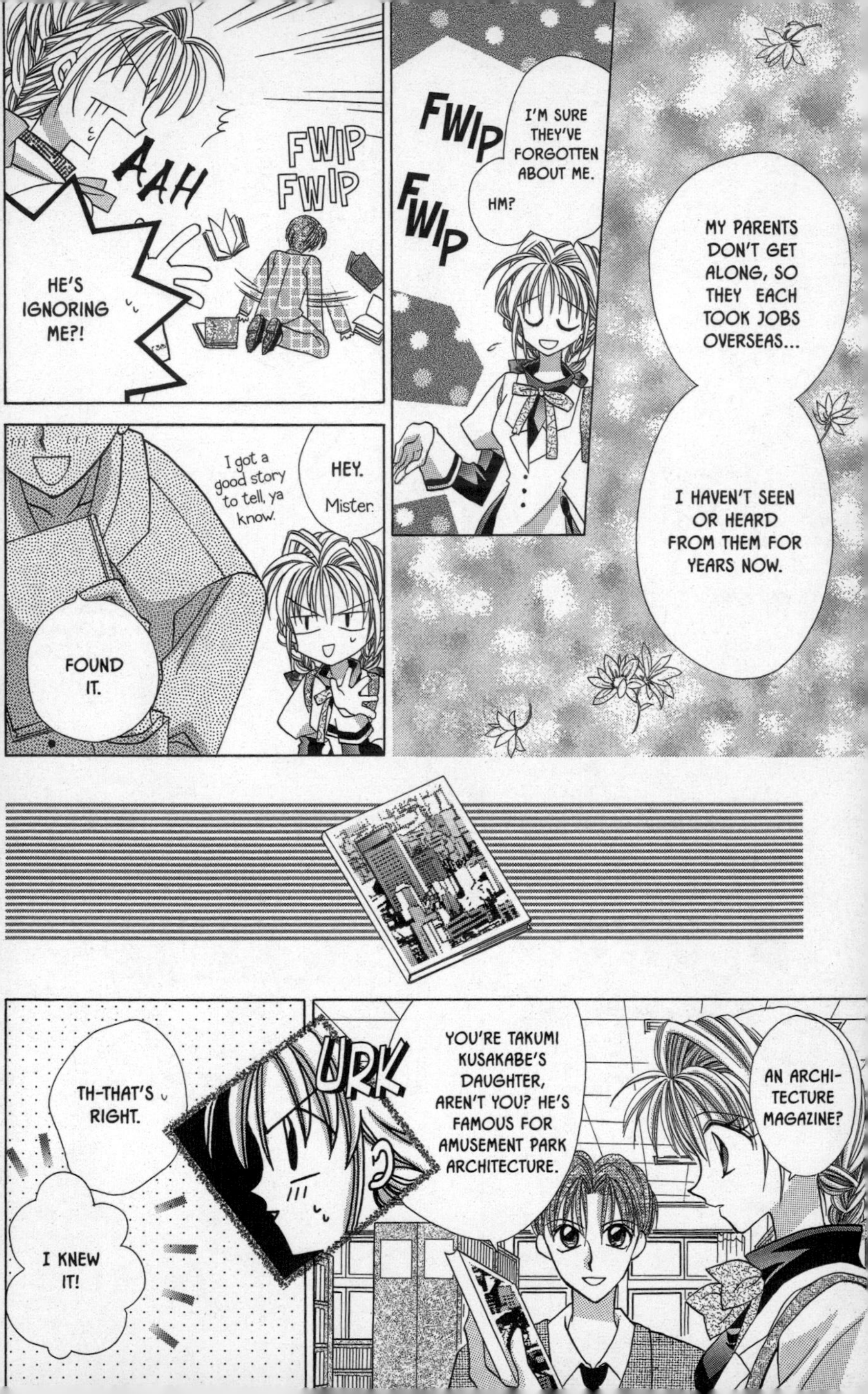
MY PARENTS DON'T GET ALONG, SO THEY EACH TOOK JOBS OVERSEAS...
I HAVEN'T SEEN OR HEARD FROM THEM FOR YEARS NOW.
FWIP
FWIP
I'M SURE THEY'VE FORGOTTEN ABOUT ME.
HM?
AAH
FWIP FWIP
HE'S IGNORING ME?!
HEY.
Mister.
I got a good story to tell, ya know.
FOUND IT.
AN ARCHI-TECTURE MAGAZINE?
YOU'RE TAKUMI KUSAKABE'S DAUGHTER, AREN'T YOU? HE'S FAMOUS FOR AMUSEMENT PARK ARCHITECTURE.
URK
TH-THAT'S RIGHT.
I KNEW IT!

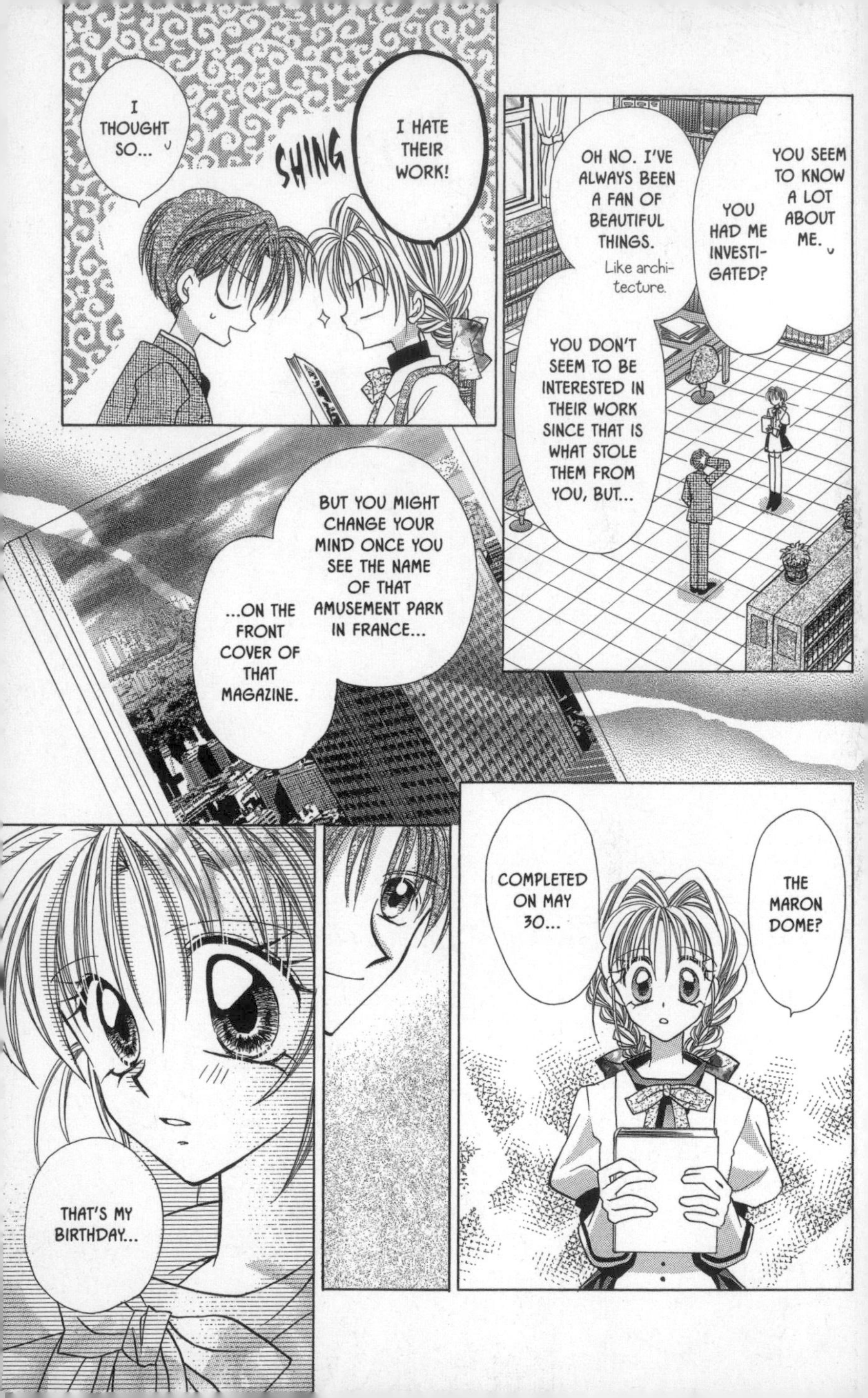
YOU SEEM TO KNOW A LOT ABOUT ME.
YOU HAD ME INVESTI-GATED?
OH NO. I'VE ALWAYS BEEN A FAN OF BEAUTIFUL THINGS.
Like archi-tecture.
YOU DON'T SEEM TO BE INTERESTED IN THEIR WORK SINCE THAT IS WHAT STOLE THEM FROM YOU, BUT...
I HATE THEIR WORK!
SHING
I THOUGHT SO...
BUT YOU MIGHT CHANGE YOUR MIND ONCE YOU SEE THE NAME OF THAT AMUSEMENT PARK IN FRANCE...
...ON THE FRONT COVER OF THAT MAGAZINE.
THE MARON DOME?
COMPLETED ON MAY 30...
THAT'S MY BIRTHDAY...

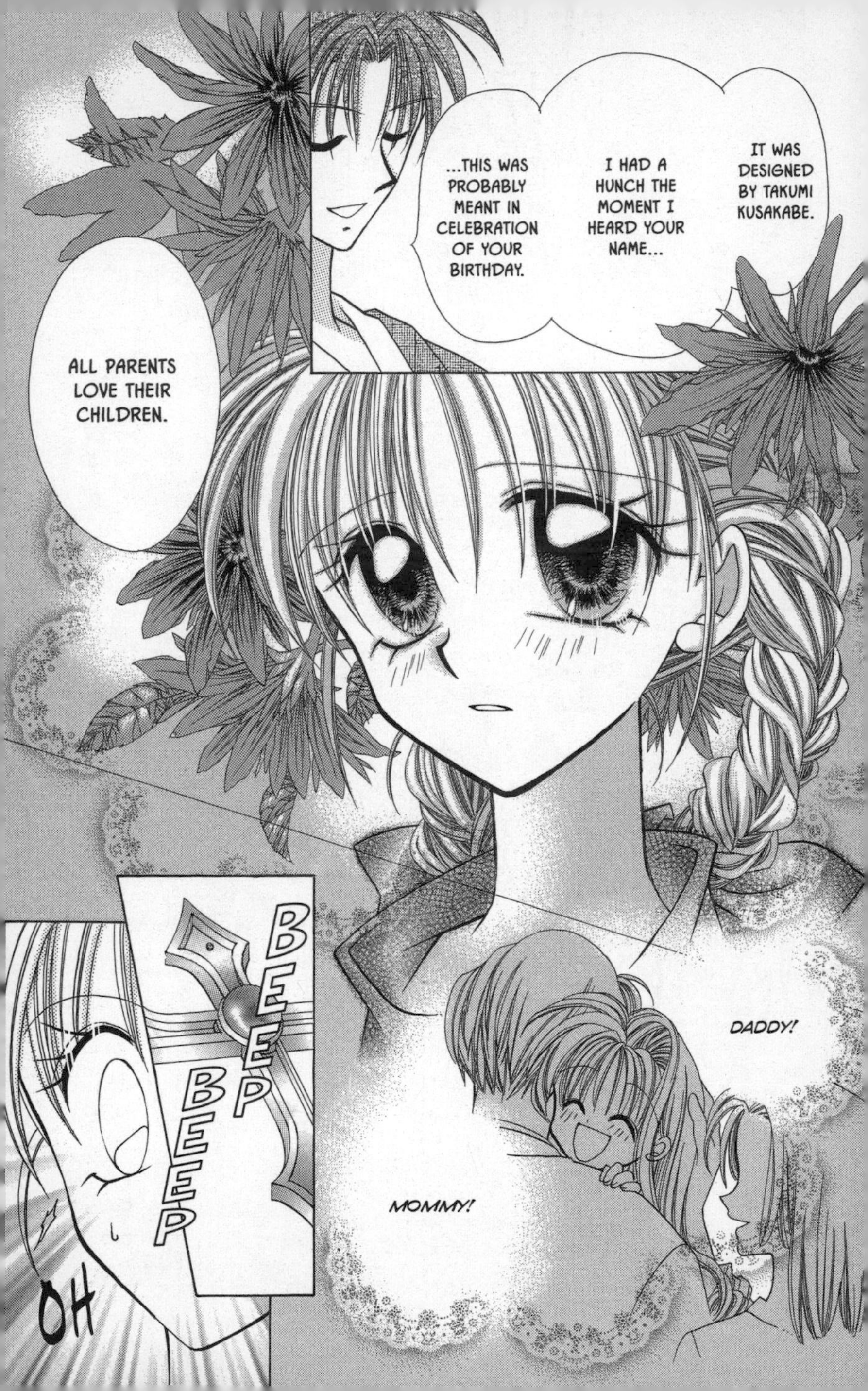
IT WAS DESIGNED BY TAKUMI KUSAKABE.
I HAD A HUNCH THE MOMENT I HEARD YOUR NAME...
...THIS WAS PROBABLY MEANT IN CELEBRATION OF YOUR BIRTHDAY.
ALL PARENTS LOVE THEIR CHILDREN.
DADDY!
MOMMY!
BEEP
BEEP
OH

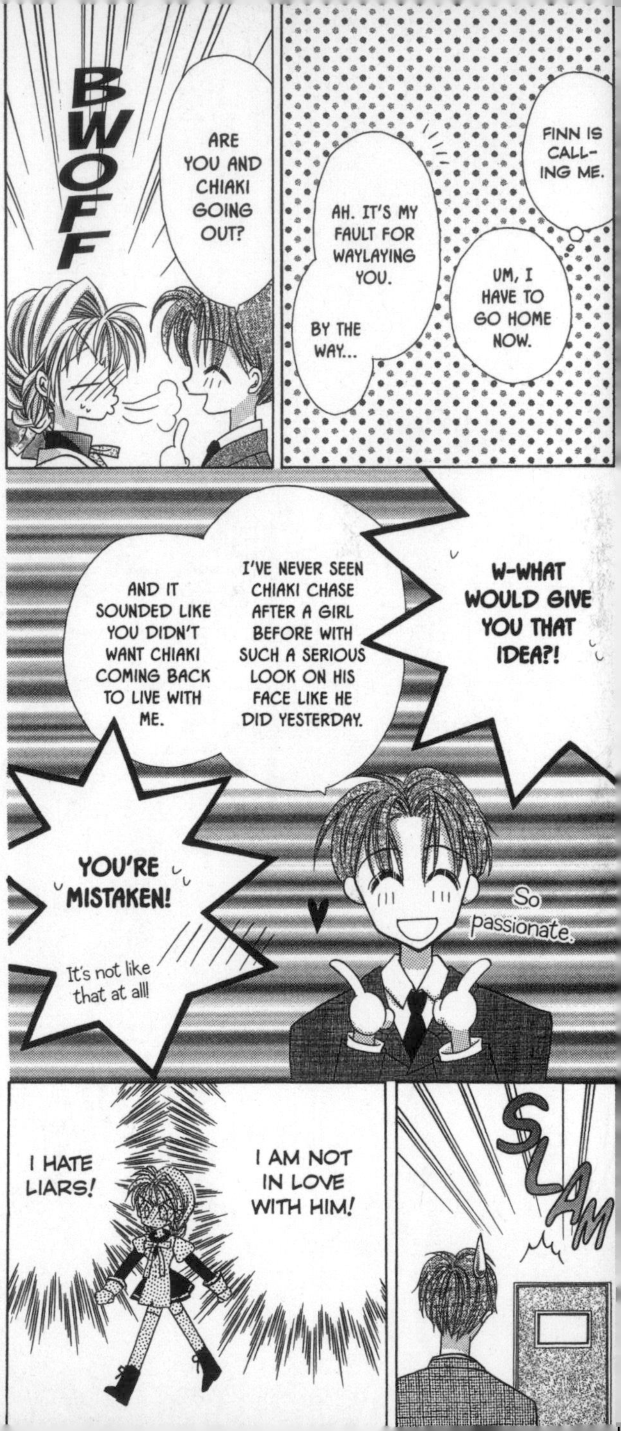
FINN IS CALLING ME.
UM, I HAVE TO GO HOME NOW.
AH. IT'S MY FAULT FOR WAYLAYING YOU.
BY THE WAY...
ARE YOU AND CHIAKI GOING OUT?
BWOFF
W-WHAT WOULD GIVE YOU THAT IDEA?!
I'VE NEVER SEEN CHIAKI CHASE AFTER A GIRL BEFORE WITH SUCH A SERIOUS LOOK ON HIS FACE LIKE HE DID YESTERDAY.
AND IT SOUNDED LIKE YOU DIDN'T WANT CHIAKI COMING BACK TO LIVE WITH ME.
So passionate.
YOU'RE MISTAKEN!
It's not like that at all!
SLAM
I AM NOT IN LOVE WITH HIM!
I HATE LIARS!

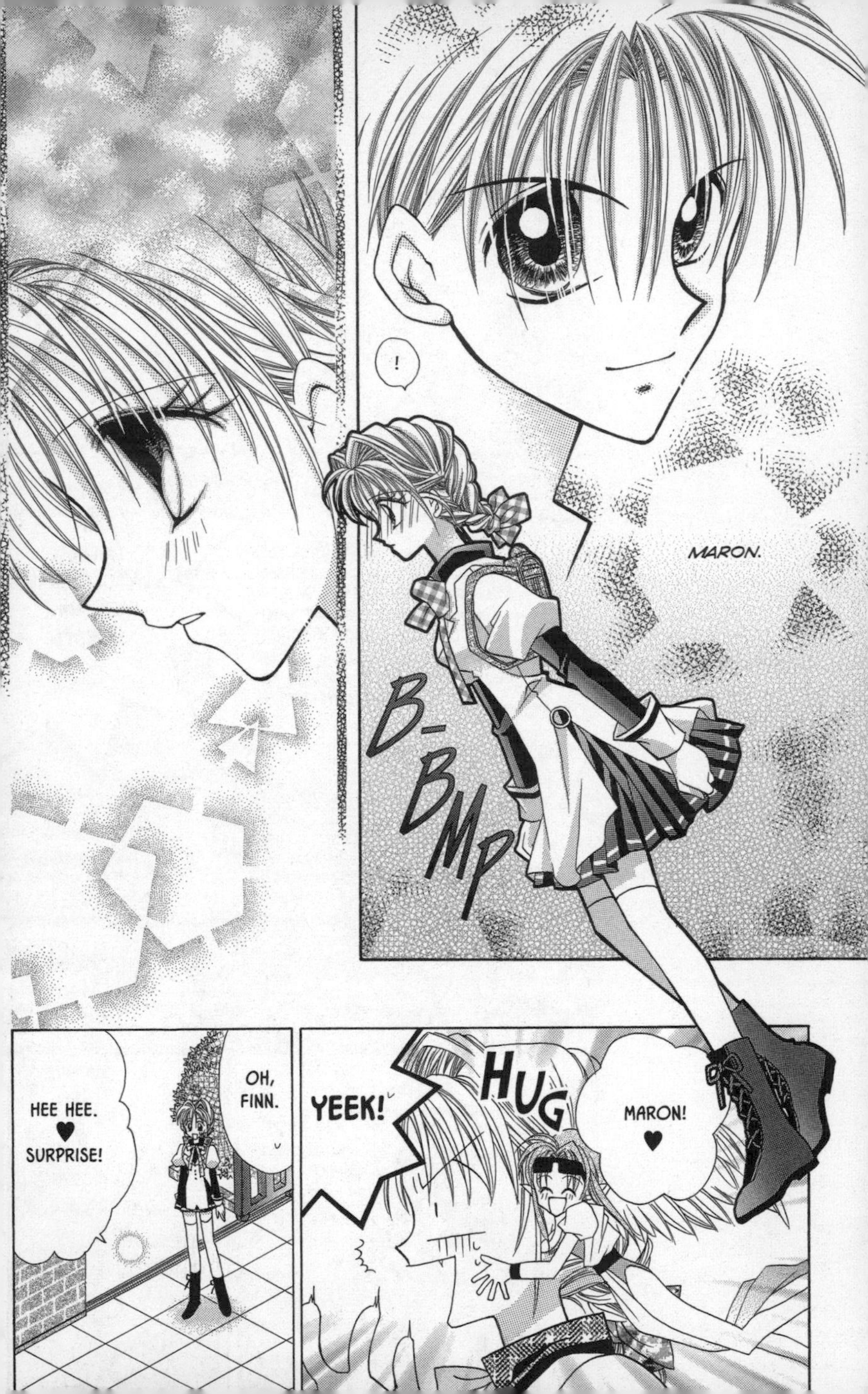
MARON.
!
B-BMP
MARON! ♥
HUG
YEEK!
OH, FINN.
HEE HEE. ♥ SURPRISE!

CHIK
WHAT IS THAT?
I'M FINN, THE PICKUP ANGEL. ♥
VROOOO
DUCKY
I ALREADY SENT THE NOTICE. YOU DON'T MIND, DO YOU?
NOPE!
GUTS!
THAT'S RIGHT! I DON'T CARE ABOUT CHIAKI!
Vroom vroom!
WE'LL DO IT TONIGHT! LET'S GO FOR IT, FINN!
THUD
OH, ONE MORE THING!
THERE WAS A MESSAGE ON YOUR ANSWERING MACHINE.

THAT'S IT, SINBAD! THAT'S THE PLACE JEANNE SENT HER NOTICE TO.

YEAH.

SO YOU'RE GOING TO FACE ME...

...MARON?

LET'S GO.

THE OCEAN HAS LAID OUT MY DESTINY...

WHO'S THERE?!

SW FF

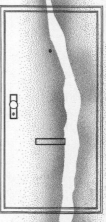

WHAT?

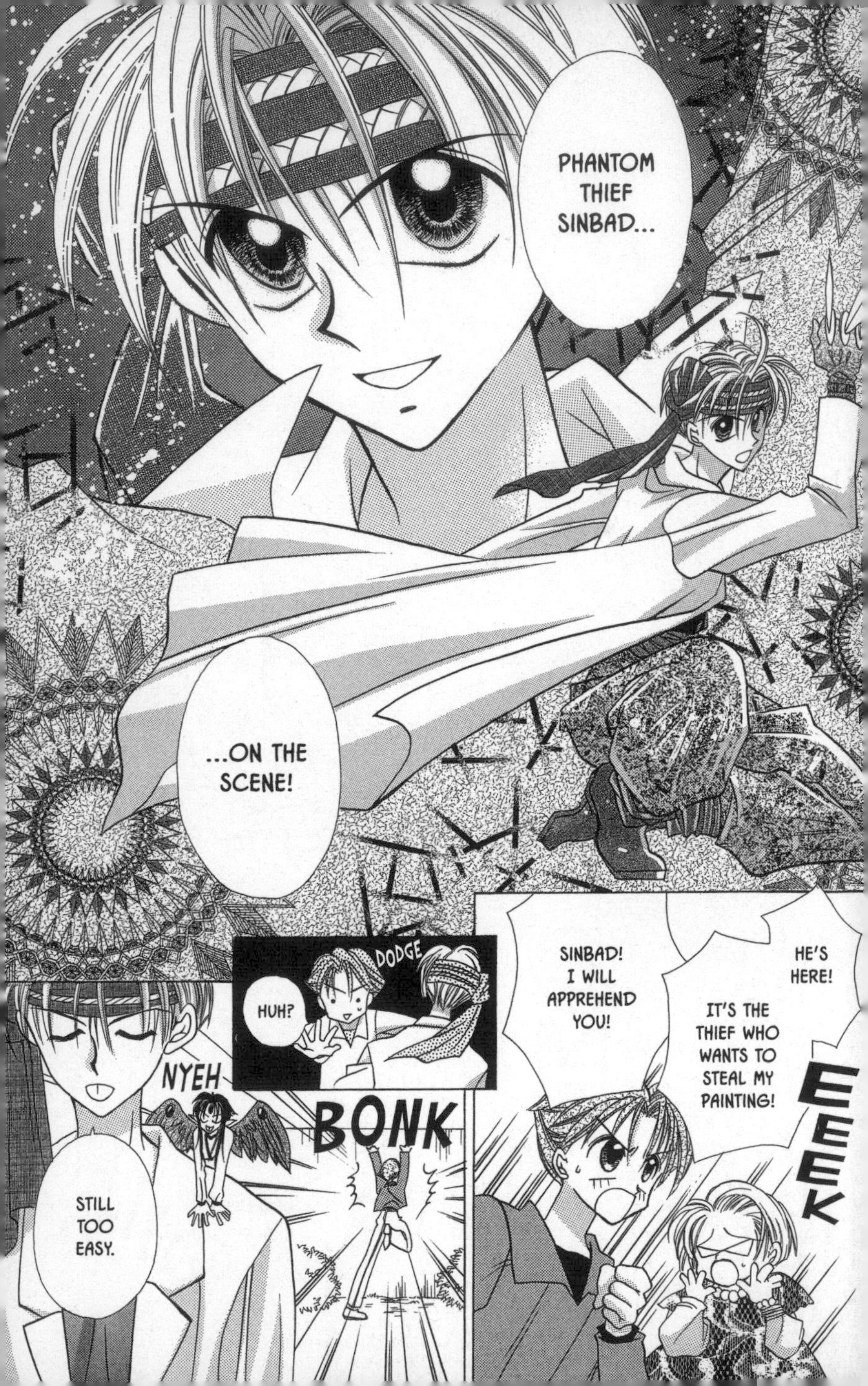
PHANTOM THIEF SINBAD...
...ON THE SCENE!
HE'S HERE!
IT'S THE THIEF WHO WANTS TO STEAL MY PAINTING!
EEEK
SINBAD! I WILL APPREHEND YOU!
DODGE
HUH?
BONK
NYEH
STILL TOO EASY.

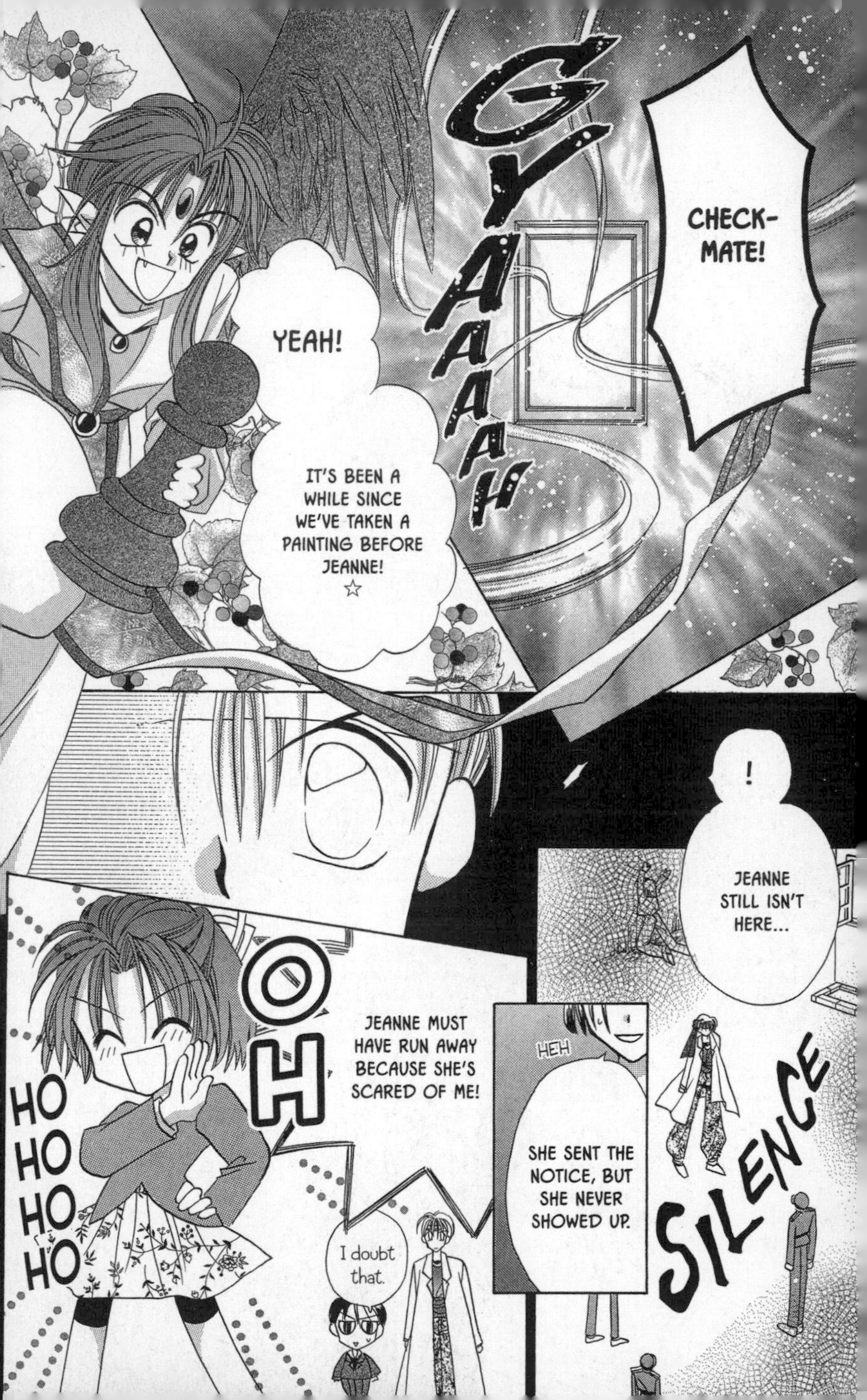
CHECK-MATE!
GYAAAAAH
YEAH!
IT'S BEEN A WHILE SINCE WE'VE TAKEN A PAINTING BEFORE JEANNE! ☆
!
JEANNE STILL ISN'T HERE...
SILENCE
HEH
SHE SENT THE NOTICE, BUT SHE NEVER SHOWED UP.
OH
HO HO HO HO
JEANNE MUST HAVE RUN AWAY BECAUSE SHE'S SCARED OF ME!
I doubt that.

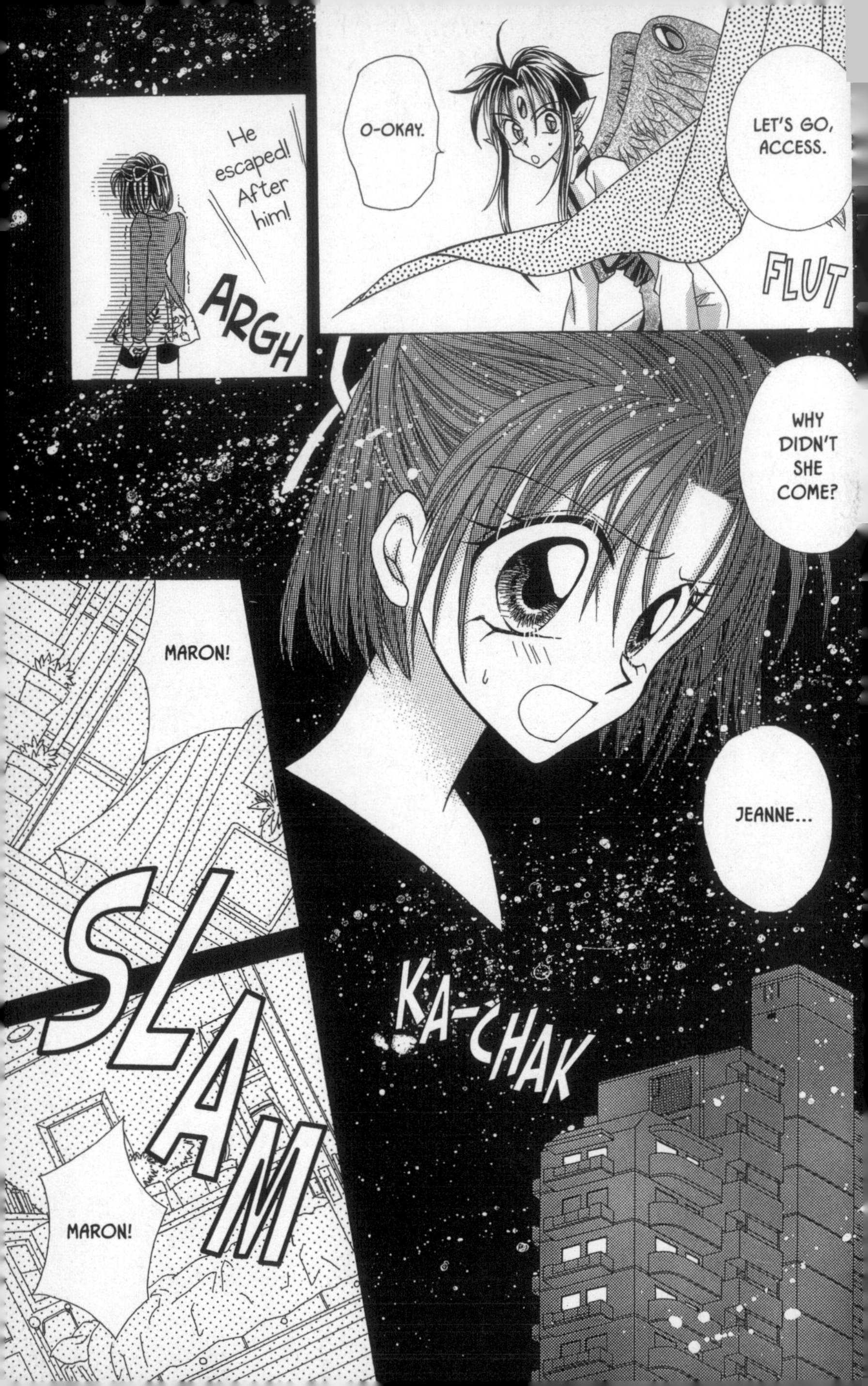
LET'S GO, ACCESS.
O-OKAY.
FLUT
He escaped! After him!
ARGH
WHY DIDN'T SHE COME?
JEANNE...
KA-CHAK
MARON!
SLAM
MARON!

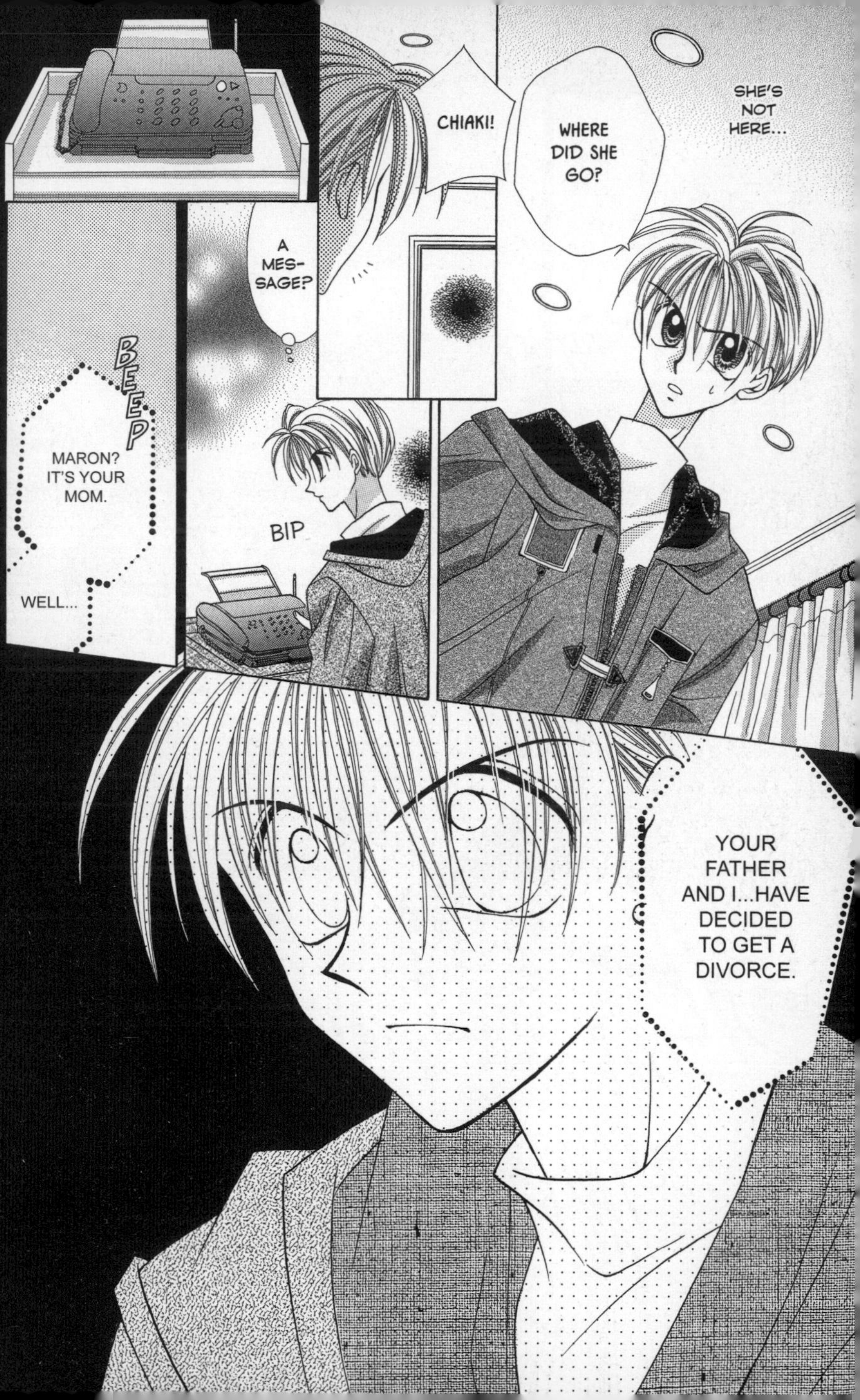
SHE'S NOT HERE...
WHERE DID SHE GO?
CHIAKI!
A MES-SAGE?
BIP
BEEP
MARON? IT'S YOUR MOM.
WELL...
YOUR FATHER AND I...HAVE DECIDED TO GET A DIVORCE.

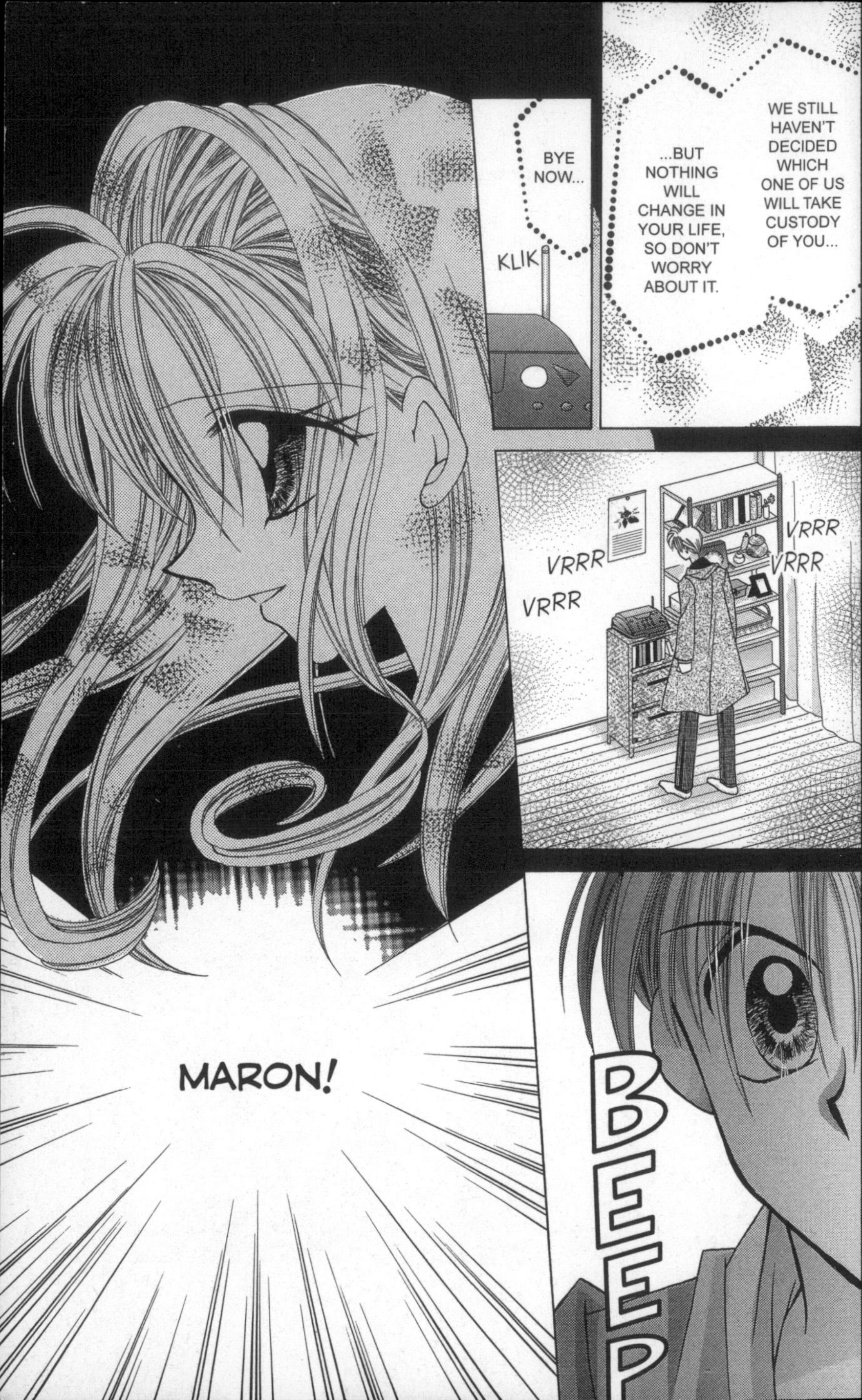
WE STILL HAVEN'T DECIDED WHICH ONE OF US WILL TAKE CUSTODY OF YOU...
...BUT NOTHING WILL CHANGE IN YOUR LIFE, SO DON'T WORRY ABOUT IT.
BYE NOW...
KLIK
VRRR
VRRR
VRRR
VRRR
BEEP
MARON!

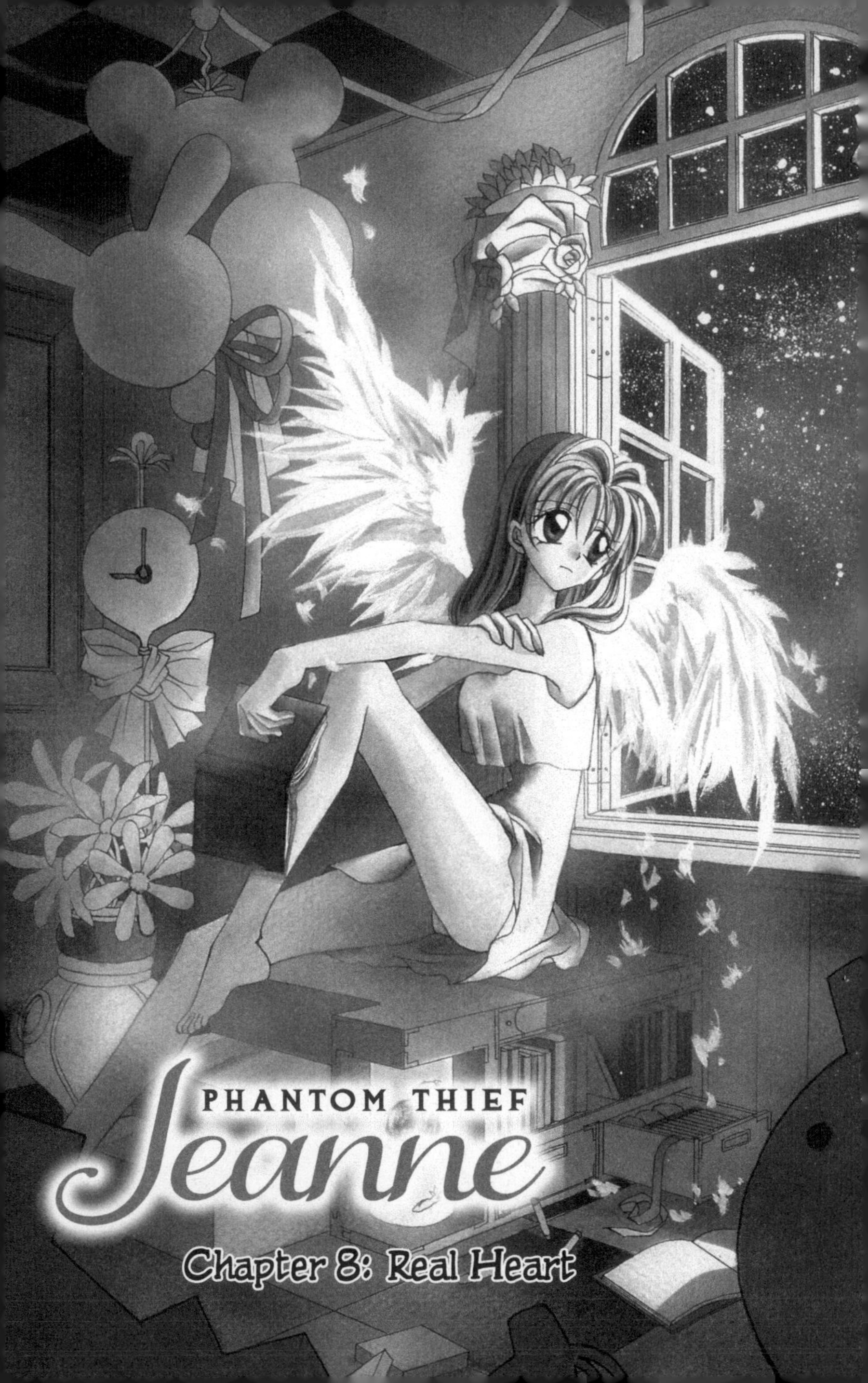
PHANTOM THIEF
Jeanne
Chapter 8: Real Heart

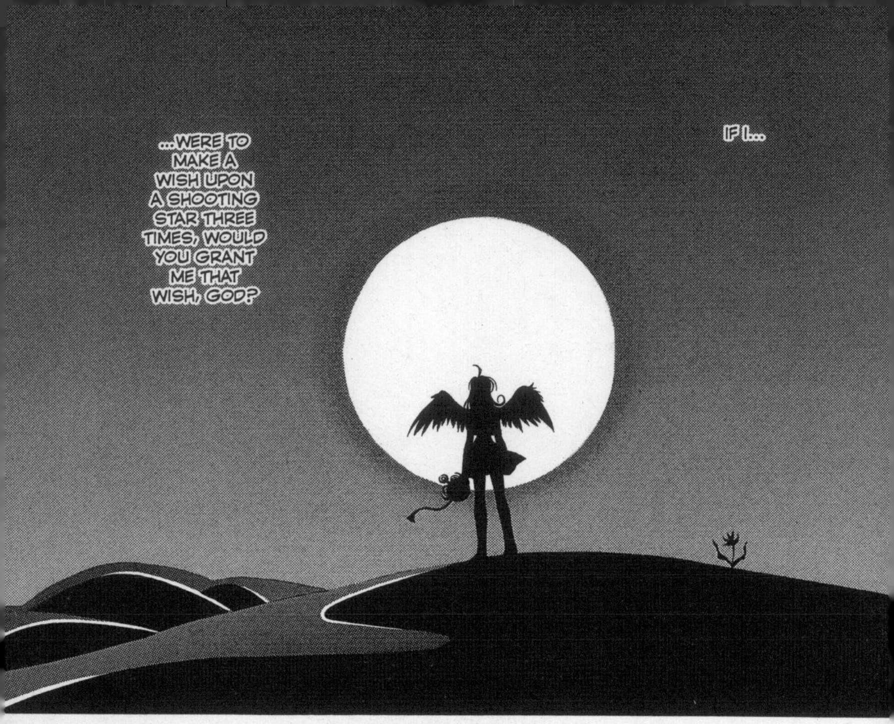
IF I...
...WERE TO MAKE A WISH UPON A SHOOTING STAR THREE TIMES, WOULD YOU GRANT ME THAT WISH, GOD?

PHANTOM
THIEF
JEANNE

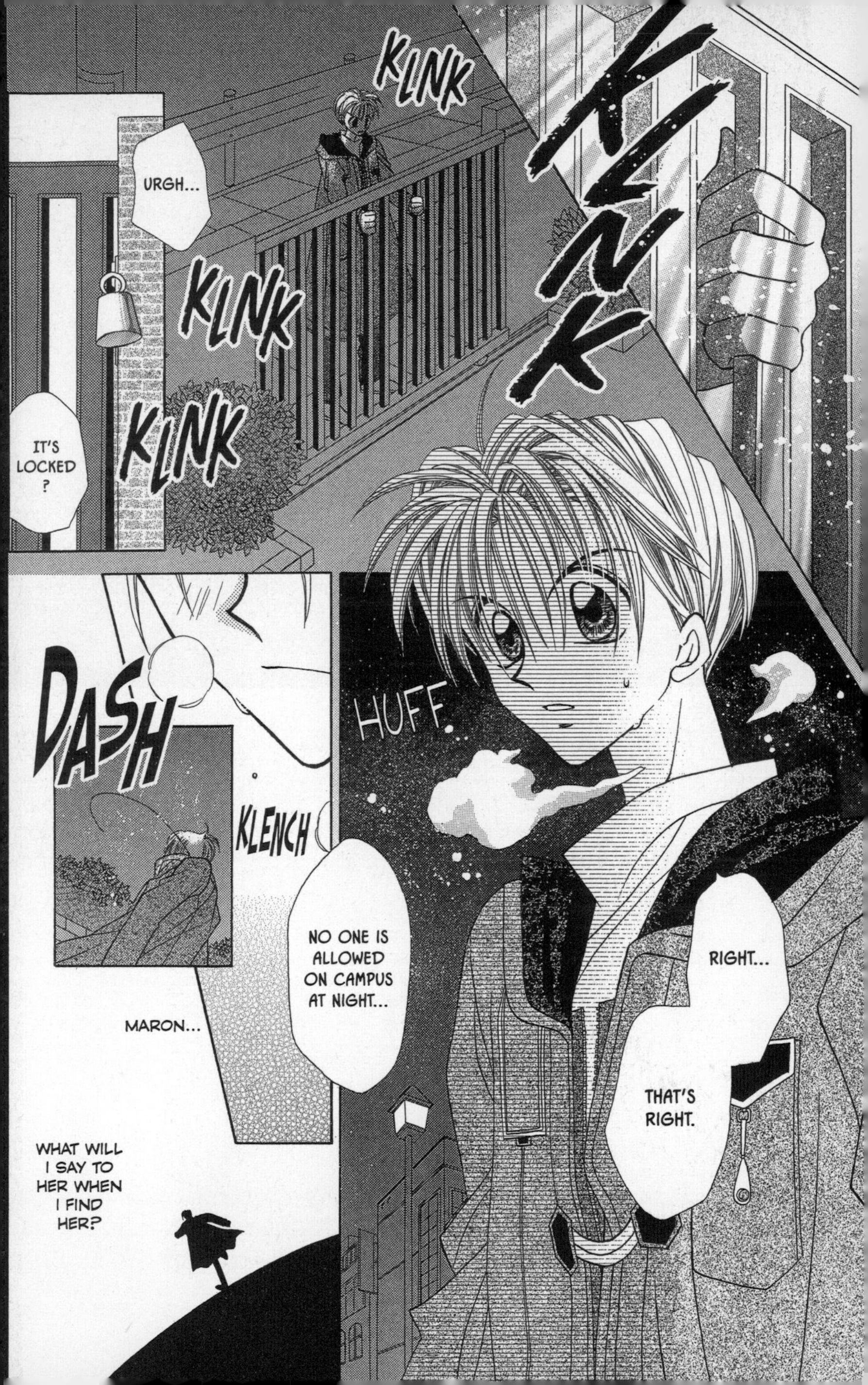
KLNK
KLNK
URGH...
KLNK
KLNK
IT'S LOCKED?
HUFF
NO ONE IS ALLOWED ON CAMPUS AT NIGHT...
RIGHT...
THAT'S RIGHT.
DASH
KLENCH
MARON...
WHAT WILL I SAY TO HER WHEN I FIND HER?

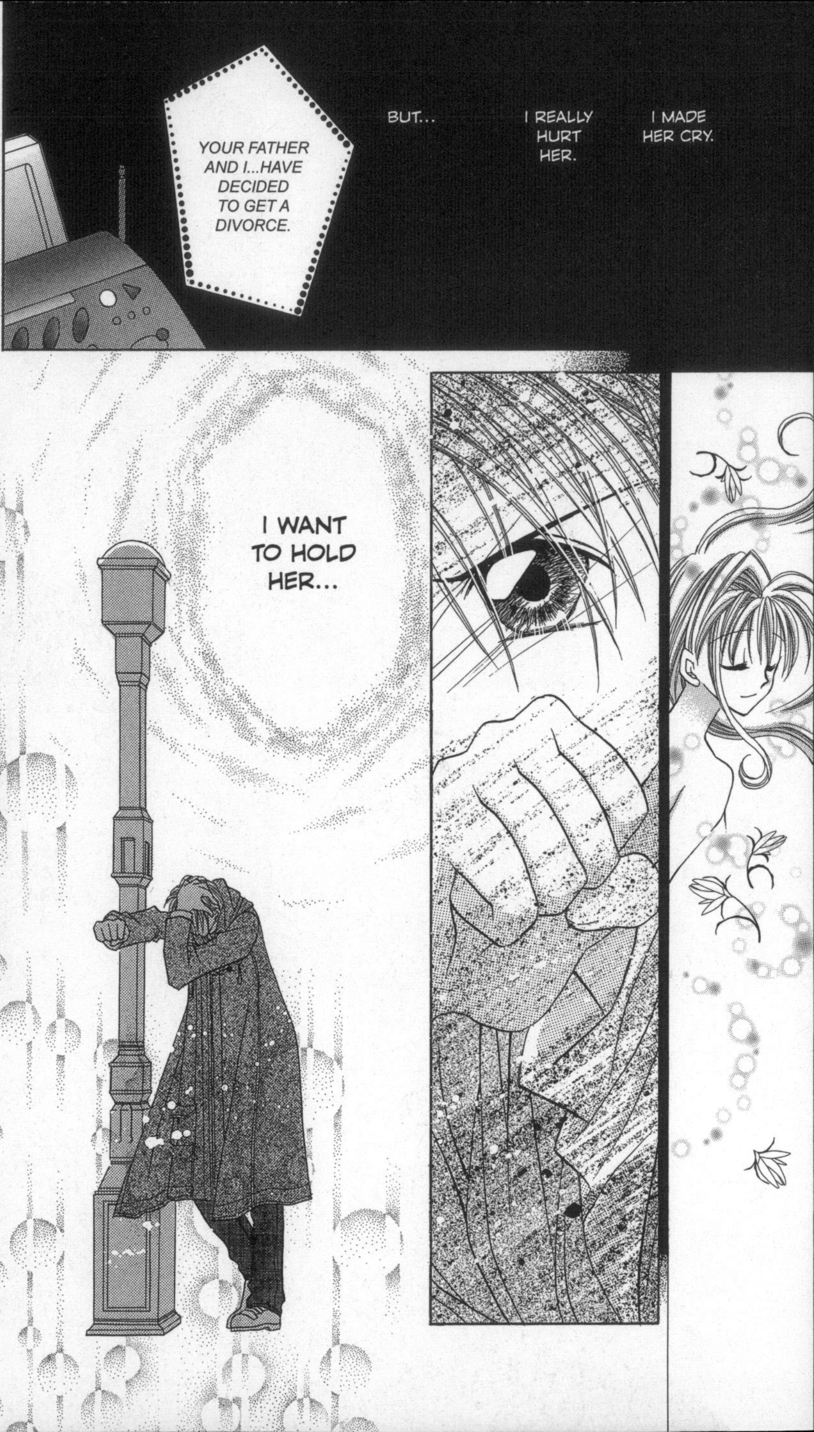
I MADE HER CRY.
I REALLY HURT HER.
BUT...
YOUR FATHER AND I...HAVE DECIDED TO GET A DIVORCE.
I WANT TO HOLD HER...

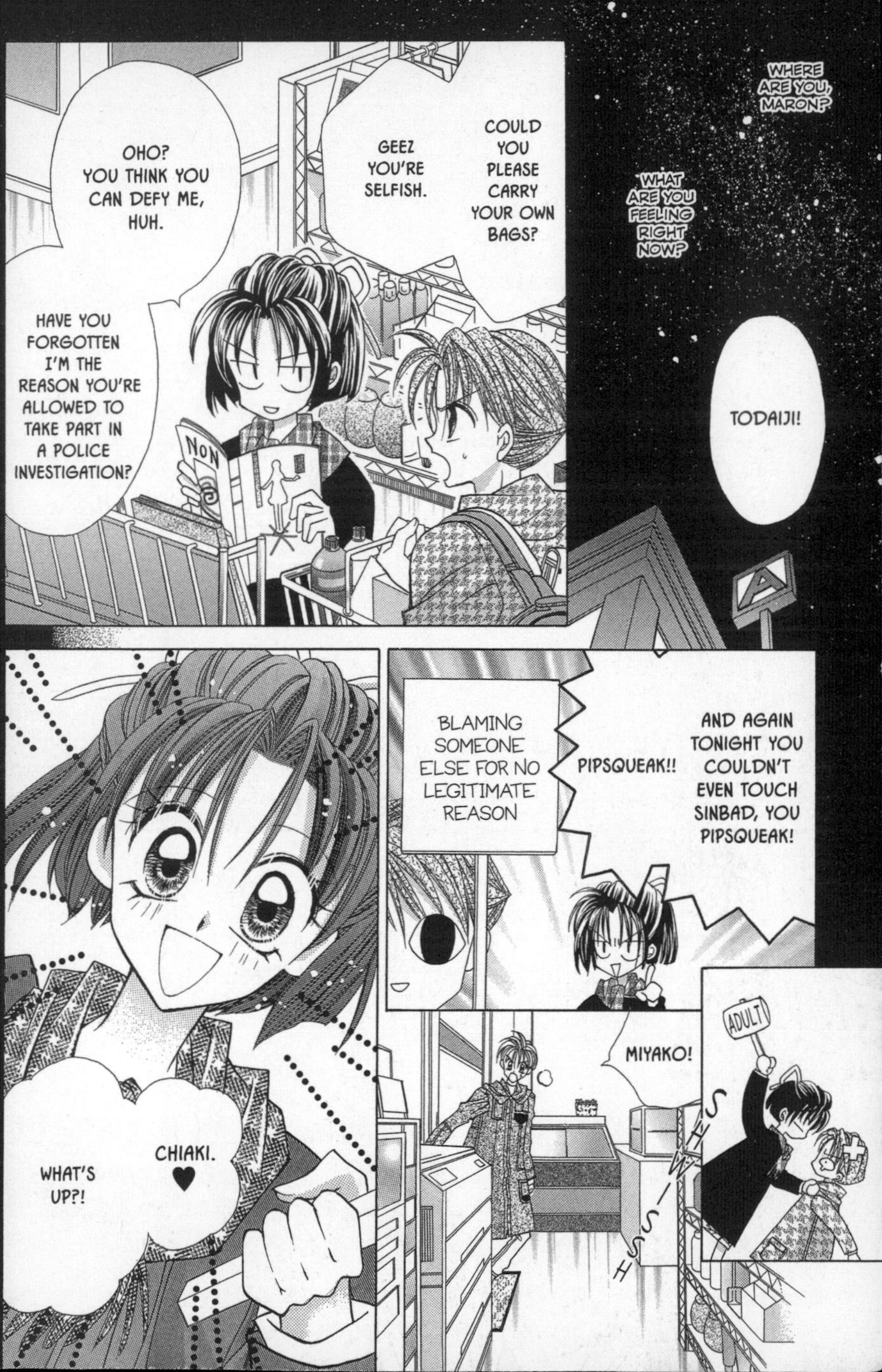
WHERE ARE YOU, MARON?
WHAT ARE YOU FEELING RIGHT NOW?
TODAIJI!
COULD YOU PLEASE CARRY YOUR OWN BAGS?
GEEZ YOU'RE SELFISH.
OHO? YOU THINK YOU CAN DEFY ME, HUH.
HAVE YOU FORGOTTEN I'M THE REASON YOU'RE ALLOWED TO TAKE PART IN A POLICE INVESTIGATION?
NON
AND AGAIN TONIGHT YOU COULDN'T EVEN TOUCH SINBAD, YOU PIPSQUEAK!
PIPSQUEAK!!
BLAMING SOMEONE ELSE FOR NO LEGITIMATE REASON
ADULT
SHH—SHH—SH
MIYAKO!
CHIAKI. ♥
WHAT'S UP?!

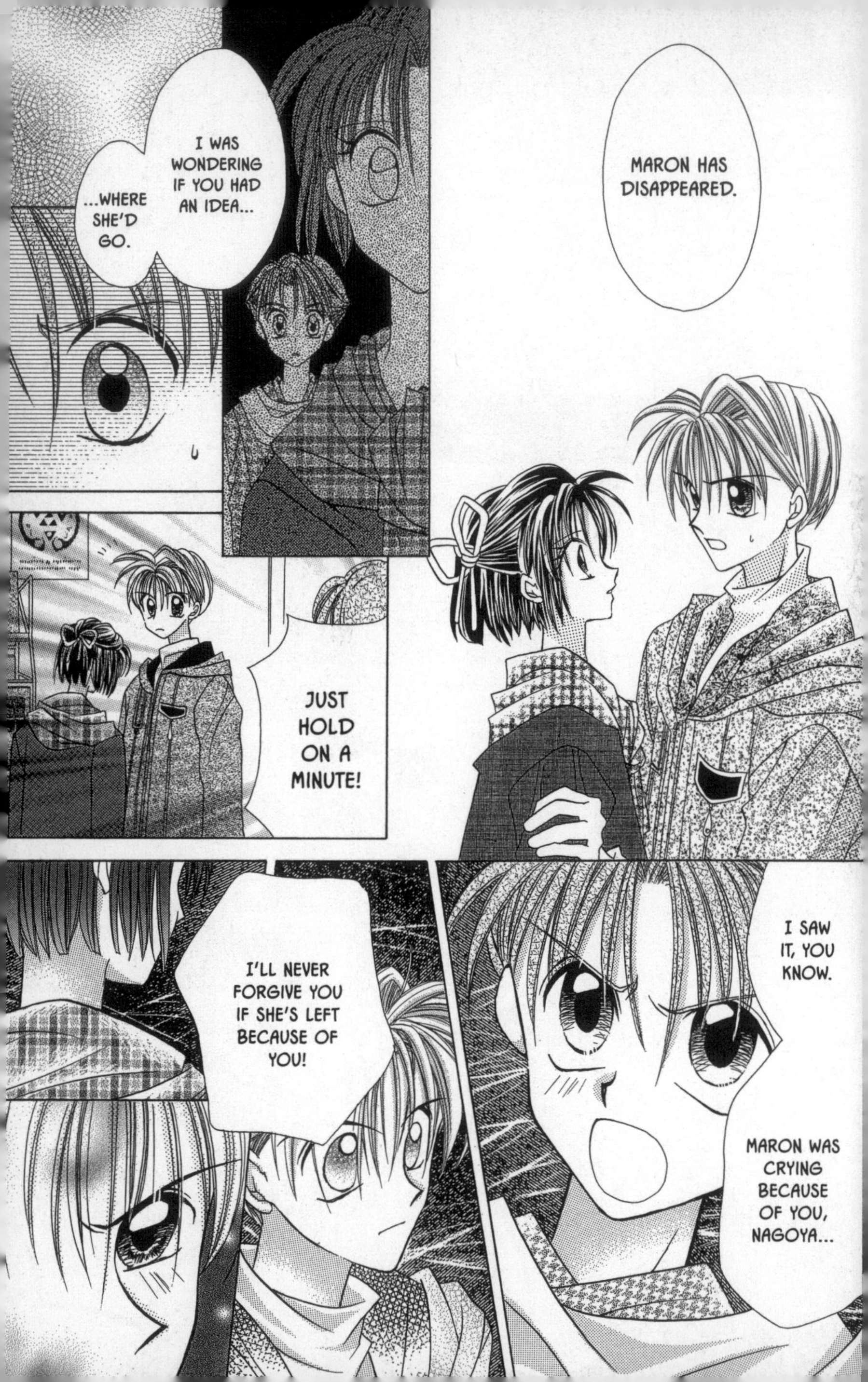
MARON HAS DISAPPEARED.
I WAS WONDERING IF YOU HAD AN IDEA...
...WHERE SHE'D GO.
JUST HOLD ON A MINUTE!
I SAW IT, YOU KNOW.
MARON WAS CRYING BECAUSE OF YOU, NAGOYA...
I'LL NEVER FORGIVE YOU IF SHE'S LEFT BECAUSE OF YOU!

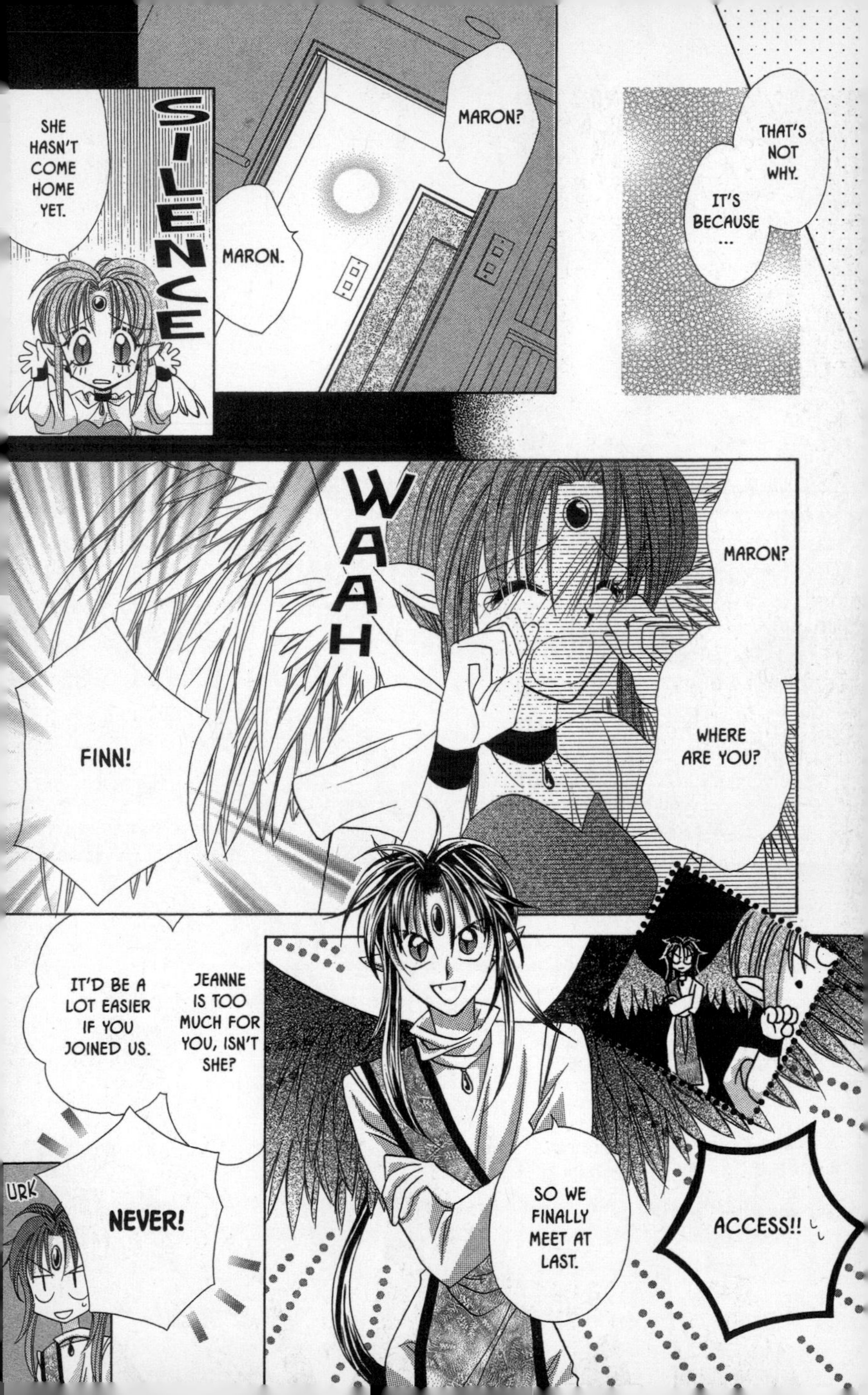

THAT'S NOT WHY.
IT'S BECAUSE ...
MARON?
MARON.
SILENCE
SHE HASN'T COME HOME YET.
MARON?
WHERE ARE YOU?
WAAH
FINN!
ACCESS!!
SO WE FINALLY MEET AT LAST.
JEANNE IS TOO MUCH FOR YOU, ISN'T SHE?
IT'D BE A LOT EASIER IF YOU JOINED US.
NEVER!
URK

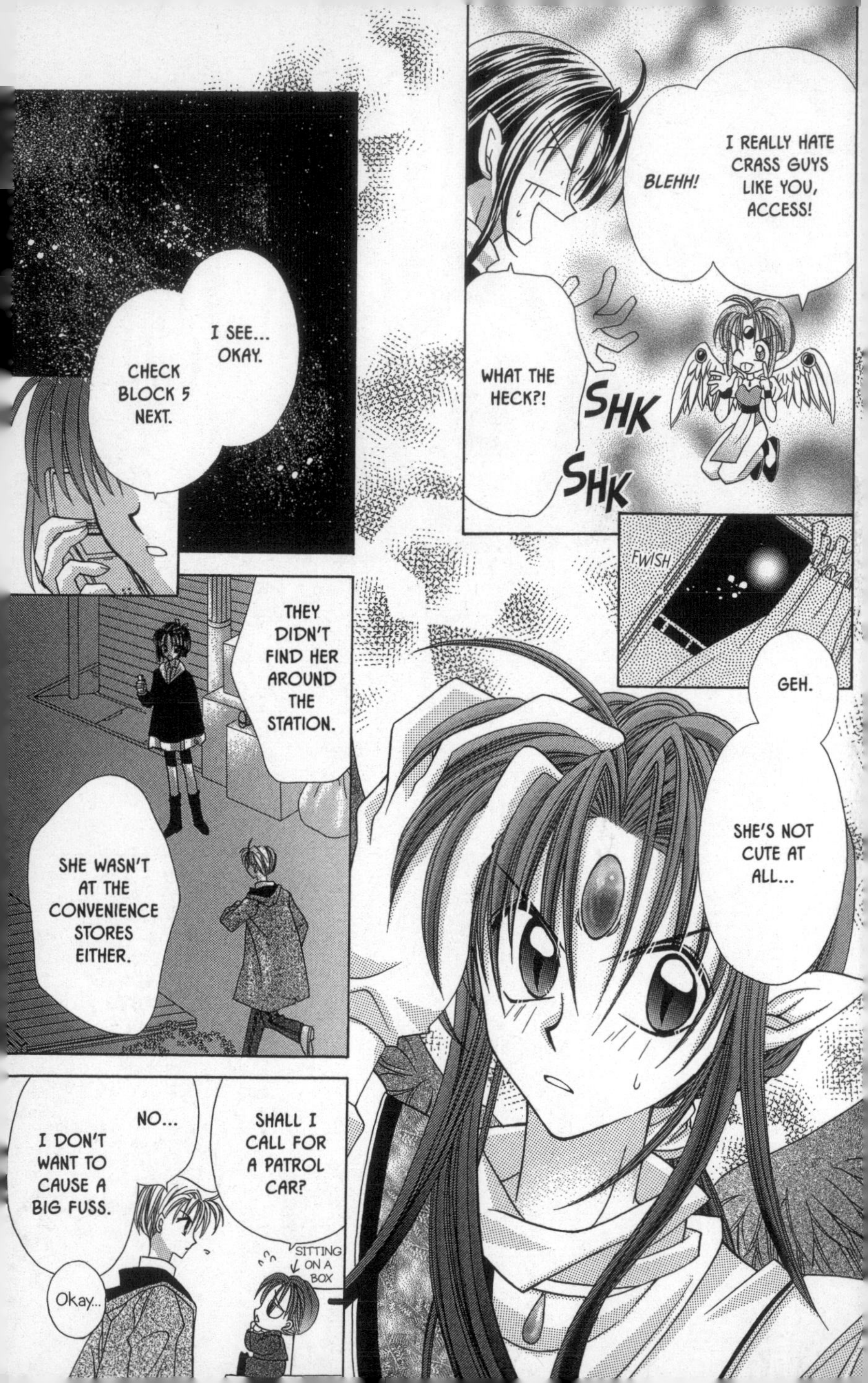
I REALLY HATE CRASS GUYS LIKE YOU, ACCESS!
BLEHH!
WHAT THE HECK?!
SHK
SHK
FWISH
GEH.
SHE'S NOT CUTE AT ALL...
I SEE... OKAY.
CHECK BLOCK 5 NEXT.
THEY DIDN'T FIND HER AROUND THE STATION.
SHE WASN'T AT THE CONVENIENCE STORES EITHER.
SHALL I CALL FOR A PATROL CAR?
NO...
I DON'T WANT TO CAUSE A BIG FUSS.
SITTING ON A BOX
Okay...

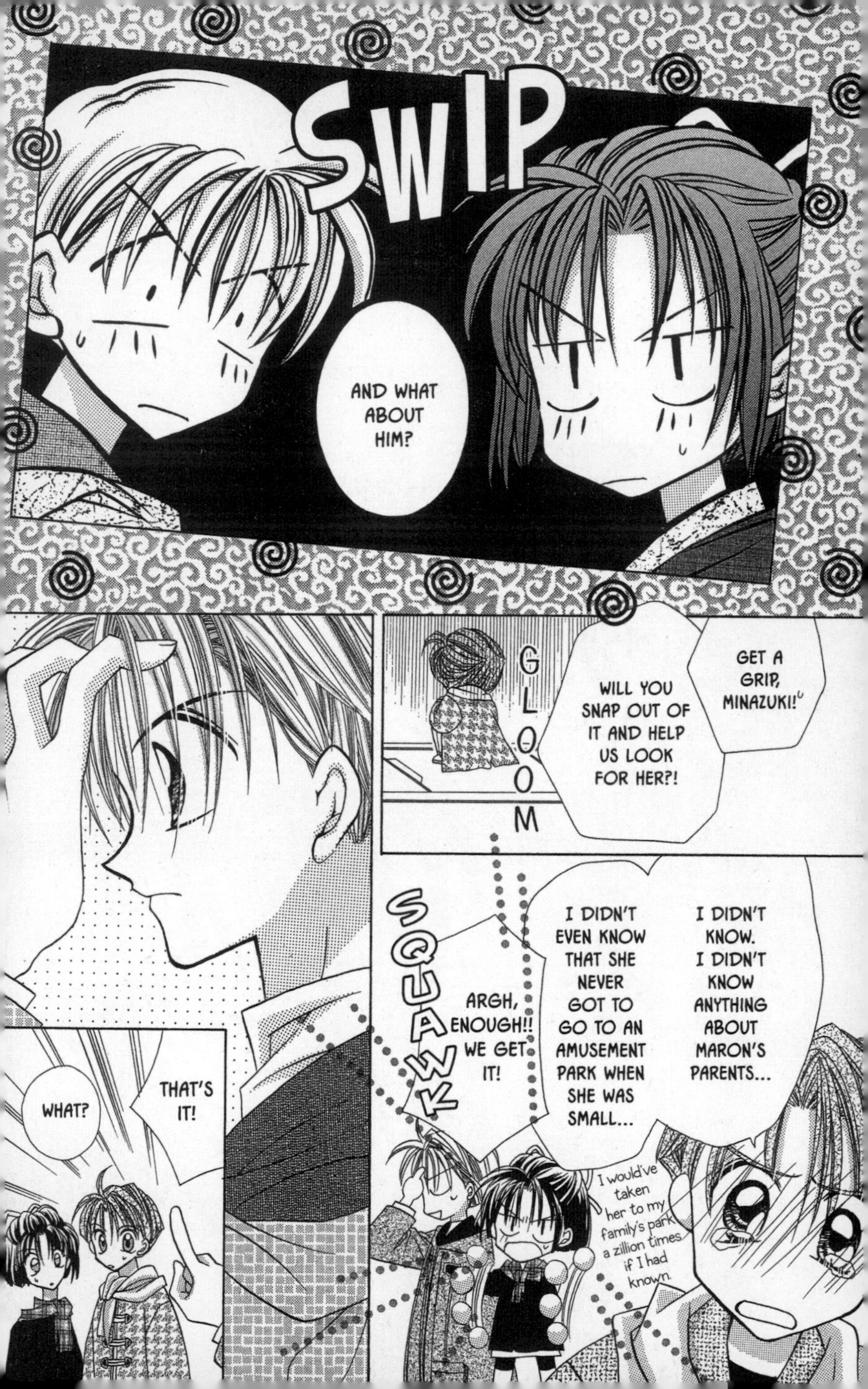
SWIP
AND WHAT ABOUT HIM?
GET A GRIP, MINAZUKI!
WILL YOU SNAP OUT OF IT AND HELP US LOOK FOR HER?!
GLOOM
I DIDN'T KNOW. I DIDN'T KNOW ANYTHING ABOUT MARON'S PARENTS...
I DIDN'T EVEN KNOW THAT SHE NEVER GOT TO GO TO AN AMUSEMENT PARK WHEN SHE WAS SMALL...
ARGH, ENOUGH!! WE GET IT!
SQUAWK
I would've taken her to my family's park a zillion times if I had known.
THAT'S IT!
WHAT?

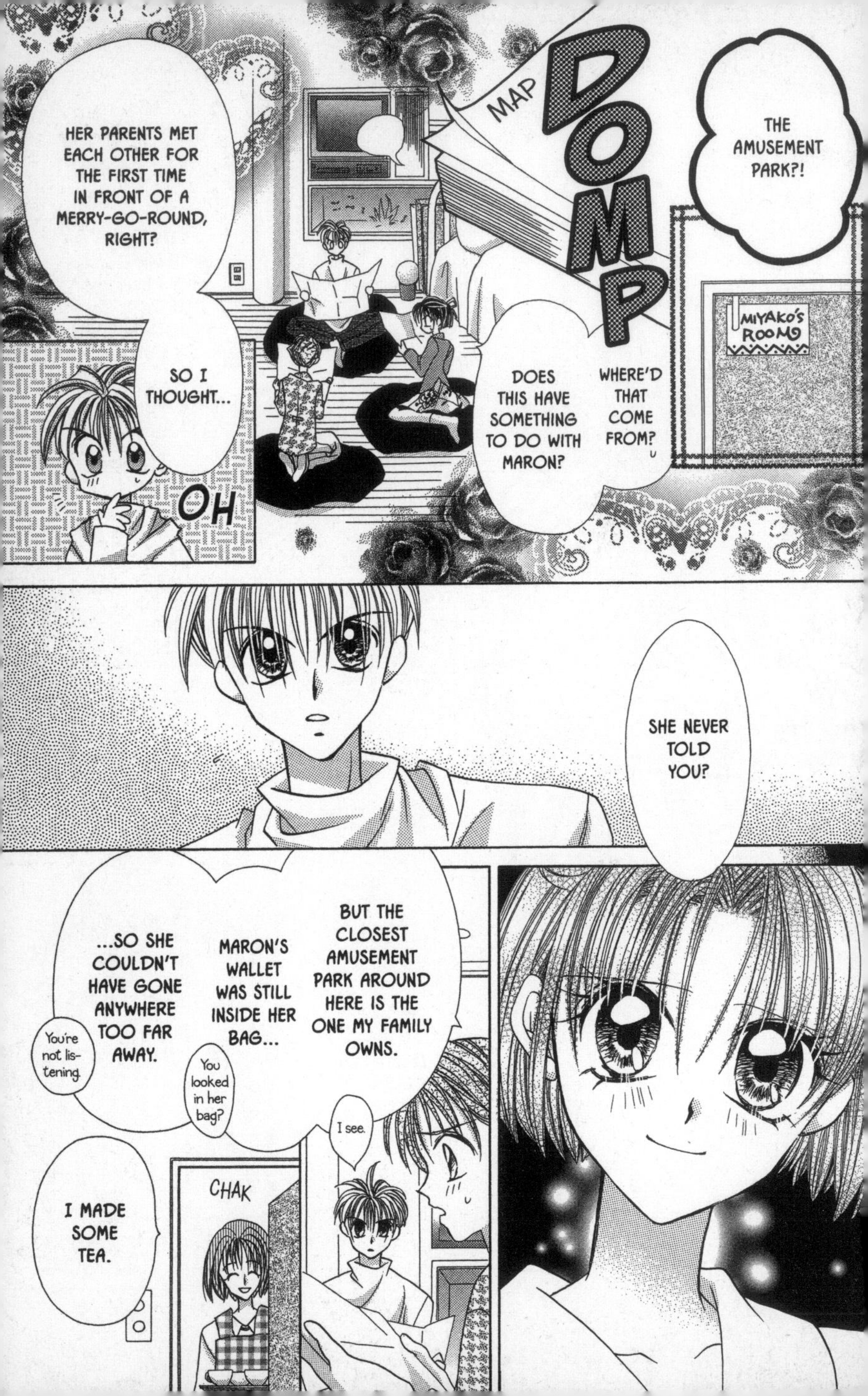
THE AMUSEMENT PARK?!
MAP
DOMP
MIYAKO'S ROOM
WHERE'D THAT COME FROM?
DOES THIS HAVE SOMETHING TO DO WITH MARON?
HER PARENTS MET EACH OTHER FOR THE FIRST TIME IN FRONT OF A MERRY-GO-ROUND, RIGHT?
SO I THOUGHT...
OH
SHE NEVER TOLD YOU?
BUT THE CLOSEST AMUSEMENT PARK AROUND HERE IS THE ONE MY FAMILY OWNS.
MARON'S WALLET WAS STILL INSIDE HER BAG...
...SO SHE COULDN'T HAVE GONE ANYWHERE TOO FAR AWAY.
You looked in her bag?
You're not listening.
I see.
CHAK
I MADE SOME TEA.

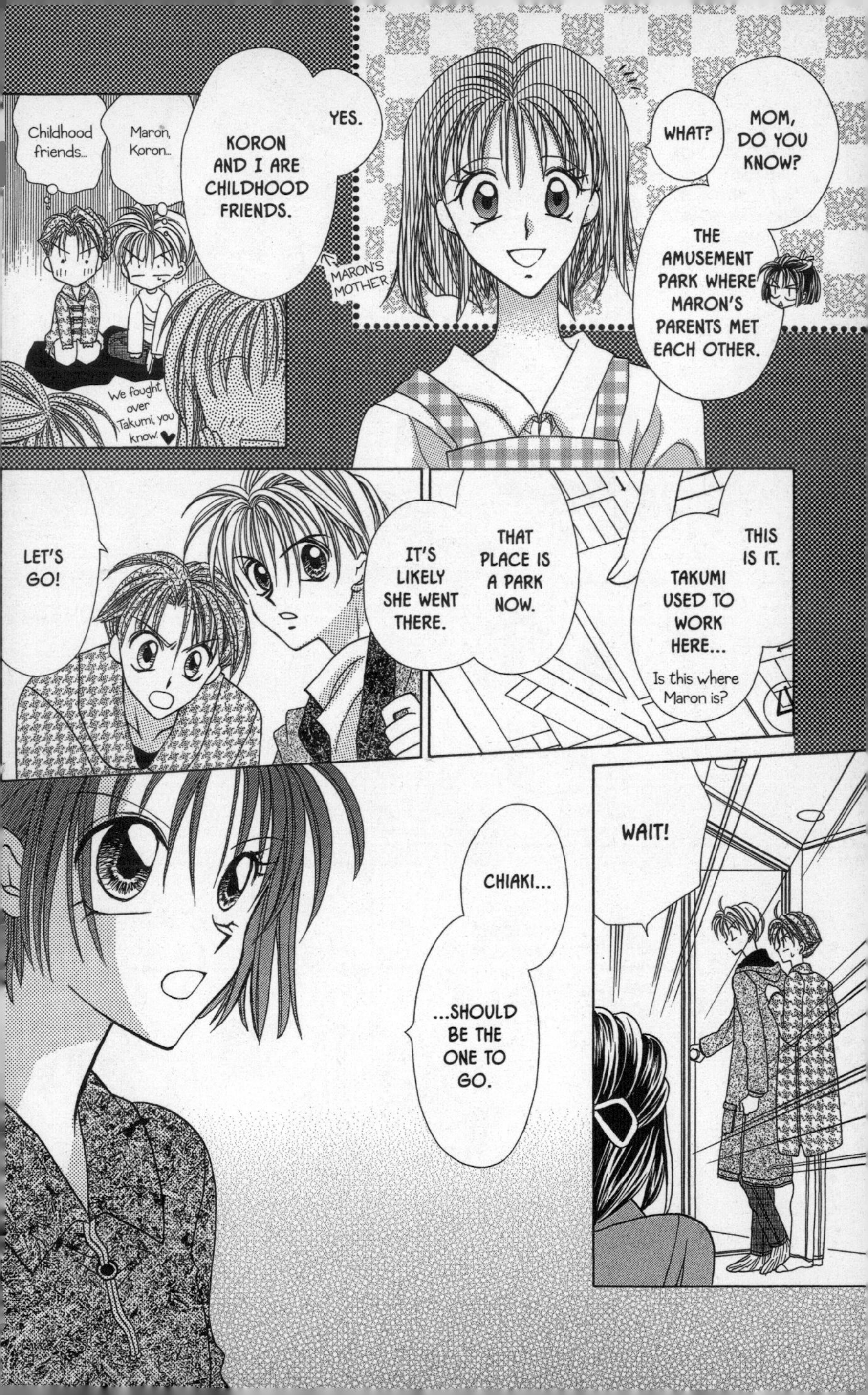
MOM, DO YOU KNOW?
WHAT?
THE AMUSEMENT PARK WHERE MARON'S PARENTS MET EACH OTHER.
MARON'S MOTHER
YES.
KORON AND I ARE CHILDHOOD FRIENDS.
Maron, Koron...
Childhood friends...
We fought over Takumi, you know. ♥
THIS IS IT.
TAKUMI USED TO WORK HERE...
Is this where Maron is?
THAT PLACE IS A PARK NOW.
IT'S LIKELY SHE WENT THERE.
LET'S GO!
WAIT!
CHIAKI...
...SHOULD BE THE ONE TO GO.

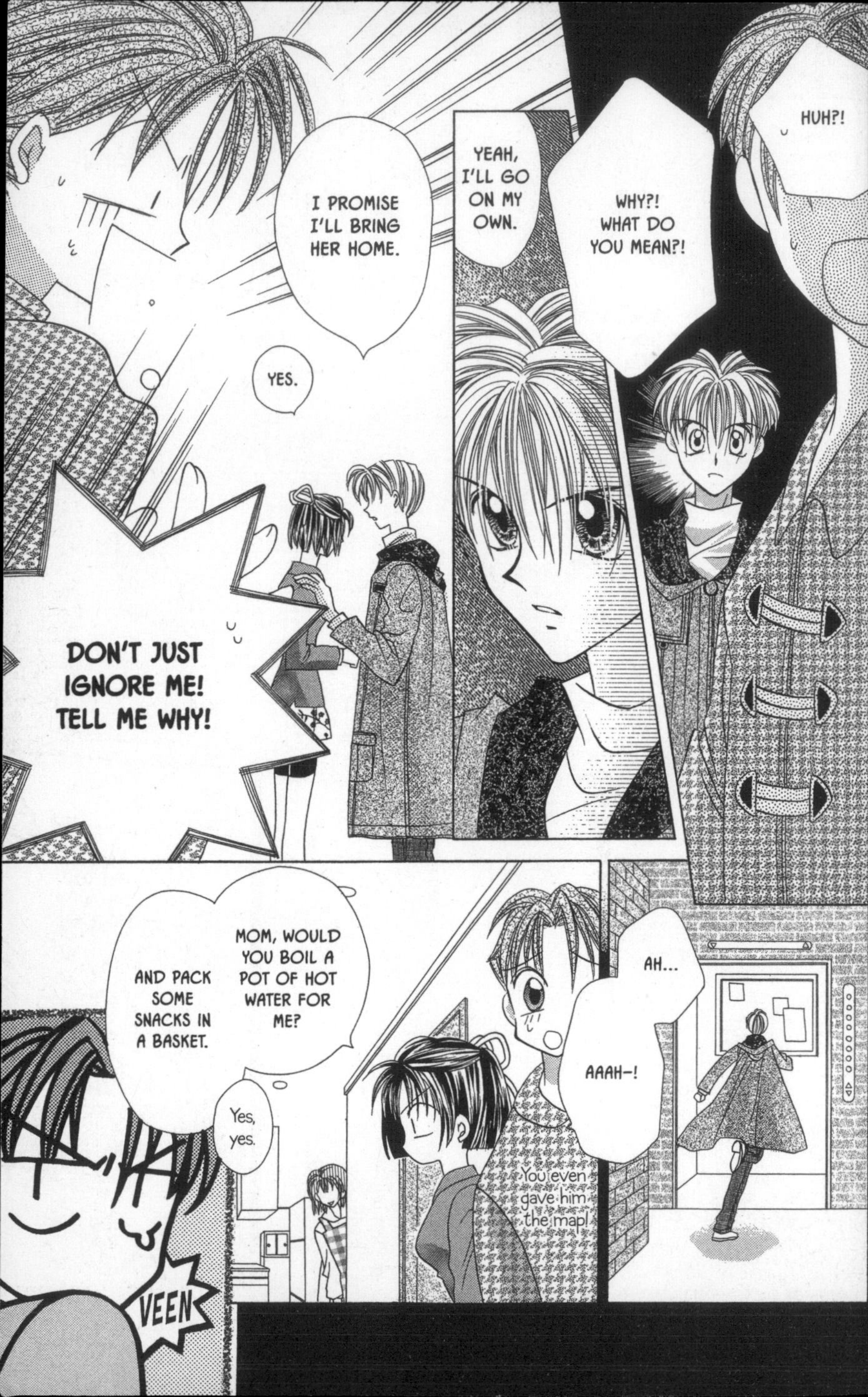
HUH?!
WHY?! WHAT DO YOU MEAN?!
YEAH, I'LL GO ON MY OWN.
I PROMISE I'LL BRING HER HOME.
YES.
DON'T JUST IGNORE ME! TELL ME WHY!
AH...
AAAH–!
You even gave him the map!
MOM, WOULD YOU BOIL A POT OF HOT WATER FOR ME?
AND PACK SOME SNACKS IN A BASKET.
Yes, yes.
VEEN

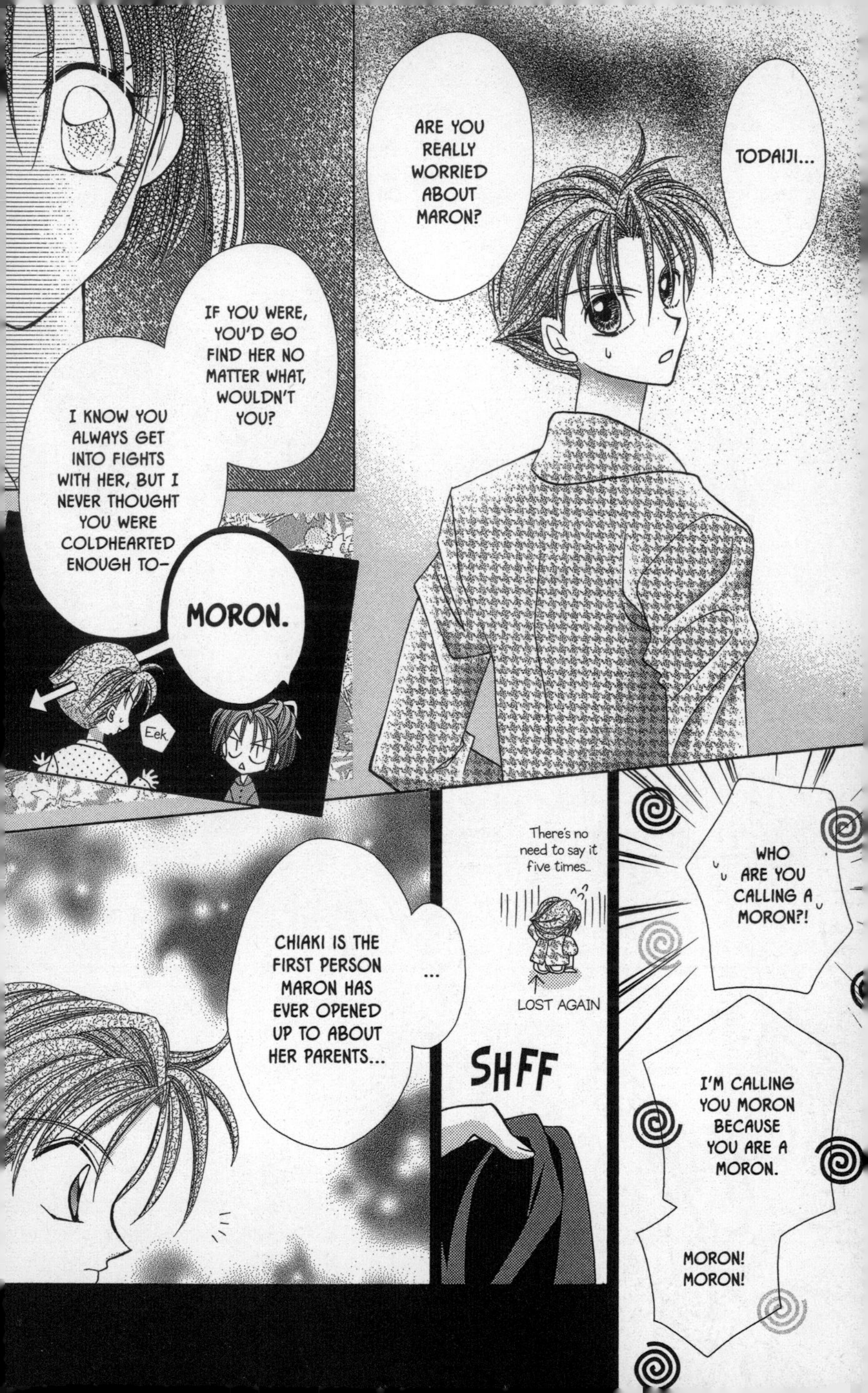
TODAIJI...
ARE YOU REALLY WORRIED ABOUT MARON?
IF YOU WERE, YOU'D GO FIND HER NO MATTER WHAT, WOULDN'T YOU?
I KNOW YOU ALWAYS GET INTO FIGHTS WITH HER, BUT I NEVER THOUGHT YOU WERE COLDHEARTED ENOUGH TO–
MORON.
Eek.
WHO ARE YOU CALLING A MORON?!
I'M CALLING YOU MORON BECAUSE YOU ARE A MORON.
MORON! MORON!
There's no need to say it five times...
LOST AGAIN
SHFF
CHIAKI IS THE FIRST PERSON MARON HAS EVER OPENED UP TO ABOUT HER PARENTS...
...

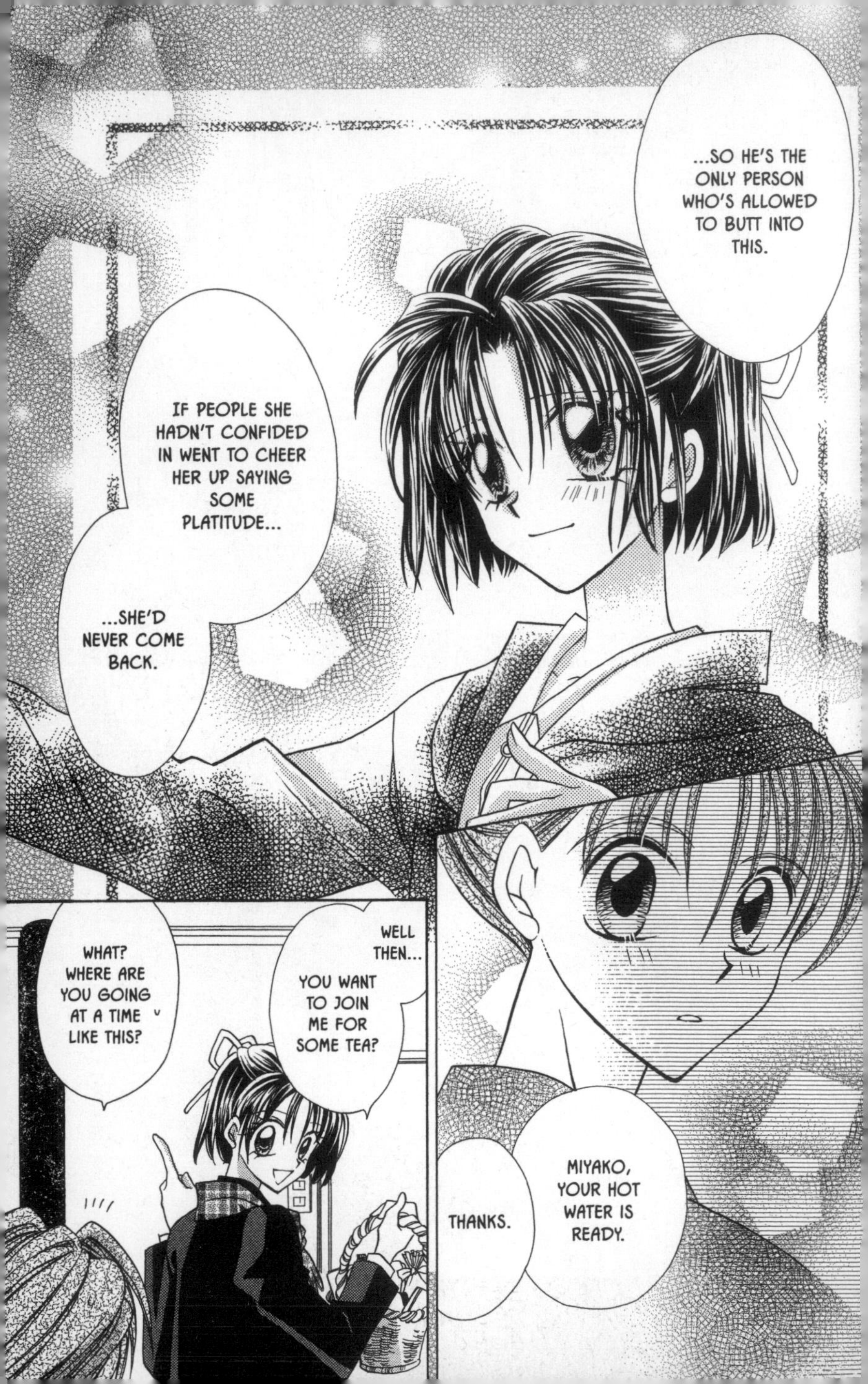
...SO HE'S THE ONLY PERSON WHO'S ALLOWED TO BUTT INTO THIS.
IF PEOPLE SHE HADN'T CONFIDED IN WENT TO CHEER HER UP SAYING SOME PLATITUDE...
...SHE'D NEVER COME BACK.
MIYAKO, YOUR HOT WATER IS READY.
THANKS.
WELL THEN...
YOU WANT TO JOIN ME FOR SOME TEA?
WHAT? WHERE ARE YOU GOING AT A TIME LIKE THIS?

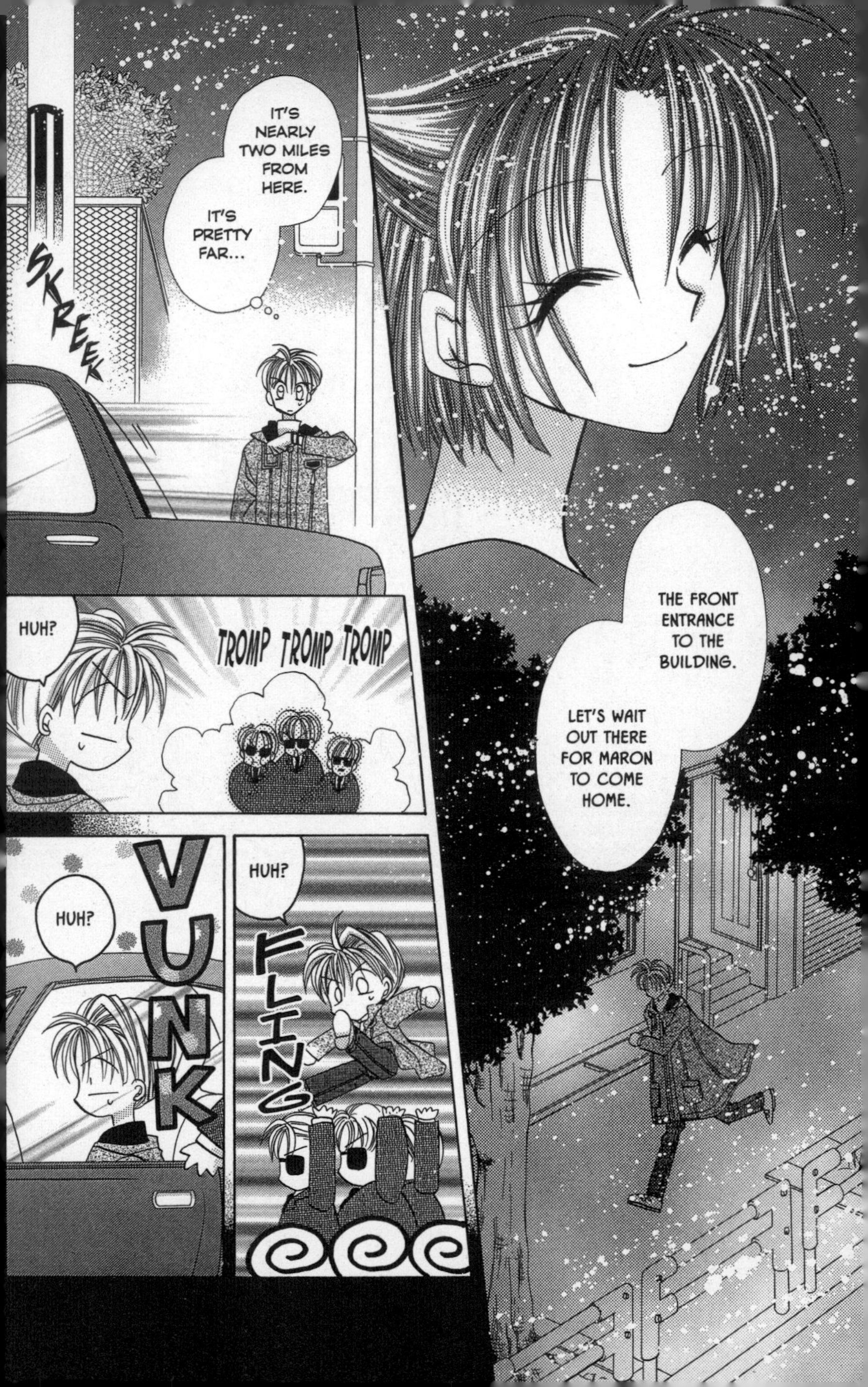
THE FRONT ENTRANCE TO THE BUILDING.
LET'S WAIT OUT THERE FOR MARON TO COME HOME.
IT'S NEARLY TWO MILES FROM HERE.
IT'S PRETTY FAR...
SKREEK
HUH?
TROMP TROMP TROMP
HUH?
FLING
HUH?
VUNK

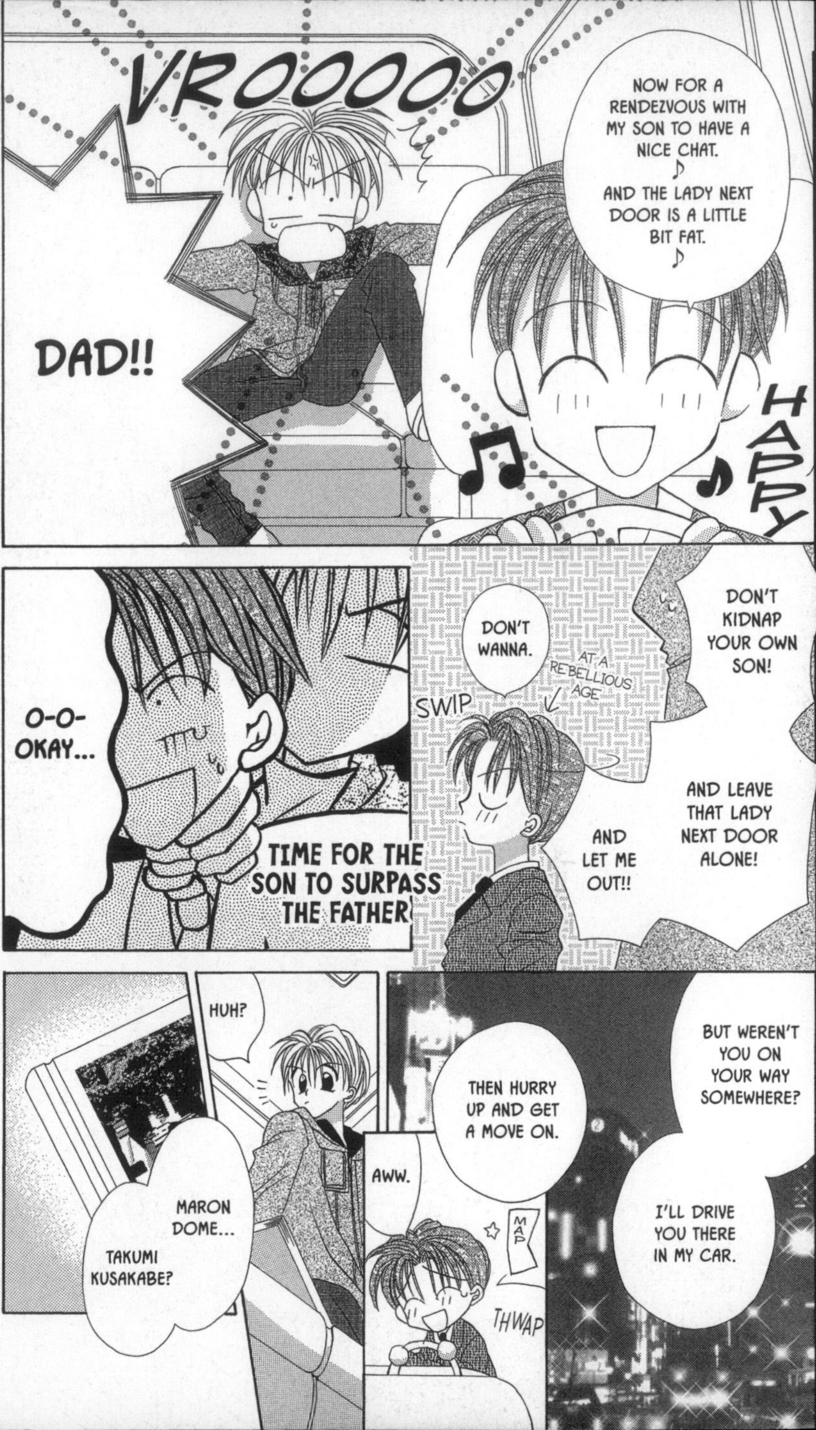
NOW FOR A RENDEZVOUS WITH MY SON TO HAVE A NICE CHAT. ♪ AND THE LADY NEXT DOOR IS A LITTLE BIT FAT. ♪
VROOOOO
HAPPY
DAD!!
DON'T KIDNAP YOUR OWN SON!
AND LEAVE THAT LADY NEXT DOOR ALONE!
AND LET ME OUT!!
DON'T WANNA.
AT A REBELLIOUS AGE
SWIP
O-O-OKAY...
TIME FOR THE SON TO SURPASS THE FATHER
BUT WEREN'T YOU ON YOUR WAY SOMEWHERE?
I'LL DRIVE YOU THERE IN MY CAR.
THEN HURRY UP AND GET A MOVE ON.
AWW.
MAP
THWAP
HUH?
MARON DOME...
TAKUMI KUSAKABE?

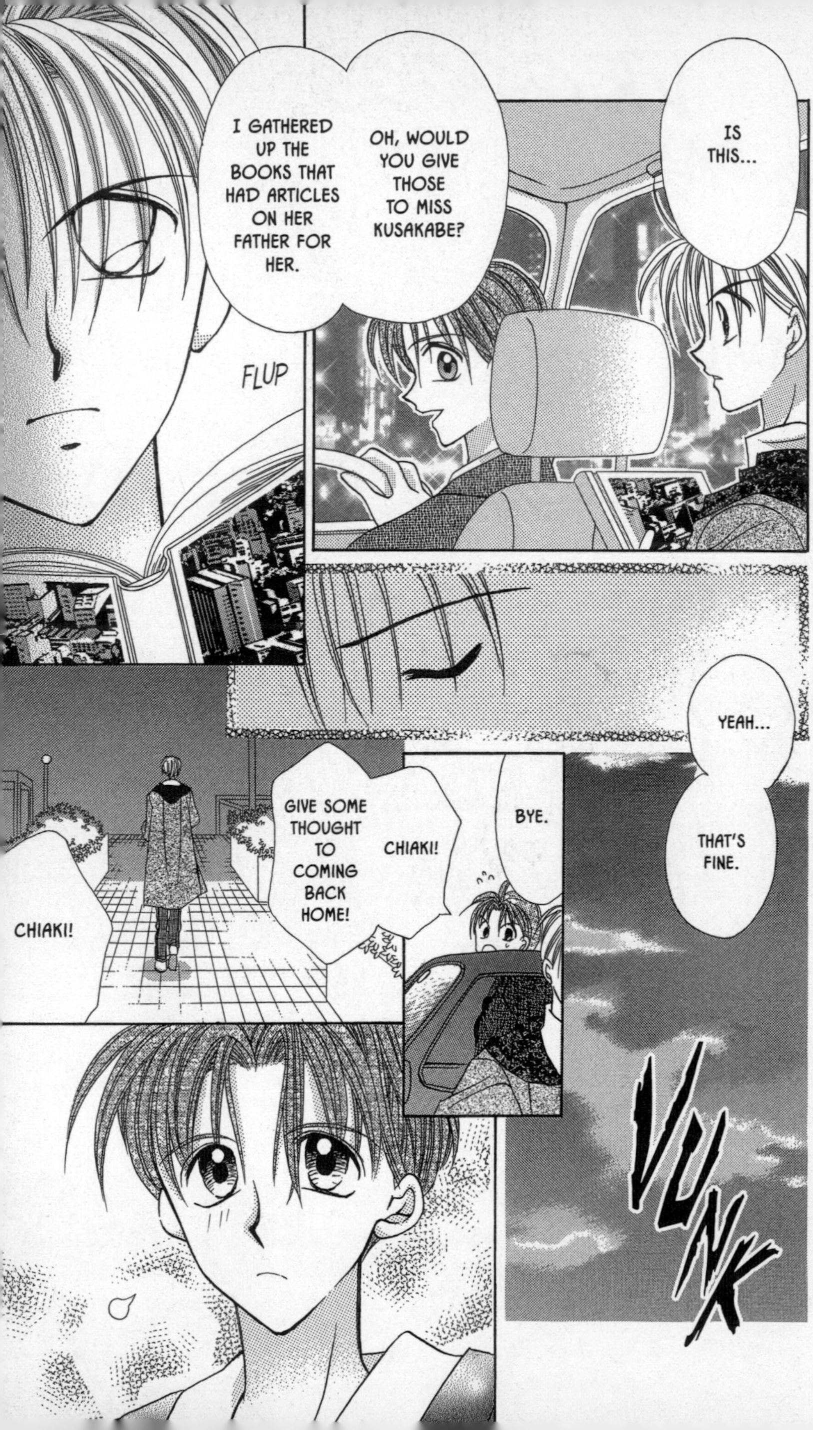
IS THIS...
OH, WOULD YOU GIVE THOSE TO MISS KUSAKABE?
I GATHERED UP THE BOOKS THAT HAD ARTICLES ON HER FATHER FOR HER.
FLUP
YEAH...
THAT'S FINE.
VUNK
BYE.
CHIAKI!
GIVE SOME THOUGHT TO COMING BACK HOME!
CHIAKI!

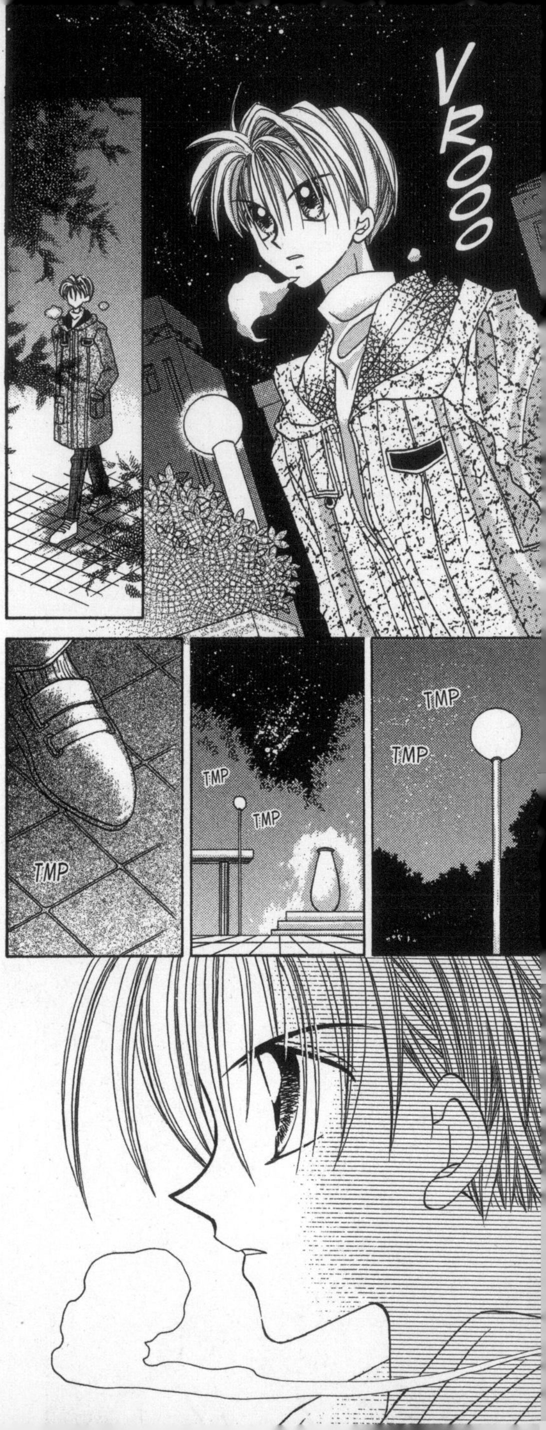
VROOO
TMP
TMP
TMP
TMP
TMP

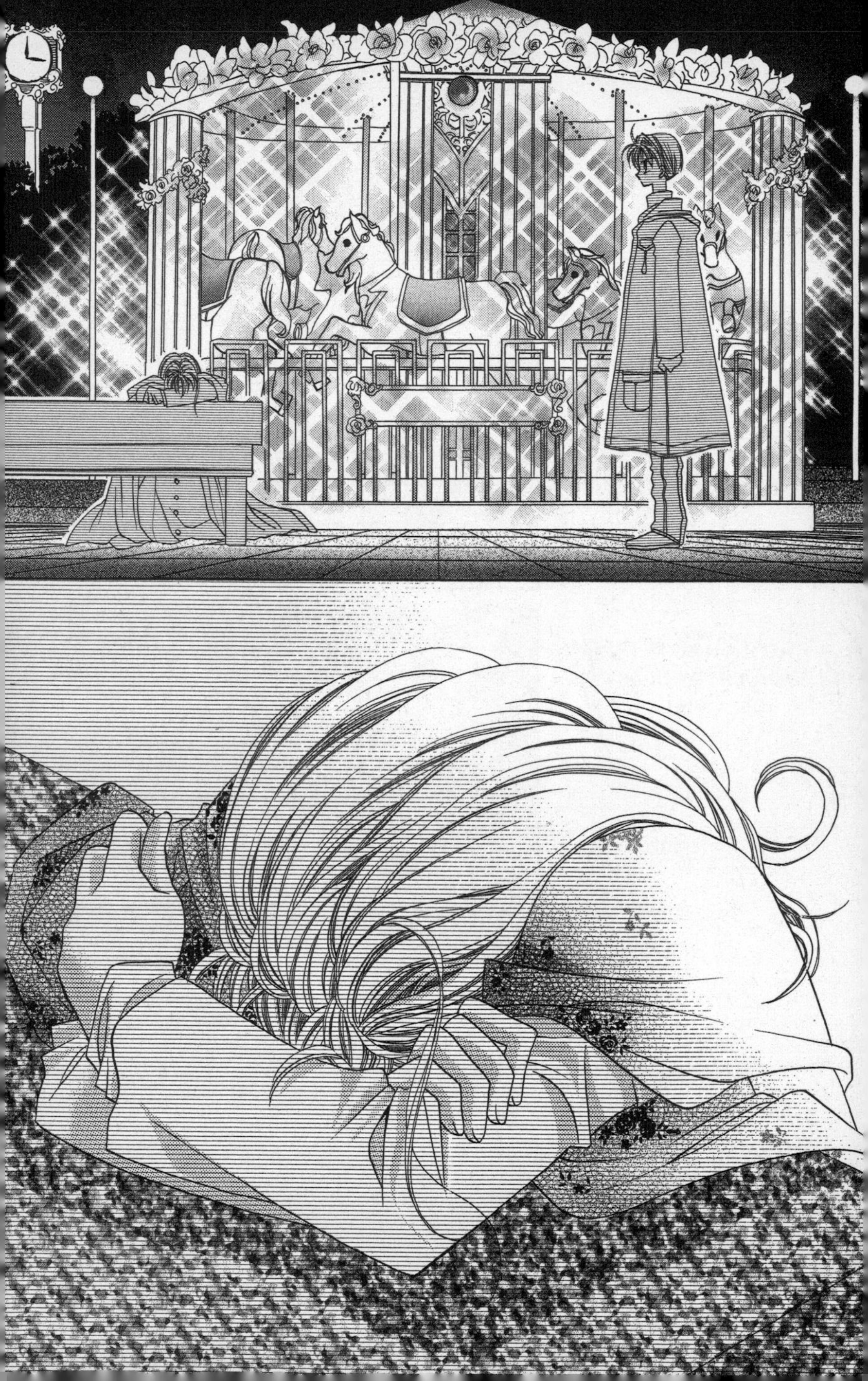

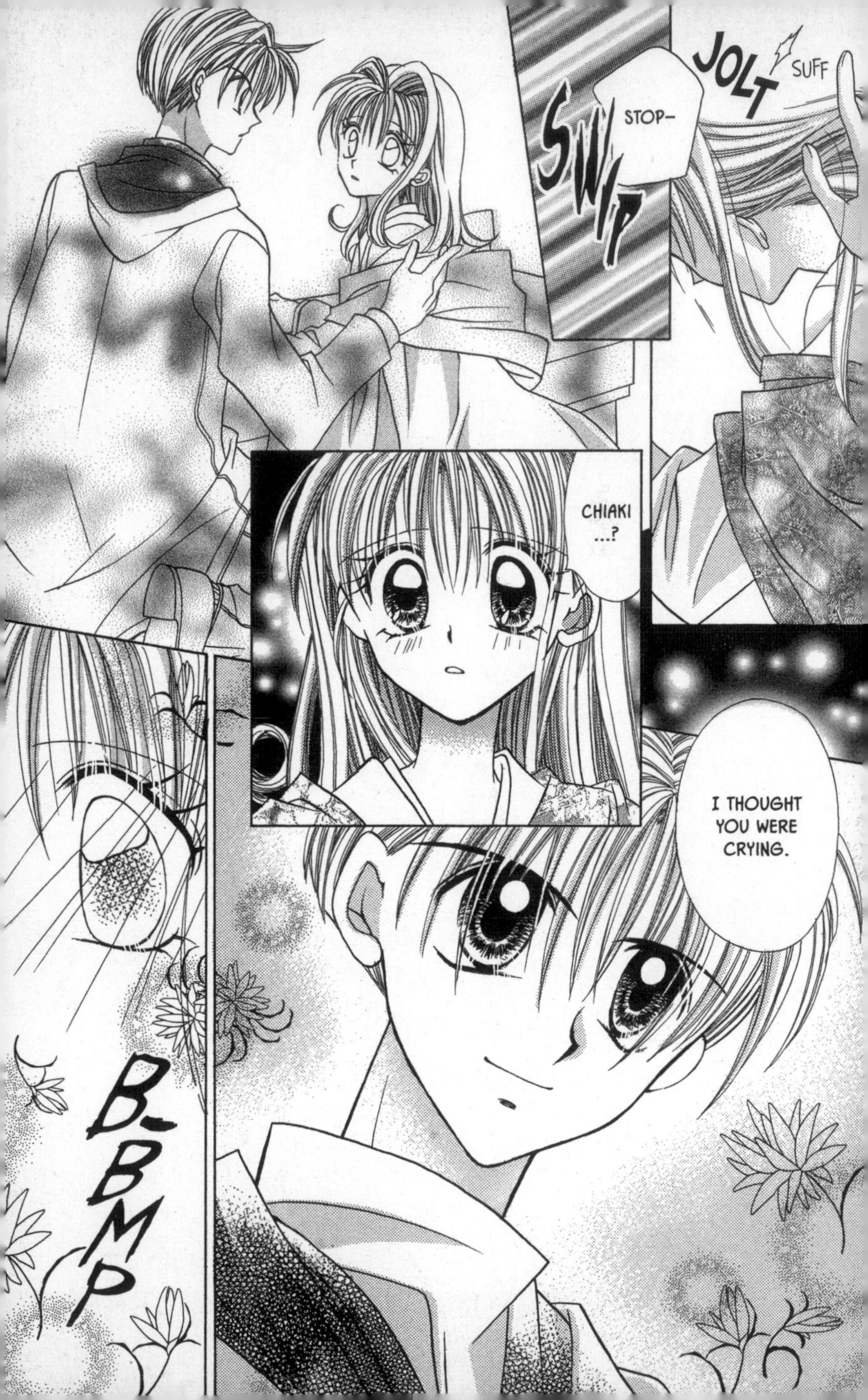
JOLT
SUFF
STOP–
SWIP
CHIAKI ...?
I THOUGHT YOU WERE CRYING.
B-BMP

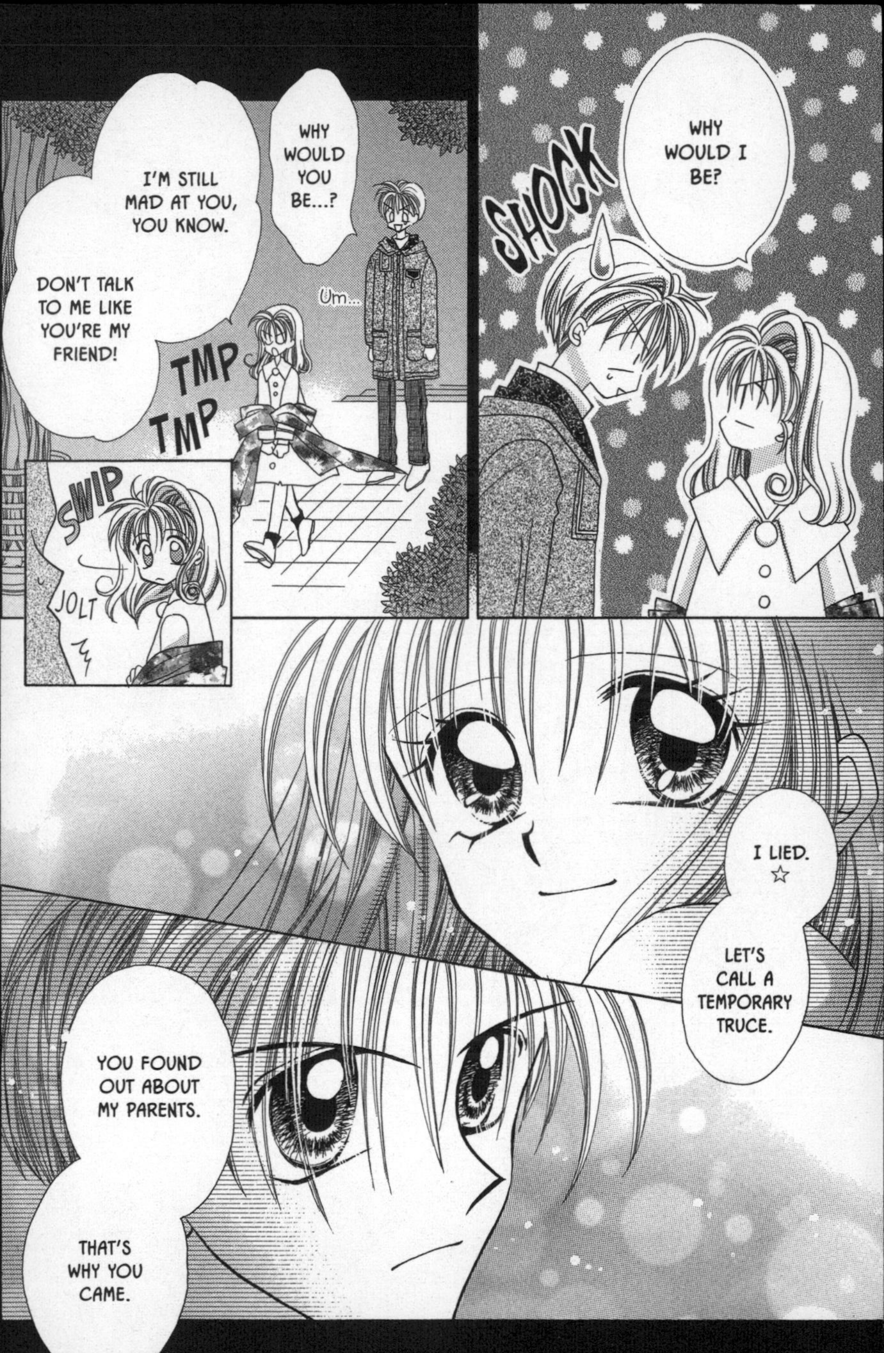
WHY WOULD I BE?
SHOCK
WHY WOULD YOU BE...?
Um...
I'M STILL MAD AT YOU, YOU KNOW.
DON'T TALK TO ME LIKE YOU'RE MY FRIEND!
TMP TMP
SWIP
JOLT
I LIED. ☆
LET'S CALL A TEMPORARY TRUCE.
YOU FOUND OUT ABOUT MY PARENTS.
THAT'S WHY YOU CAME.

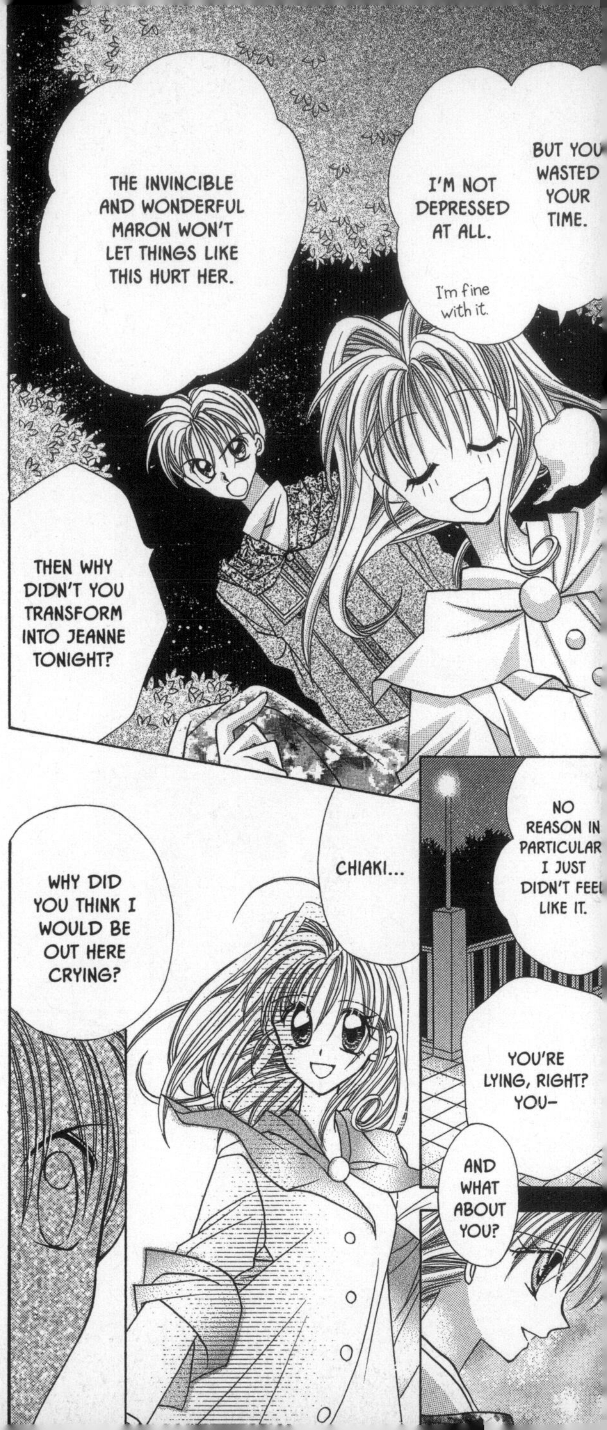
BUT YOU WASTED YOUR TIME.
I'M NOT DEPRESSED AT ALL.
I'm fine with it.
THE INVINCIBLE AND WONDERFUL MARON WON'T LET THINGS LIKE THIS HURT HER.
THEN WHY DIDN'T YOU TRANSFORM INTO JEANNE TONIGHT?
NO REASON IN PARTICULAR I JUST DIDN'T FEEL LIKE IT.
YOU'RE LYING, RIGHT? YOU–
AND WHAT ABOUT YOU?
CHIAKI...
WHY DID YOU THINK I WOULD BE OUT HERE CRYING?

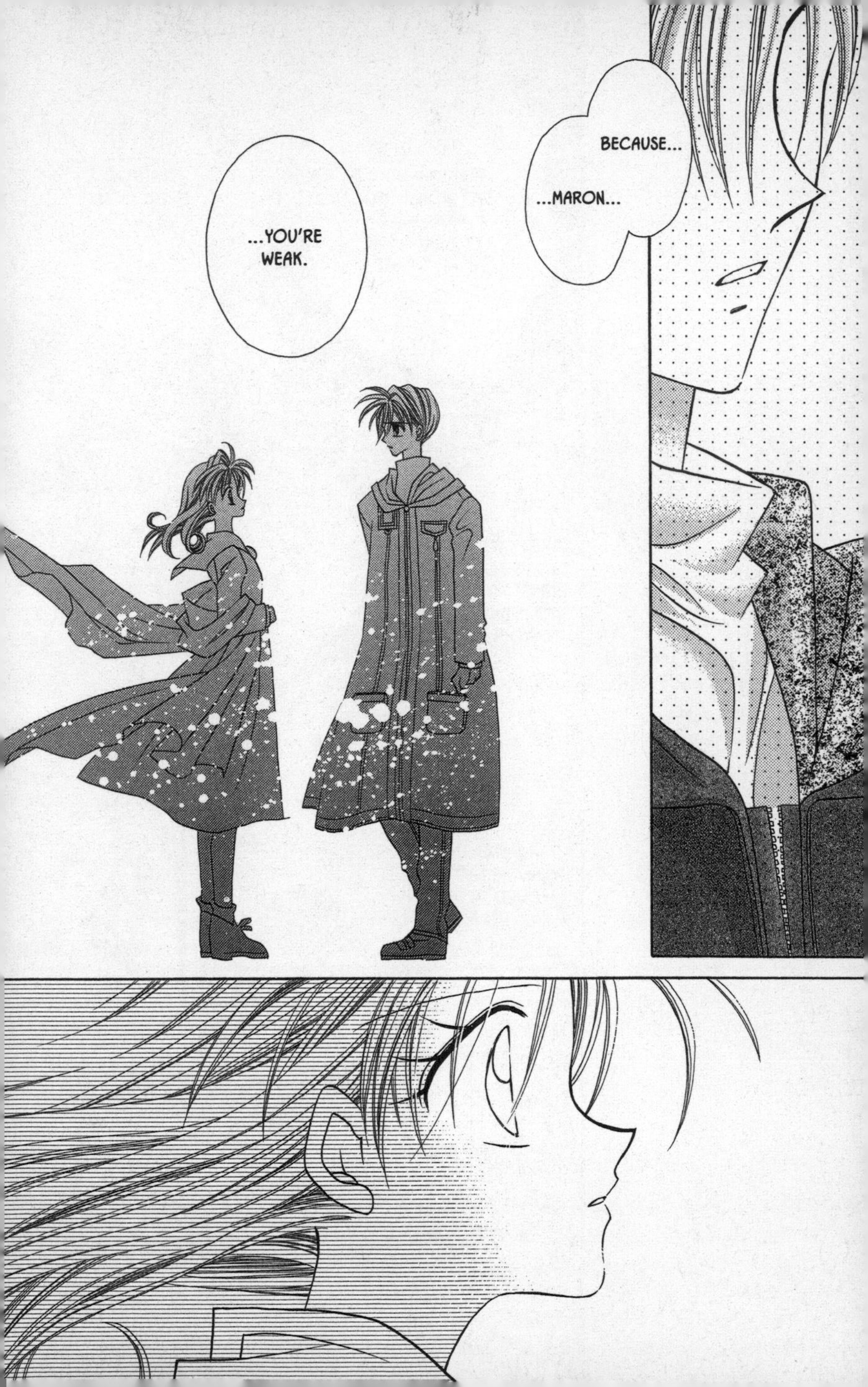
BECAUSE...
...MARON...
...YOU'RE WEAK.

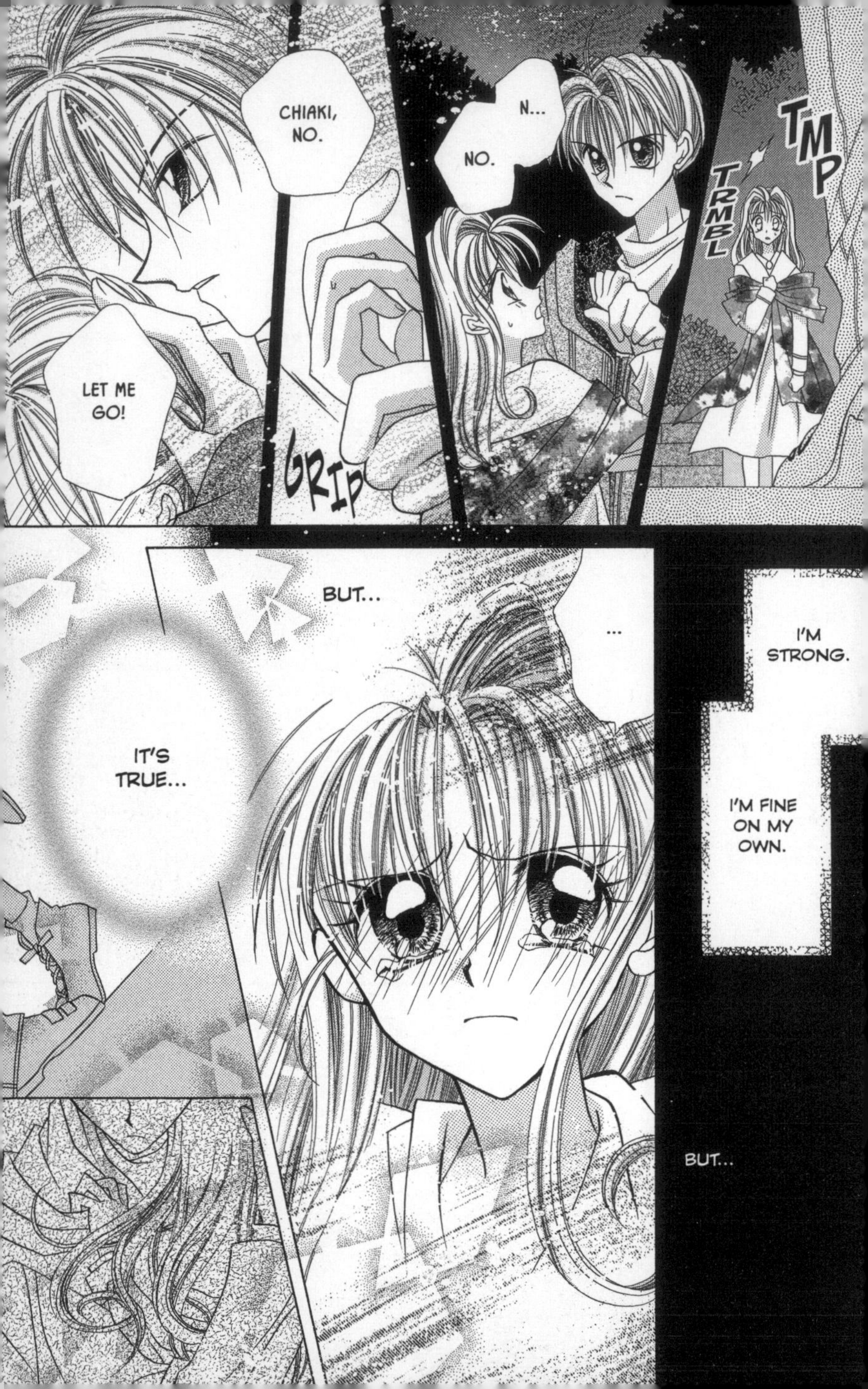
TMP
TRMBL
N...
NO.
CHIAKI, NO.
GRIP
LET ME GO!
I'M STRONG.
I'M FINE ON MY OWN.
BUT...
BUT...
...
IT'S TRUE...

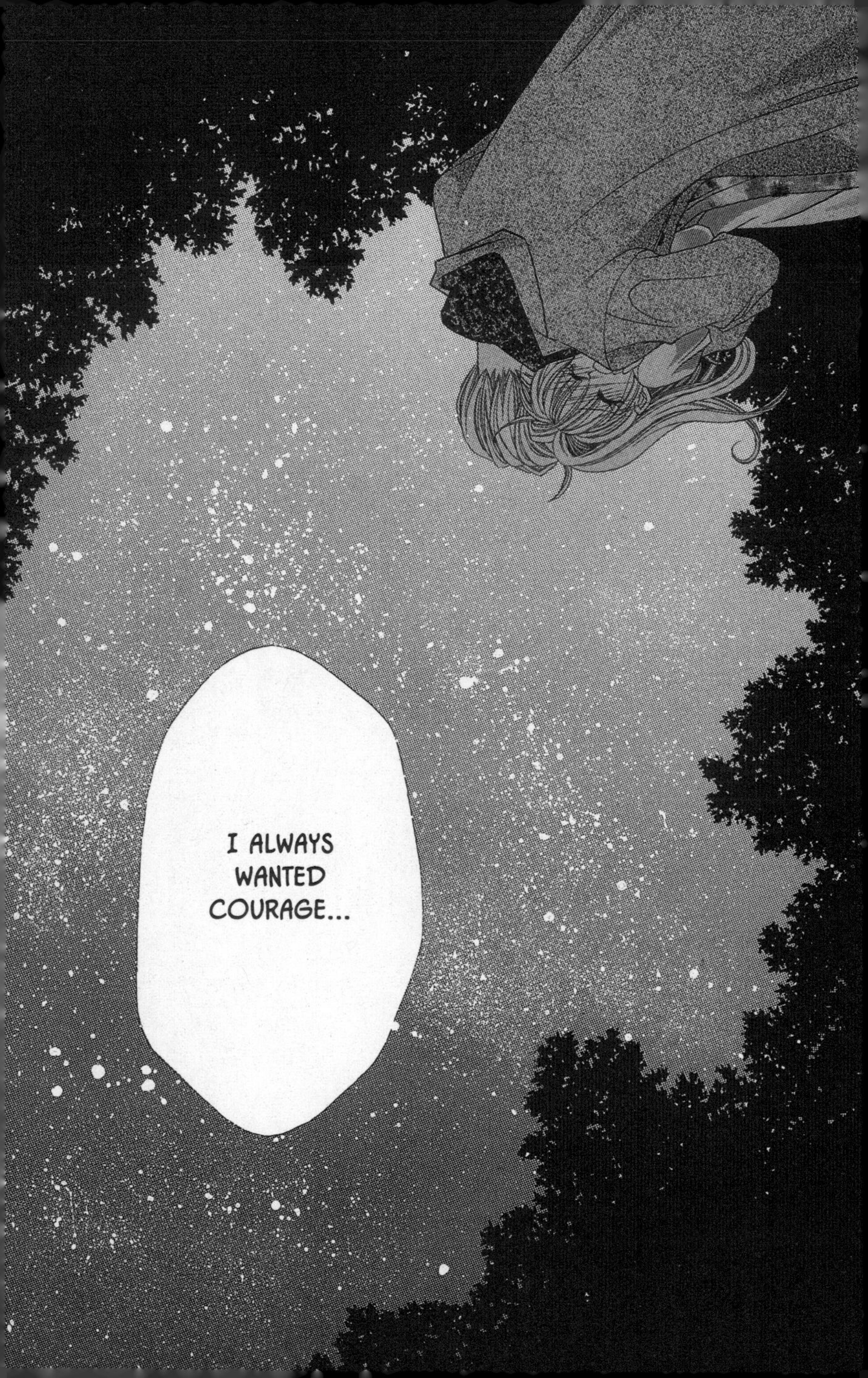
I ALWAYS WANTED COURAGE...

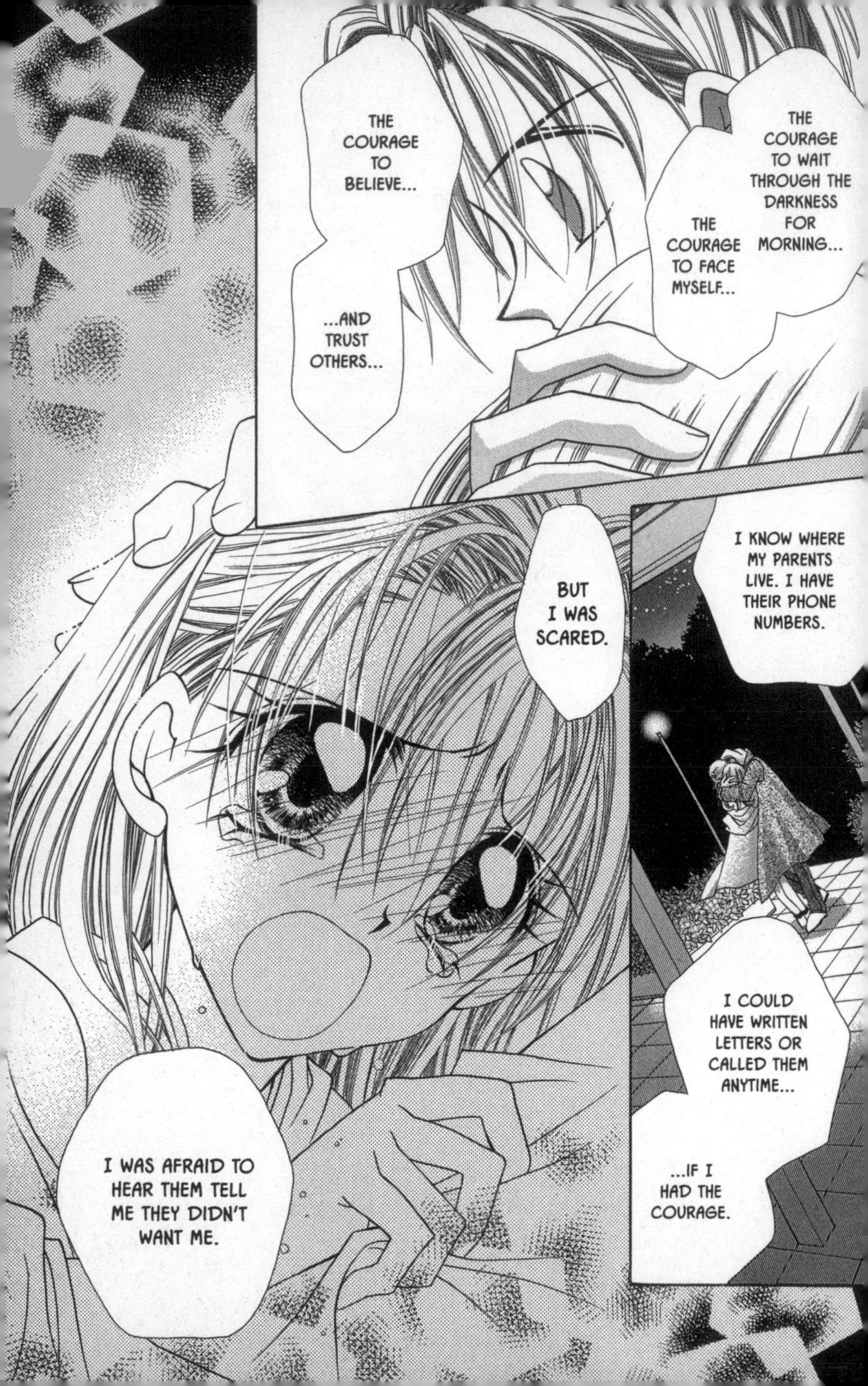
THE COURAGE TO WAIT THROUGH THE DARKNESS FOR MORNING...
THE COURAGE TO FACE MYSELF...
THE COURAGE TO BELIEVE...
...AND TRUST OTHERS...
I KNOW WHERE MY PARENTS LIVE. I HAVE THEIR PHONE NUMBERS.
I COULD HAVE WRITTEN LETTERS OR CALLED THEM ANYTIME...
...IF I HAD THE COURAGE.
BUT I WAS SCARED.
I WAS AFRAID TO HEAR THEM TELL ME THEY DIDN'T WANT ME.

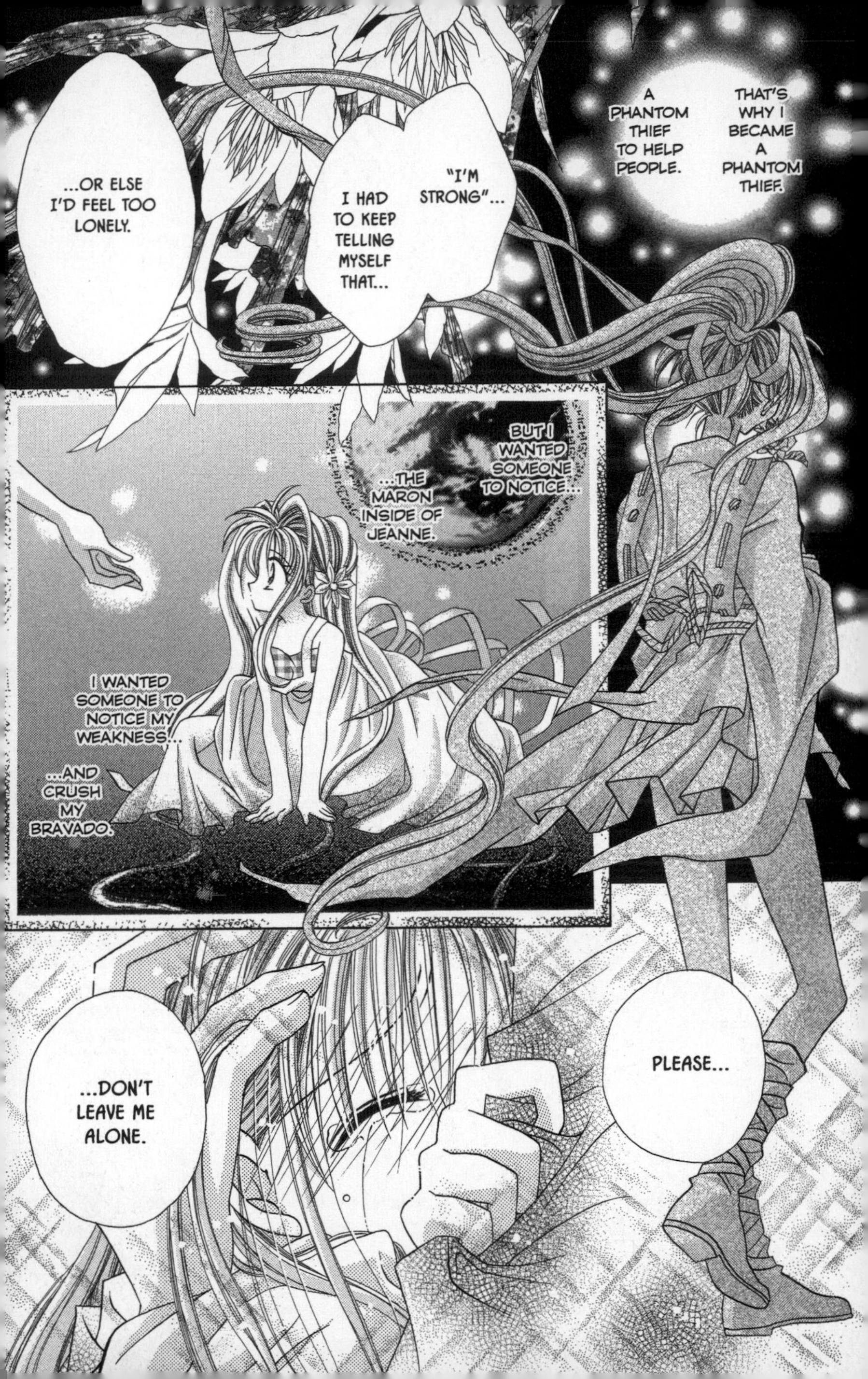
THAT'S WHY I BECAME A PHANTOM THIEF.
A PHANTOM THIEF TO HELP PEOPLE.
"I'M STRONG"...
I HAD TO KEEP TELLING MYSELF THAT...
...OR ELSE I'D FEEL TOO LONELY.
BUT I WANTED SOMEONE TO NOTICE...
...THE MARON INSIDE OF JEANNE.
I WANTED SOMEONE TO NOTICE MY WEAKNESS...
...AND CRUSH MY BRAVADO.
PLEASE...
...DON'T LEAVE ME ALONE.

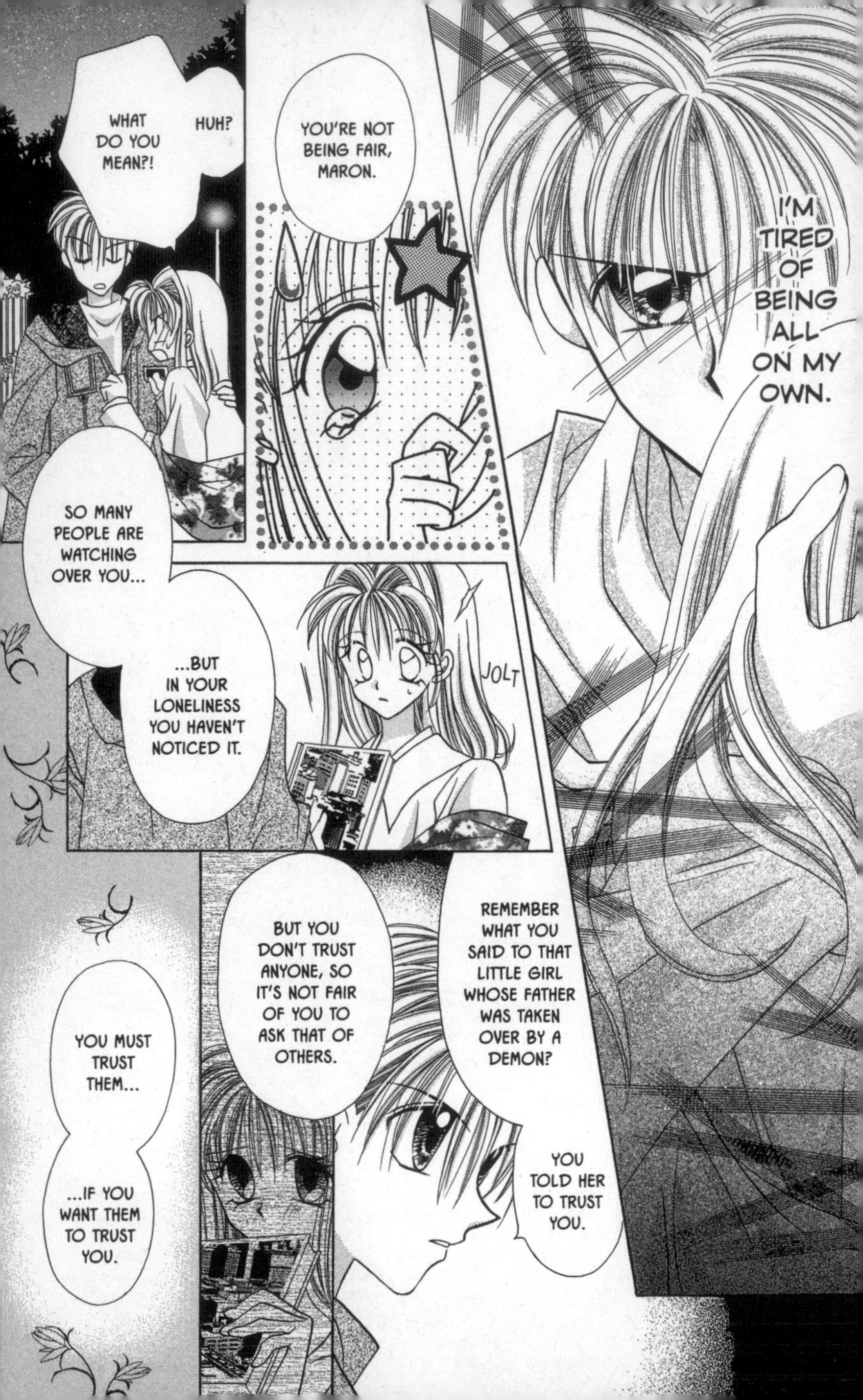
I'M TIRED OF BEING ALL ON MY OWN.
YOU'RE NOT BEING FAIR, MARON.
HUH?
WHAT DO YOU MEAN?!
SO MANY PEOPLE ARE WATCHING OVER YOU...
JOLT
...BUT IN YOUR LONELINESS YOU HAVEN'T NOTICED IT.
REMEMBER WHAT YOU SAID TO THAT LITTLE GIRL WHOSE FATHER WAS TAKEN OVER BY A DEMON?
BUT YOU DON'T TRUST ANYONE, SO IT'S NOT FAIR OF YOU TO ASK THAT OF OTHERS.
YOU TOLD HER TO TRUST YOU.
YOU MUST TRUST THEM...
...IF YOU WANT THEM TO TRUST YOU.

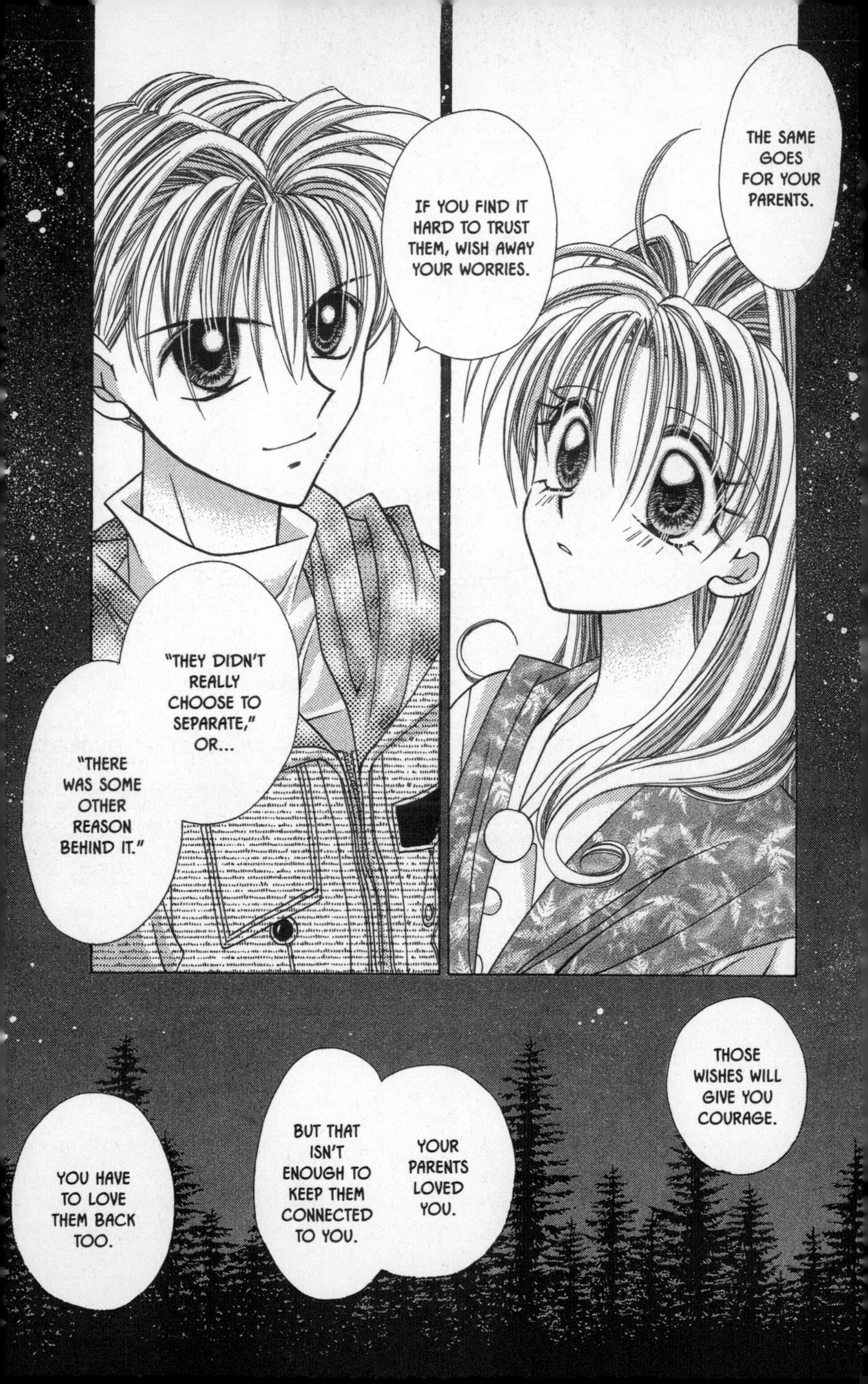
THE SAME GOES FOR YOUR PARENTS.
IF YOU FIND IT HARD TO TRUST THEM, WISH AWAY YOUR WORRIES.
"THEY DIDN'T REALLY CHOOSE TO SEPARATE," OR...
"THERE WAS SOME OTHER REASON BEHIND IT."
THOSE WISHES WILL GIVE YOU COURAGE.
YOUR PARENTS LOVED YOU.
BUT THAT ISN'T ENOUGH TO KEEP THEM CONNECTED TO YOU.
YOU HAVE TO LOVE THEM BACK TOO.

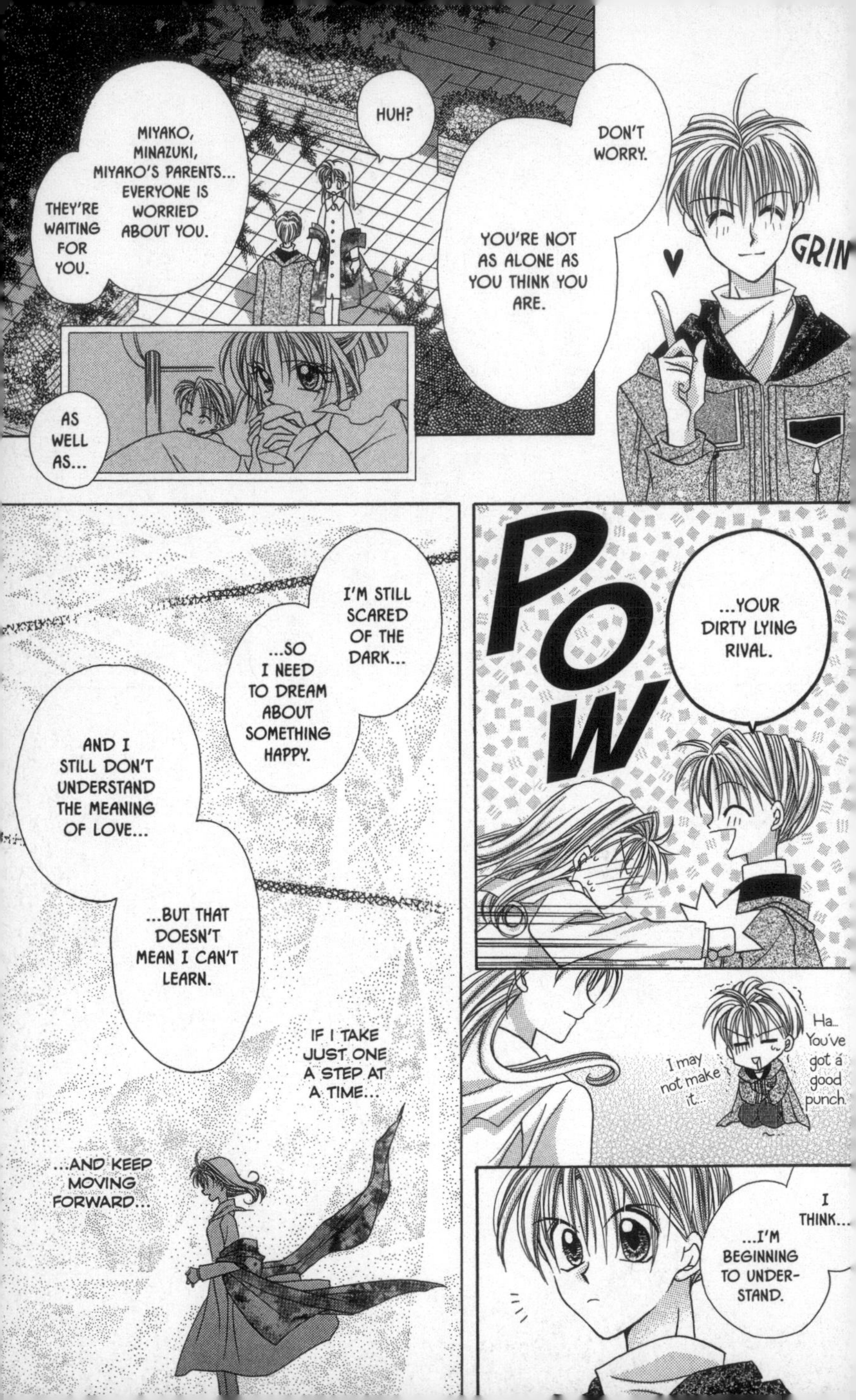
DON'T WORRY.
YOU'RE NOT AS ALONE AS YOU THINK YOU ARE.
GRIN
HUH?
MIYAKO, MINAZUKI, MIYAKO'S PARENTS... EVERYONE IS WORRIED ABOUT YOU.
THEY'RE WAITING FOR YOU.
AS WELL AS...
...YOUR DIRTY LYING RIVAL.
POW
Ha... You've got a good punch.
I may not make it...
I THINK...
...I'M BEGINNING TO UNDER-STAND.
I'M STILL SCARED OF THE DARK...
...SO I NEED TO DREAM ABOUT SOMETHING HAPPY.
AND I STILL DON'T UNDERSTAND THE MEANING OF LOVE...
...BUT THAT DOESN'T MEAN I CAN'T LEARN.
IF I TAKE JUST ONE A STEP AT A TIME...
...AND KEEP MOVING FORWARD...

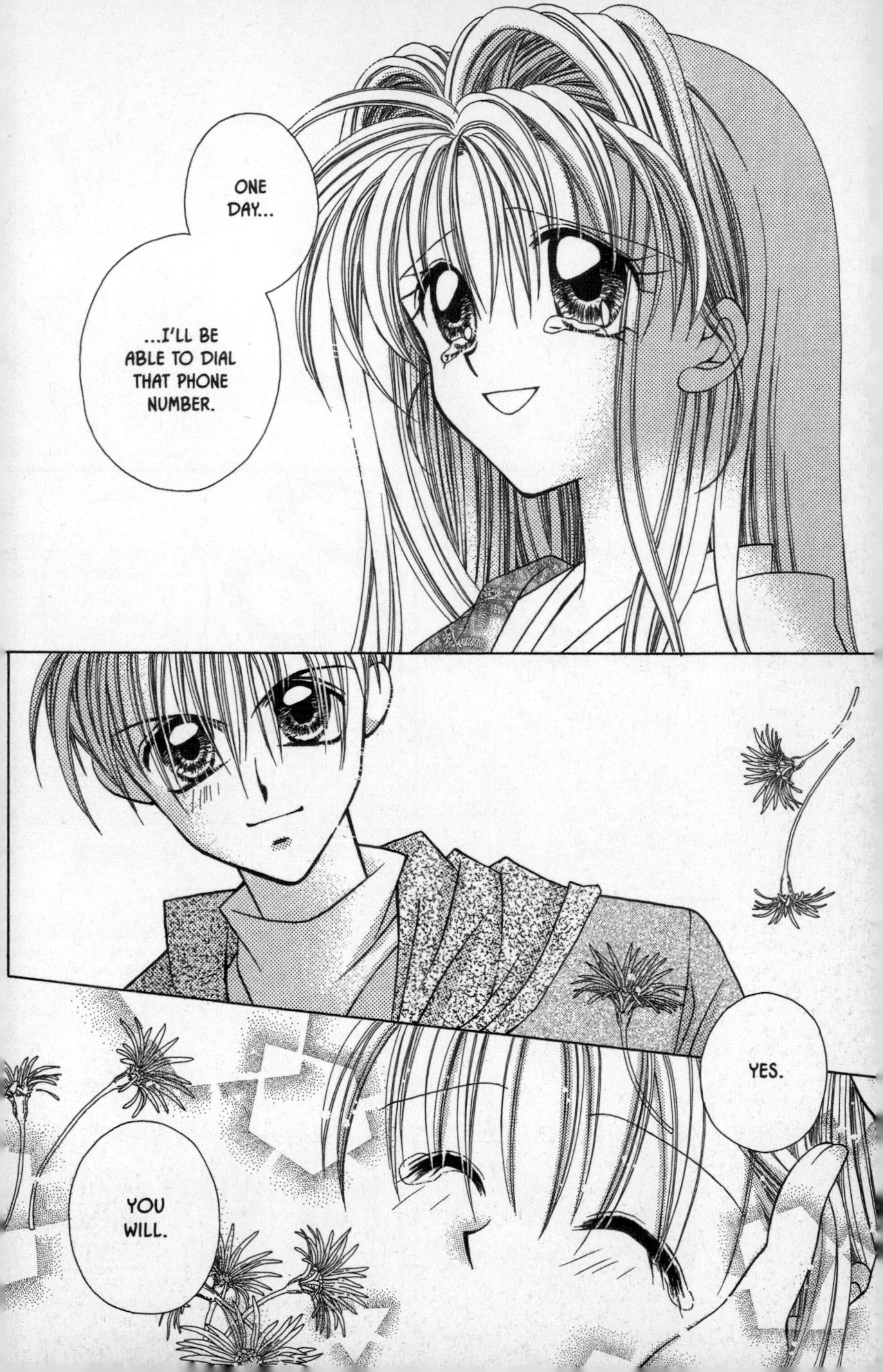
ONE DAY...
...I'LL BE ABLE TO DIAL THAT PHONE NUMBER.
YES.
YOU WILL.

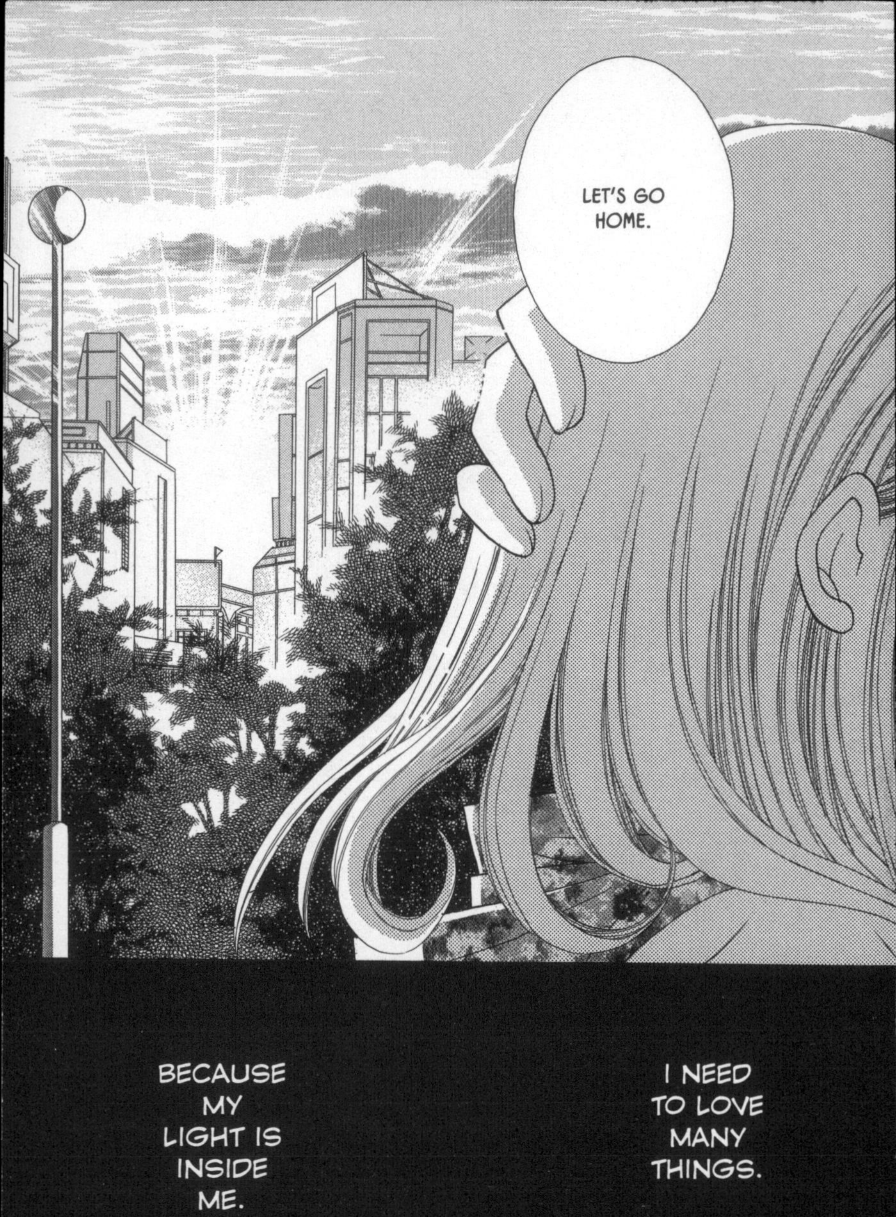
LET'S GO HOME.
I NEED TO LOVE MANY THINGS.
BECAUSE MY LIGHT IS INSIDE ME.

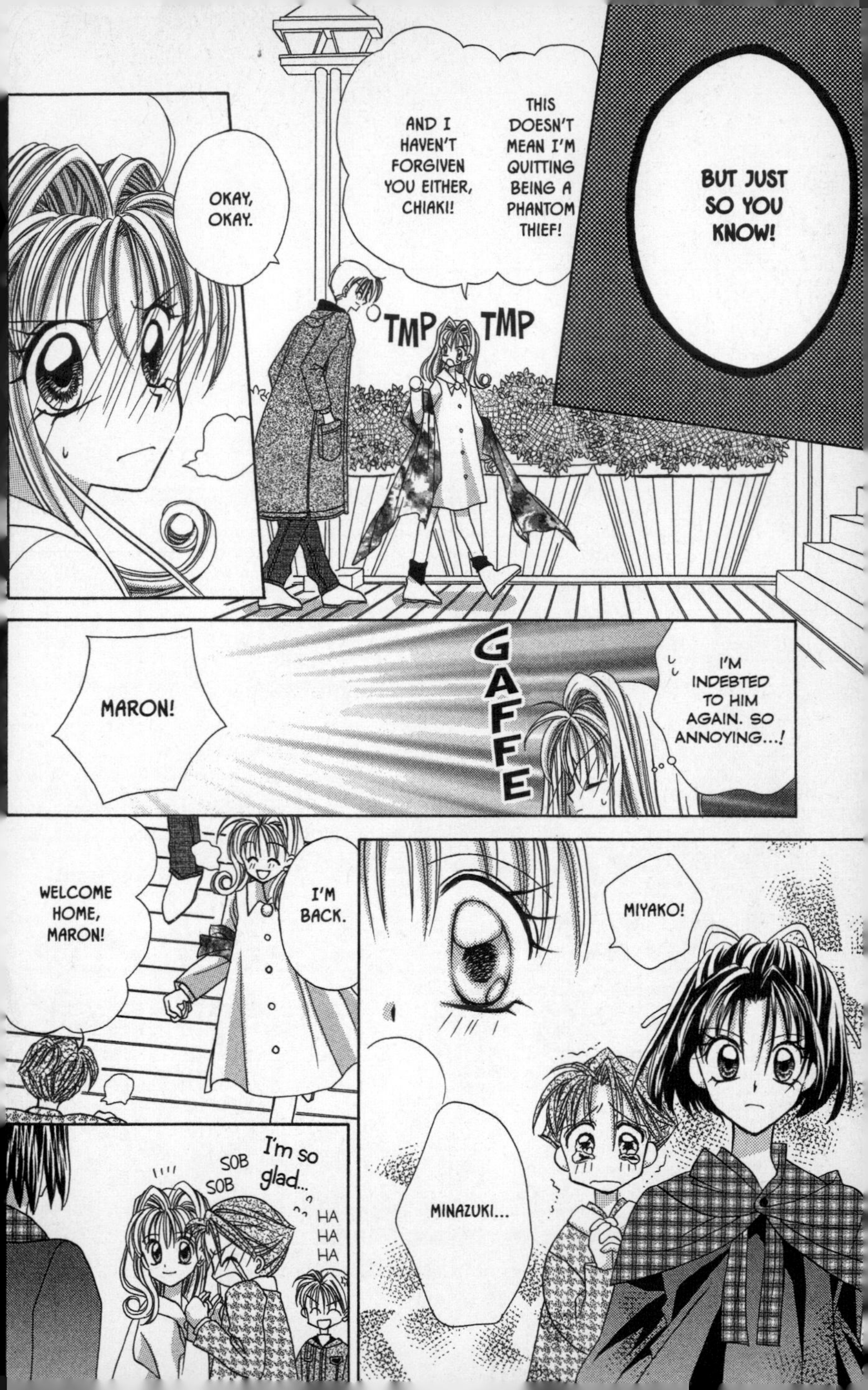
BUT JUST SO YOU KNOW!
THIS DOESN'T MEAN I'M QUITTING BEING A PHANTOM THIEF!
AND I HAVEN'T FORGIVEN YOU EITHER, CHIAKI!
TMP TMP
OKAY, OKAY.
I'M INDEBTED TO HIM AGAIN. SO ANNOYING...!
GAFFE
MARON!
MIYAKO!
MINAZUKI...
I'M BACK.
WELCOME HOME, MARON!
I'm so glad...
SOB SOB
HA HA HA

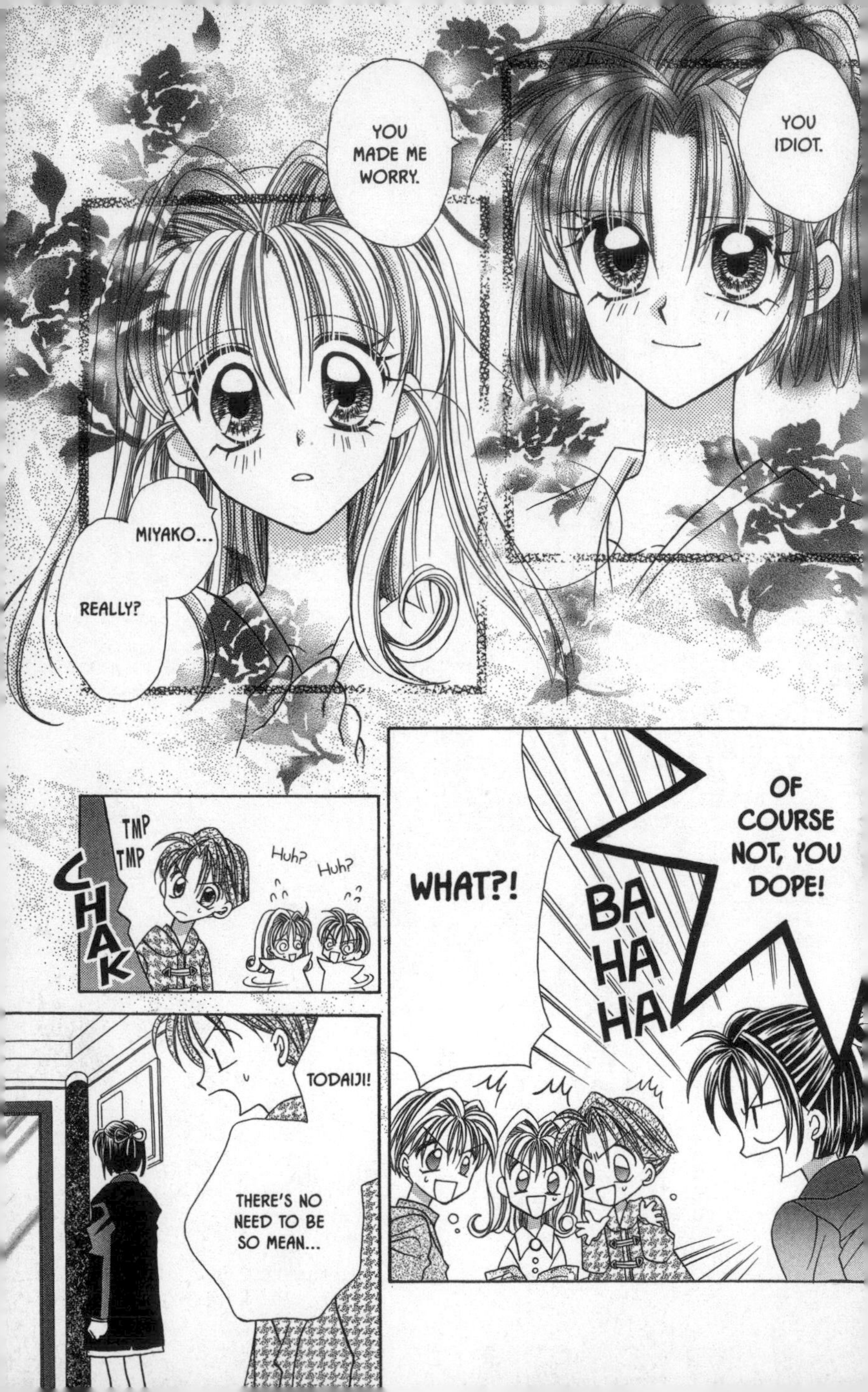
YOU IDIOT.
YOU MADE ME WORRY.
MIYAKO... REALLY?
OF COURSE NOT, YOU DOPE!
BA HA HA
WHAT?!
TMP TMP
CHAK
Huh?
Huh?
TODAIJI!
THERE'S NO NEED TO BE SO MEAN...

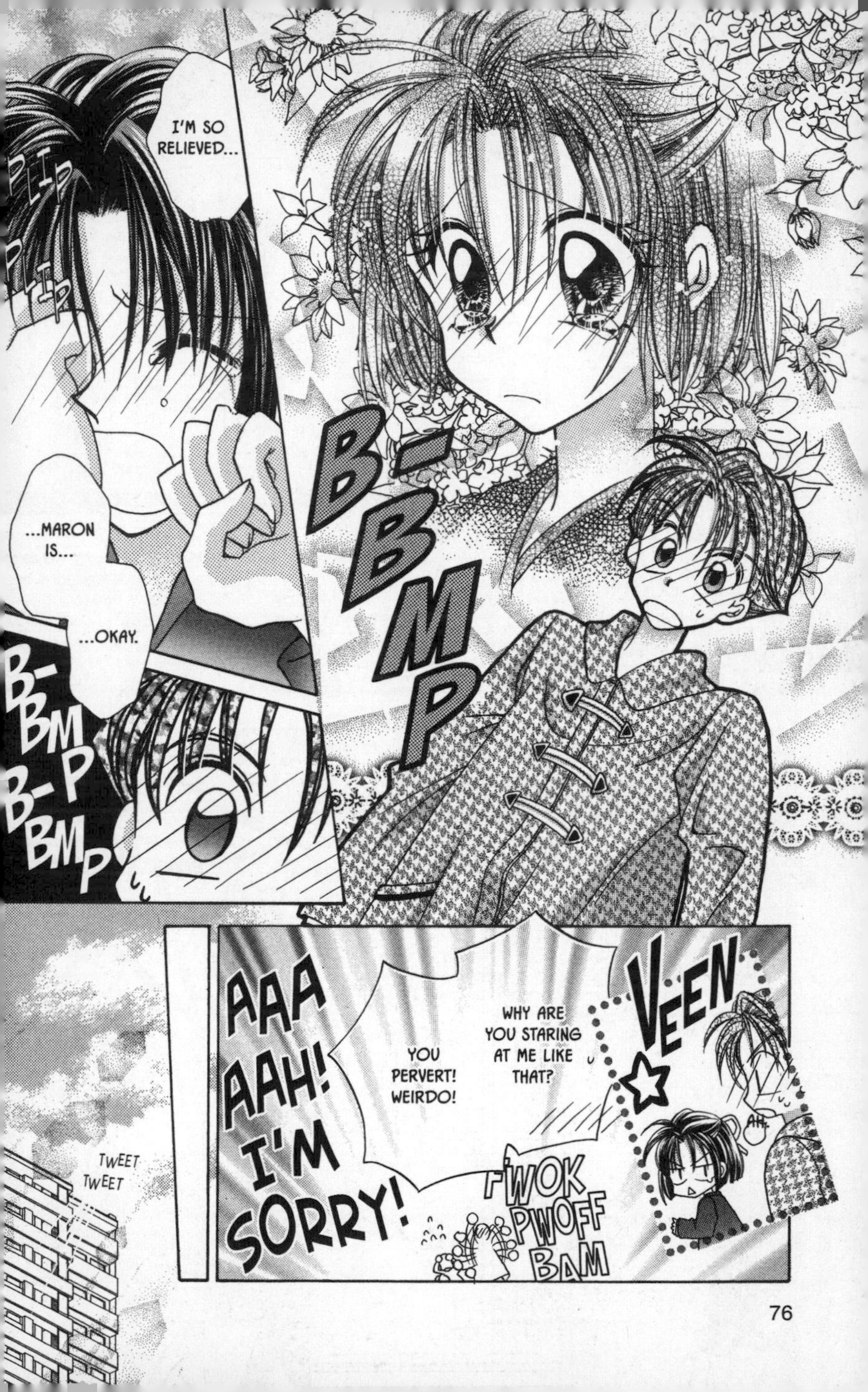
B-B-MP
I'M SO RELIEVED...
PLIP PLIP
...MARON IS...
...OKAY.
B-BMP B-BMP
VEEN
AH.
WHY ARE YOU STARING AT ME LIKE THAT?
YOU PERVERT! WEIRDO!
AAAAAH! I'M SORRY!
FWOK PWOFF BAM
TWEET TWEET

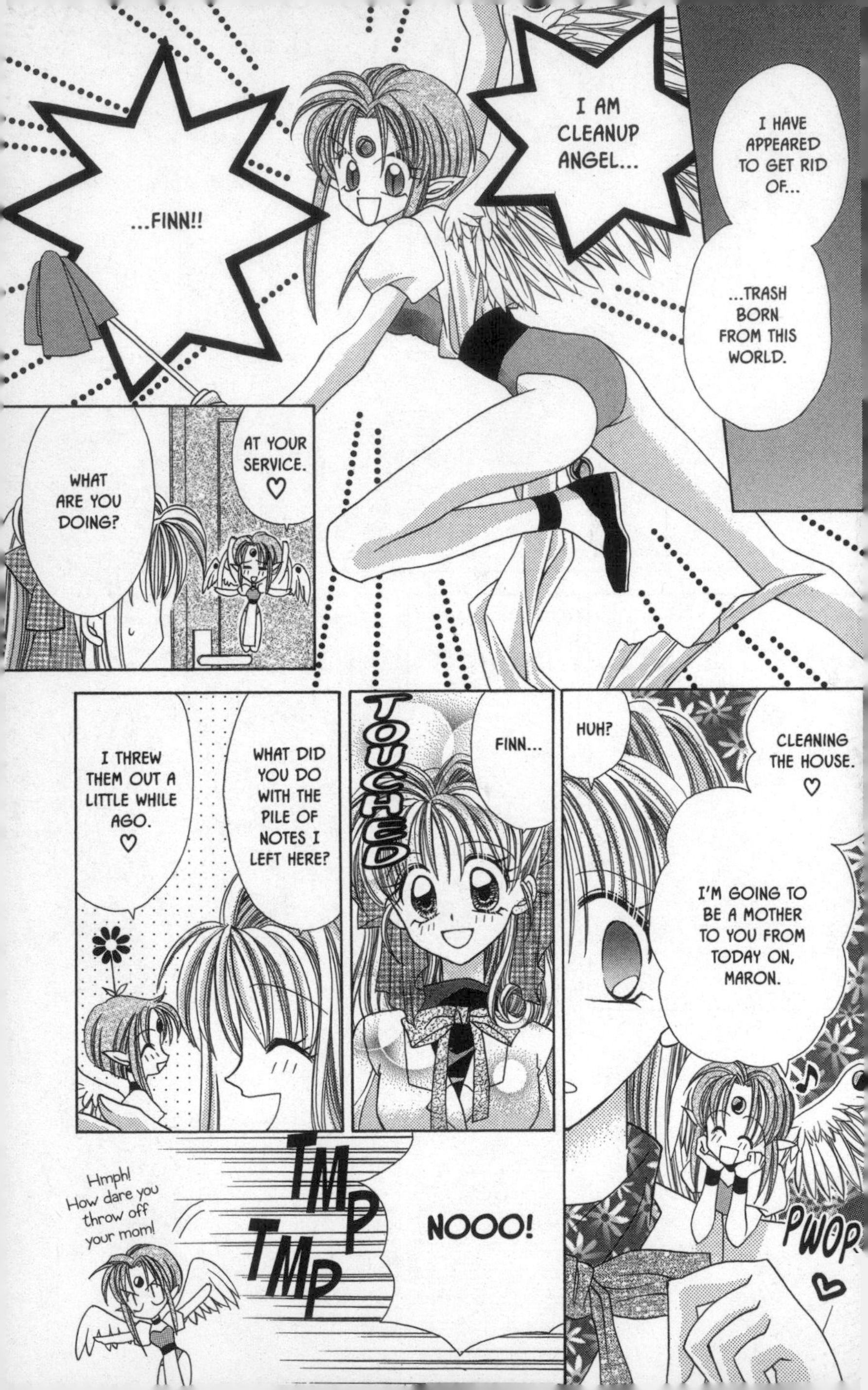
I AM CLEANUP ANGEL...
...FINN!!
I HAVE APPEARED TO GET RID OF...
...TRASH BORN FROM THIS WORLD.
AT YOUR SERVICE. ♡
WHAT ARE YOU DOING?
CLEANING THE HOUSE. ♡
HUH?
I'M GOING TO BE A MOTHER TO YOU FROM TODAY ON, MARON.
PWOP ♡
TOUCHED
FINN...
WHAT DID YOU DO WITH THE PILE OF NOTES I LEFT HERE?
I THREW THEM OUT A LITTLE WHILE AGO. ♡
NOOO!
TMP TMP
Hmph! How dare you throw off your mom!

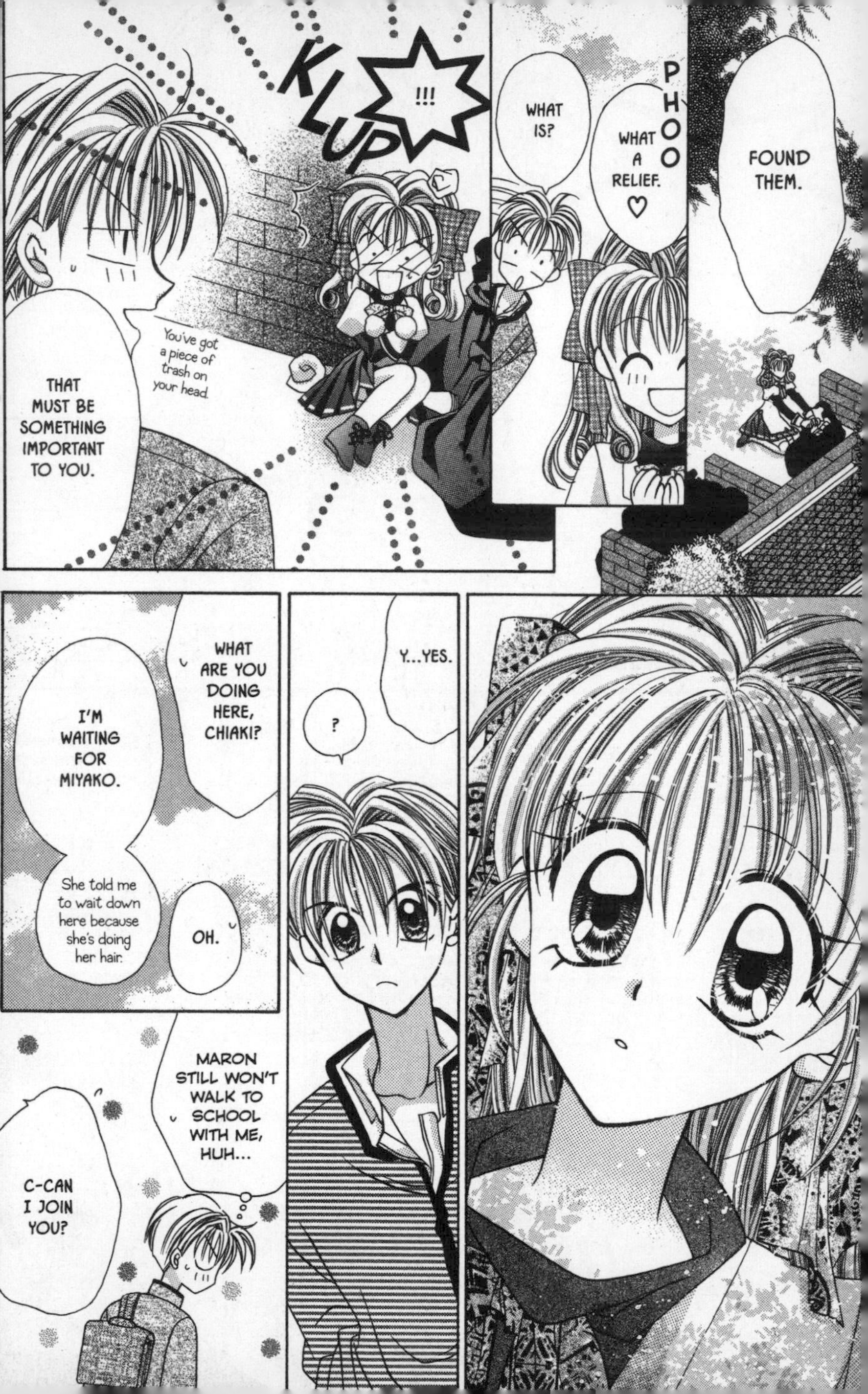
FOUND THEM.
PHOO
WHAT A RELIEF. ♡
WHAT IS?
KLUP
!!!
You've got a piece of trash on your head.
THAT MUST BE SOMETHING IMPORTANT TO YOU.
Y...YES.
?
WHAT ARE YOU DOING HERE, CHIAKI?
I'M WAITING FOR MIYAKO.
She told me to wait down here because she's doing her hair.
OH.
MARON STILL WON'T WALK TO SCHOOL WITH ME, HUH...
C-CAN I JOIN YOU?

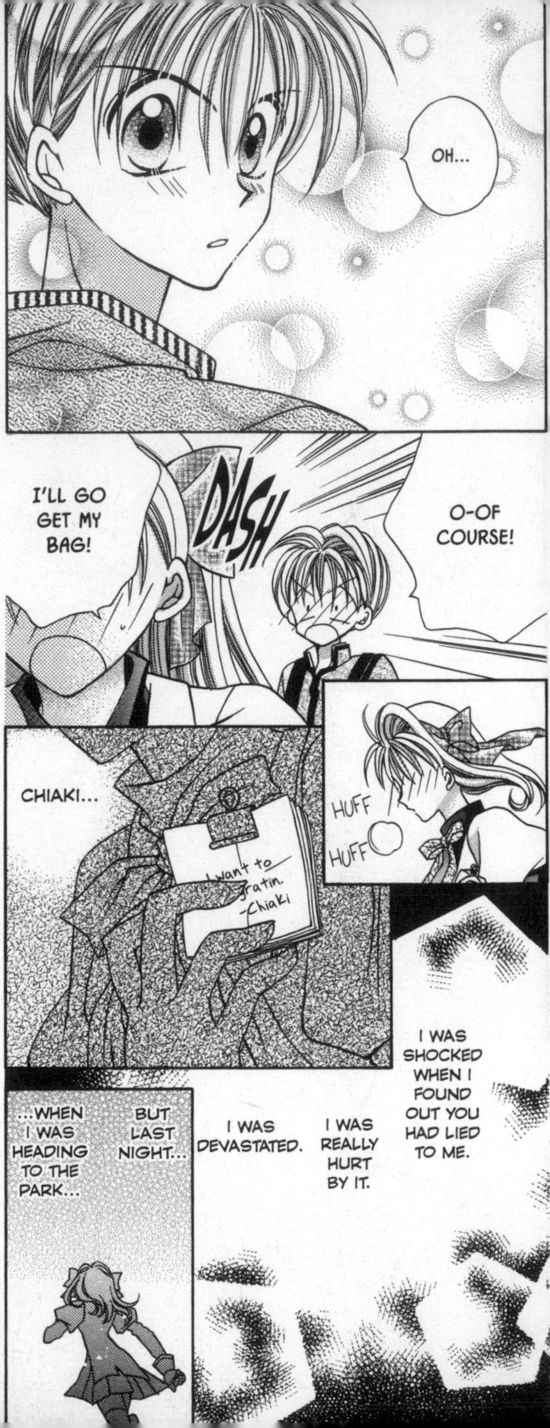
OH...
O-OF COURSE!
DASH
I'LL GO GET MY BAG!
HUFF
HUFF
CHIAKI...
I want to gratin. -Chiaki
I WAS SHOCKED WHEN I FOUND OUT YOU HAD LIED TO ME.
I WAS REALLY HURT BY IT.
I WAS DEVASTATED.
BUT LAST NIGHT...
...WHEN I WAS HEADING TO THE PARK...

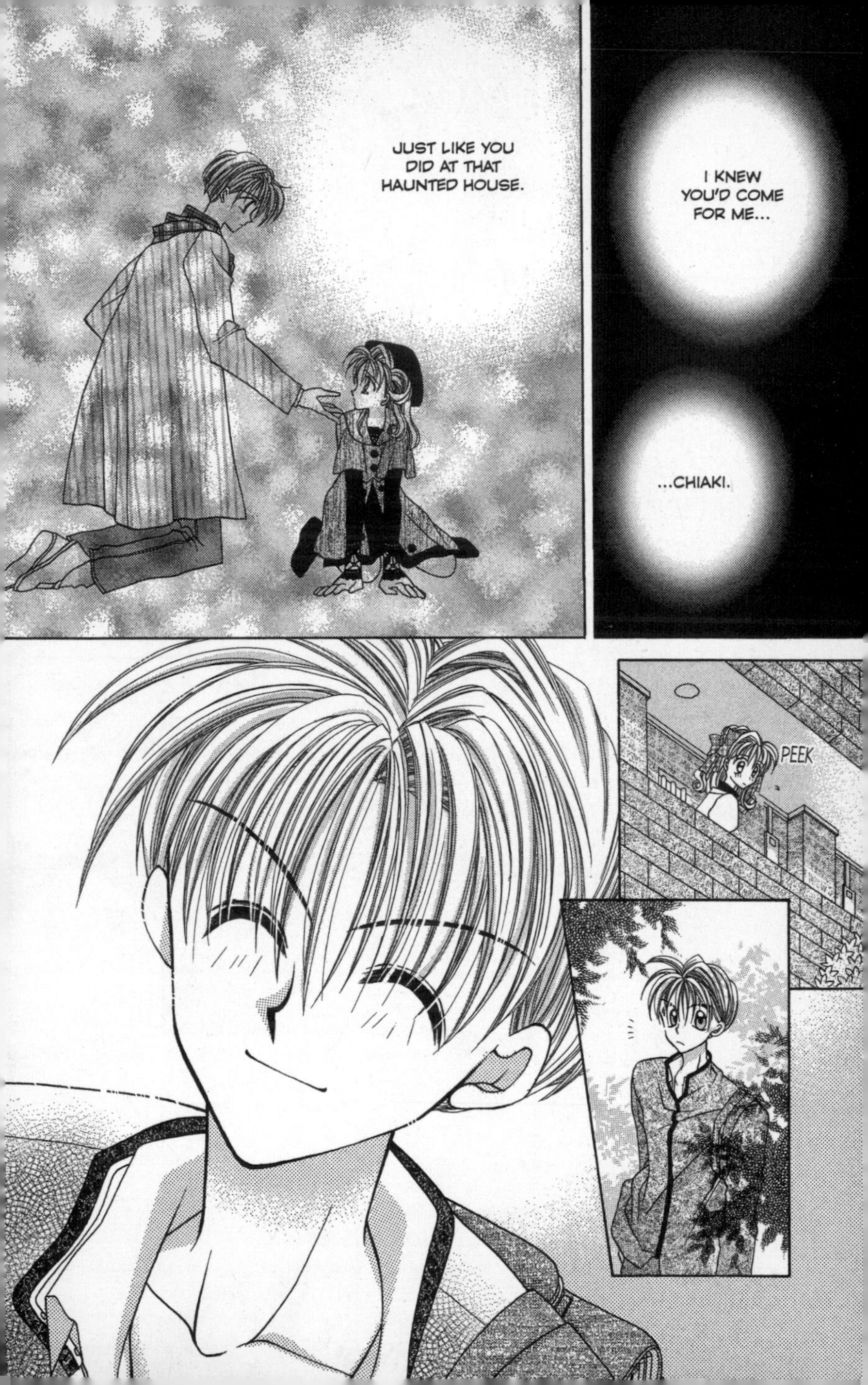
I KNEW YOU'D COME FOR ME...
...CHIAKI.
JUST LIKE YOU DID AT THAT HAUNTED HOUSE.
PEEK

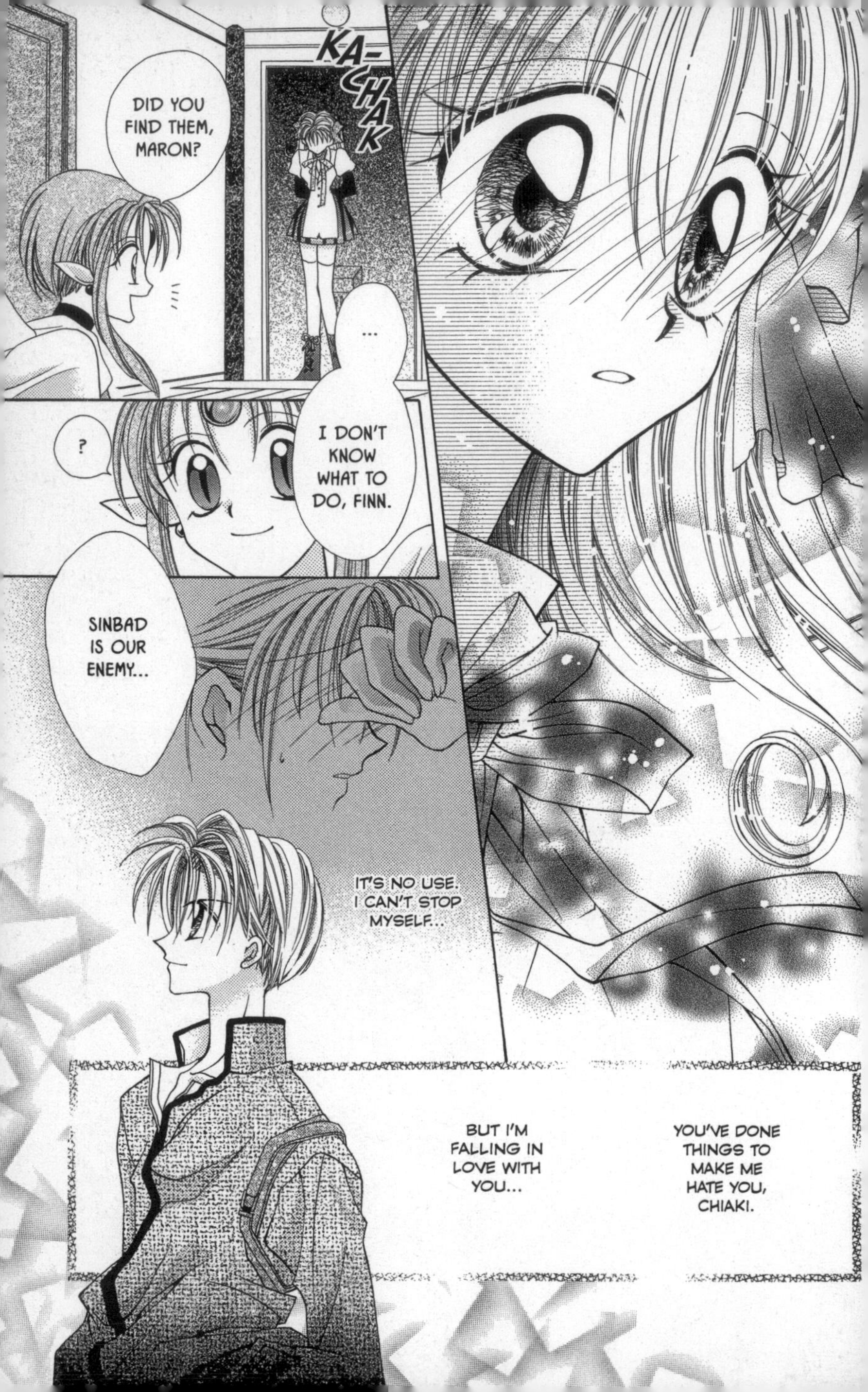
KA-CHAK
DID YOU FIND THEM, MARON?
...
?
I DON'T KNOW WHAT TO DO, FINN.
SINBAD IS OUR ENEMY...
IT'S NO USE. I CAN'T STOP MYSELF...
YOU'VE DONE THINGS TO MAKE ME HATE YOU, CHIAKI.
BUT I'M FALLING IN LOVE WITH YOU...

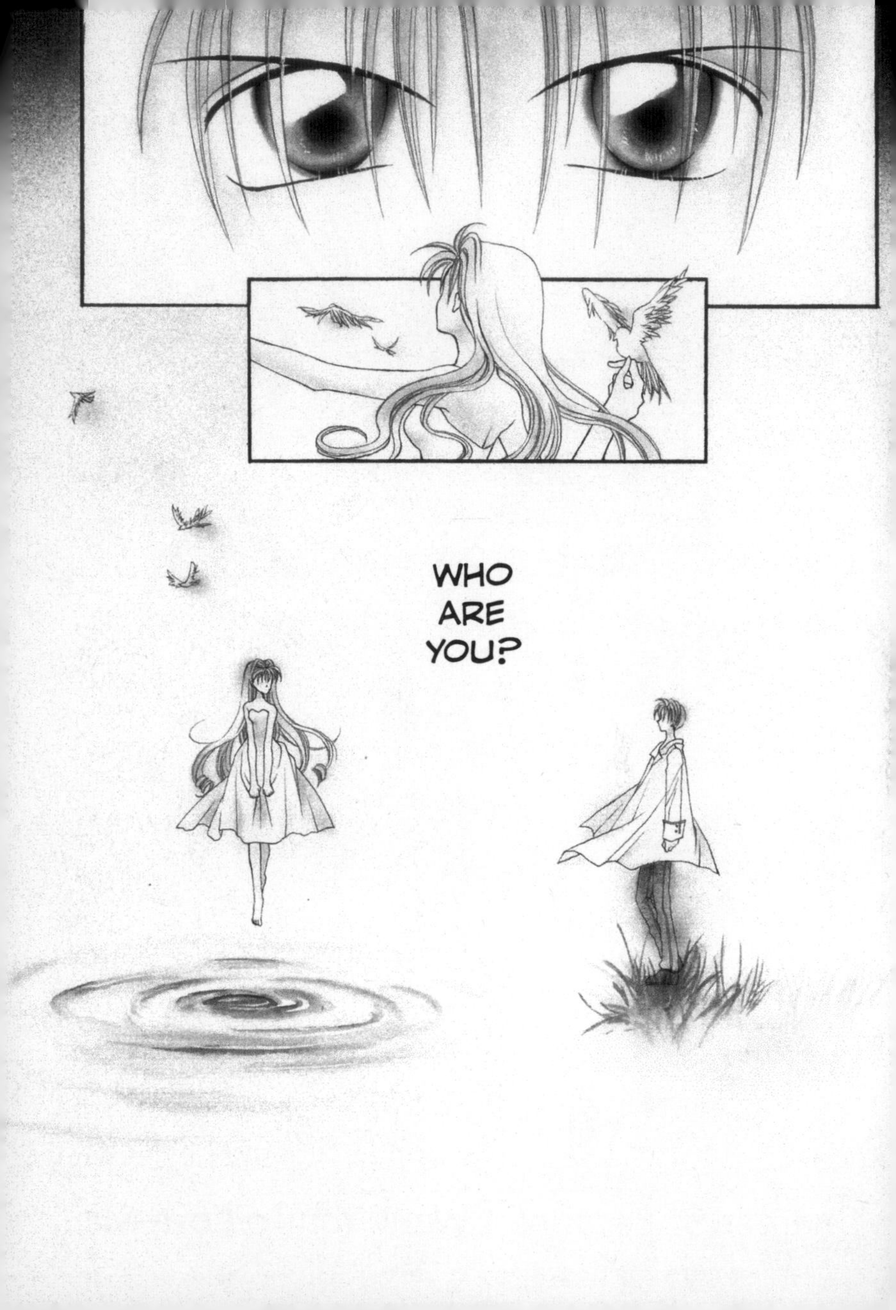
WHO ARE YOU?

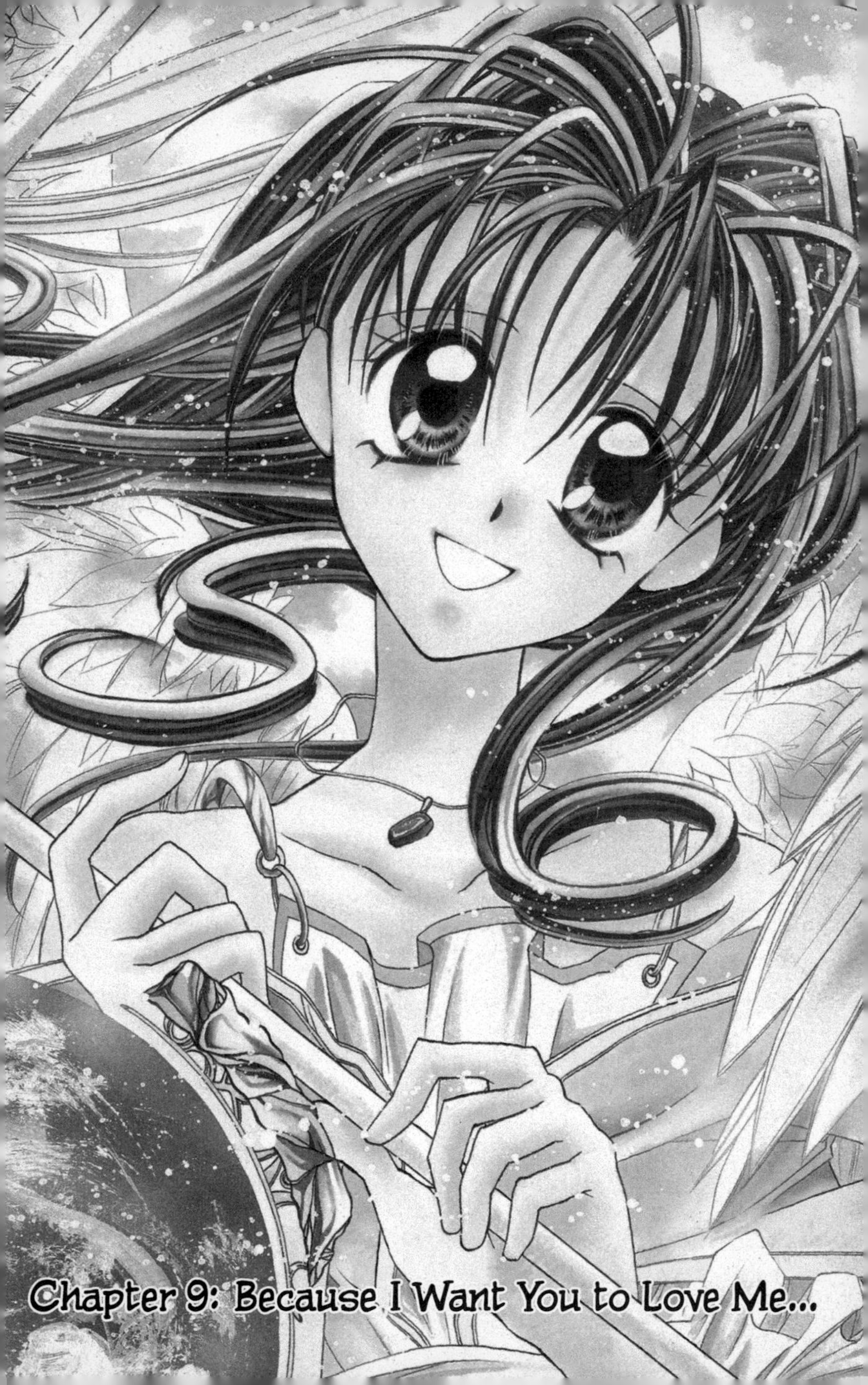
Chapter 9: Because I Want You to Love Me...

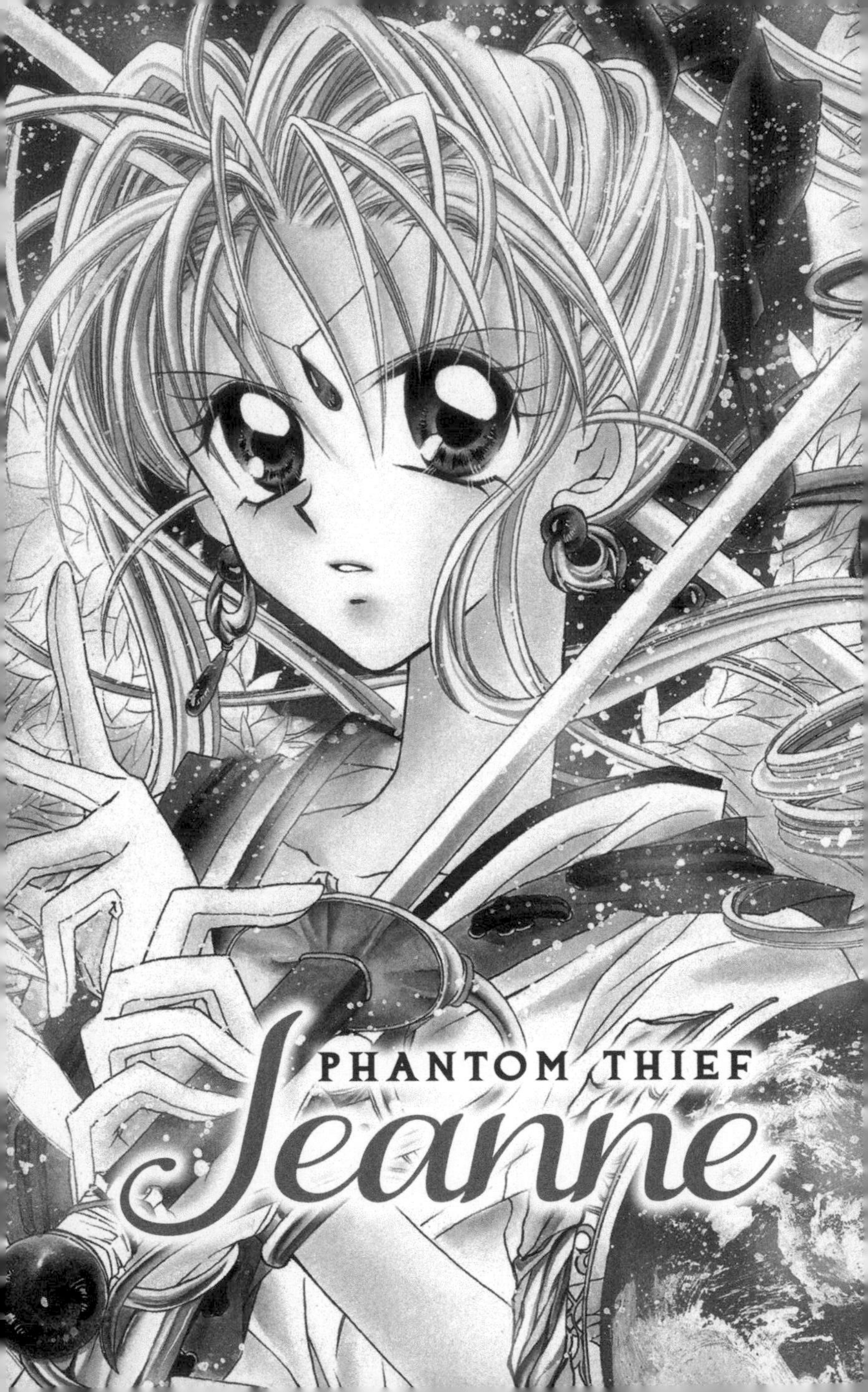
PHANTOM THIEF
Jeanne

SHEEN

PHANTOM
THIEF
JEANNE

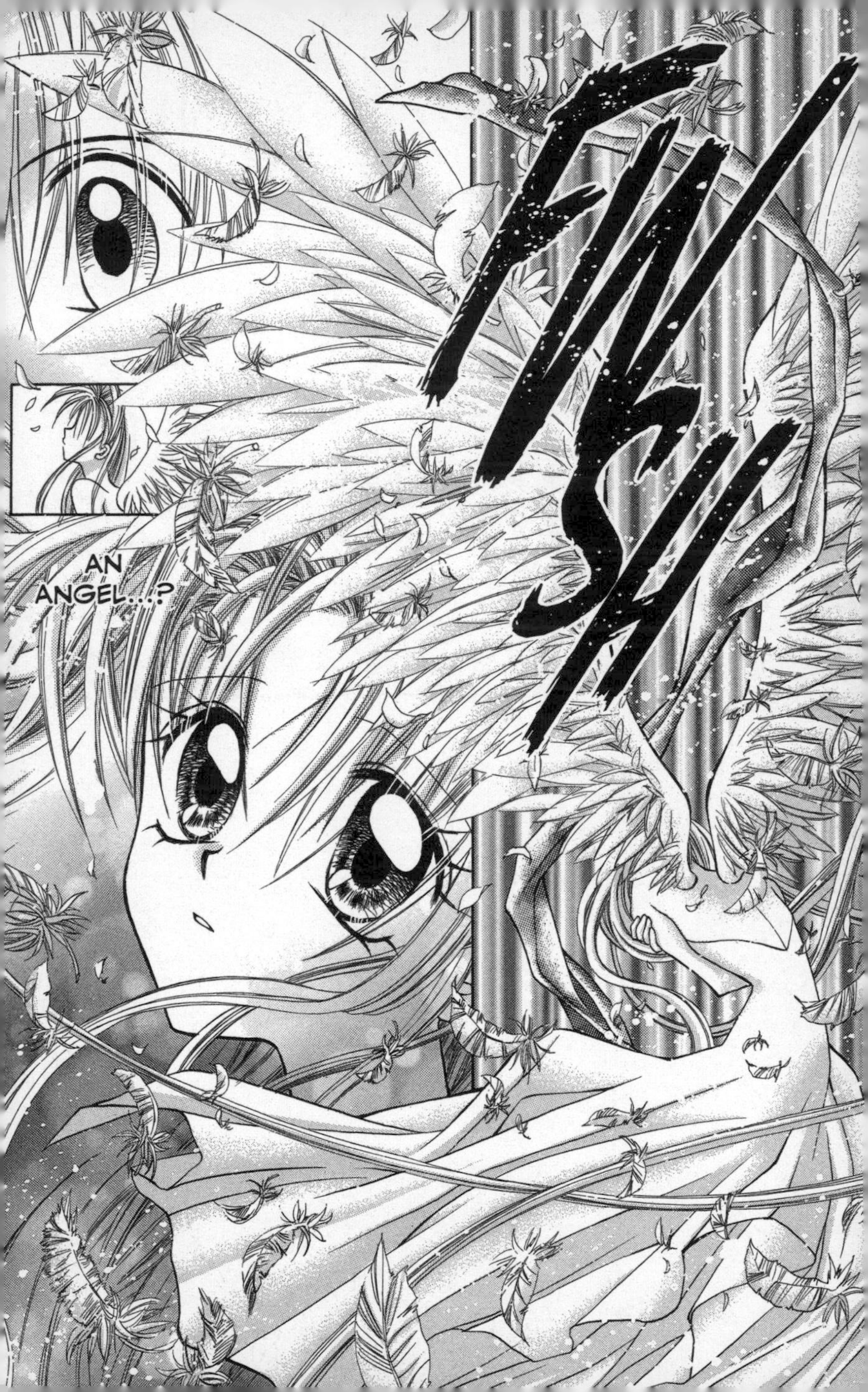
FWISH
AN ANGEL...?

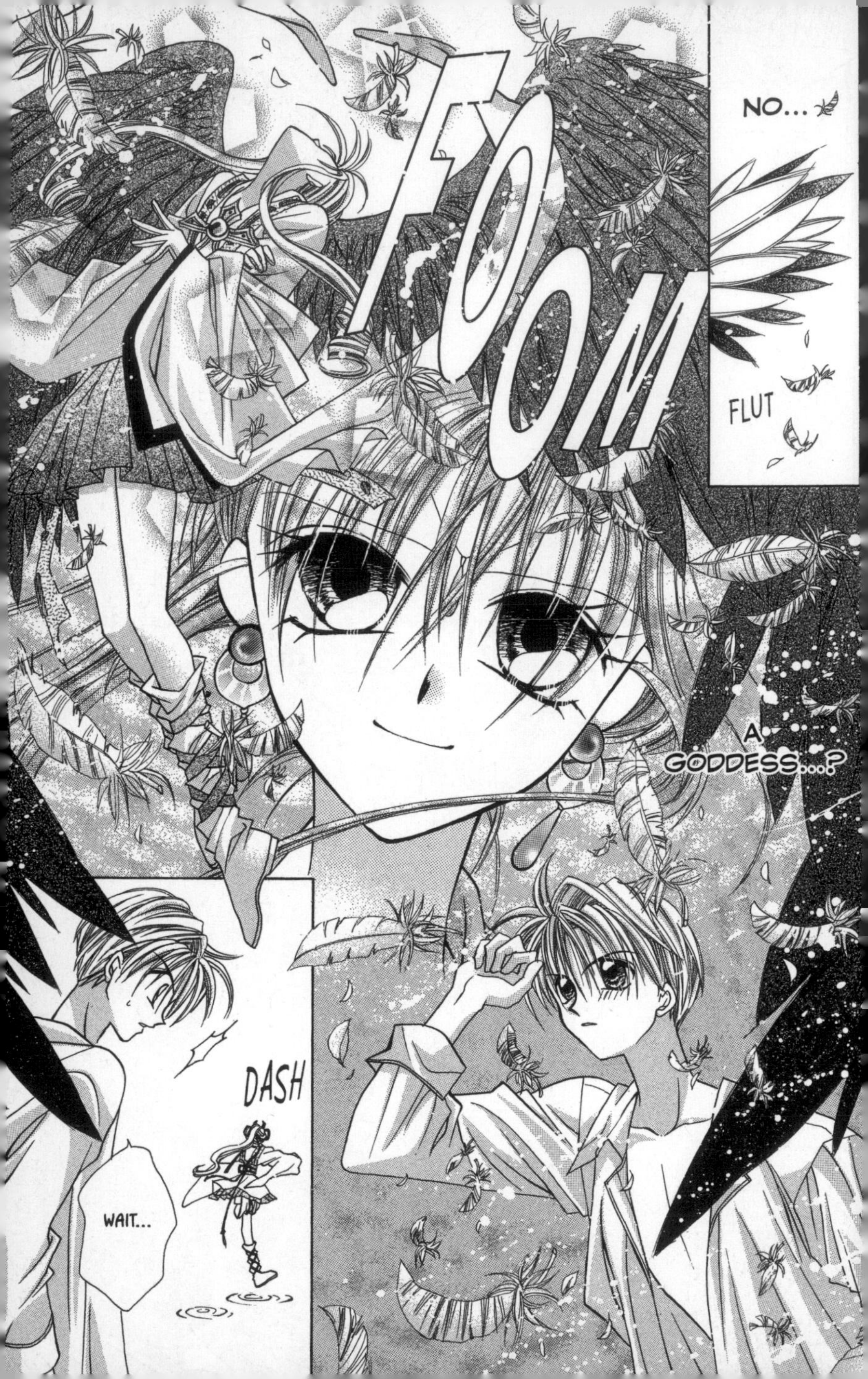
NO...
FLUT
FOOM
A GODDESS...?
DASH
WAIT...

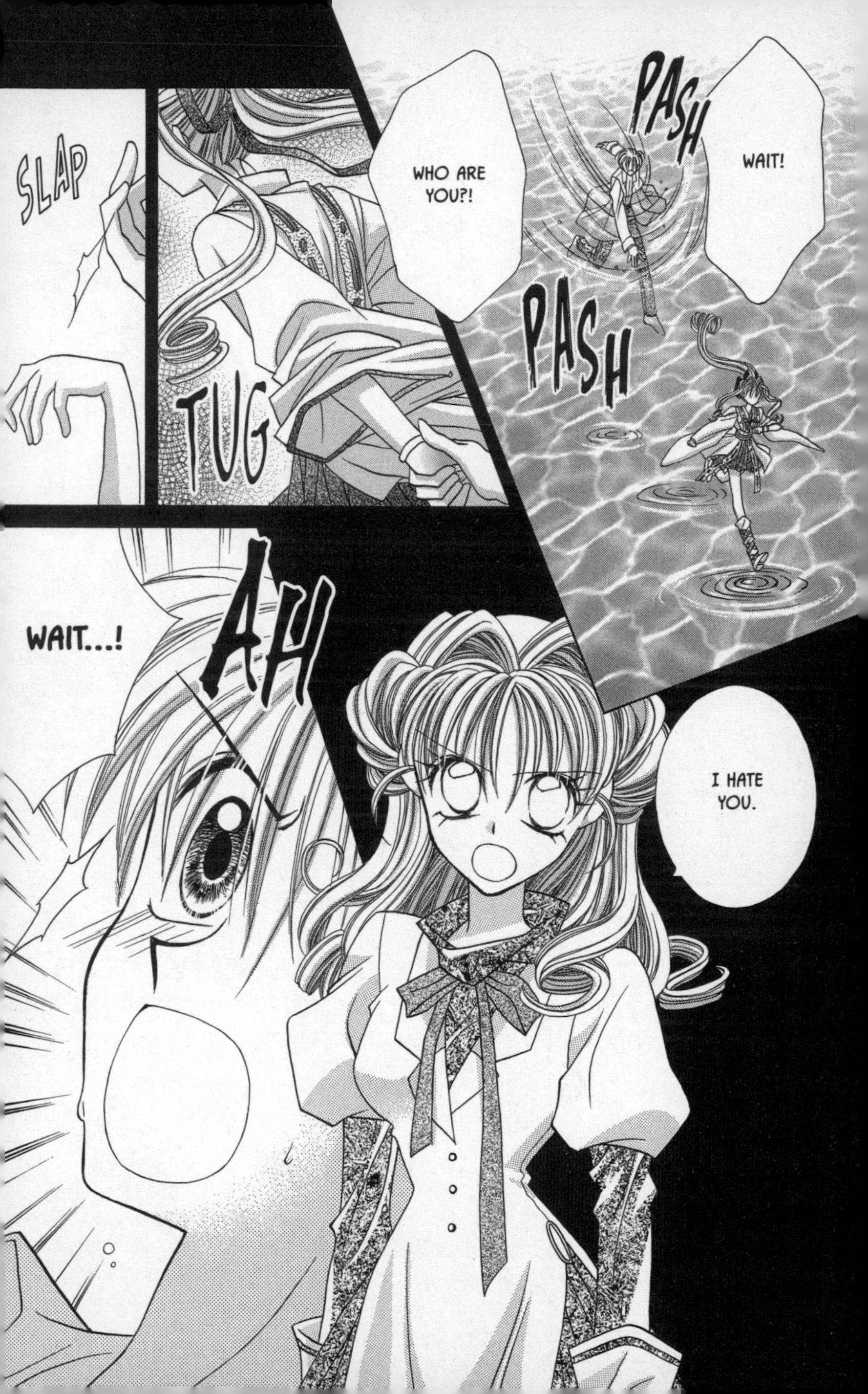
PASH
WAIT!
PASH
WHO ARE YOU?!
TUG
SLAP
I HATE YOU.
AH
WAIT...!

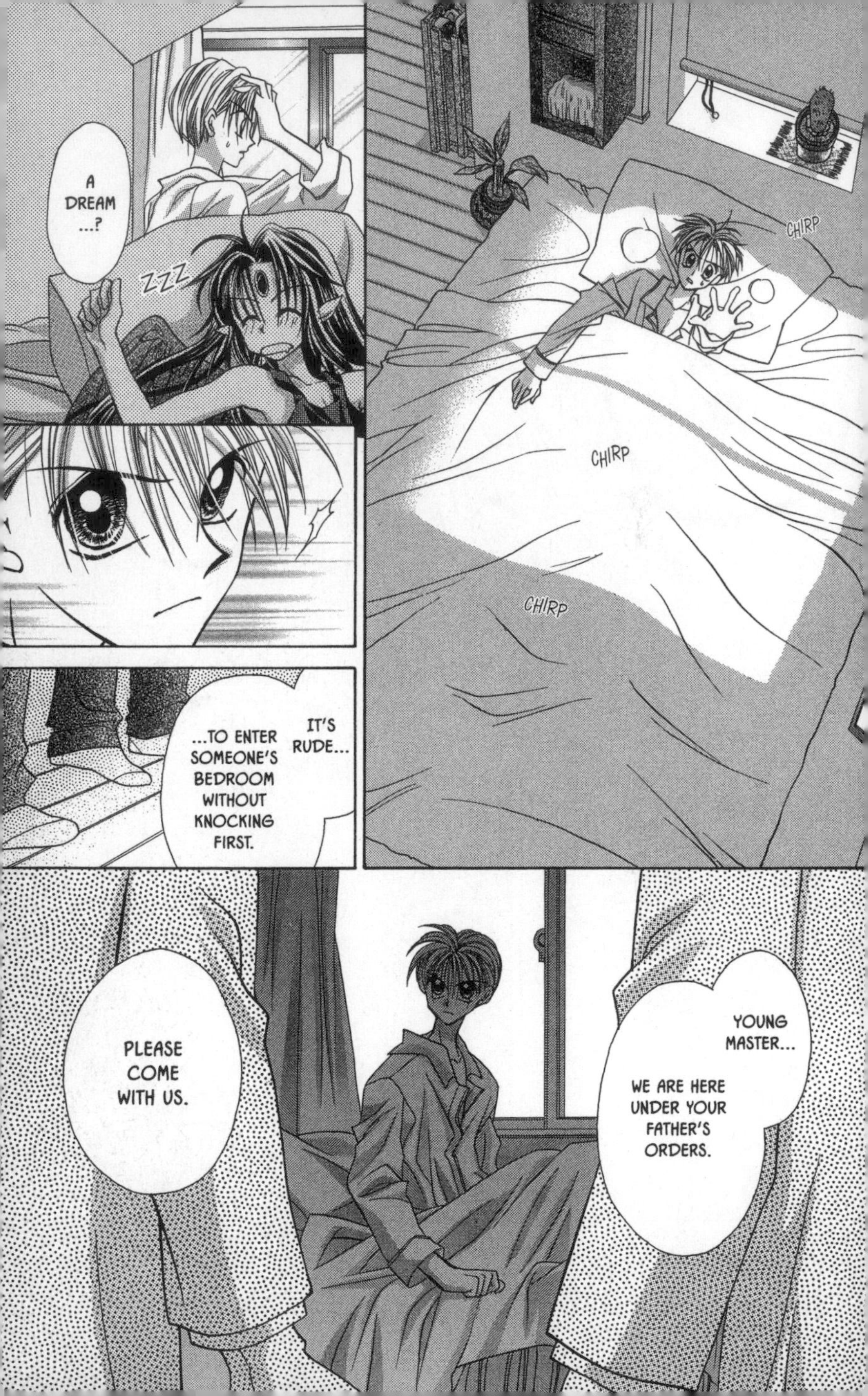
CHIRP
CHIRP
CHIRP
A DREAM ...?
ZZZ
IT'S RUDE...
...TO ENTER SOMEONE'S BEDROOM WITHOUT KNOCKING FIRST.
YOUNG MASTER...
WE ARE HERE UNDER YOUR FATHER'S ORDERS.
PLEASE COME WITH US.

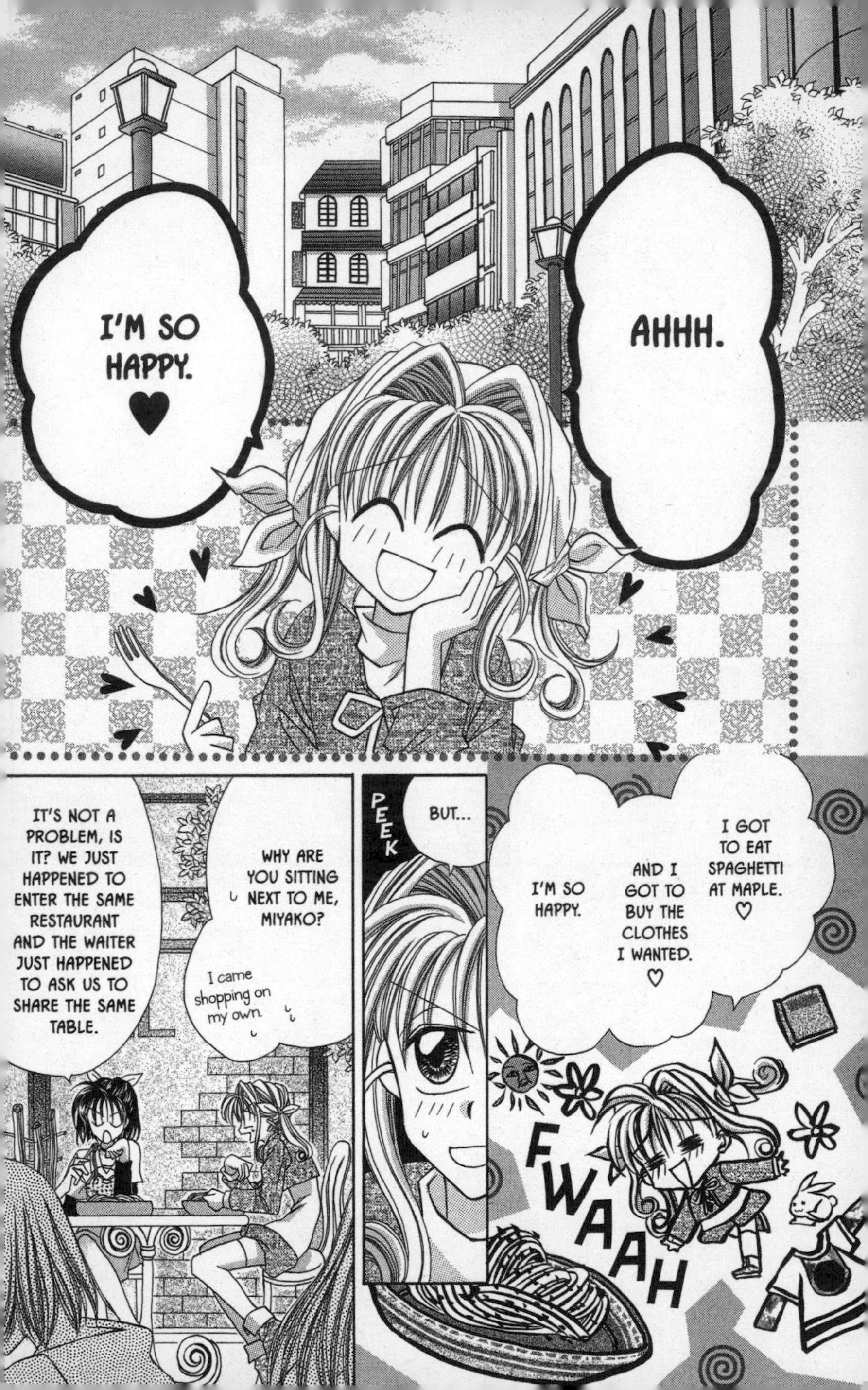
AHHH.
I'M SO HAPPY. ♥
I GOT TO EAT SPAGHETTI AT MAPLE. ♡
AND I GOT TO BUY THE CLOTHES I WANTED. ♡
I'M SO HAPPY.
FWAAAH
PEEK
BUT...
WHY ARE YOU SITTING NEXT TO ME, MIYAKO?
I came shopping on my own.
IT'S NOT A PROBLEM, IS IT? WE JUST HAPPENED TO ENTER THE SAME RESTAURANT AND THE WAITER JUST HAPPENED TO ASK US TO SHARE THE SAME TABLE.

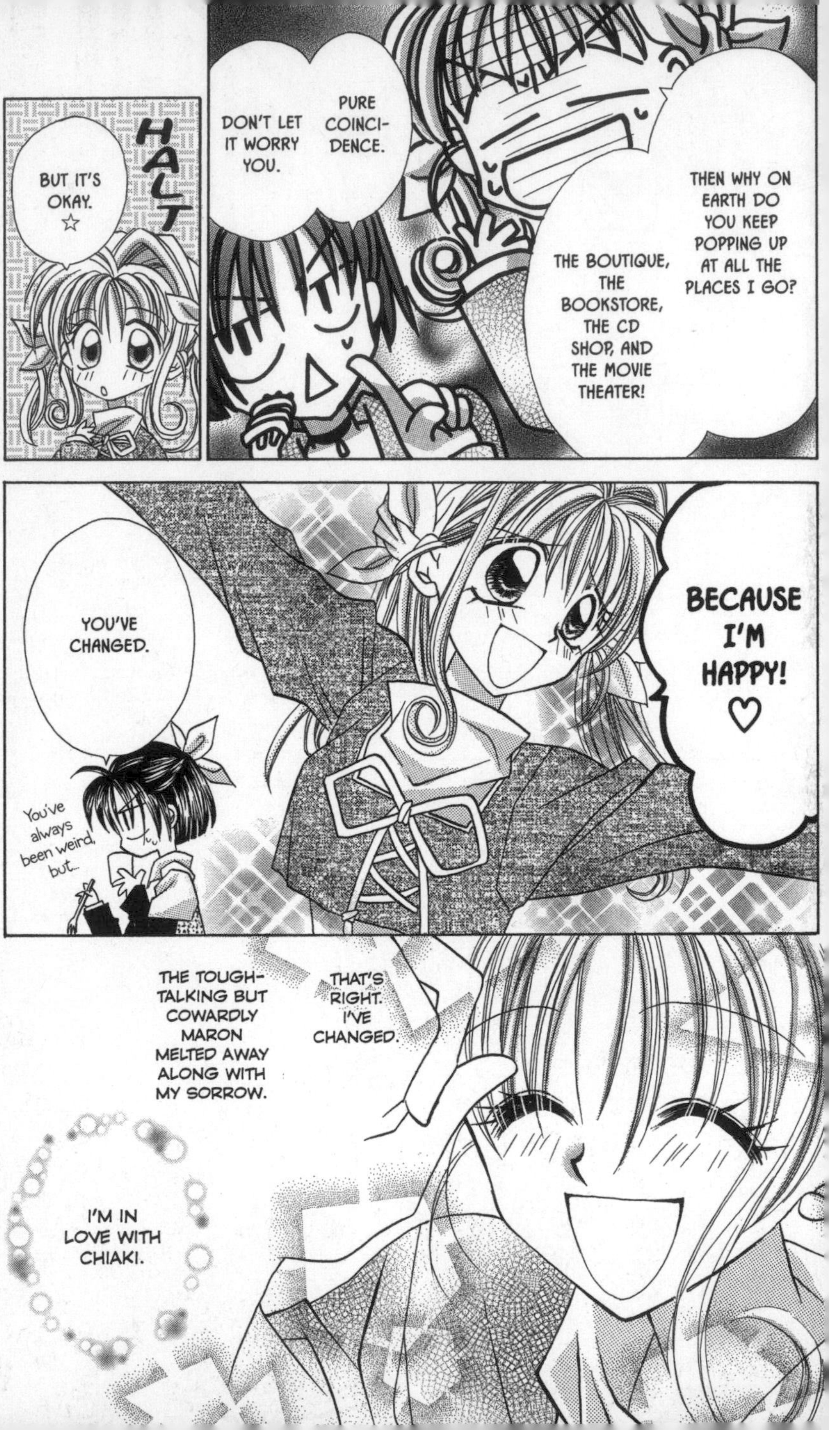
THEN WHY ON EARTH DO YOU KEEP POPPING UP AT ALL THE PLACES I GO?
THE BOUTIQUE, THE BOOKSTORE, THE CD SHOP, AND THE MOVIE THEATER!
PURE COINCI-DENCE.
DON'T LET IT WORRY YOU.
HALT
BUT IT'S OKAY. ☆
BECAUSE I'M HAPPY! ♡
YOU'VE CHANGED.
You've always been weird, but...
THAT'S RIGHT. I'VE CHANGED.
THE TOUGH-TALKING BUT COWARDLY MARON MELTED AWAY ALONG WITH MY SORROW.
I'M IN LOVE WITH CHIAKI.

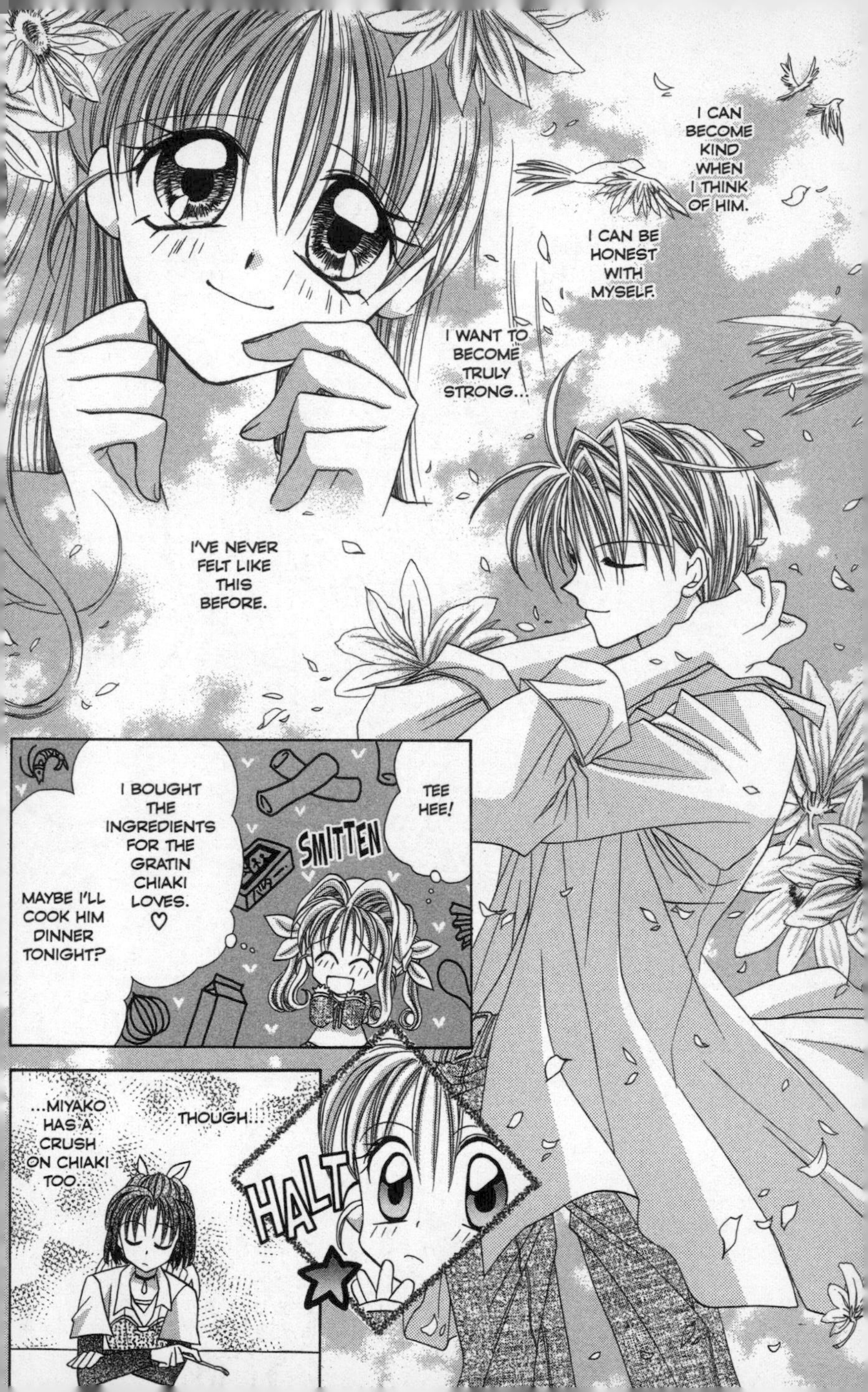
I CAN BECOME KIND WHEN I THINK OF HIM.
I CAN BE HONEST WITH MYSELF.
I WANT TO BECOME TRULY STRONG...
I'VE NEVER FELT LIKE THIS BEFORE.
TEE HEE!
SMITTEN
I BOUGHT THE INGREDIENTS FOR THE GRATIN CHIAKI LOVES. ♡
MAYBE I'LL COOK HIM DINNER TONIGHT?
HALT
THOUGH...
...MIYAKO HAS A CRUSH ON CHIAKI TOO...

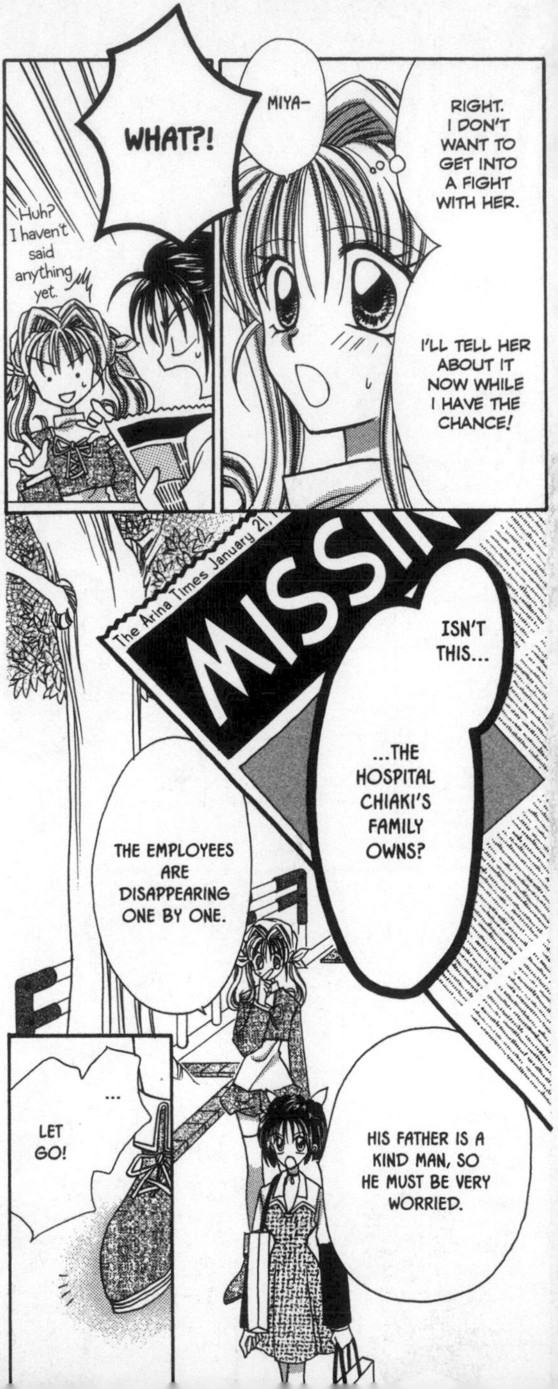
MIYA–
RIGHT. I DON'T WANT TO GET INTO A FIGHT WITH HER.
I'LL TELL HER ABOUT IT NOW WHILE I HAVE THE CHANCE!
WHAT?!
Huh? I haven't said anything yet.
The Arina Times January 21,
MISSI
ISN'T THIS...
...THE HOSPITAL CHIAKI'S FAMILY OWNS?
THE EMPLOYEES ARE DISAPPEARING ONE BY ONE.
HIS FATHER IS A KIND MAN, SO HE MUST BE VERY WORRIED.
...
LET GO!

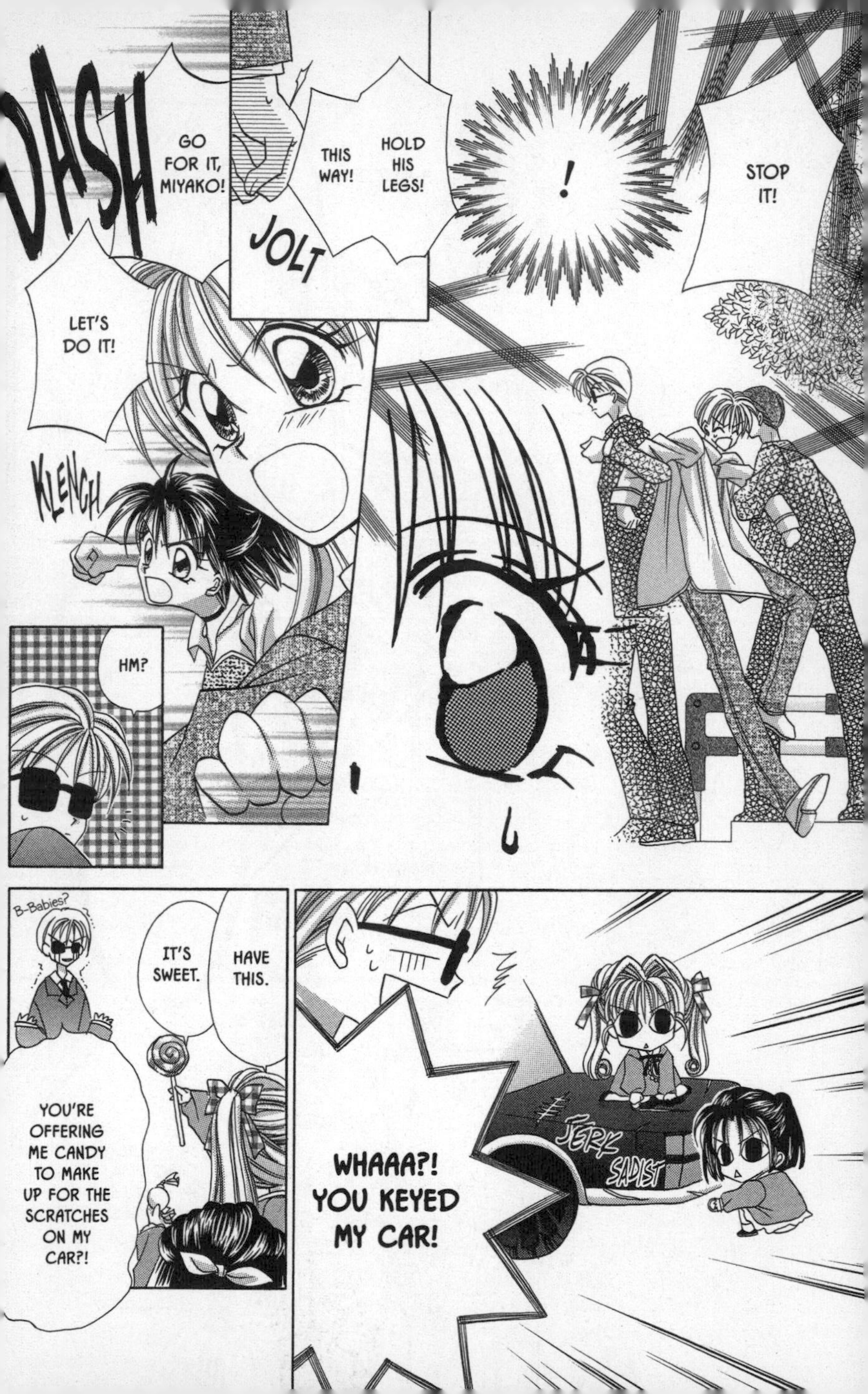
STOP IT!
!
HOLD HIS LEGS!
THIS WAY!
JOLT
GO FOR IT, MIYAKO!
DASH
LET'S DO IT!
KLENCH
HM?
WHAAA?! YOU KEYED MY CAR!
JERK
SADIST
HAVE THIS.
IT'S SWEET.
B-Babies?
YOU'RE OFFERING ME CANDY TO MAKE UP FOR THE SCRATCHES ON MY CAR?!

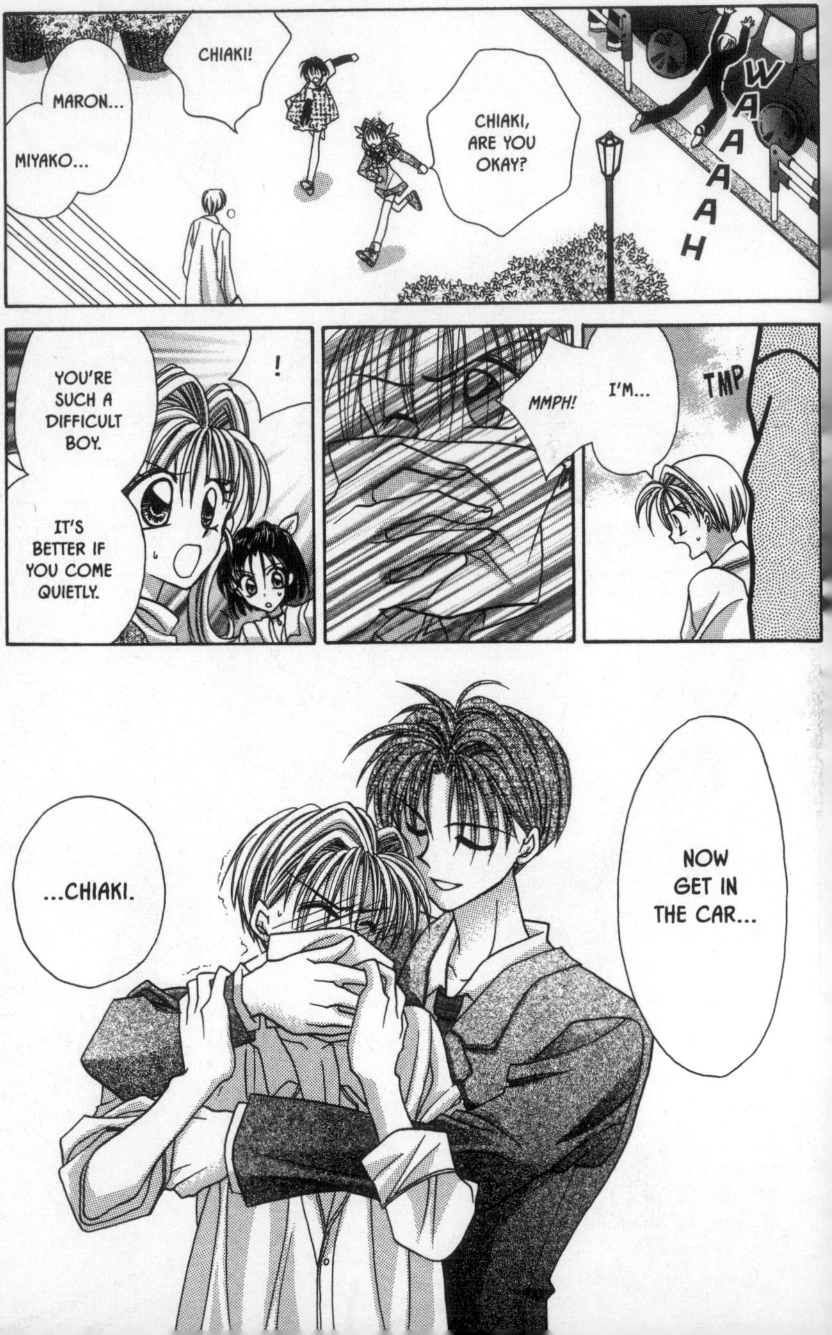
WAAAAH
CHIAKI, ARE YOU OKAY?
CHIAKI!
MARON...
MIYAKO...
TMP
I'M...
MMPH!
!
YOU'RE SUCH A DIFFICULT BOY.
IT'S BETTER IF YOU COME QUIETLY.
NOW GET IN THE CAR...
...CHIAKI.

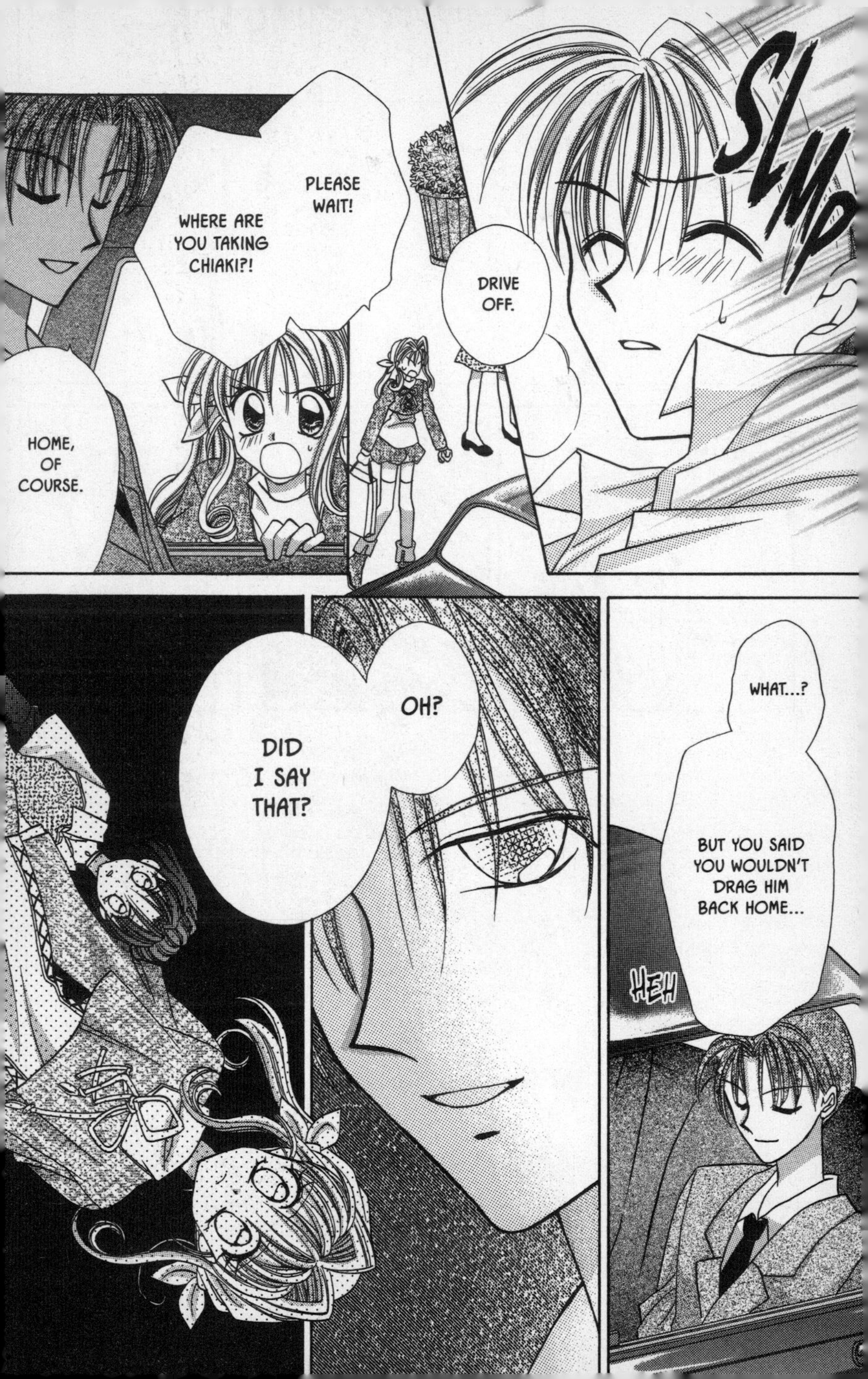
SLMP
DRIVE OFF.
PLEASE WAIT!
WHERE ARE YOU TAKING CHIAKI?!
HOME, OF COURSE.
WHAT...?
BUT YOU SAID YOU WOULDN'T DRAG HIM BACK HOME...
HEH
OH?
DID I SAY THAT?

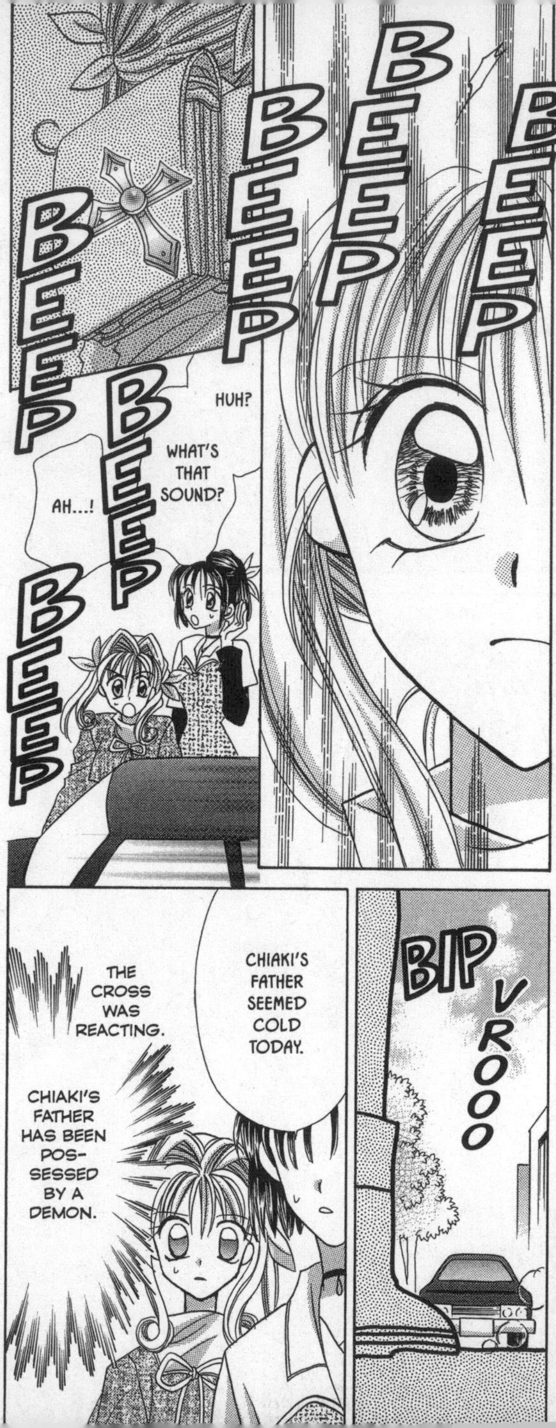
BEEP
BEEP
BEEP
BEEP
BEEP
BEEP
HUH?
WHAT'S THAT SOUND?
AH...!
BIP
VROOO
CHIAKI'S FATHER SEEMED COLD TODAY.
THE CROSS WAS REACTING.
CHIAKI'S FATHER HAS BEEN POS-SESSED BY A DEMON.

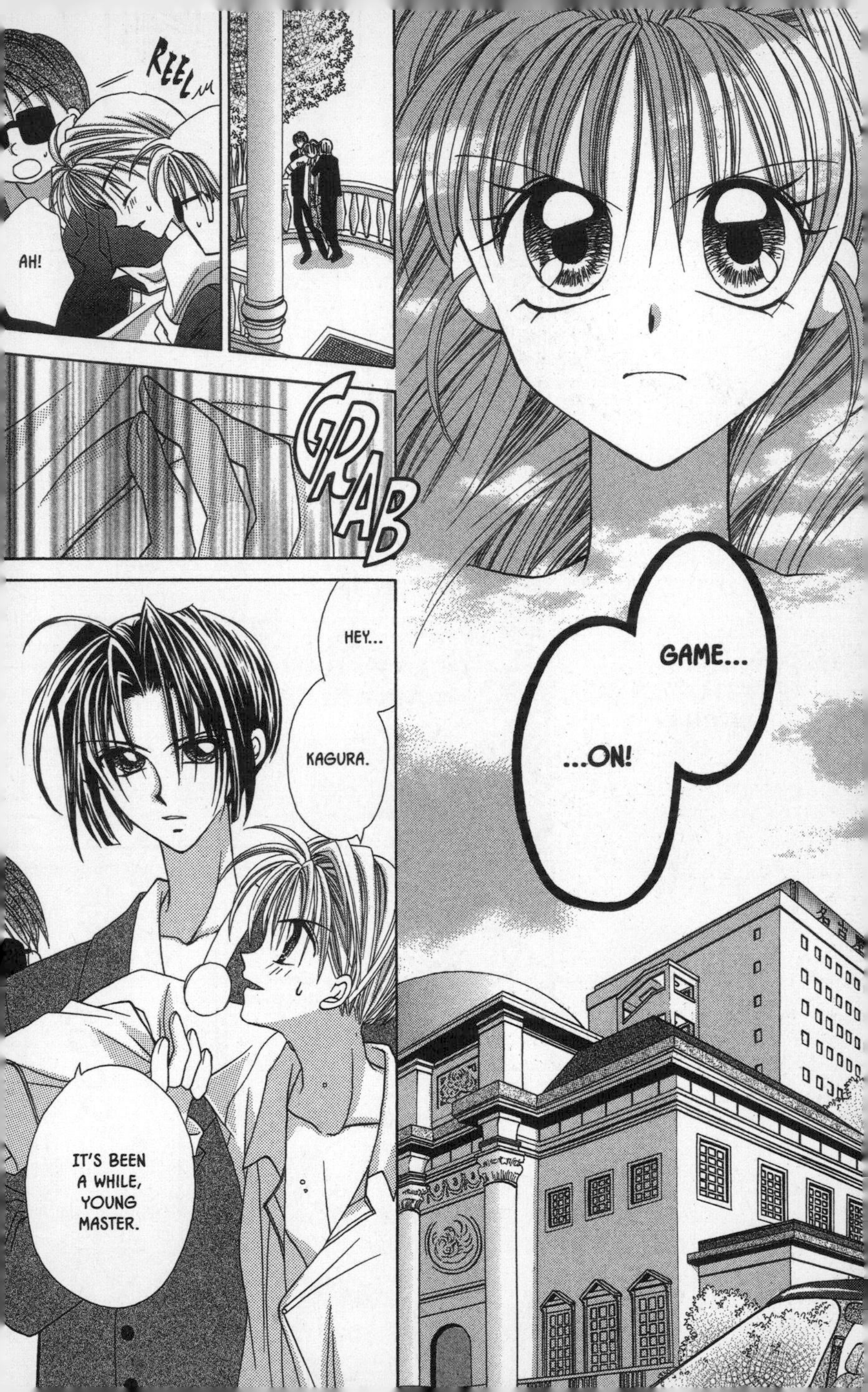
GAME...
...ON!
REEL
AH!
GRAB
HEY...
KAGURA.
IT'S BEEN A WHILE, YOUNG MASTER.

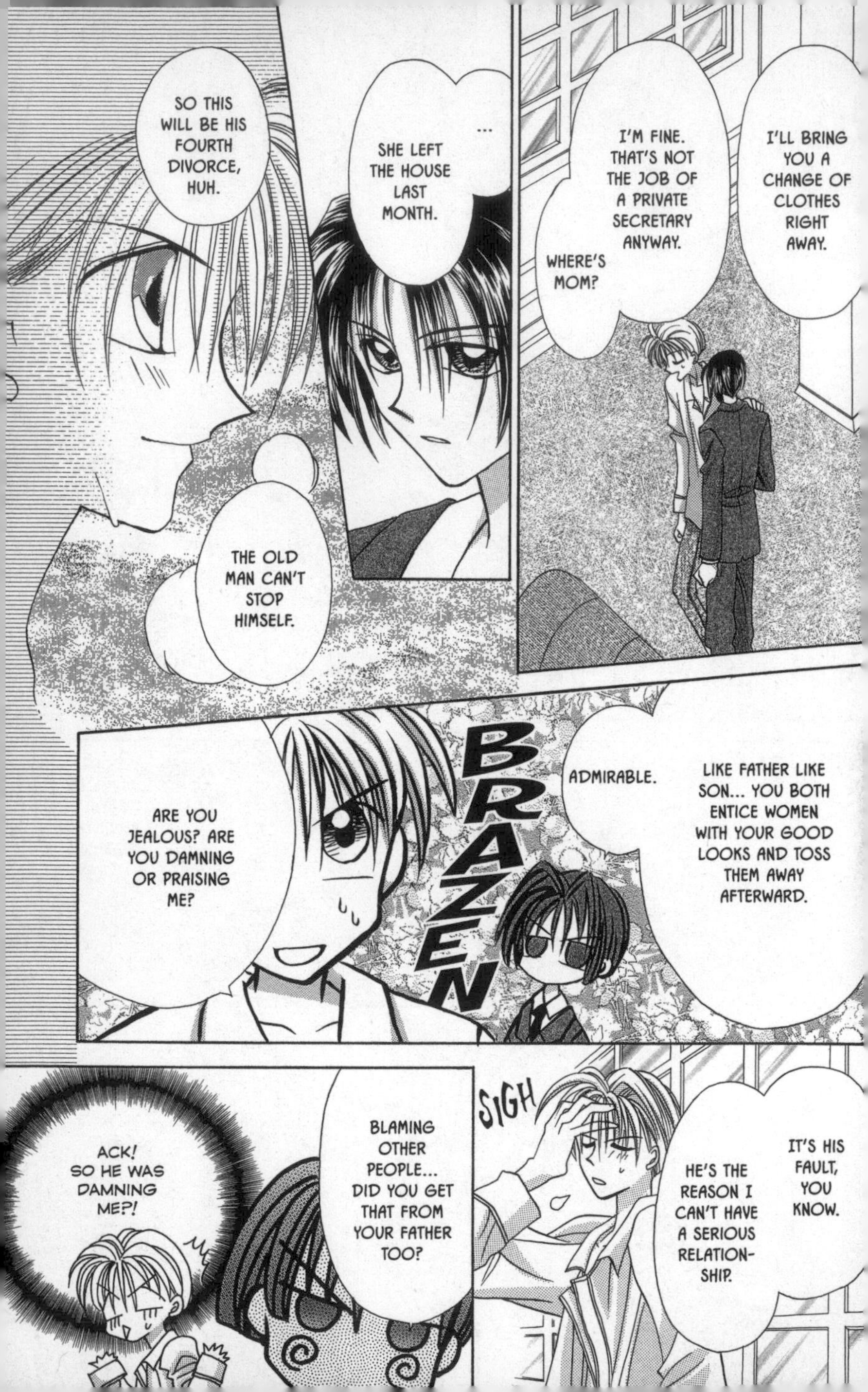
I'LL BRING YOU A CHANGE OF CLOTHES RIGHT AWAY.
I'M FINE. THAT'S NOT THE JOB OF A PRIVATE SECRETARY ANYWAY.
WHERE'S MOM?
...
SHE LEFT THE HOUSE LAST MONTH.
SO THIS WILL BE HIS FOURTH DIVORCE, HUH.
THE OLD MAN CAN'T STOP HIMSELF.
LIKE FATHER LIKE SON... YOU BOTH ENTICE WOMEN WITH YOUR GOOD LOOKS AND TOSS THEM AWAY AFTERWARD.
ADMIRABLE.
BRAZEN
ARE YOU JEALOUS? ARE YOU DAMNING OR PRAISING ME?
IT'S HIS FAULT, YOU KNOW.
HE'S THE REASON I CAN'T HAVE A SERIOUS RELATIONSHIP.
SIGH
BLAMING OTHER PEOPLE... DID YOU GET THAT FROM YOUR FATHER TOO?
ACK! SO HE WAS DAMNING ME?!

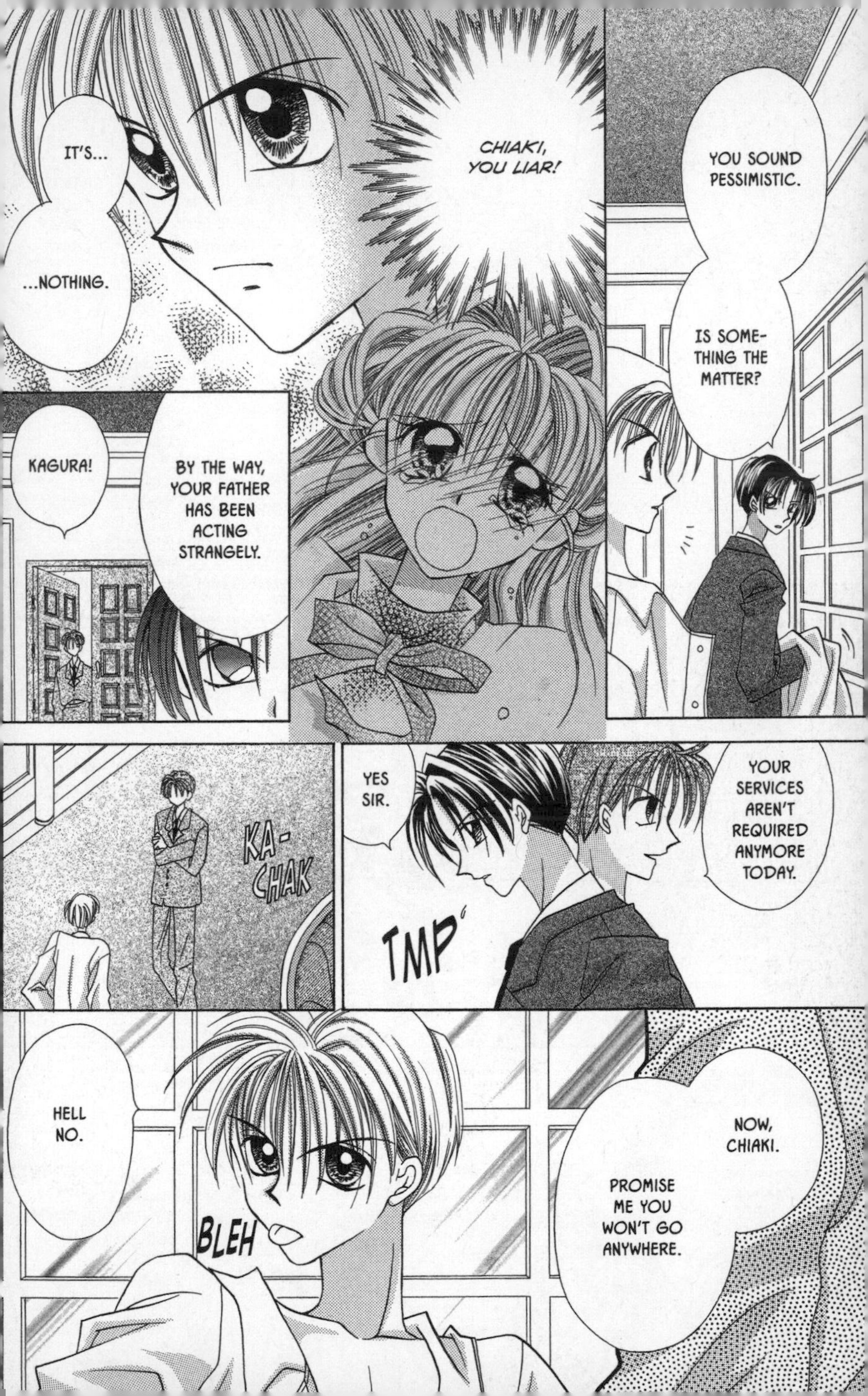
YOU SOUND PESSIMISTIC.
IS SOME-THING THE MATTER?
IT'S...
...NOTHING.
CHIAKI, YOU LIAR!
BY THE WAY, YOUR FATHER HAS BEEN ACTING STRANGELY.
KAGURA!
YOUR SERVICES AREN'T REQUIRED ANYMORE TODAY.
YES SIR.
TMP
KA-CHAK
NOW, CHIAKI.
PROMISE ME YOU WON'T GO ANYWHERE.
BLEH
HELL NO.

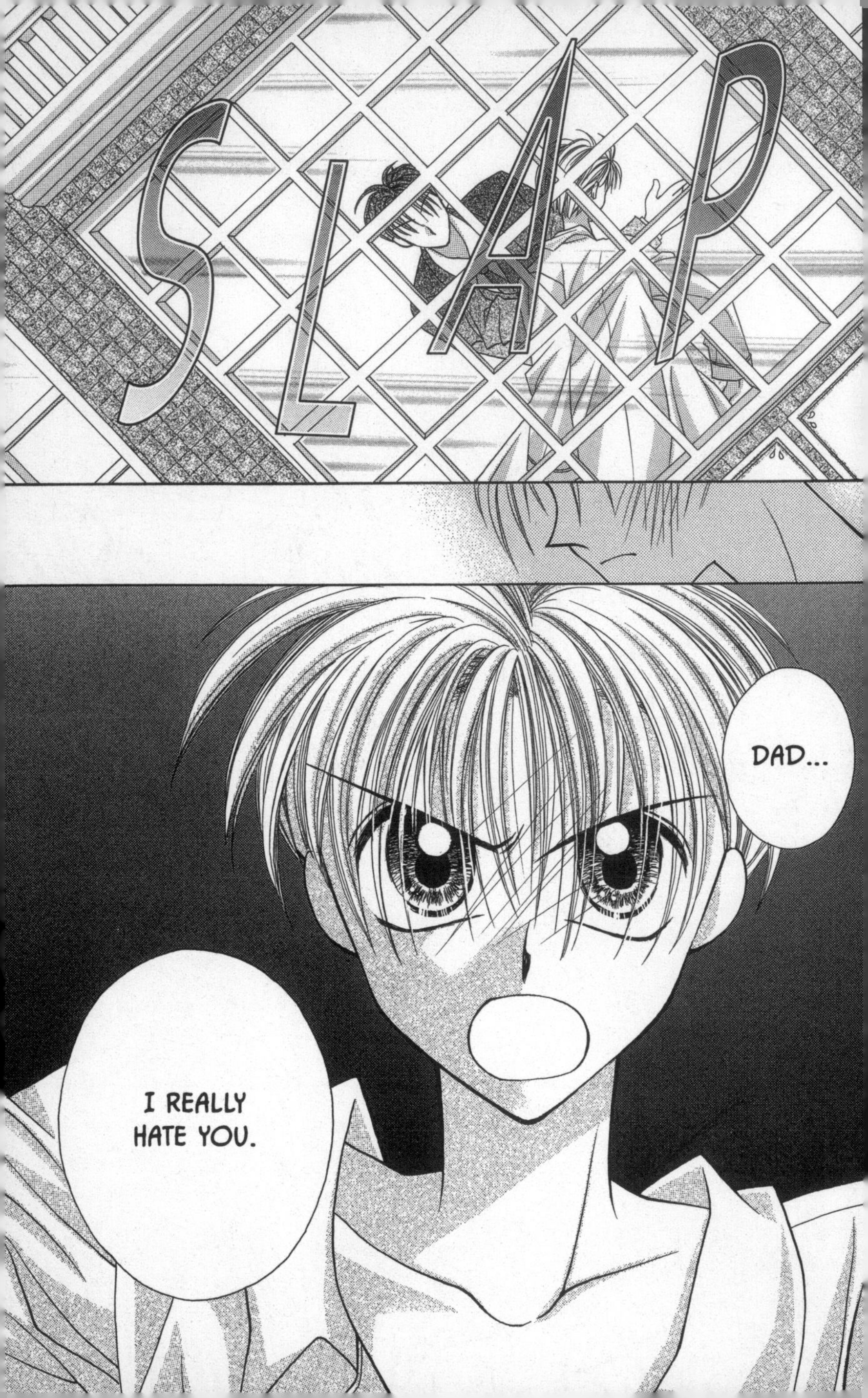
SLAP
DAD...
I REALLY HATE YOU.

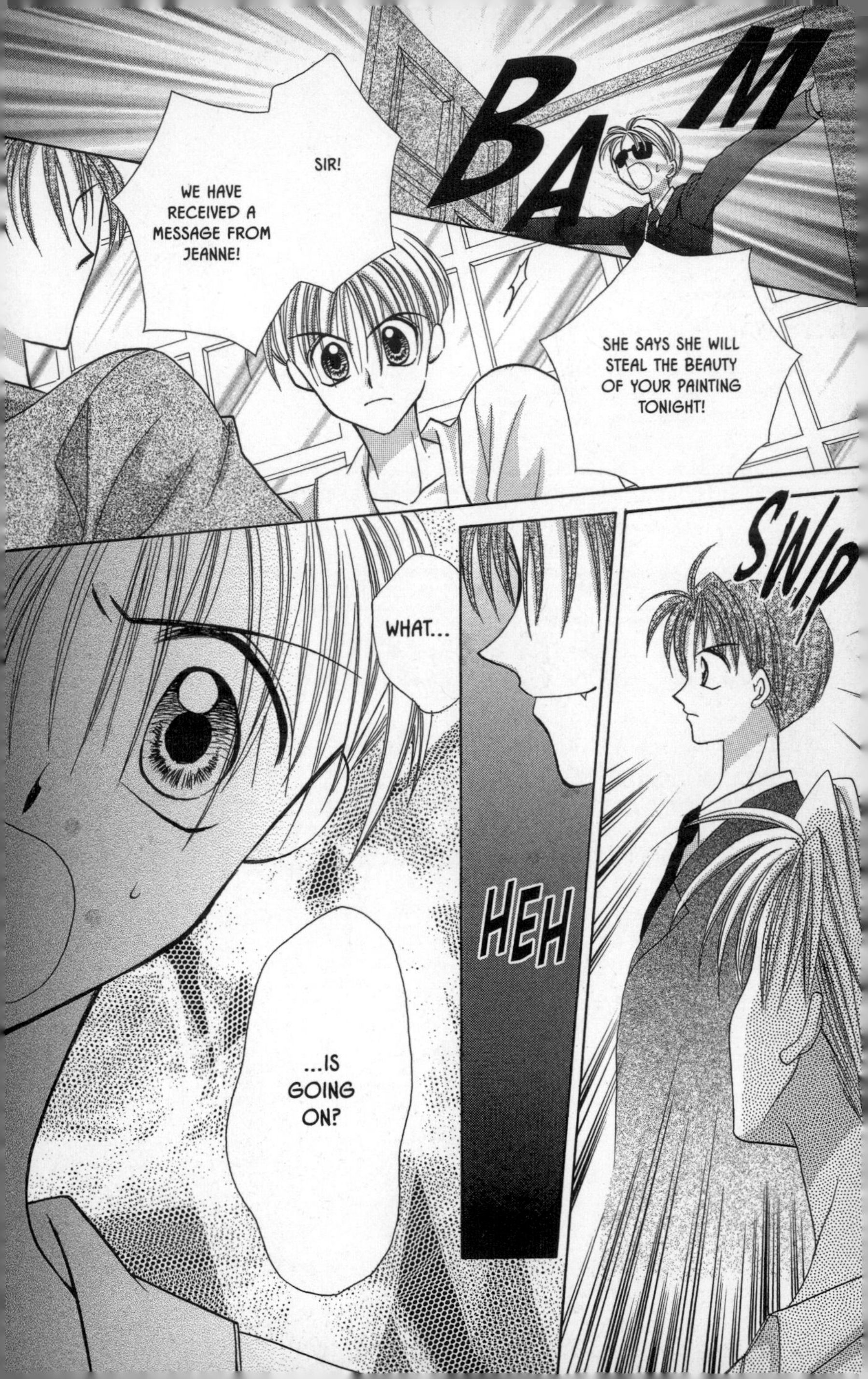
BAM
SIR!
WE HAVE RECEIVED A MESSAGE FROM JEANNE!
SHE SAYS SHE WILL STEAL THE BEAUTY OF YOUR PAINTING TONIGHT!
SWIP
HEH
WHAT...
...IS GOING ON?

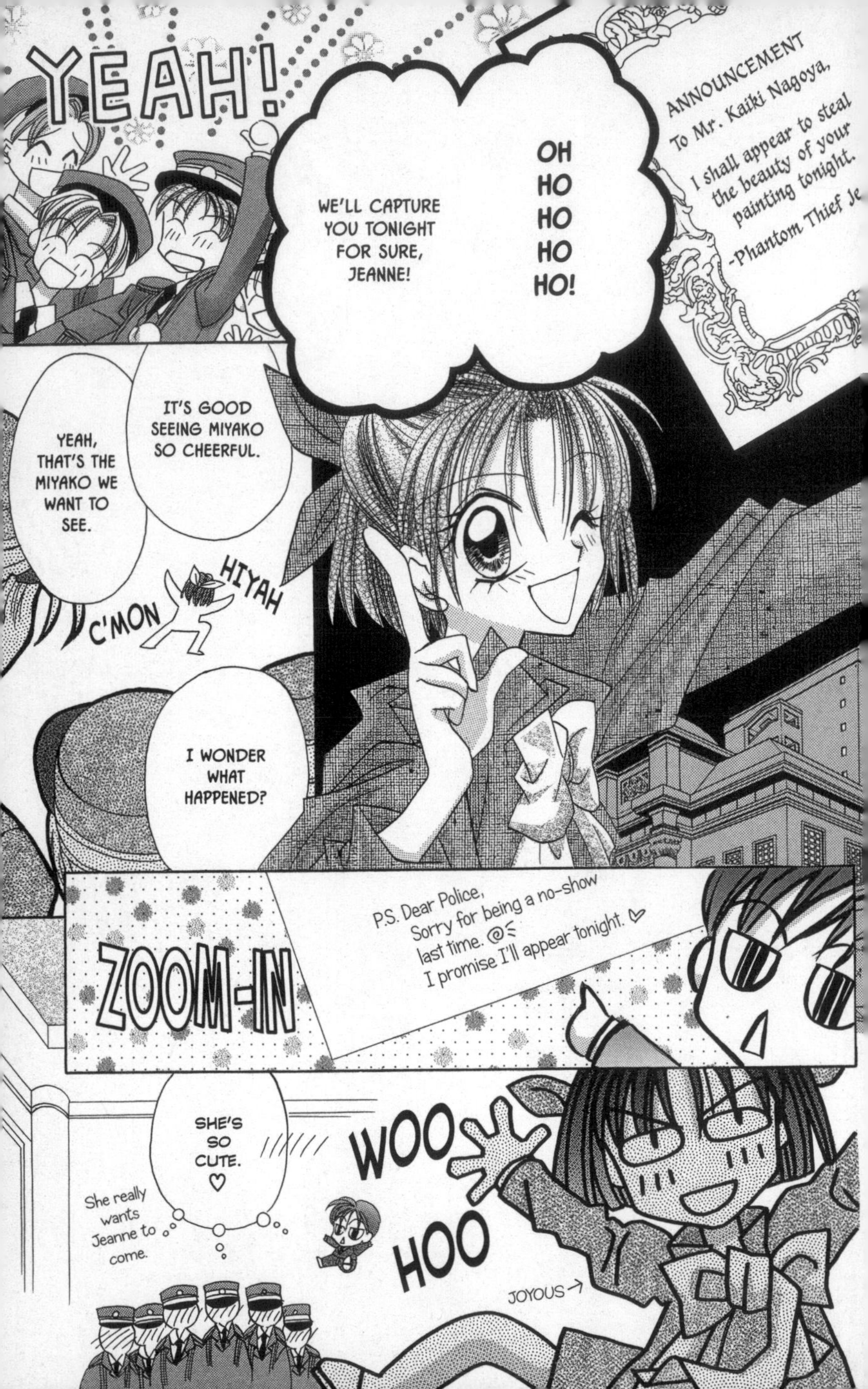
ANNOUNCEMENT
To Mr. Kaiki Nagoya,
I shall appear to steal the beauty of your painting tonight.
-Phantom Thief Je
OH HO HO HO HO!
WE'LL CAPTURE YOU TONIGHT FOR SURE, JEANNE!
YEAH!
IT'S GOOD SEEING MIYAKO SO CHEERFUL.
YEAH, THAT'S THE MIYAKO WE WANT TO SEE.
HIYAH
C'MON
I WONDER WHAT HAPPENED?
P.S. Dear Police,
Sorry for being a no-show last time.
I promise I'll appear tonight. ♥
ZOOM-IN
JOYOUS
WOO HOO
SHE'S SO CUTE. ♥
She really wants Jeanne to come.

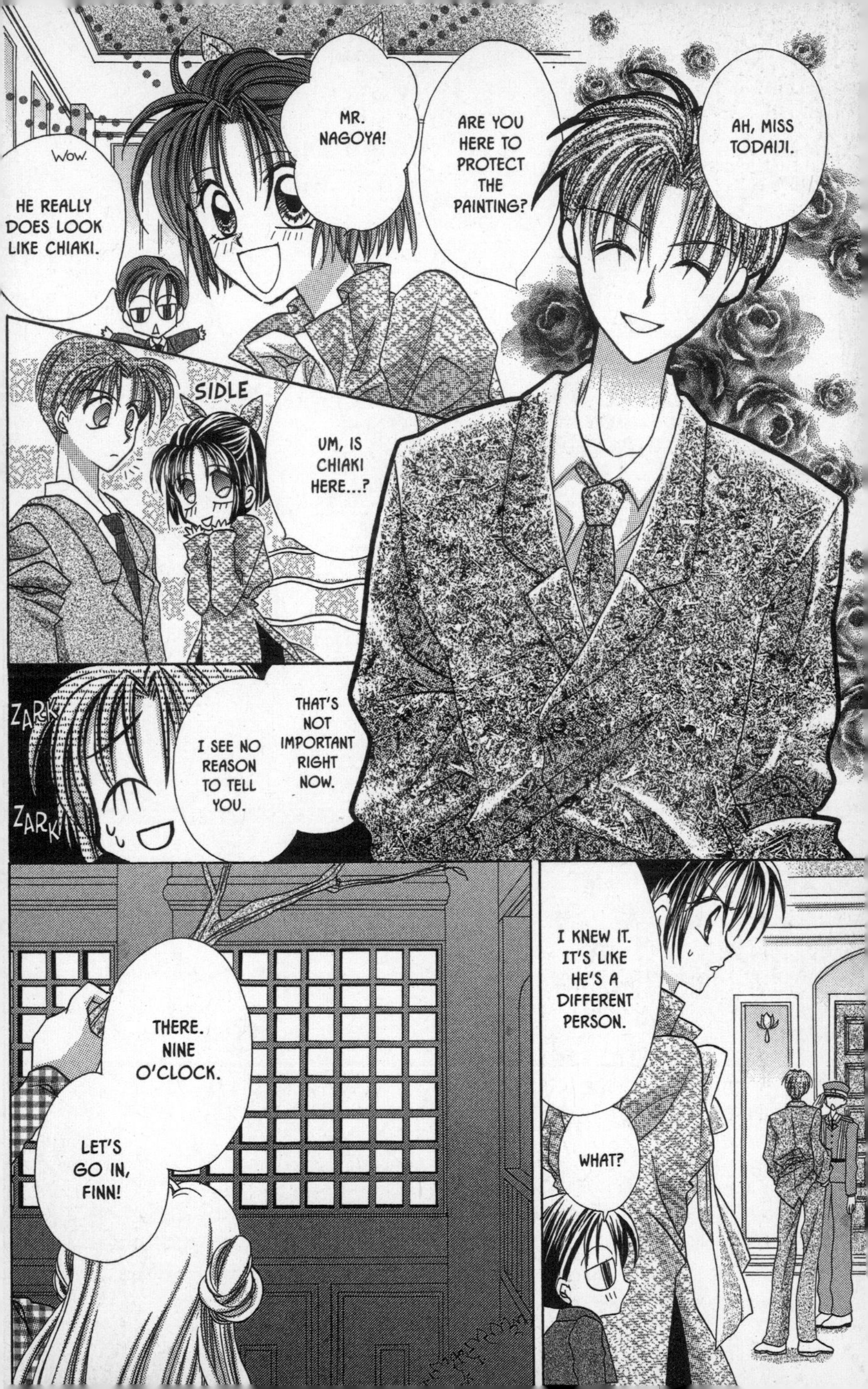
AH, MISS TODAIJI.
ARE YOU HERE TO PROTECT THE PAINTING?
MR. NAGOYA!
Wow.
HE REALLY DOES LOOK LIKE CHIAKI.
SIDLE
UM, IS CHIAKI HERE...?
THAT'S NOT IMPORTANT RIGHT NOW.
I SEE NO REASON TO TELL YOU.
ZARK
ZARK
I KNEW IT. IT'S LIKE HE'S A DIFFERENT PERSON.
WHAT?
THERE. NINE O'CLOCK.
LET'S GO IN, FINN!

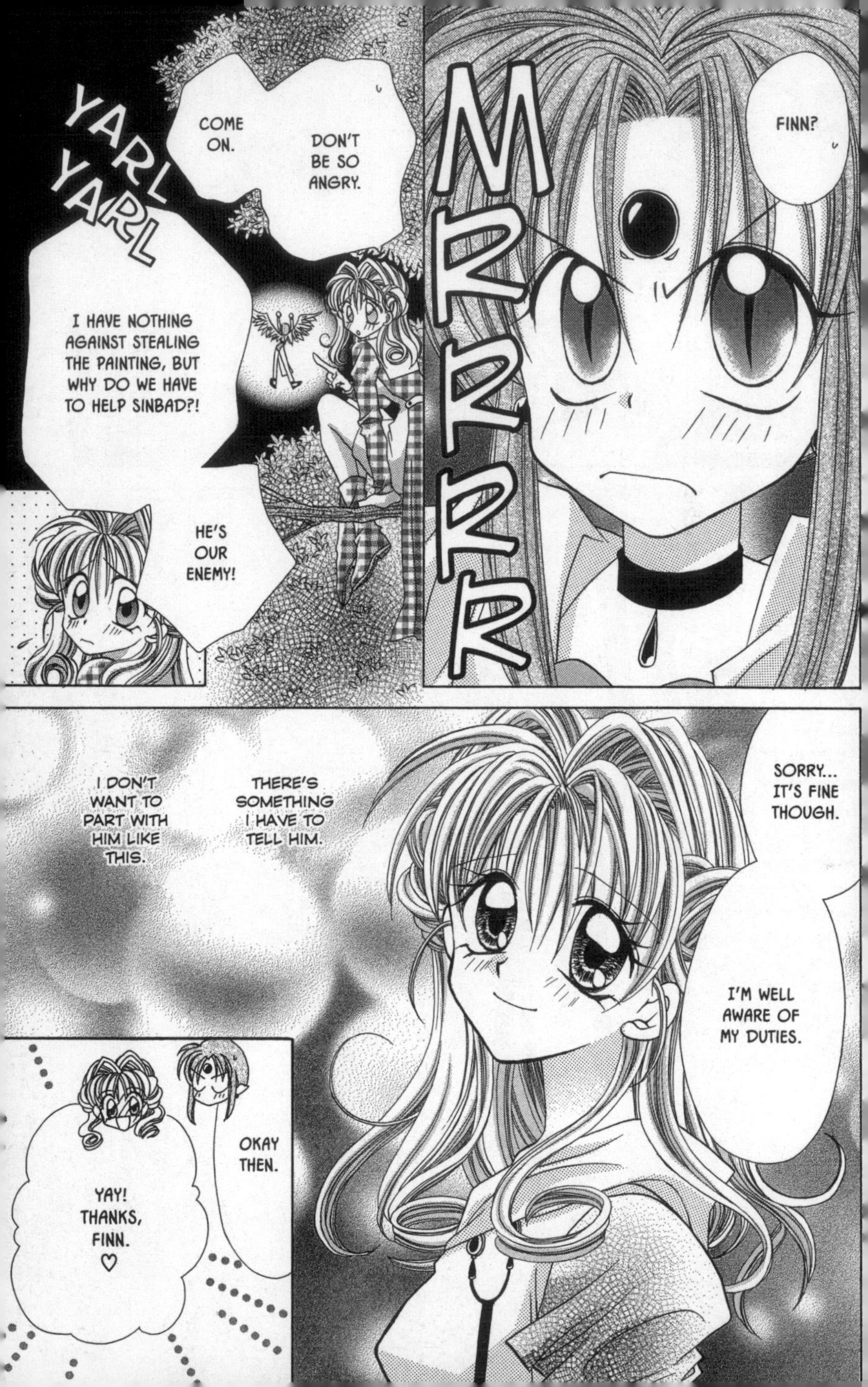
FINN?
MRRRR
COME ON. DON'T BE SO ANGRY.
YARL YARL
I HAVE NOTHING AGAINST STEALING THE PAINTING, BUT WHY DO WE HAVE TO HELP SINBAD?!
HE'S OUR ENEMY!
SORRY... IT'S FINE THOUGH.
I'M WELL AWARE OF MY DUTIES.
THERE'S SOMETHING I HAVE TO TELL HIM.
I DON'T WANT TO PART WITH HIM LIKE THIS.
OKAY THEN.
YAY! THANKS, FINN. ♡

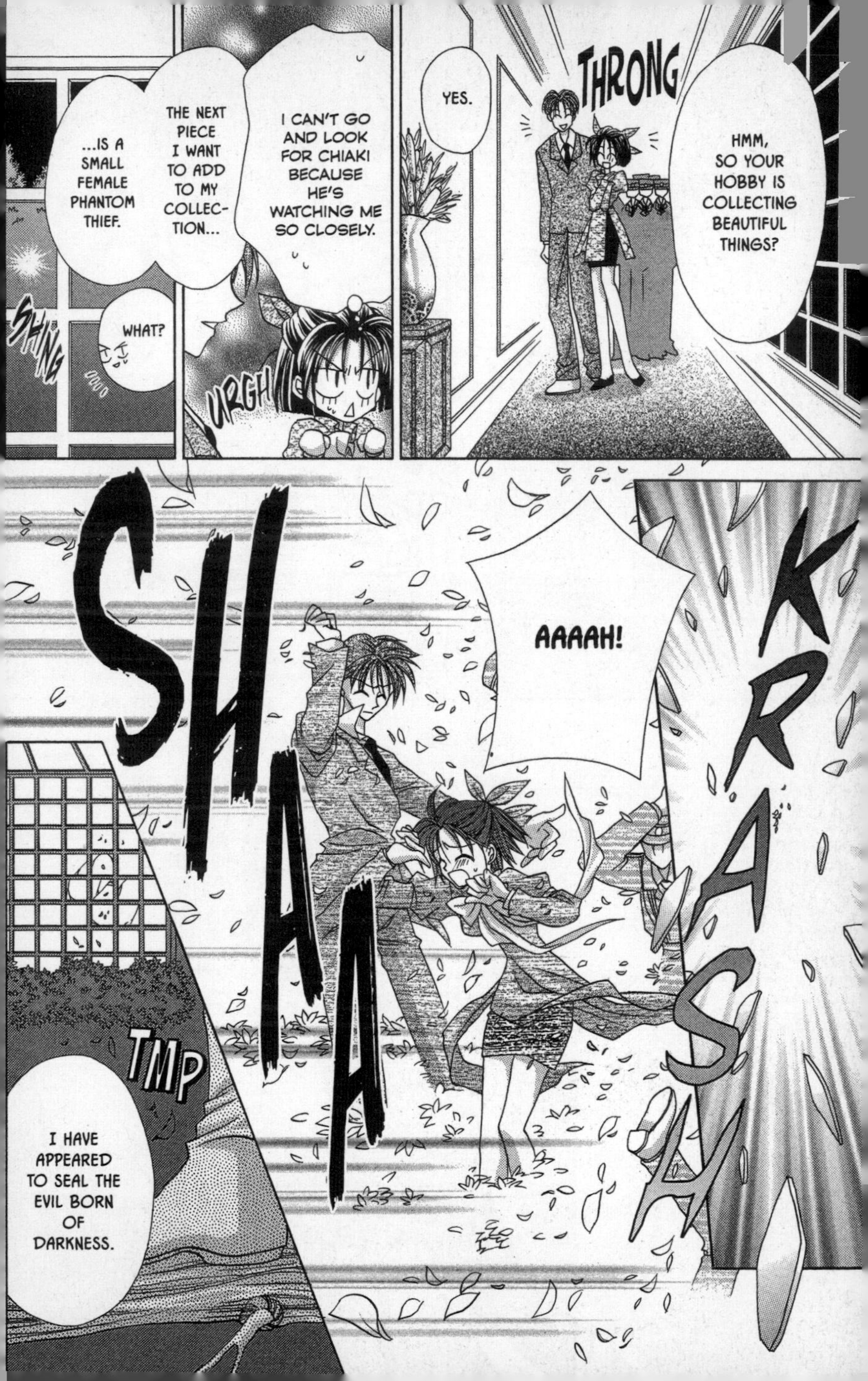
THRONG
HMM, SO YOUR HOBBY IS COLLECTING BEAUTIFUL THINGS?
YES.
I CAN'T GO AND LOOK FOR CHIAKI BECAUSE HE'S WATCHING ME SO CLOSELY.
URGH
THE NEXT PIECE I WANT TO ADD TO MY COLLECTION...
...IS A SMALL FEMALE PHANTOM THIEF.
WHAT?
SHING
KRASH
AAAAH!
SHAA
TMP
I HAVE APPEARED TO SEAL THE EVIL BORN OF DARKNESS.

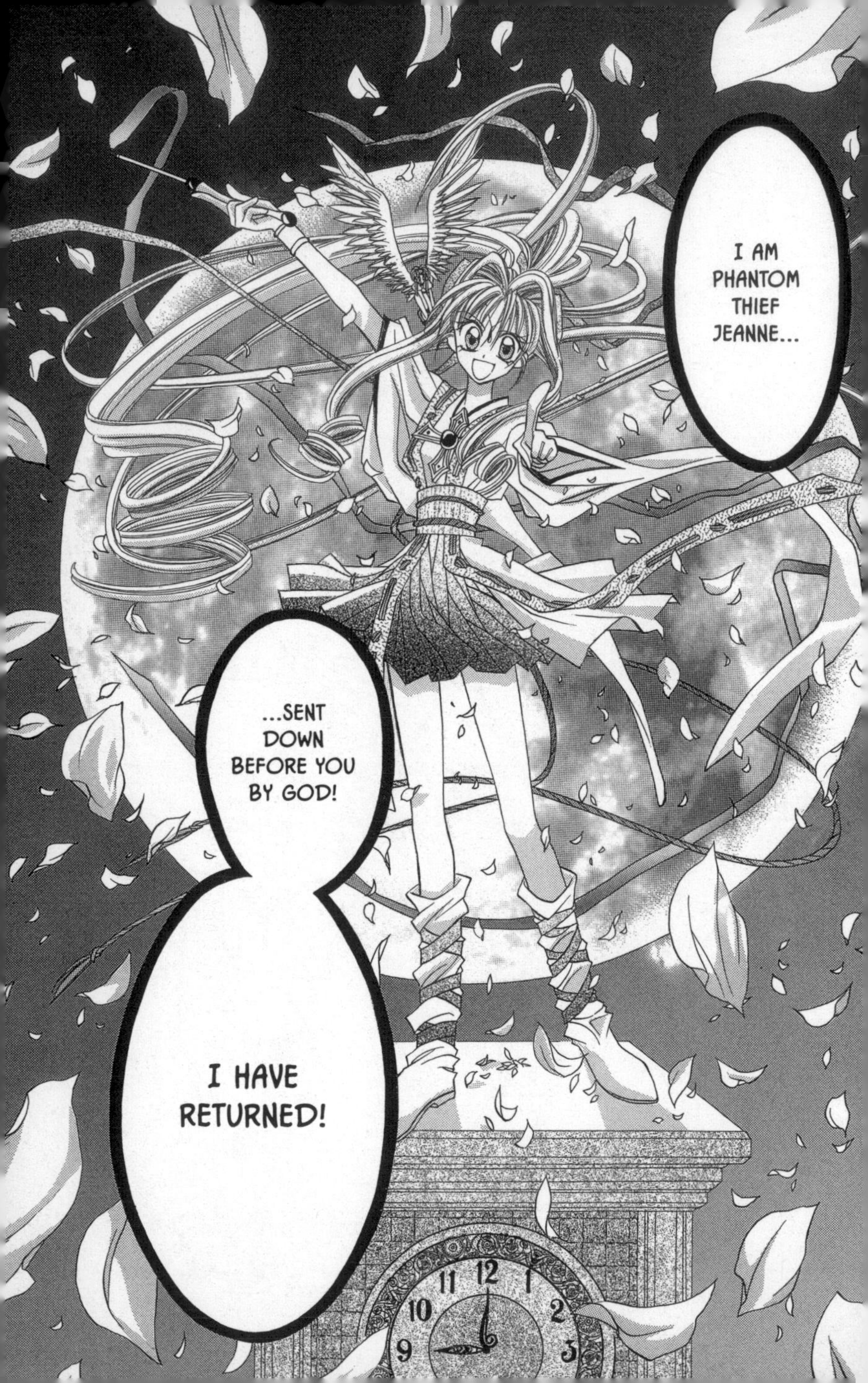
I AM PHANTOM THIEF JEANNE...
...SENT DOWN BEFORE YOU BY GOD!
I HAVE RETURNED!
11 12 1
10 2
9 3

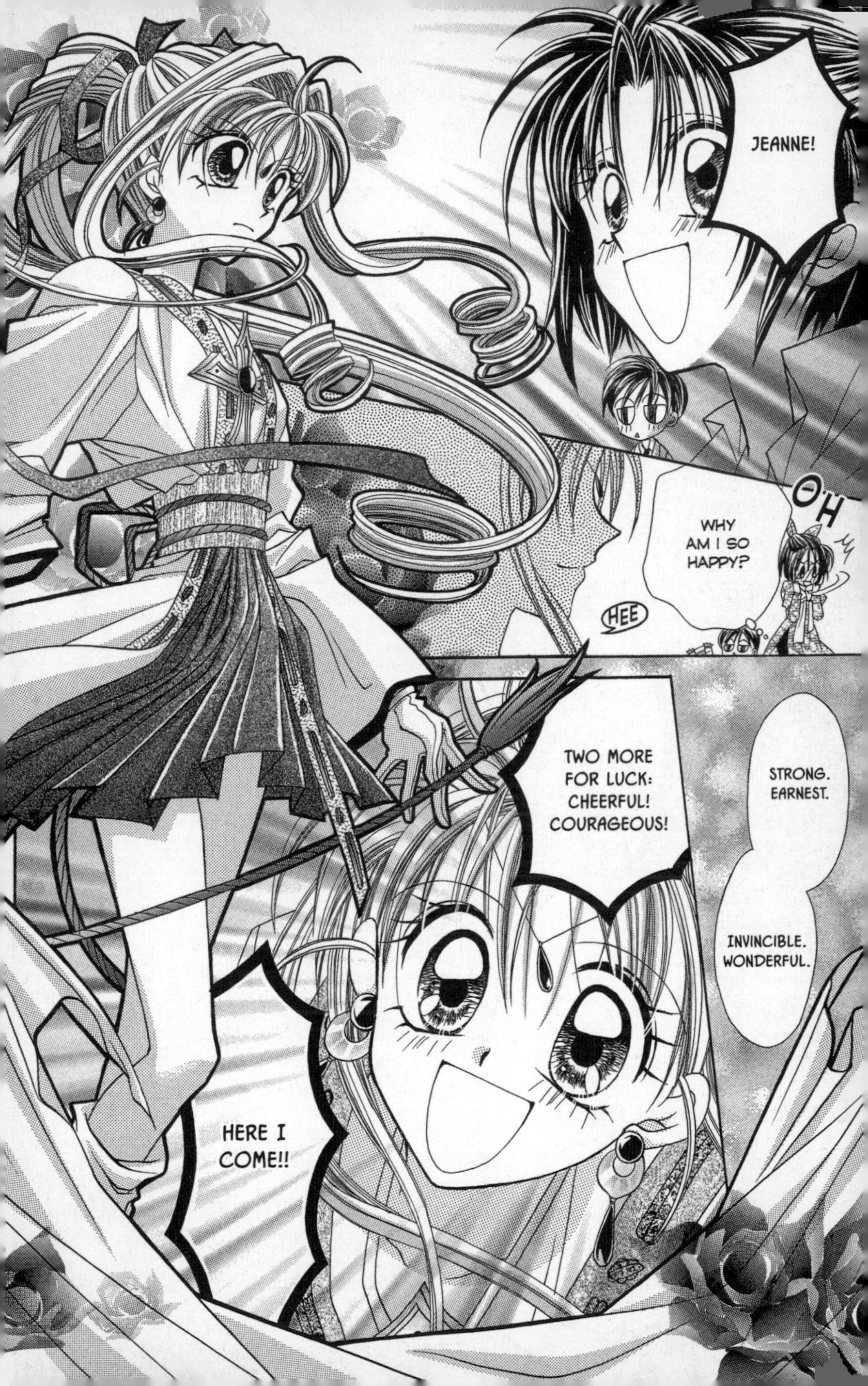
JEANNE!
OH
WHY AM I SO HAPPY?
HEE
STRONG. EARNEST.
INVINCIBLE. WONDERFUL.
TWO MORE FOR LUCK: CHEERFUL! COURAGEOUS!
HERE I COME!!

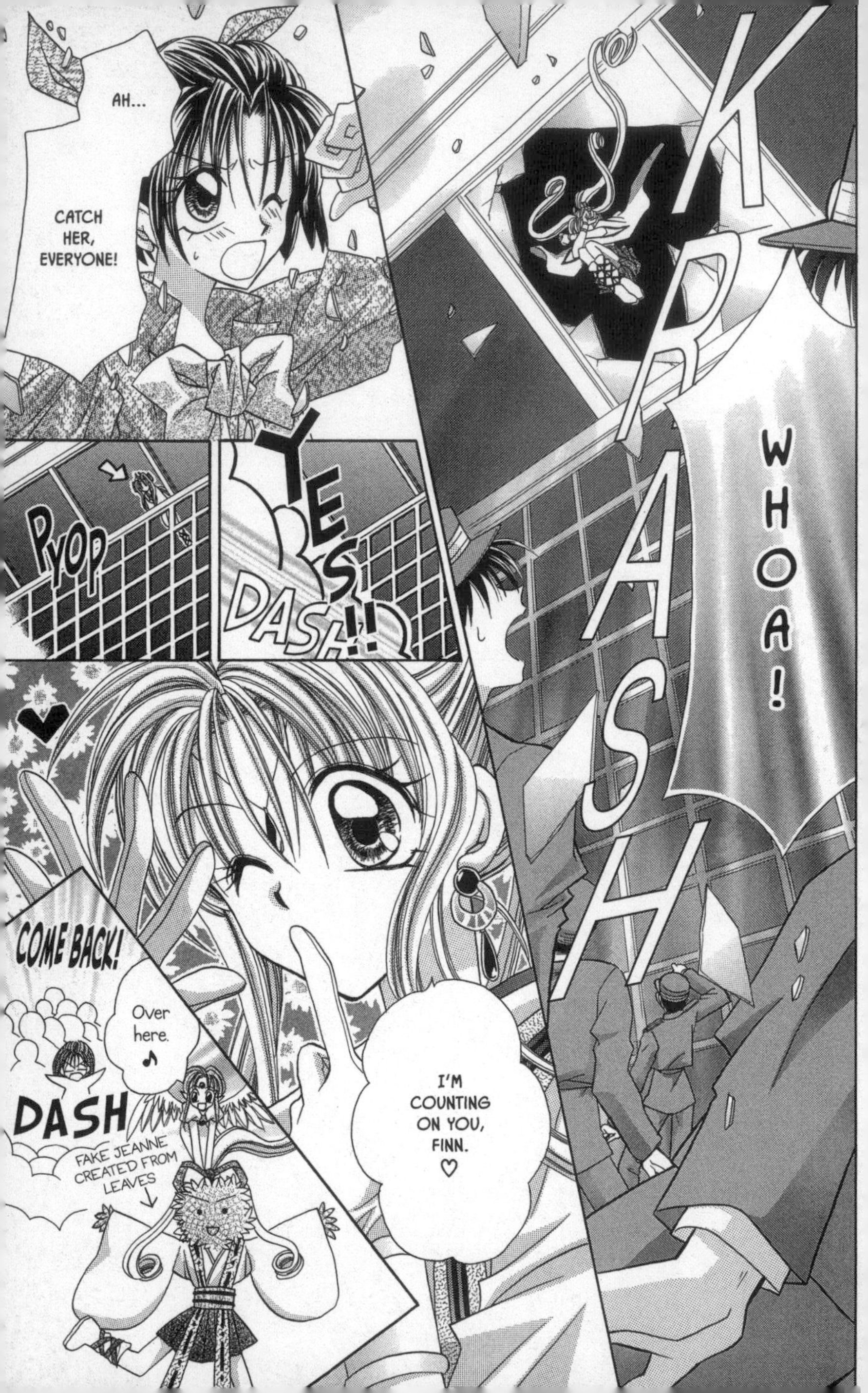
KRASH
WHOA!
AH...
CATCH HER, EVERYONE!
YES
DASH!!
PYOP
I'M COUNTING ON YOU, FINN. ♡
COME BACK!
Over here. ♪
DASH
FAKE JEANNE CREATED FROM LEAVES

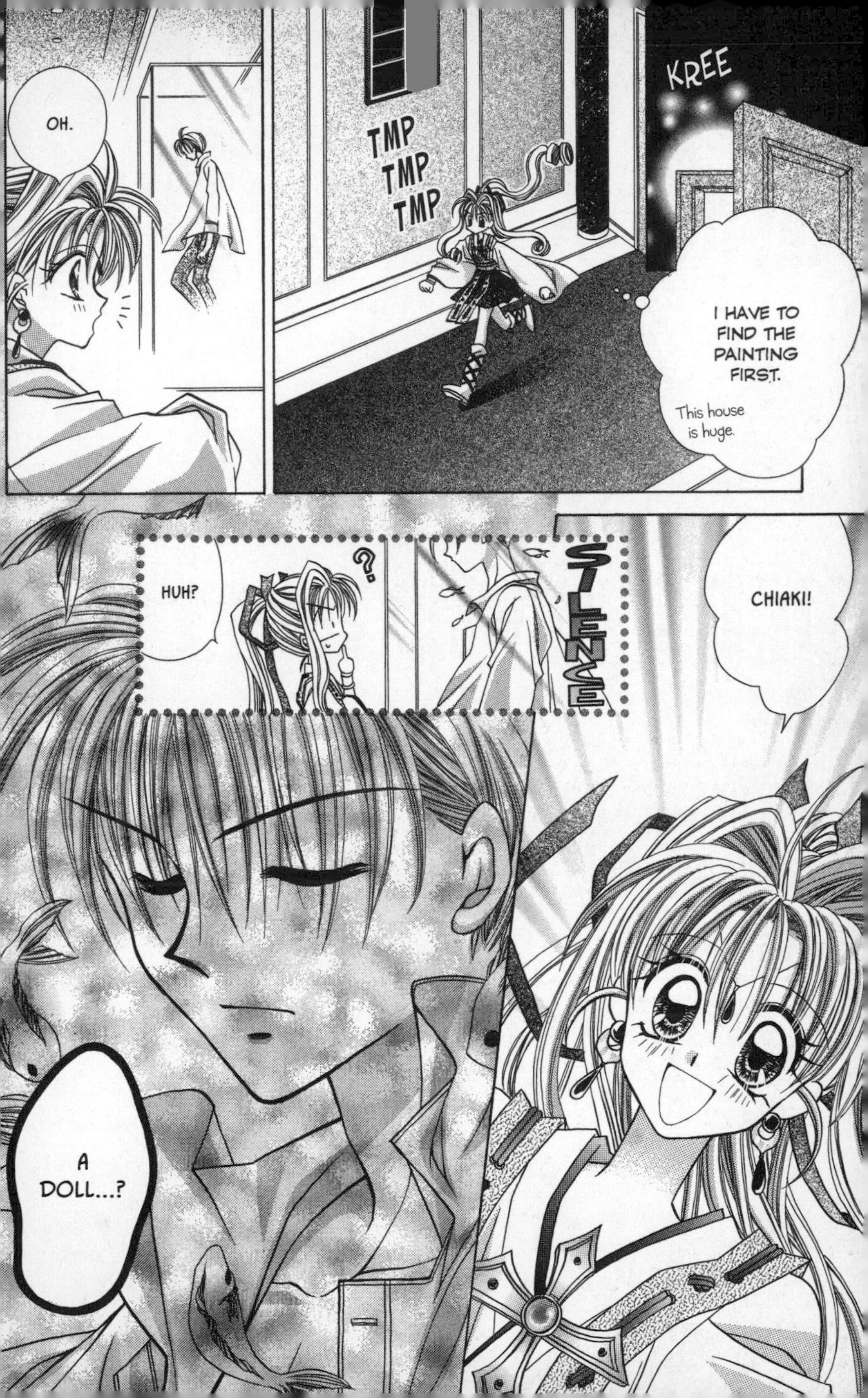
KREE
I HAVE TO FIND THE PAINTING FIRST.
This house is huge.
TMP TMP TMP
OH.
CHIAKI!
SILENCE
?
HUH?
A DOLL...?

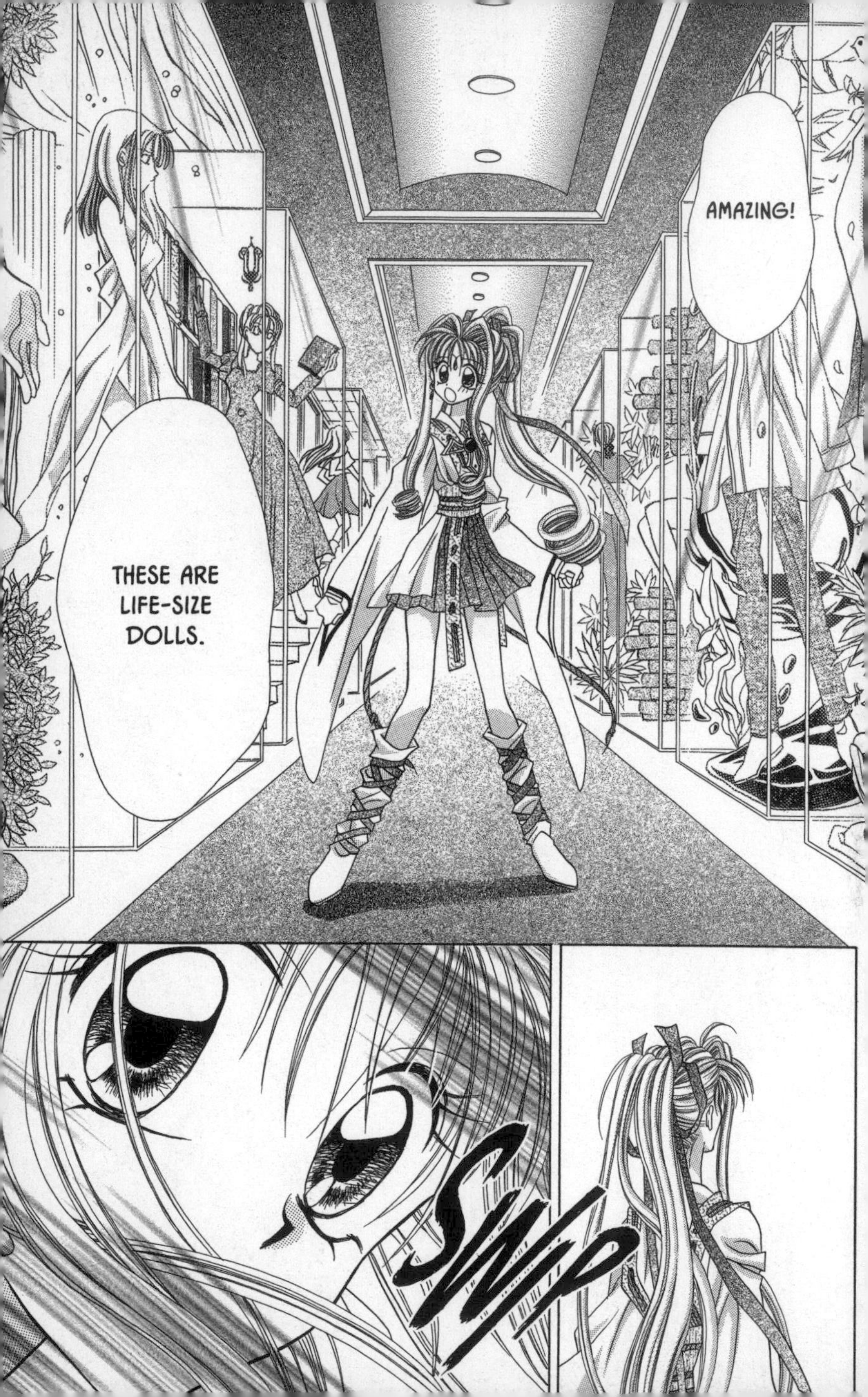
AMAZING!
THESE ARE LIFE-SIZE DOLLS.
SNIP

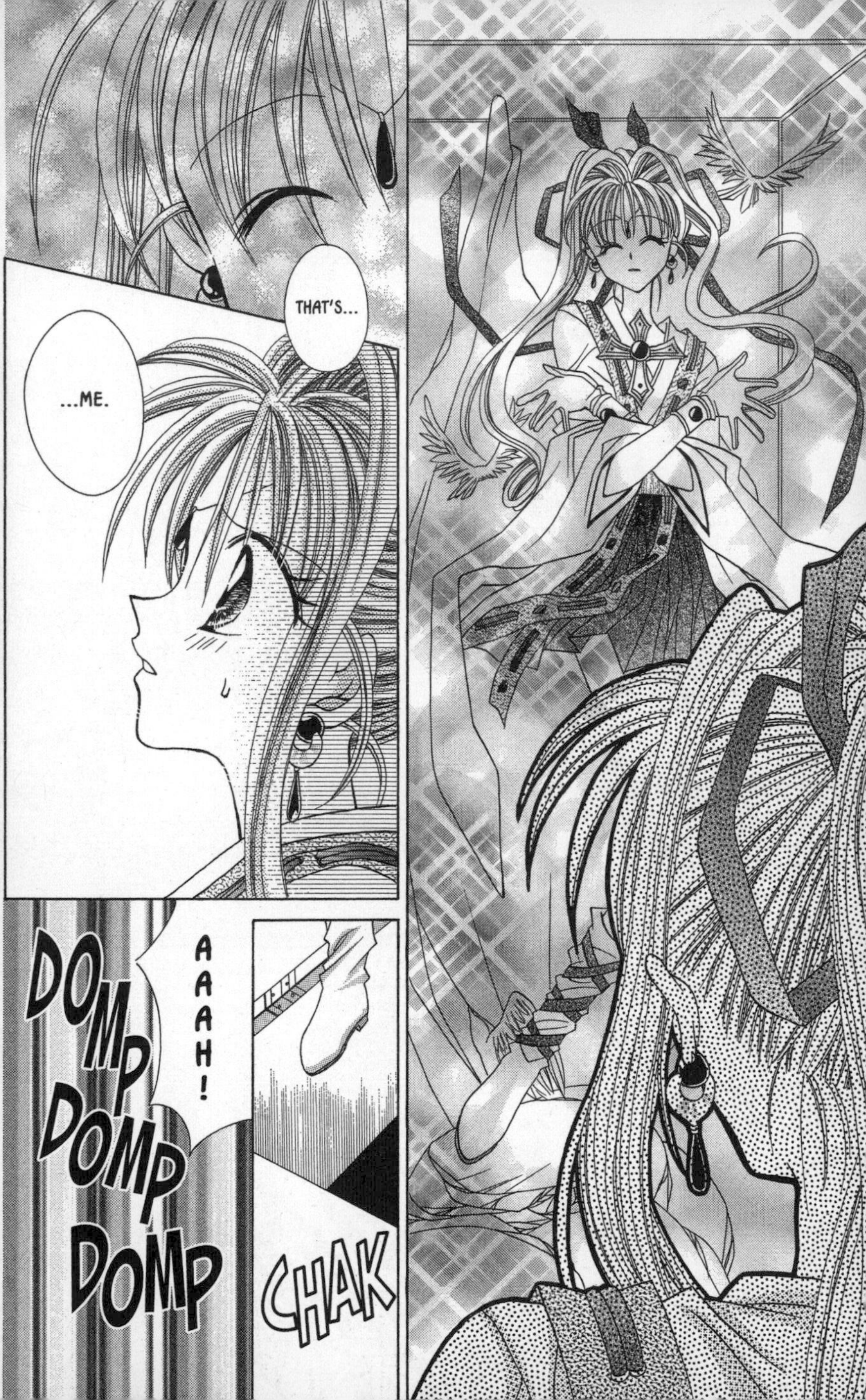
THAT'S...
...ME.
CHAK
AAAAH!
DOMP DOMP DOMP

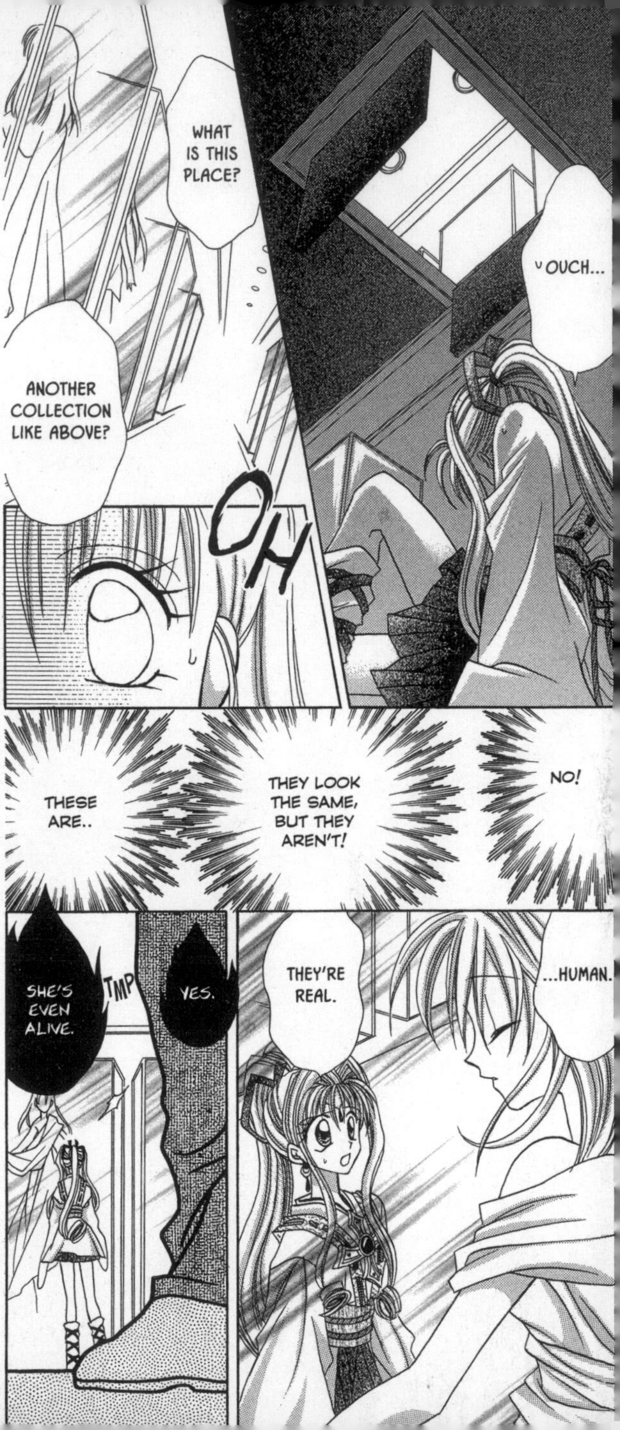
OUCH...
WHAT IS THIS PLACE?
ANOTHER COLLECTION LIKE ABOVE?
OH
NO!
THEY LOOK THE SAME, BUT THEY AREN'T!
THESE ARE..
...HUMAN.
THEY'RE REAL.
YES.
TMP
SHE'S EVEN ALIVE.

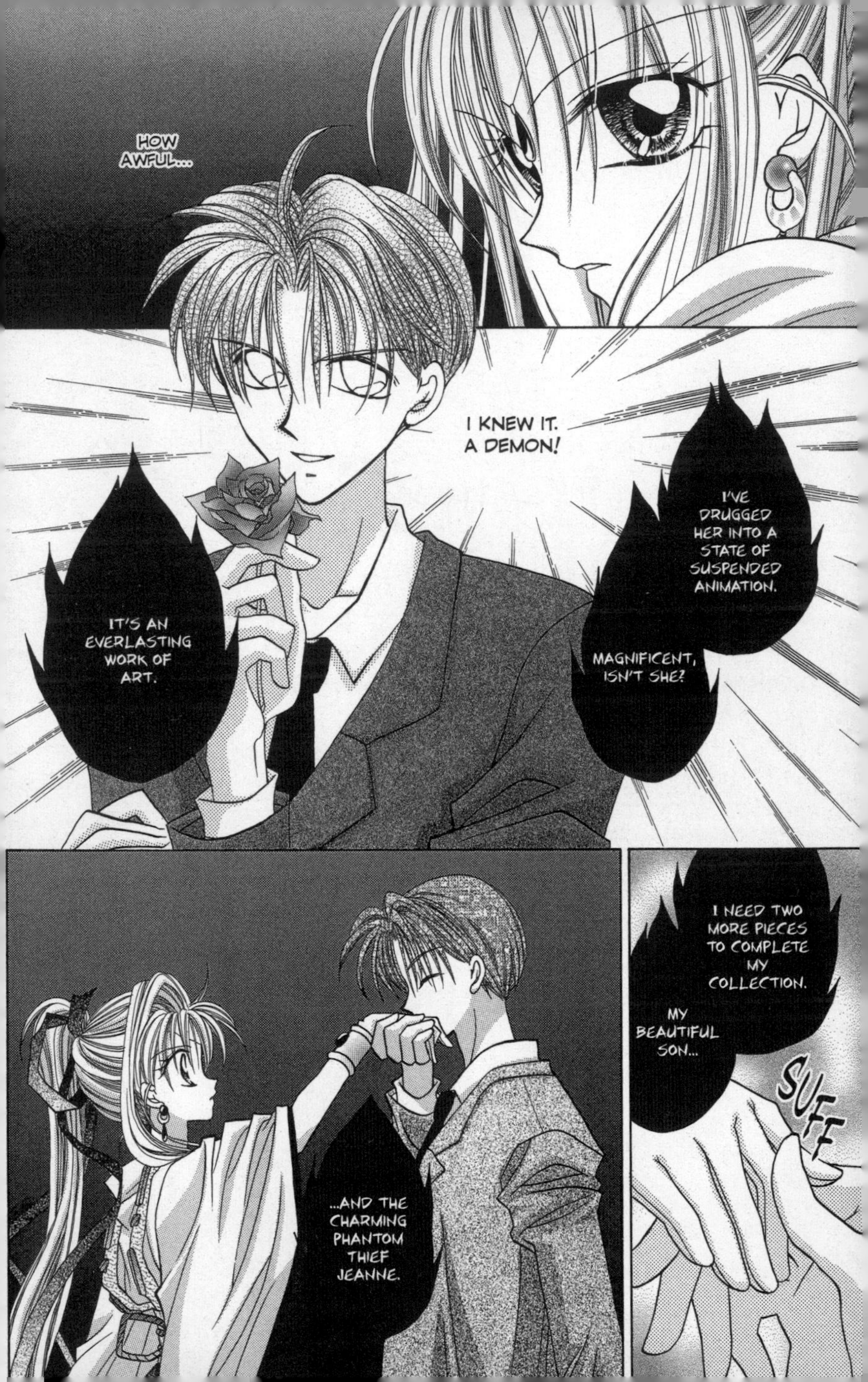
HOW AWFUL...
I KNEW IT. A DEMON!
I'VE DRUGGED HER INTO A STATE OF SUSPENDED ANIMATION.
MAGNIFICENT, ISN'T SHE?
IT'S AN EVERLASTING WORK OF ART.
I NEED TWO MORE PIECES TO COMPLETE MY COLLECTION.
MY BEAUTIFUL SON...
SUFF
...AND THE CHARMING PHANTOM THIEF JEANNE.

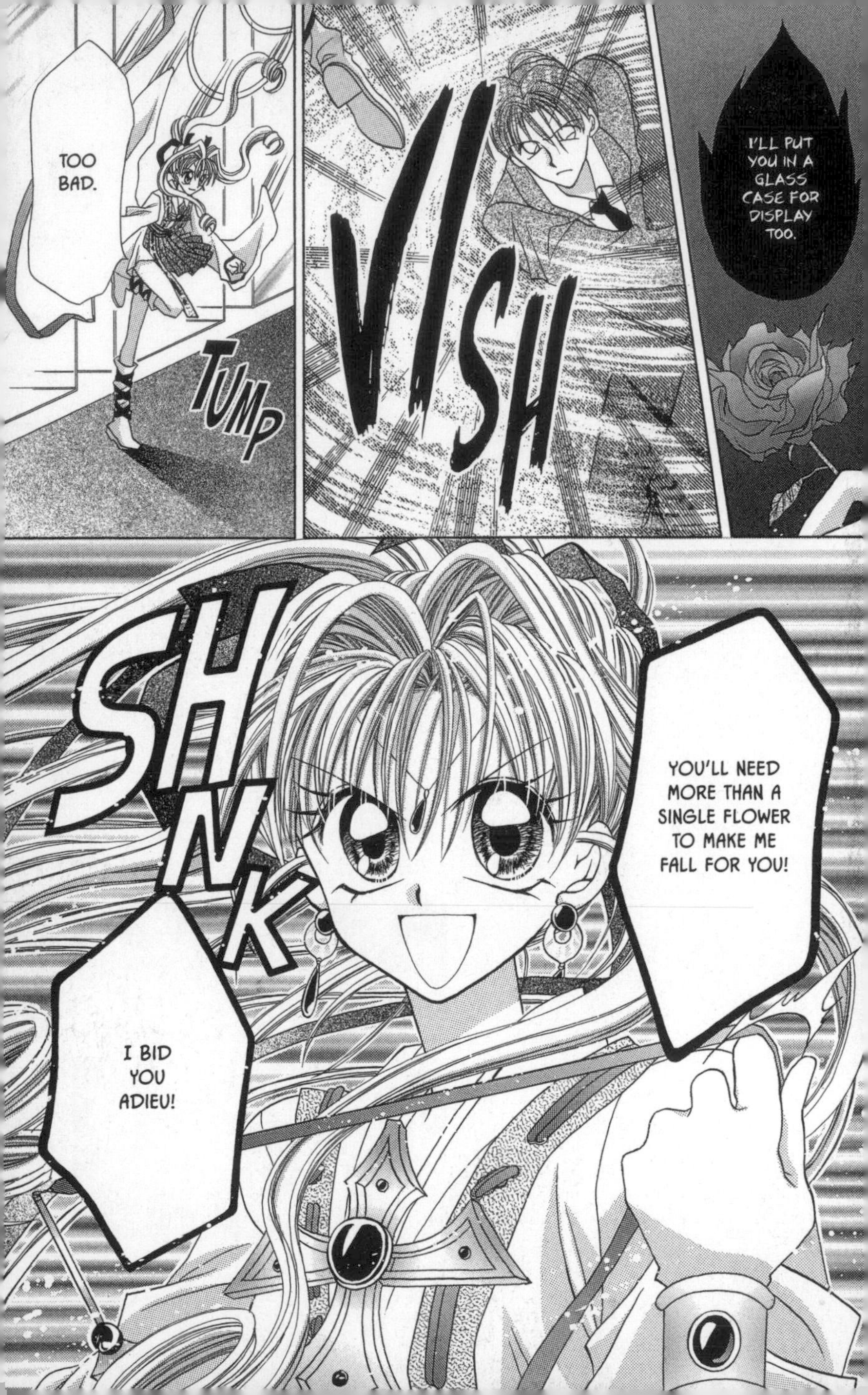
I'LL PUT YOU IN A GLASS CASE FOR DISPLAY TOO.
VISH
TOO BAD.
TUMP
YOU'LL NEED MORE THAN A SINGLE FLOWER TO MAKE ME FALL FOR YOU!
SHNK
I BID YOU ADIEU!

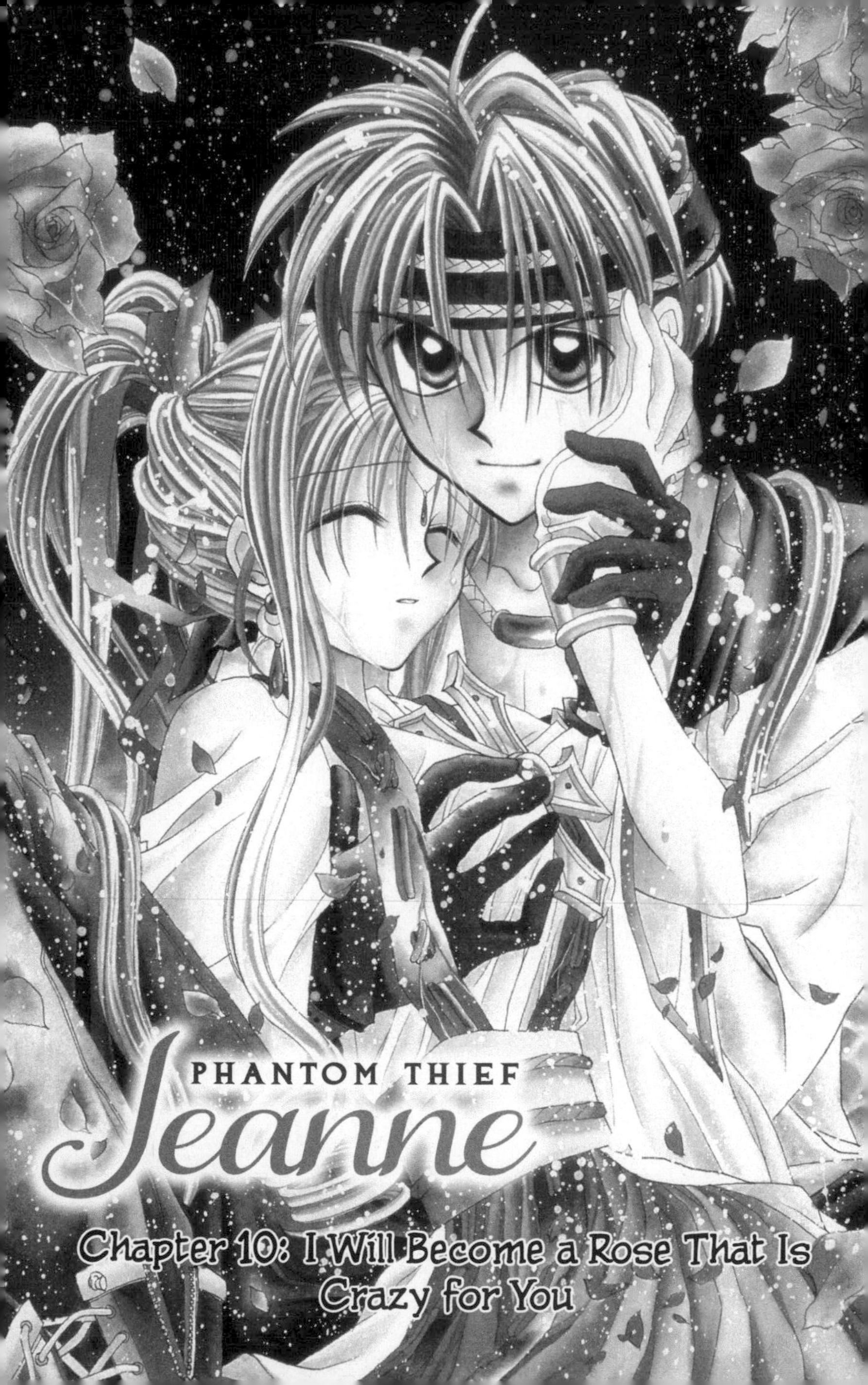
PHANTOM THIEF
Jeanne
Chapter 10: I Will Become a Rose That Is Crazy for You

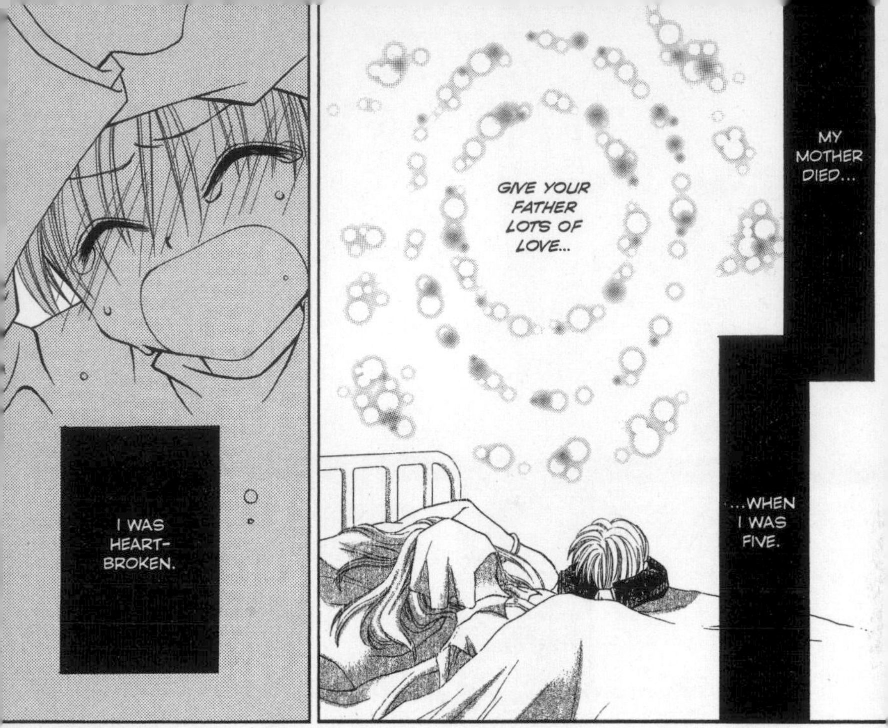
MY MOTHER DIED...
GIVE YOUR FATHER LOTS OF LOVE...
...WHEN I WAS FIVE.
I WAS HEART-BROKEN.

PHANTOM THIEF JEANNE

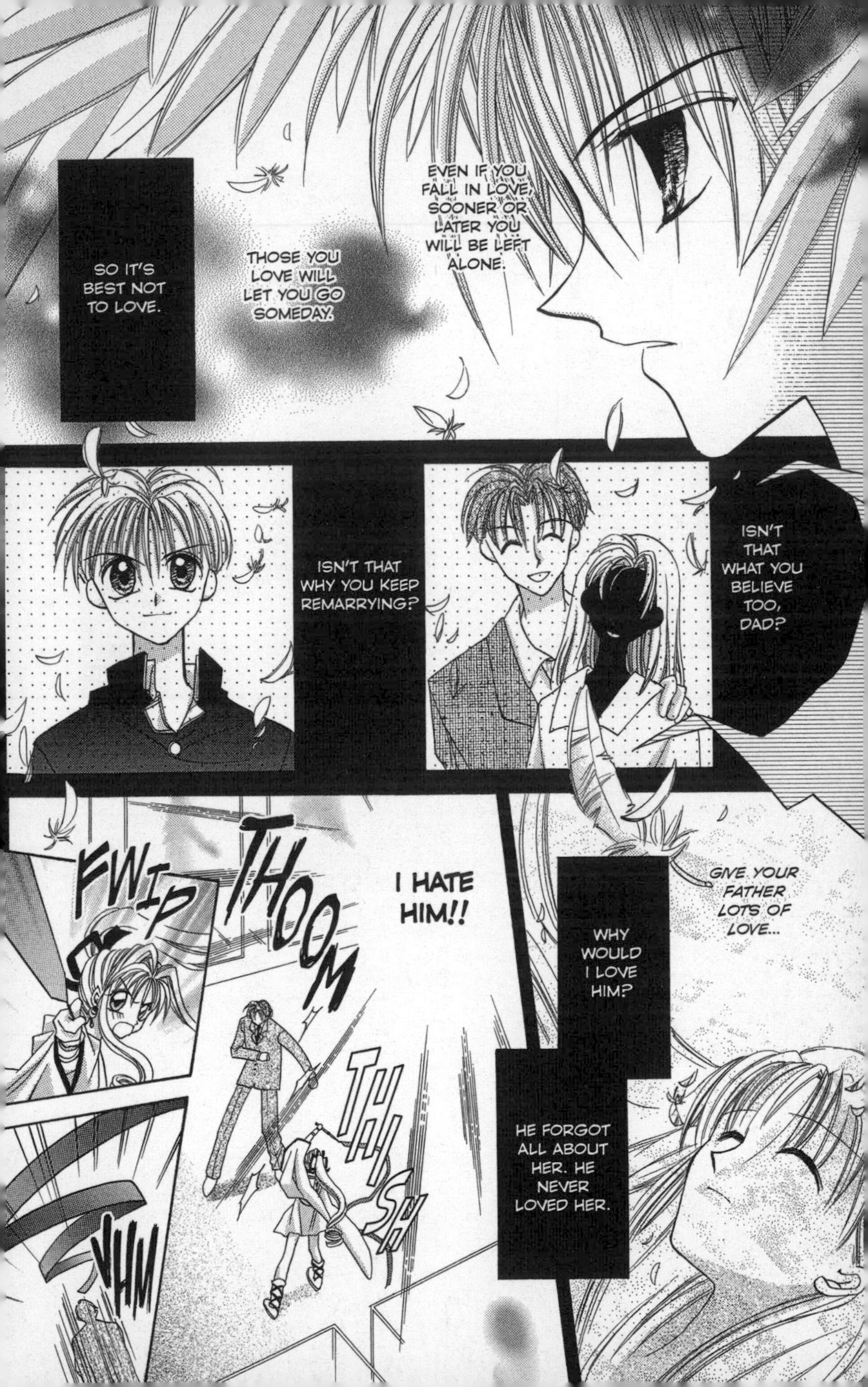
EVEN IF YOU FALL IN LOVE, SOONER OR LATER YOU WILL BE LEFT ALONE.
THOSE YOU LOVE WILL LET YOU GO SOMEDAY.
SO IT'S BEST NOT TO LOVE.
ISN'T THAT WHAT YOU BELIEVE TOO, DAD?
ISN'T THAT WHY YOU KEEP REMARRYING?
GIVE YOUR FATHER LOTS OF LOVE...
WHY WOULD I LOVE HIM?
HE FORGOT ALL ABOUT HER. HE NEVER LOVED HER.
I HATE HIM!!
THOOM
FWIP
THHSH
VHM

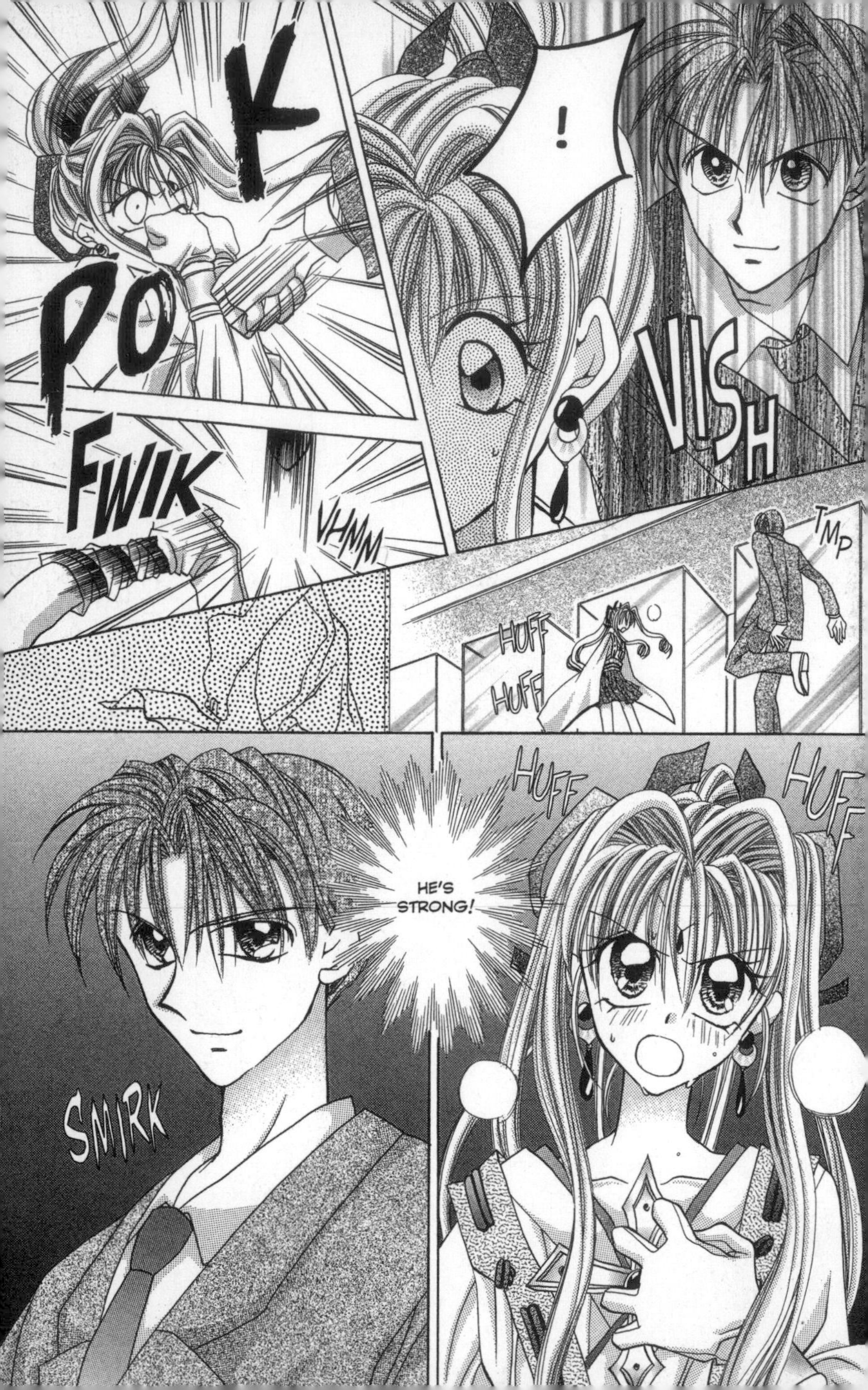
!
VISH
POK
FWIK
VHNN
TMP
HUFF
HUFF
HUFF
HUFF
HE'S STRONG!
SMIRK

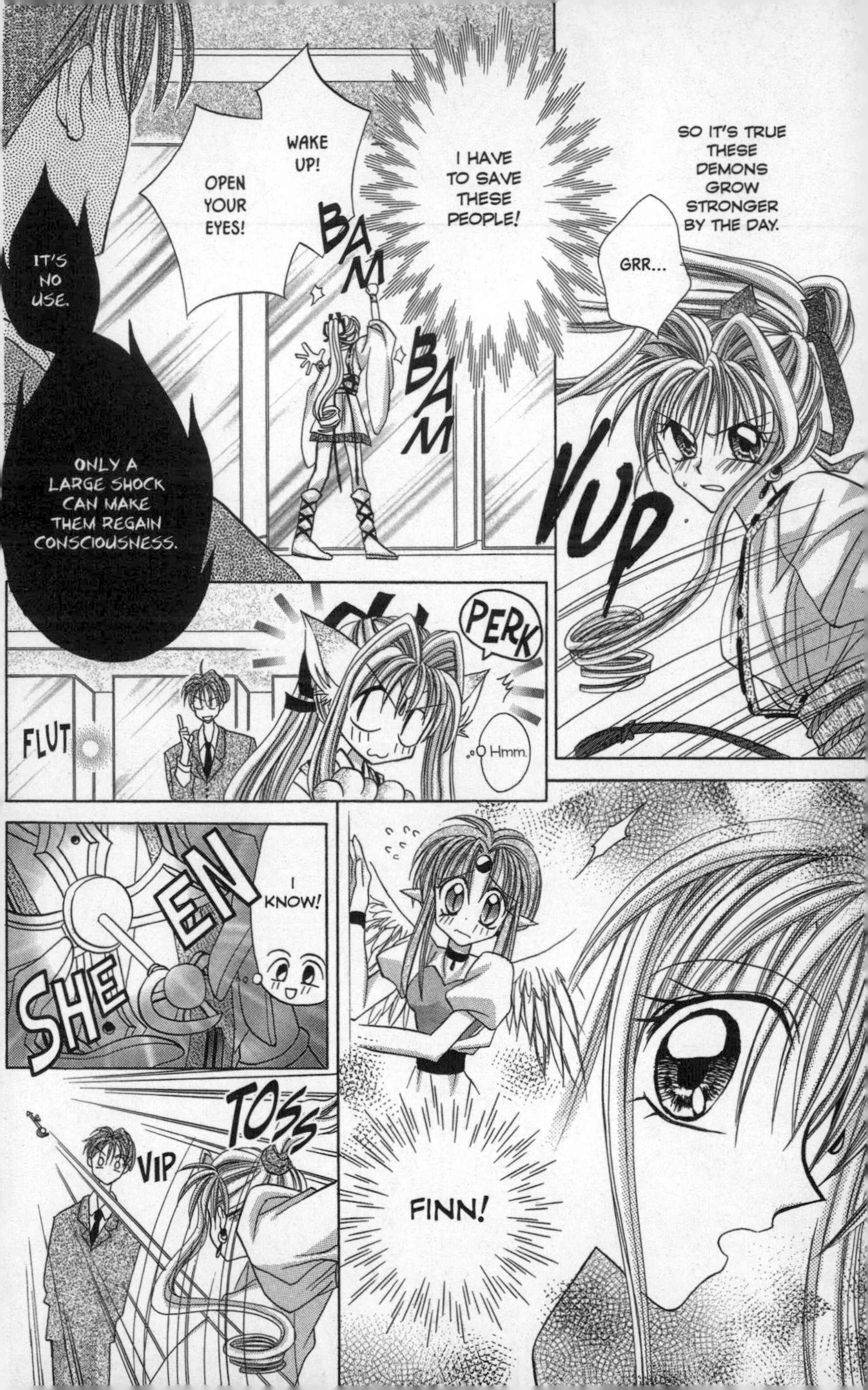
SO IT'S TRUE THESE DEMONS GROW STRONGER BY THE DAY.
GRR...
VUP
I HAVE TO SAVE THESE PEOPLE!
WAKE UP!
OPEN YOUR EYES!
BAM
BAM
BAM
IT'S NO USE.
ONLY A LARGE SHOCK CAN MAKE THEM REGAIN CONSCIOUSNESS.
PERK
Hmm.
FLUT
FINN!
I KNOW!
SHEEN
TOSS
VIP

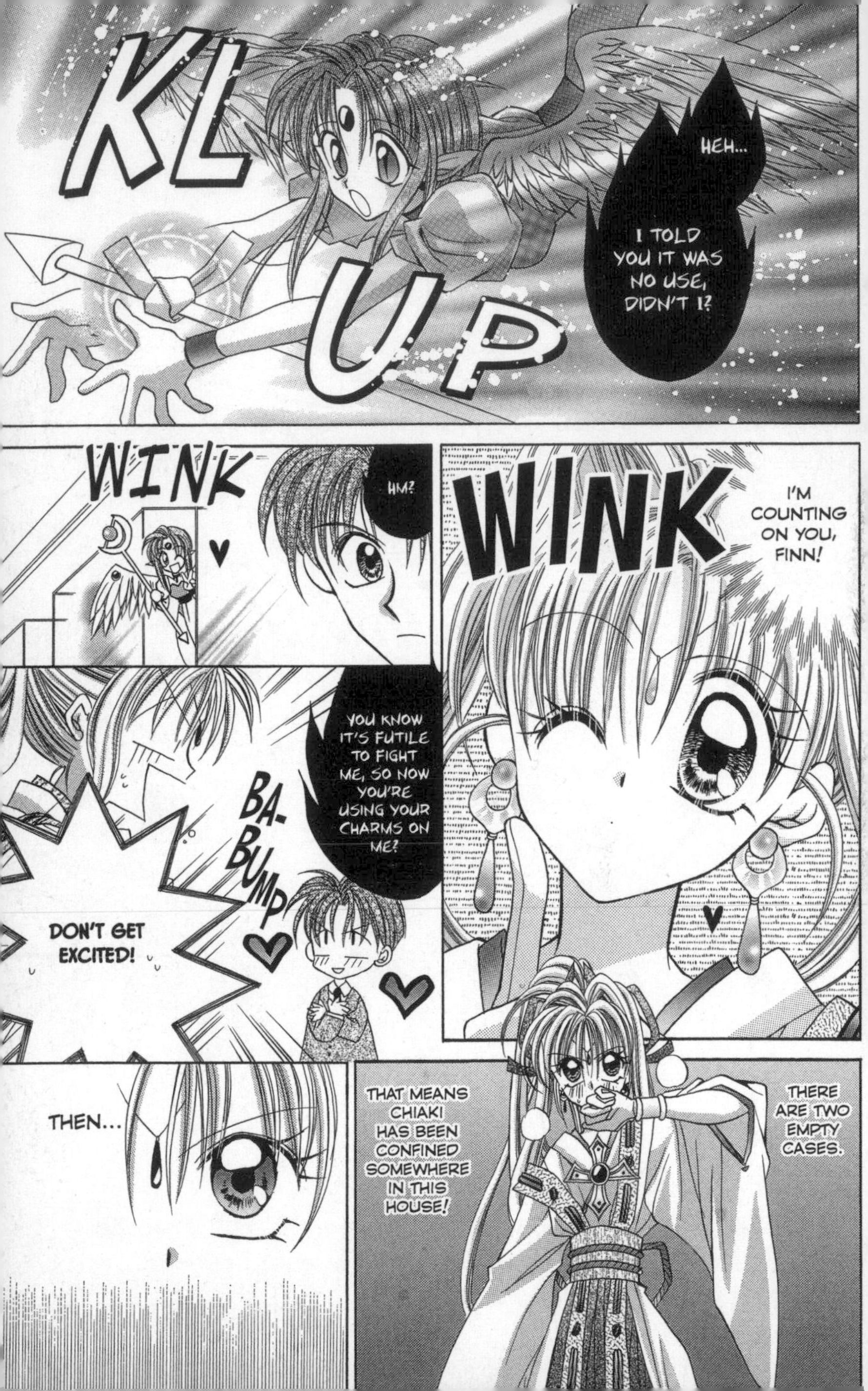
HEH...
I TOLD YOU IT WAS NO USE, DIDN'T I?
KL
UP
I'M COUNTING ON YOU, FINN!
WINK
HM?
WINK
YOU KNOW IT'S FUTILE TO FIGHT ME, SO NOW YOU'RE USING YOUR CHARMS ON ME?
BA-BUMP
DON'T GET EXCITED!
THERE ARE TWO EMPTY CASES.
THAT MEANS CHIAKI HAS BEEN CONFINED SOMEWHERE IN THIS HOUSE!
THEN...

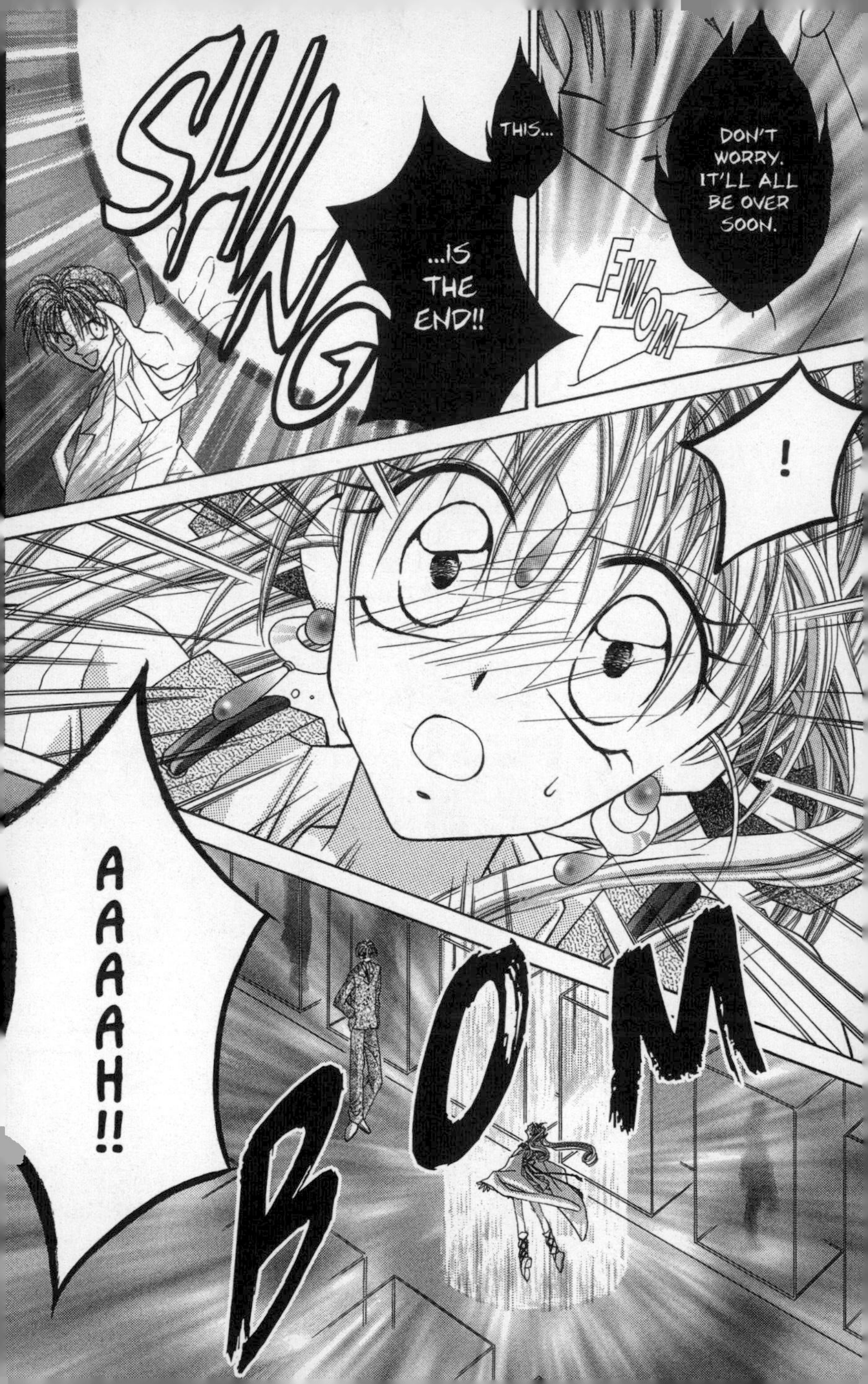
DON'T WORRY. IT'LL ALL BE OVER SOON.
FWOM
THIS...
SHING
...IS THE END!!
!
BOOM
AAAAAH!!

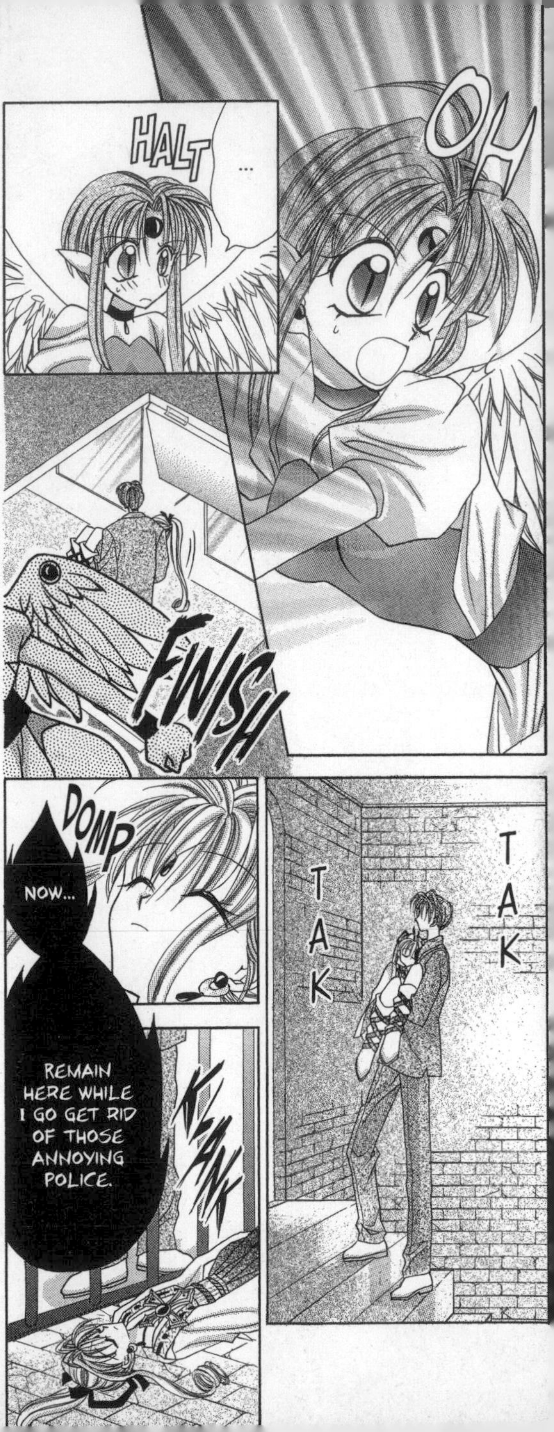
OH
HALT
...
FWISH
TAK
TAK
DOMP
NOW...
REMAIN HERE WHILE I GO GET RID OF THOSE ANNOYING POLICE.
KLANK

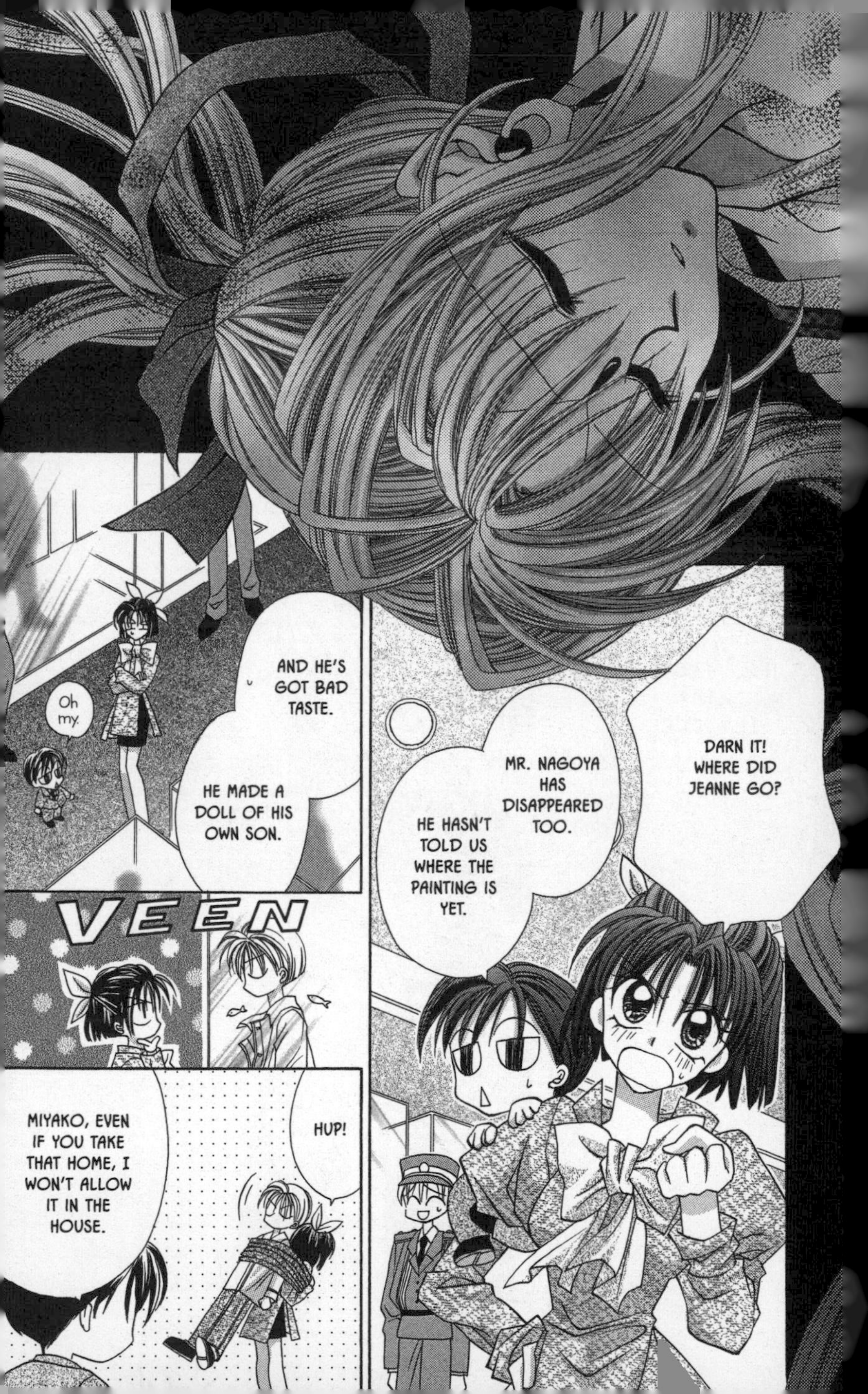

DARN IT! WHERE DID JEANNE GO?
MR. NAGOYA HAS DISAPPEARED TOO.
HE HASN'T TOLD US WHERE THE PAINTING IS YET.
AND HE'S GOT BAD TASTE.
HE MADE A DOLL OF HIS OWN SON.
Oh my.
VEEN
HUP!
MIYAKO, EVEN IF YOU TAKE THAT HOME, I WON'T ALLOW IT IN THE HOUSE.

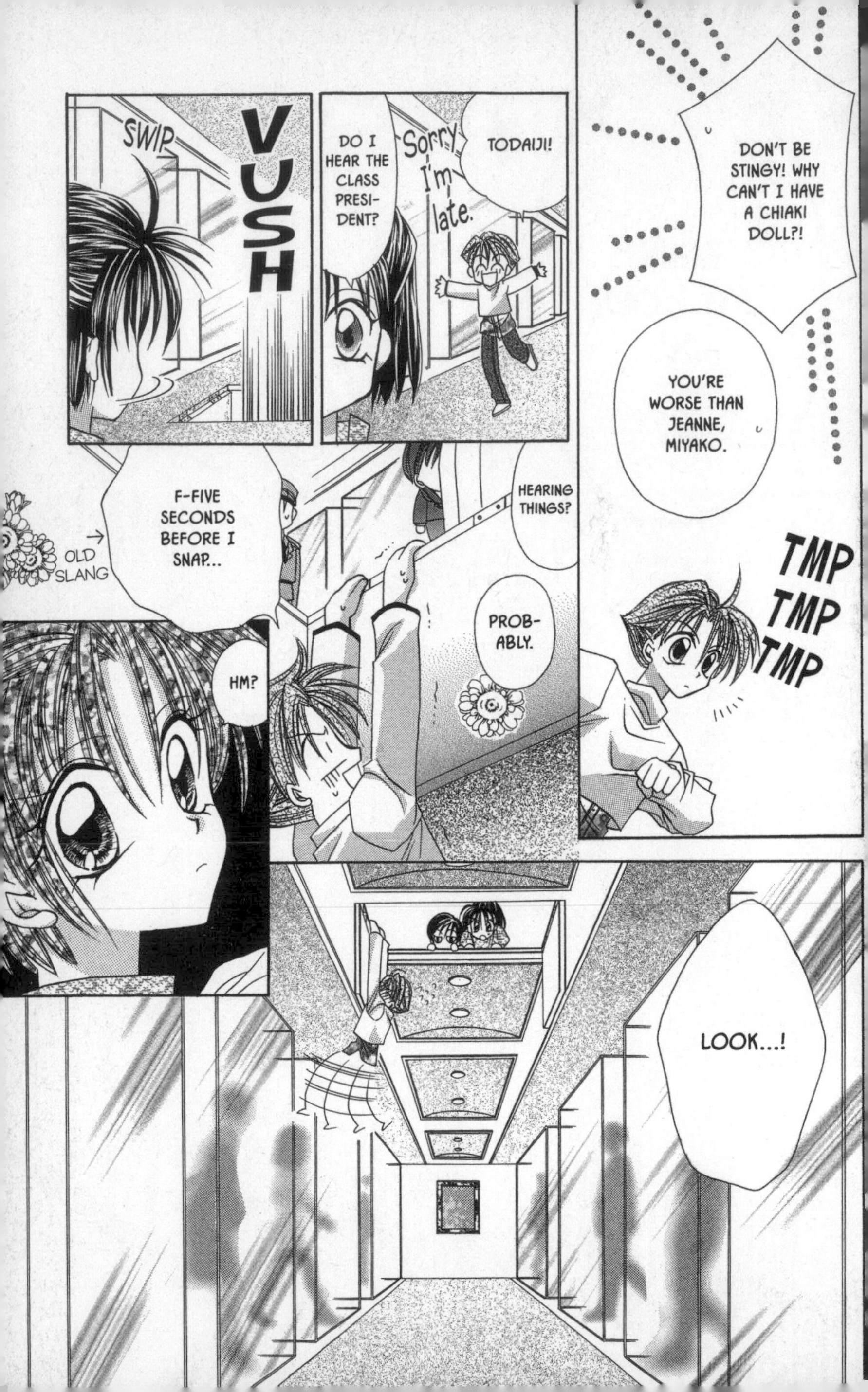
DON'T BE STINGY! WHY CAN'T I HAVE A CHIAKI DOLL?!
YOU'RE WORSE THAN JEANNE, MIYAKO.
TMP TMP TMP
TODAIJI!
Sorry, I'm late.
DO I HEAR THE CLASS PRESIDENT?
SWIP
VUSH
HEARING THINGS?
PROBABLY.
F-FIVE SECONDS BEFORE I SNAP...
OLD SLANG
HM?
LOOK...!

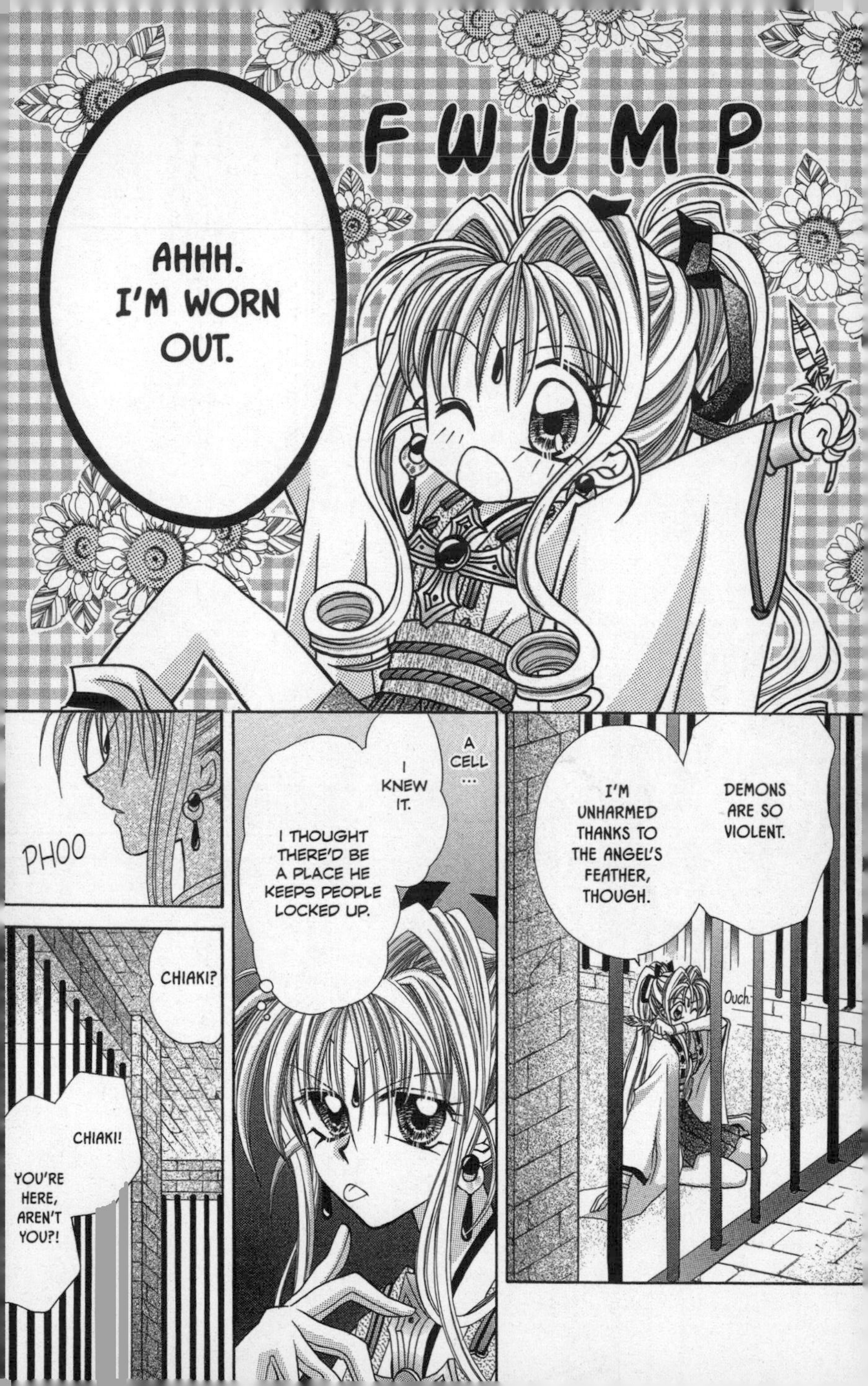
FWUMP
AHHH. I'M WORN OUT.
DEMONS ARE SO VIOLENT.
I'M UNHARMED THANKS TO THE ANGEL'S FEATHER, THOUGH.
Ouch.
A CELL...
I KNEW IT.
I THOUGHT THERE'D BE A PLACE HE KEEPS PEOPLE LOCKED UP.
PHOO
CHIAKI?
CHIAKI!
YOU'RE HERE, AREN'T YOU?!

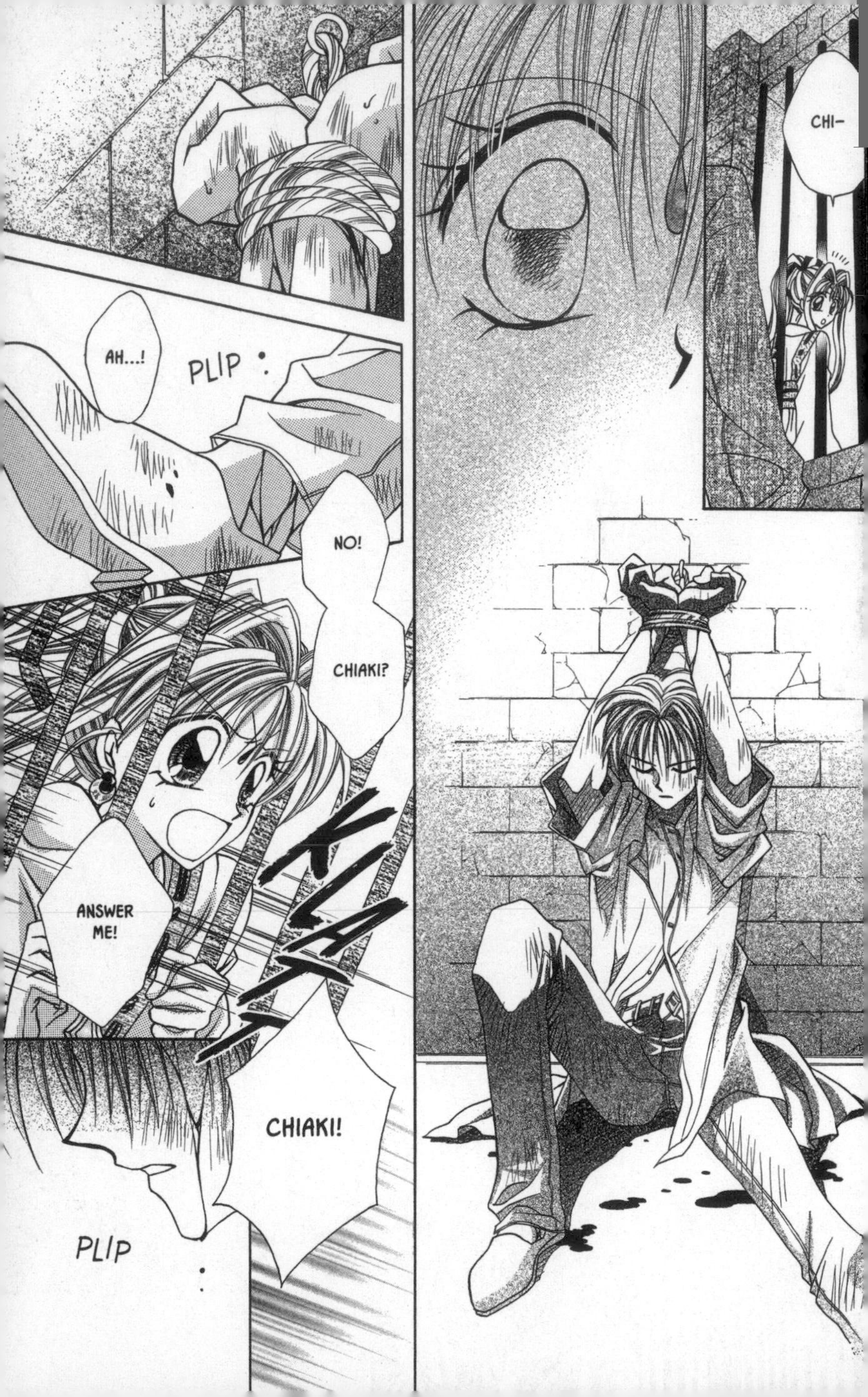
CHI–
AH...!
PLIP
NO!
CHIAKI?
ANSWER ME!
KLATT
CHIAKI!
PLIP

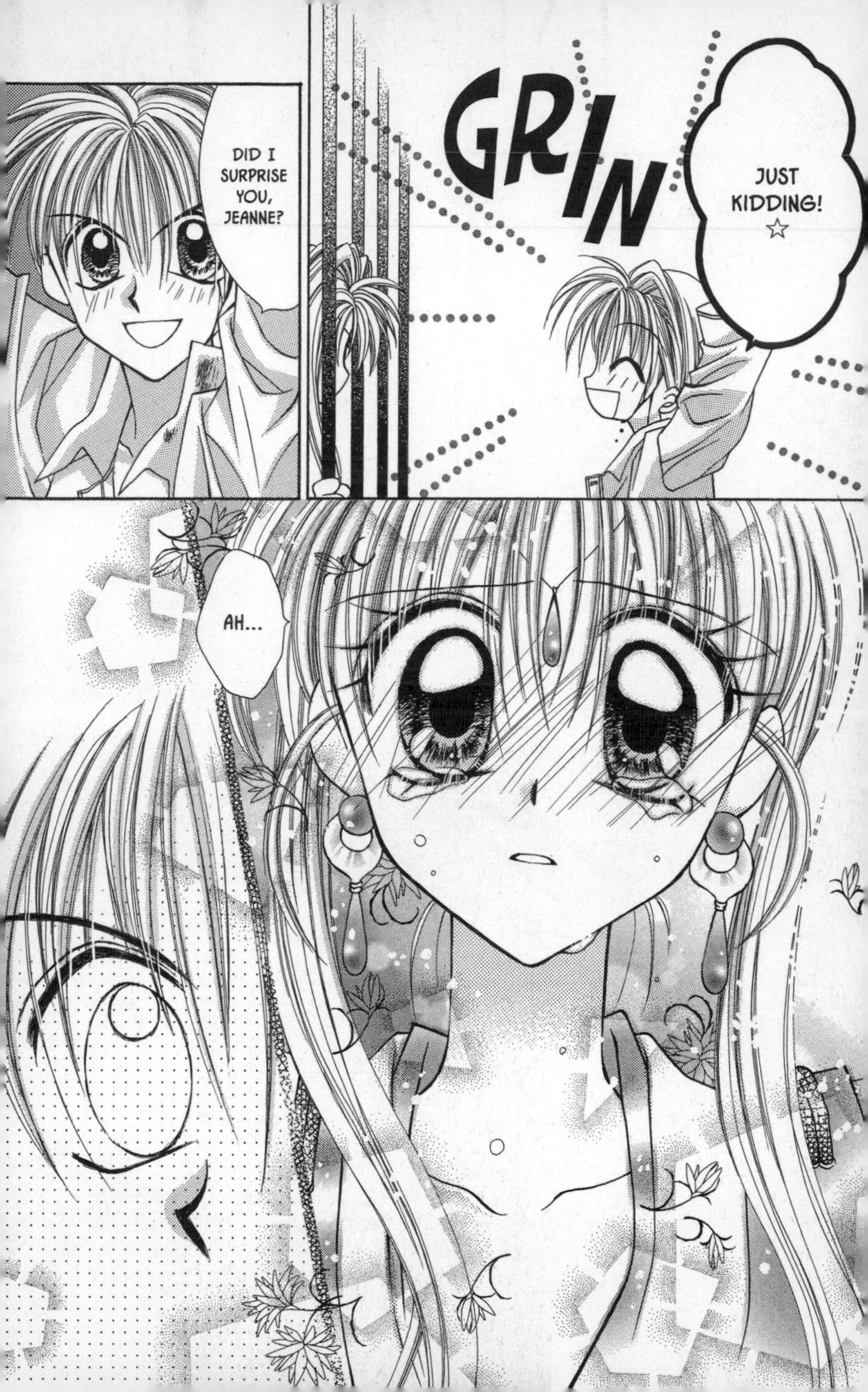
GRIN
JUST KIDDING! ☆
DID I SURPRISE YOU, JEANNE?
AH...

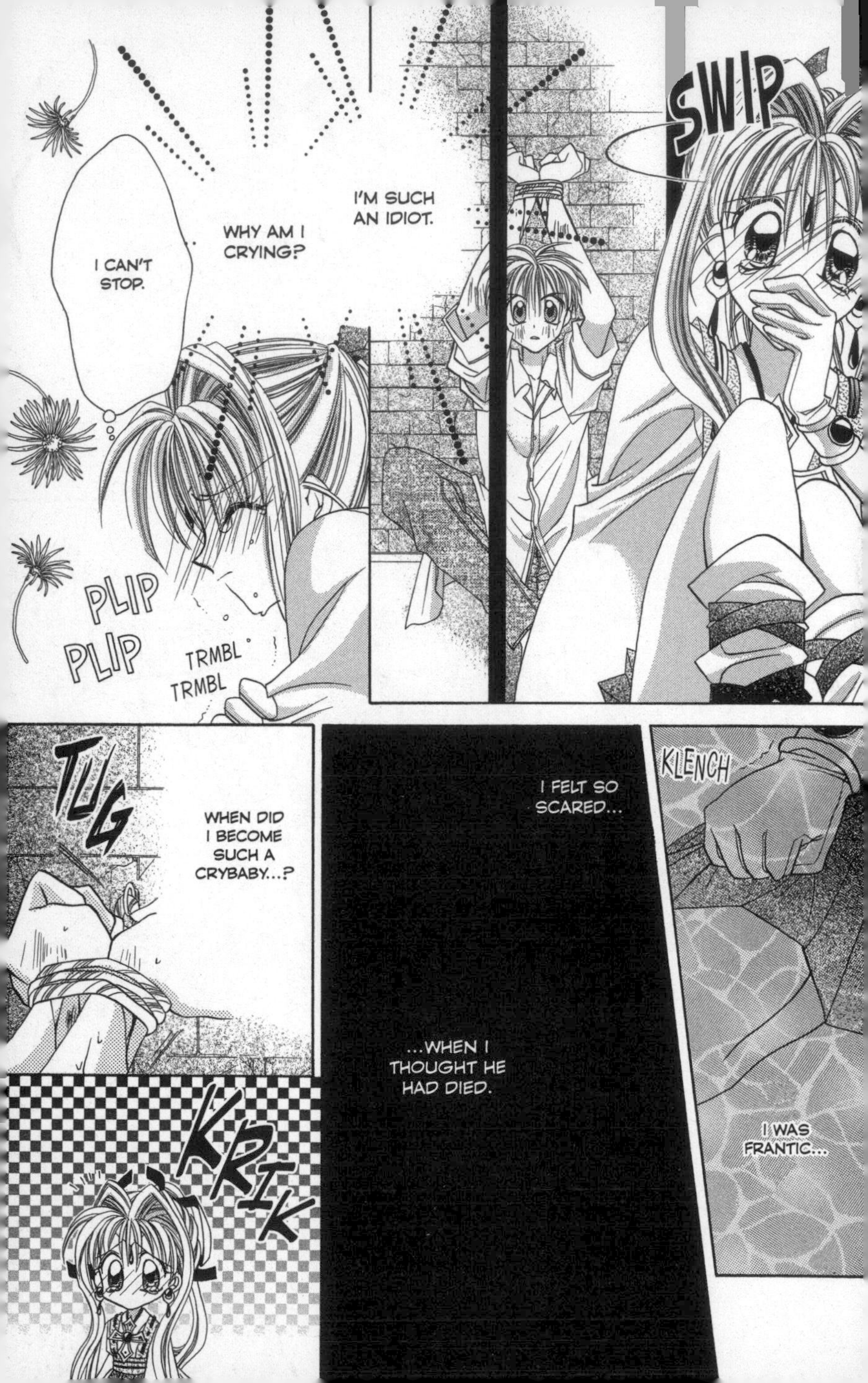
SWIP
I'M SUCH AN IDIOT.
WHY AM I CRYING?
I CAN'T STOP.
PLIP PLIP
TRMBL TRMBL
KLENCH
I WAS FRANTIC...
I FELT SO SCARED...
...WHEN I THOUGHT HE HAD DIED.
TUG
WHEN DID I BECOME SUCH A CRYBABY...?
KRIK

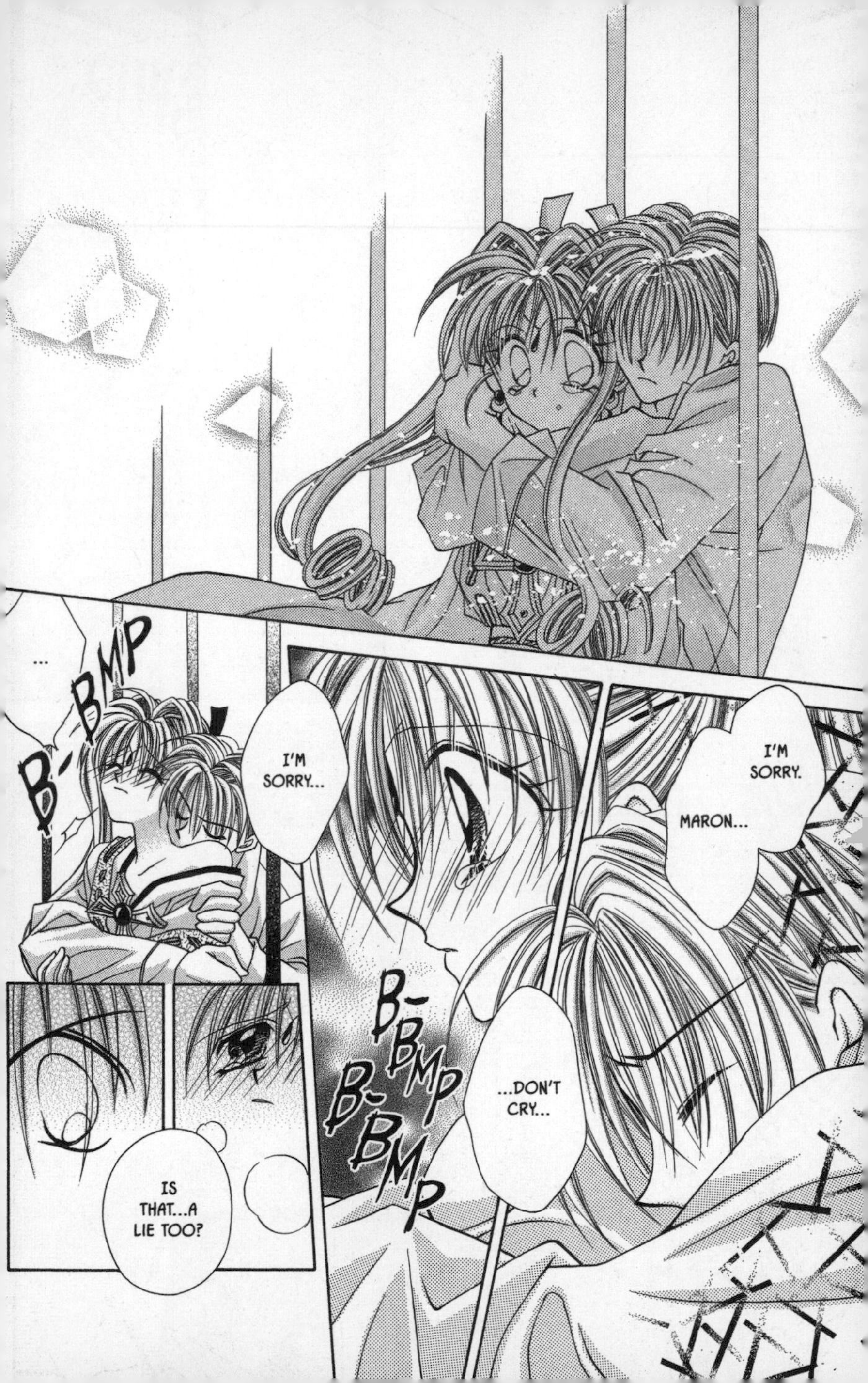
I'M SORRY.
MARON...
I'M SORRY...
...DON'T CRY...
B-BMP B-BMP
...
B-BMP
IS THAT...A LIE TOO?

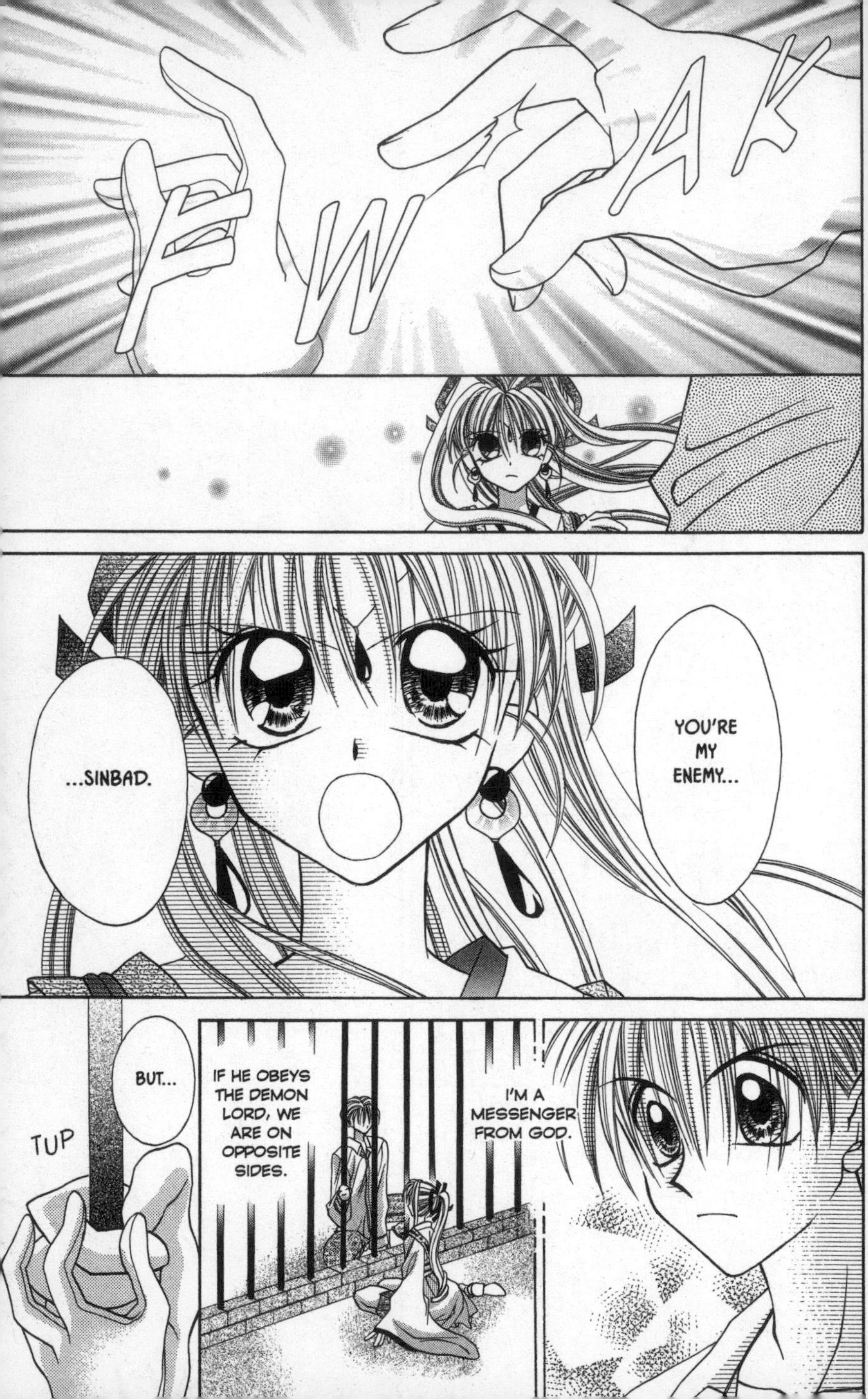
FWAK
YOU'RE MY ENEMY...
...SINBAD.
I'M A MESSENGER FROM GOD.
IF HE OBEYS THE DEMON LORD, WE ARE ON OPPOSITE SIDES.
BUT...
TUP

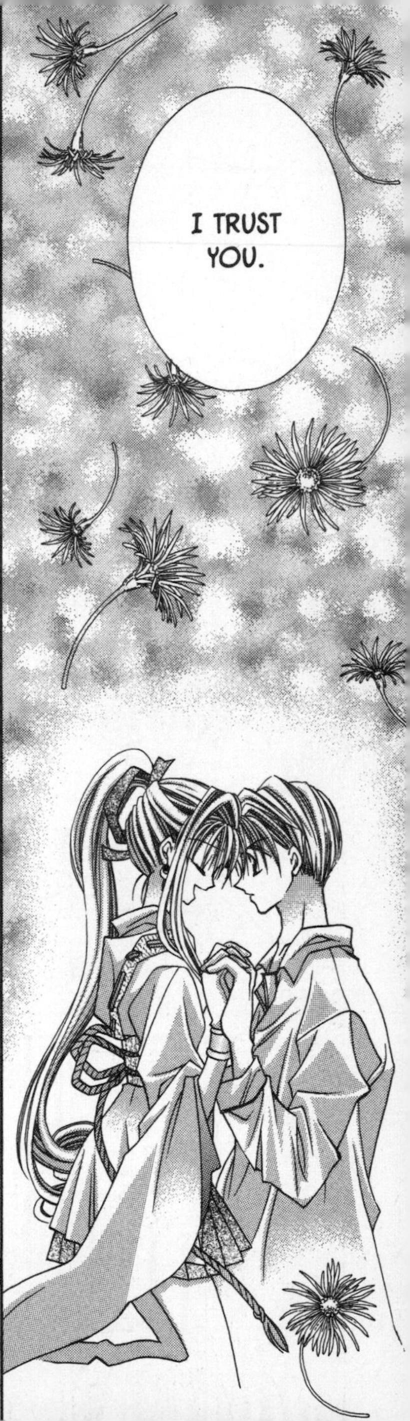
I TRUST YOU.

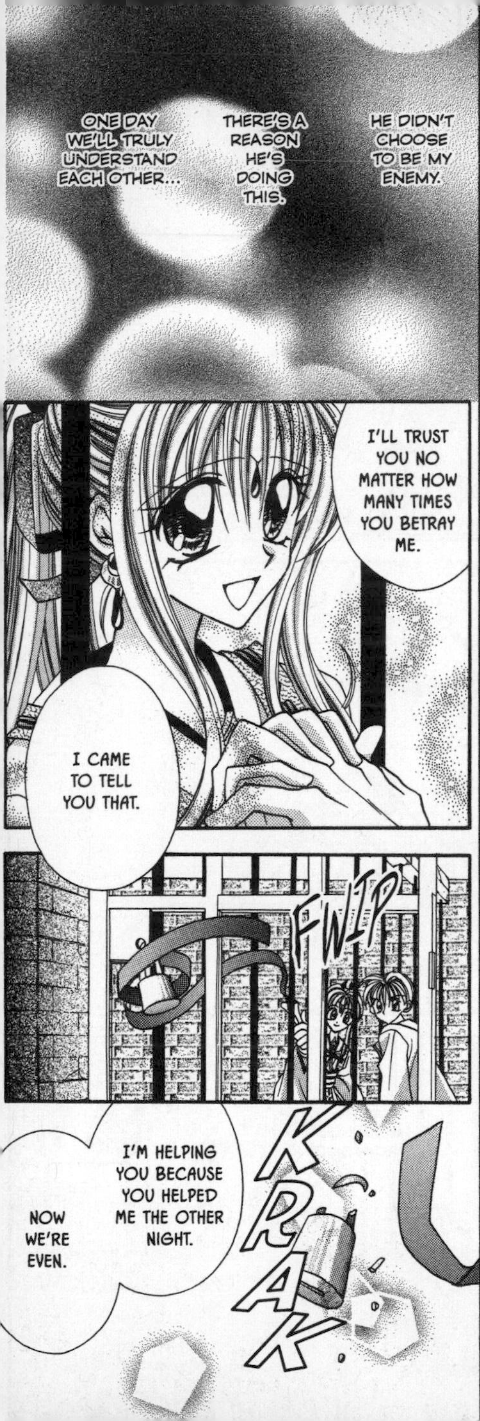
HE DIDN'T CHOOSE TO BE MY ENEMY.
THERE'S A REASON HE'S DOING THIS.
ONE DAY WE'LL TRULY UNDERSTAND EACH OTHER...
I'LL TRUST YOU NO MATTER HOW MANY TIMES YOU BETRAY ME.
I CAME TO TELL YOU THAT.
FWIP
KRAK
I'M HELPING YOU BECAUSE YOU HELPED ME THE OTHER NIGHT.
NOW WE'RE EVEN.

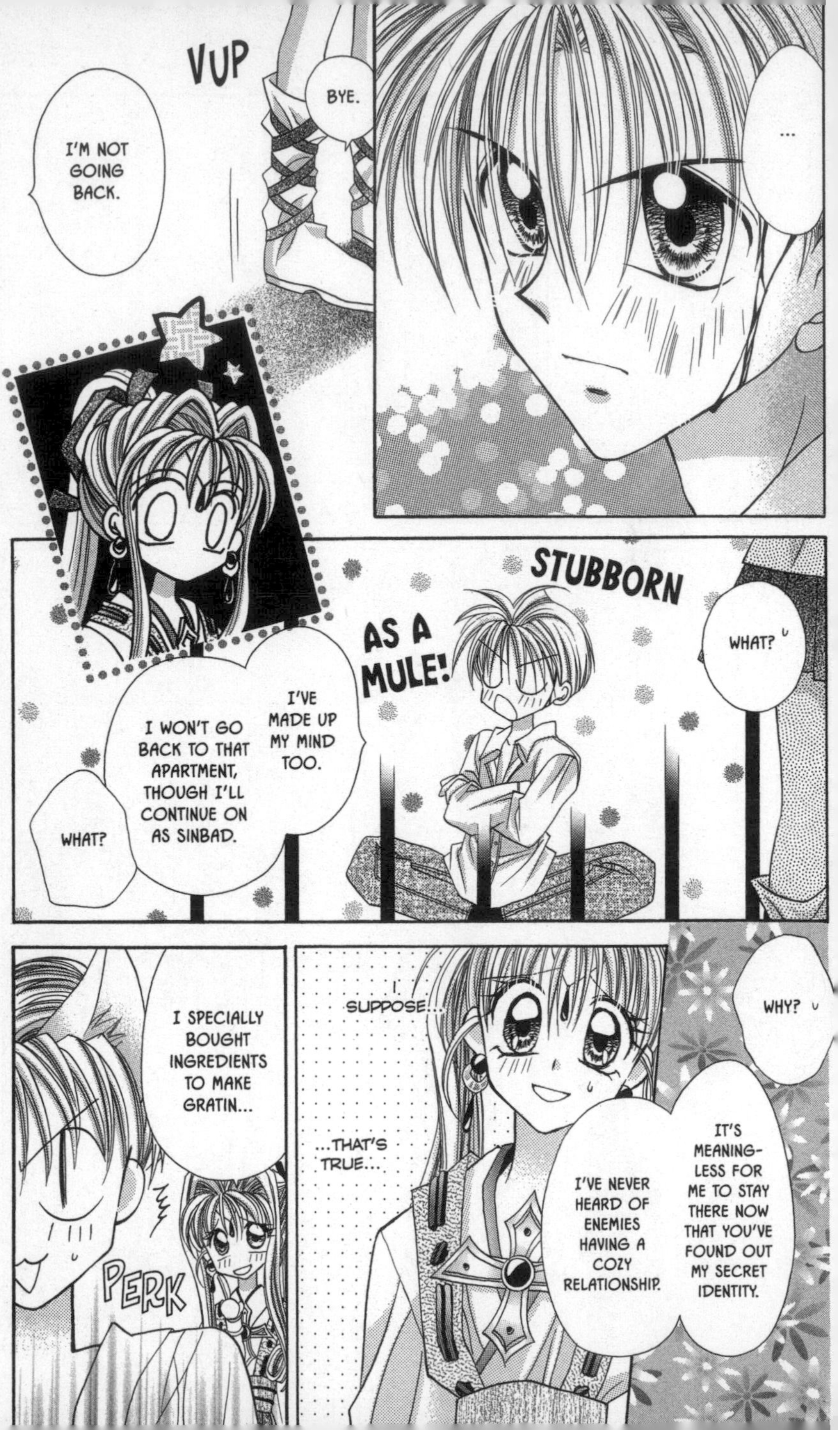
...
BYE.
VUP
I'M NOT GOING BACK.
WHAT?
STUBBORN AS A MULE!
I'VE MADE UP MY MIND TOO.
I WON'T GO BACK TO THAT APARTMENT, THOUGH I'LL CONTINUE ON AS SINBAD.
WHAT?
WHY?
IT'S MEANING-LESS FOR ME TO STAY THERE NOW THAT YOU'VE FOUND OUT MY SECRET IDENTITY.
I'VE NEVER HEARD OF ENEMIES HAVING A COZY RELATIONSHIP.
I. SUPPOSE...
...THAT'S TRUE...
I SPECIALLY BOUGHT INGREDIENTS TO MAKE GRATIN...
PERK

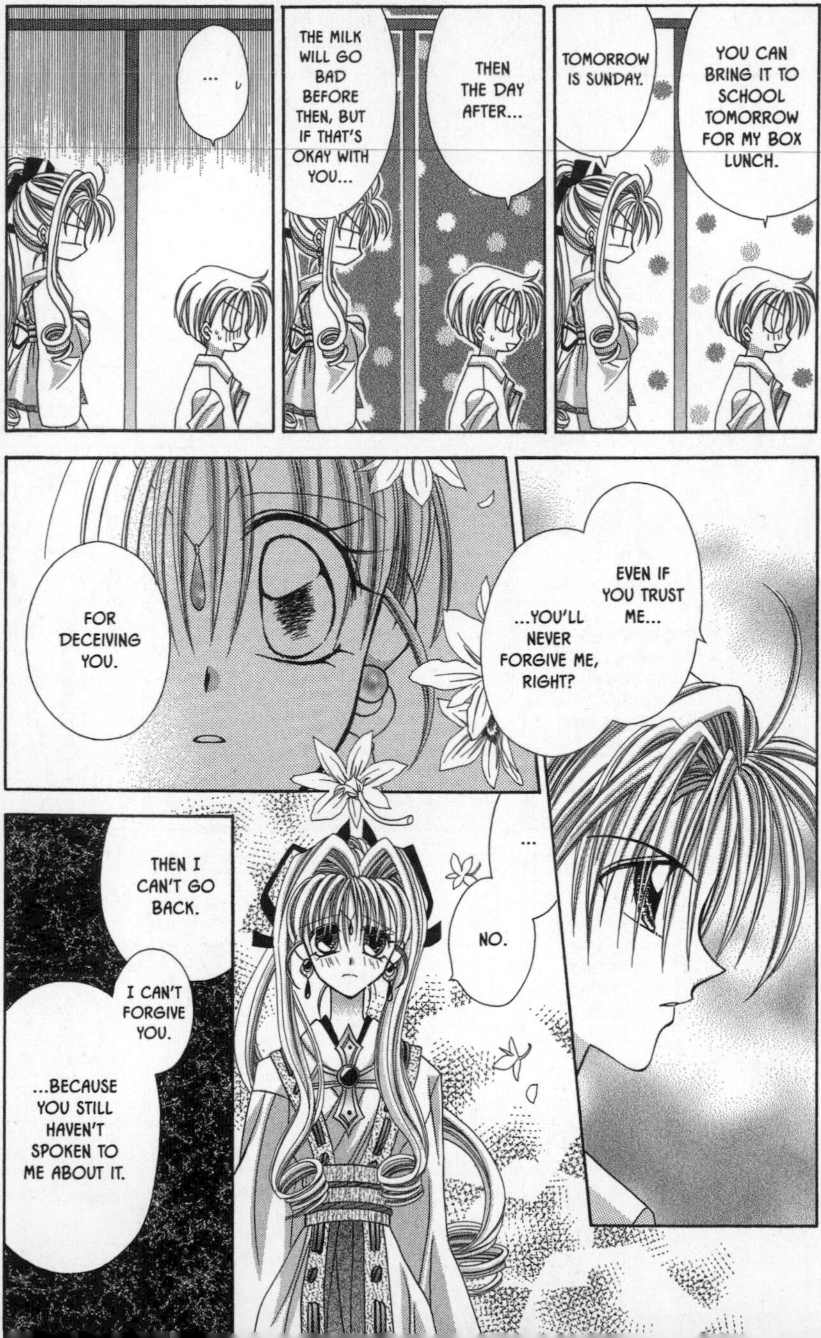
YOU CAN BRING IT TO SCHOOL TOMORROW FOR MY BOX LUNCH.
TOMORROW IS SUNDAY.
THEN THE DAY AFTER...
THE MILK WILL GO BAD BEFORE THEN, BUT IF THAT'S OKAY WITH YOU...
...
EVEN IF YOU TRUST ME...
...YOU'LL NEVER FORGIVE ME, RIGHT?
...
NO.
FOR DECEIVING YOU.
THEN I CAN'T GO BACK.
I CAN'T FORGIVE YOU.
...BECAUSE YOU STILL HAVEN'T SPOKEN TO ME ABOUT IT.

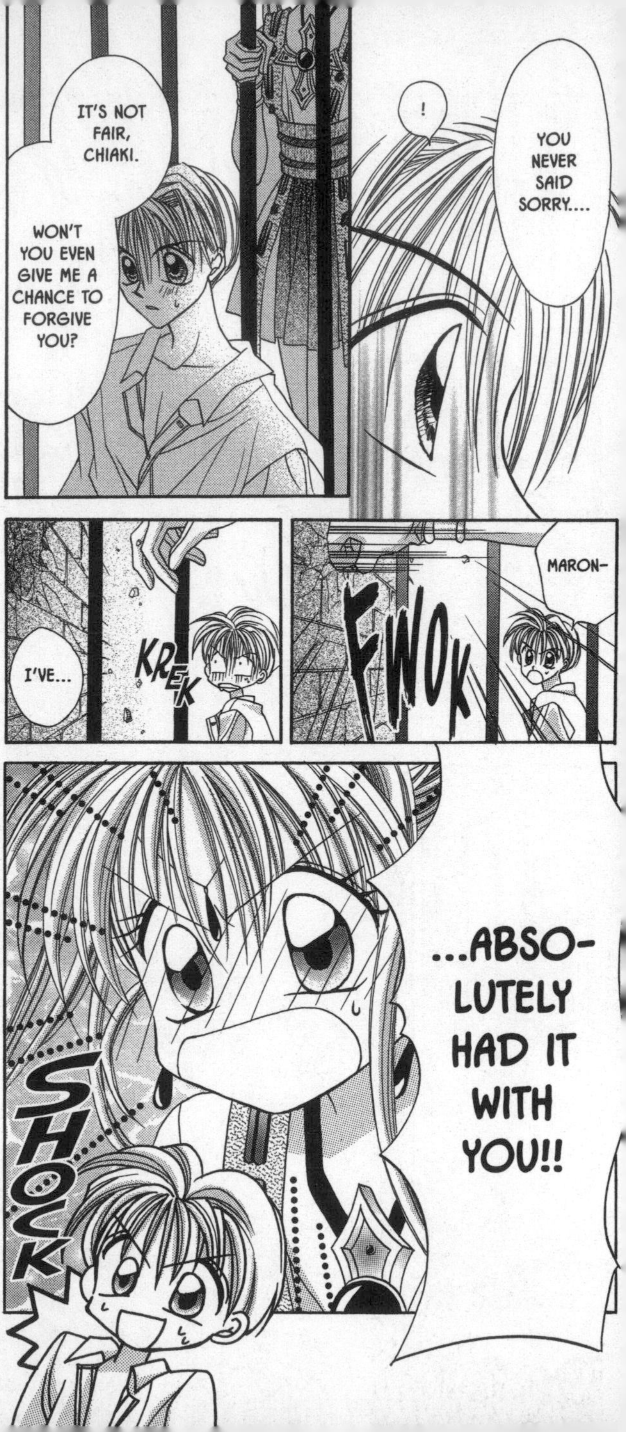
YOU NEVER SAID SORRY....
!
IT'S NOT FAIR, CHIAKI.
WON'T YOU EVEN GIVE ME A CHANCE TO FORGIVE YOU?
MARON-
FWOK
KREK
I'VE...
...ABSO-LUTELY HAD IT WITH YOU!!
SHOCK

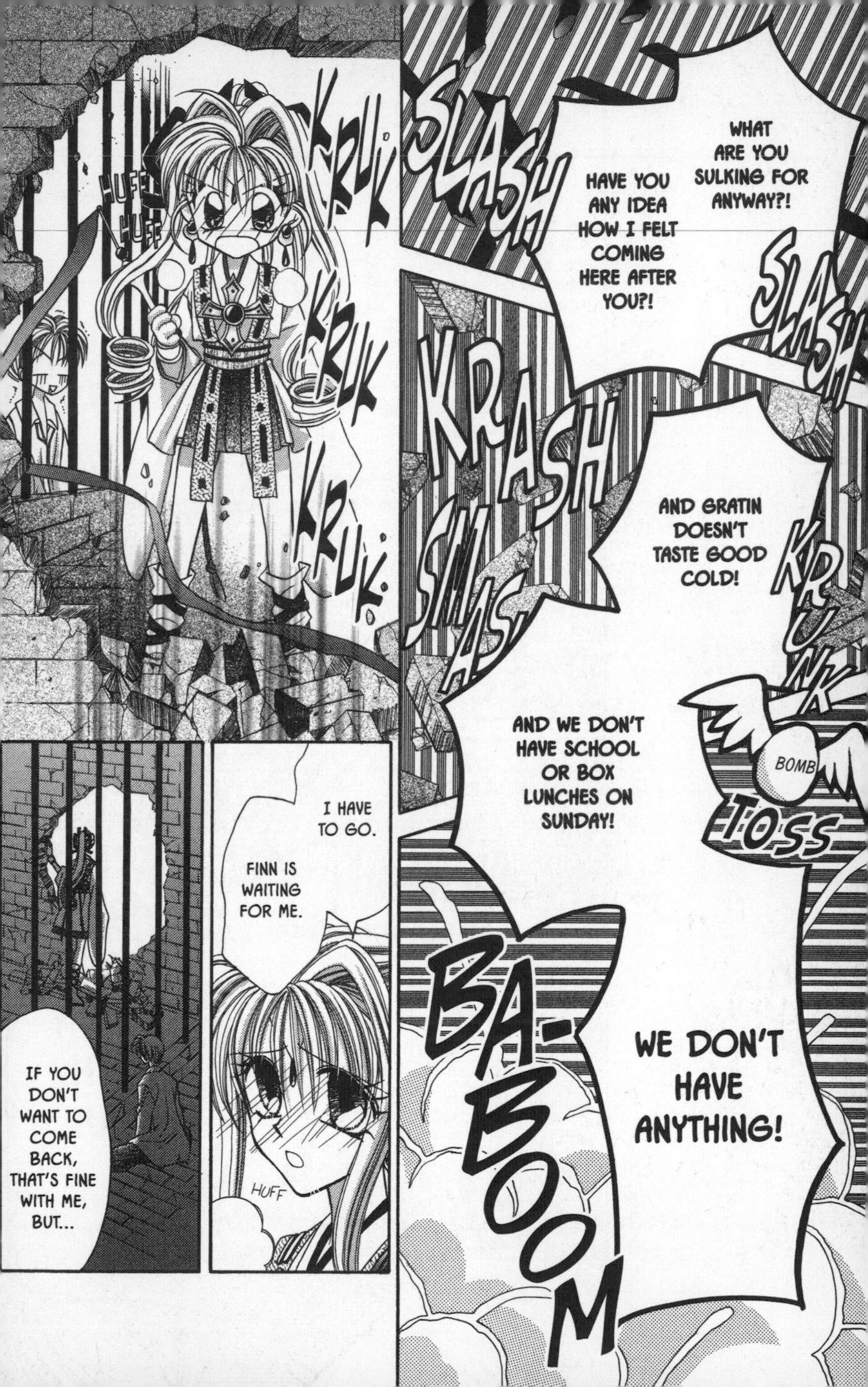
WHAT ARE YOU SULKING FOR ANYWAY?!
SLASH
HAVE YOU ANY IDEA HOW I FELT COMING HERE AFTER YOU?!
SLASH
KRASH
SMASH
AND GRATIN DOESN'T TASTE GOOD COLD!
KRUNK
AND WE DON'T HAVE SCHOOL OR BOX LUNCHES ON SUNDAY!
BOMB
TOSS
WE DON'T HAVE ANYTHING!
BA-BOOM
KRUK
KRUK
KRUK
HUFF HUFF
I HAVE TO GO.
FINN IS WAITING FOR ME.
HUFF
IF YOU DON'T WANT TO COME BACK, THAT'S FINE WITH ME, BUT...

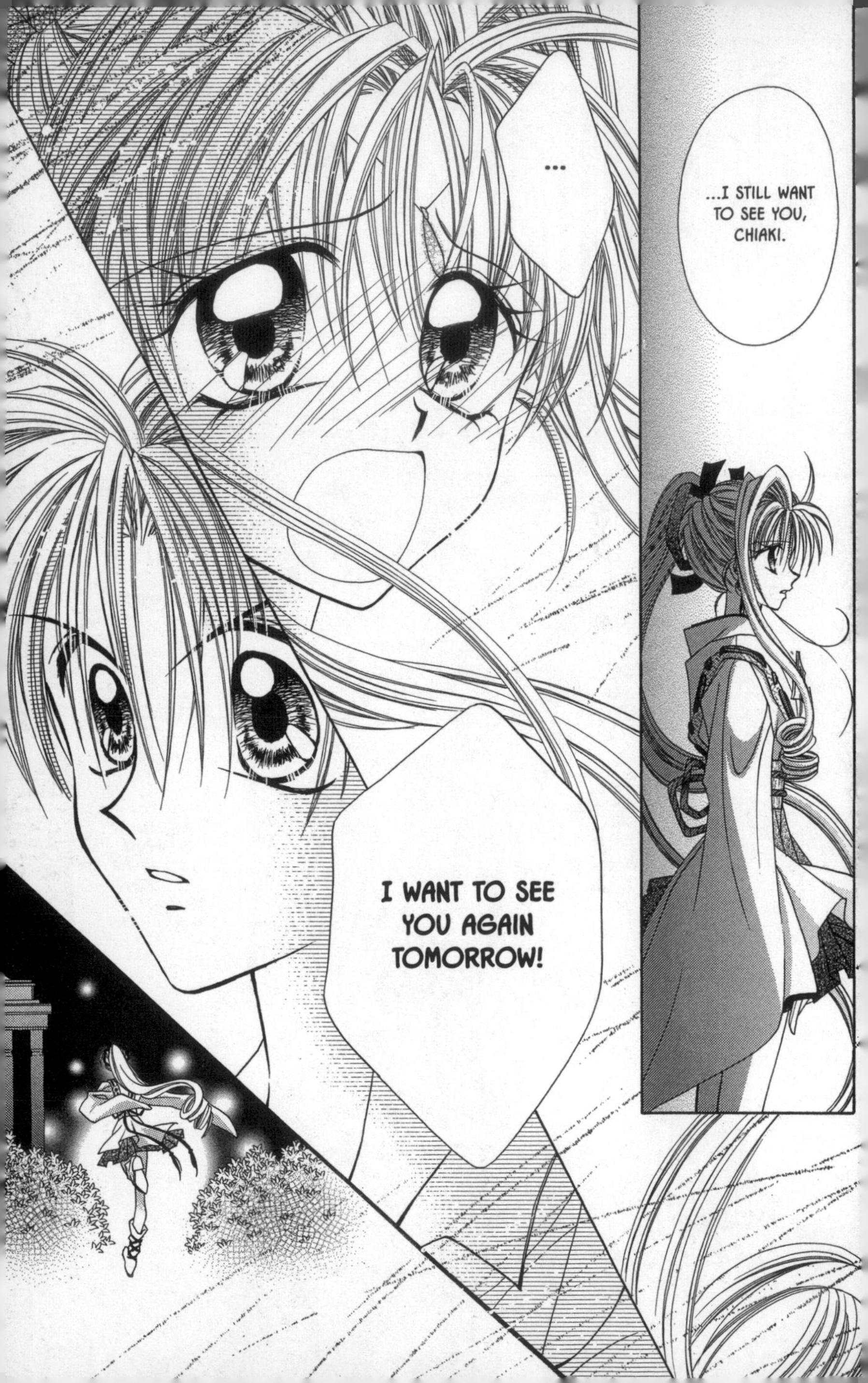
...I STILL WANT TO SEE YOU, CHIAKI.
...
I WANT TO SEE YOU AGAIN TOMORROW!

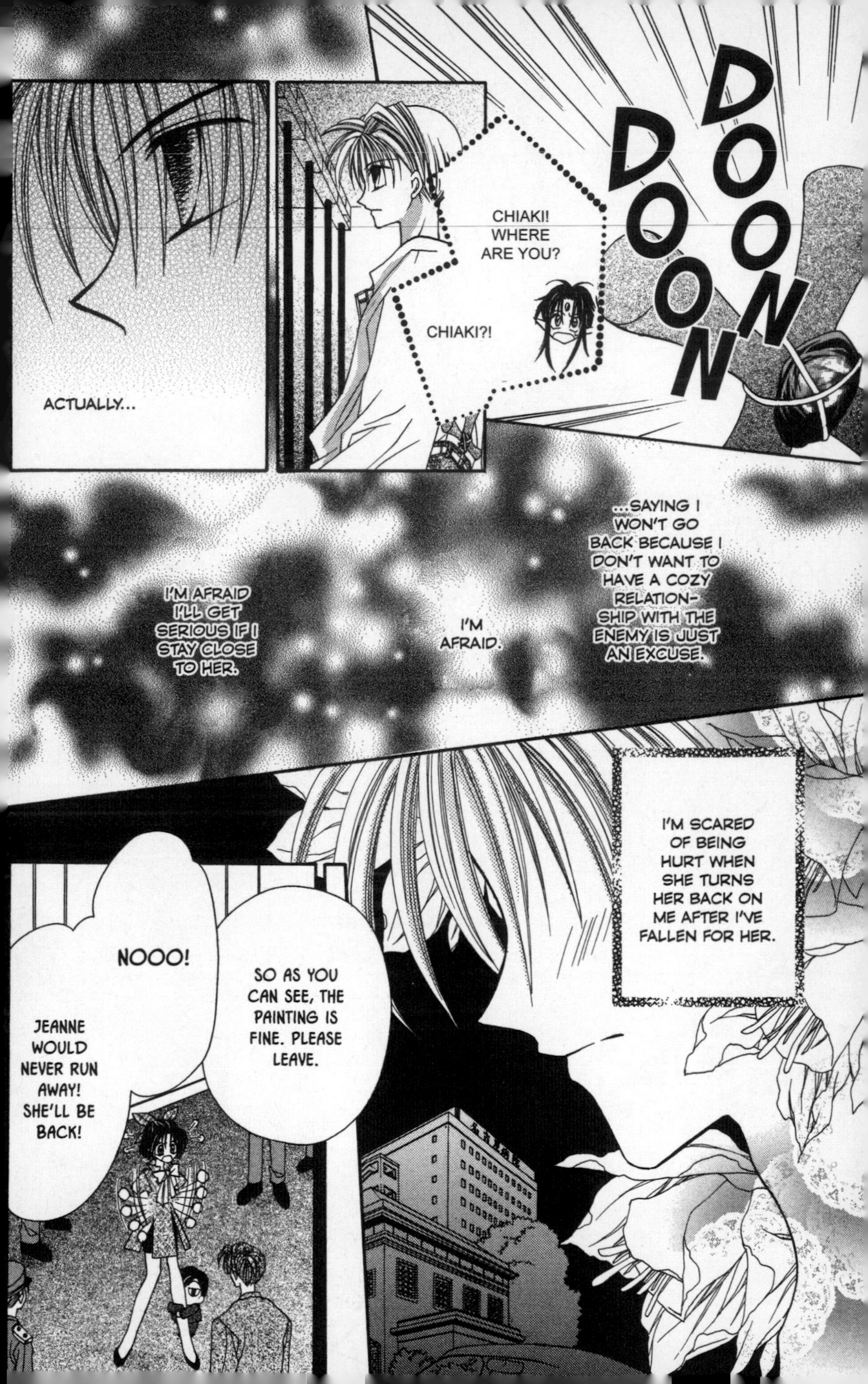
DOON DOON
CHIAKI! WHERE ARE YOU?
CHIAKI?!
ACTUALLY...
...SAYING I WON'T GO BACK BECAUSE I DON'T WANT TO HAVE A COZY RELATION-SHIP WITH THE ENEMY IS JUST AN EXCUSE.
I'M AFRAID.
I'M AFRAID I'LL GET SERIOUS IF I STAY CLOSE TO HER.
I'M SCARED OF BEING HURT WHEN SHE TURNS HER BACK ON ME AFTER I'VE FALLEN FOR HER.
SO AS YOU CAN SEE, THE PAINTING IS FINE. PLEASE LEAVE.
NOOO!
JEANNE WOULD NEVER RUN AWAY! SHE'LL BE BACK!

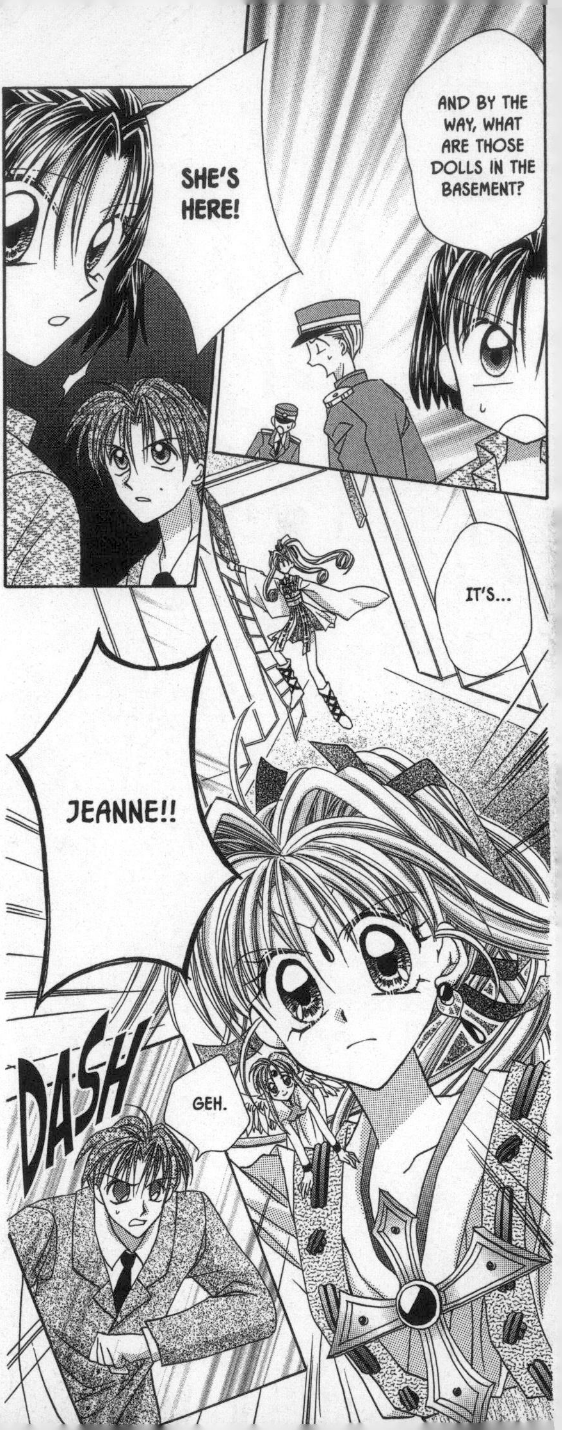
AND BY THE WAY, WHAT ARE THOSE DOLLS IN THE BASEMENT?
SHE'S HERE!
IT'S...
JEANNE!!
DASH
GEH.

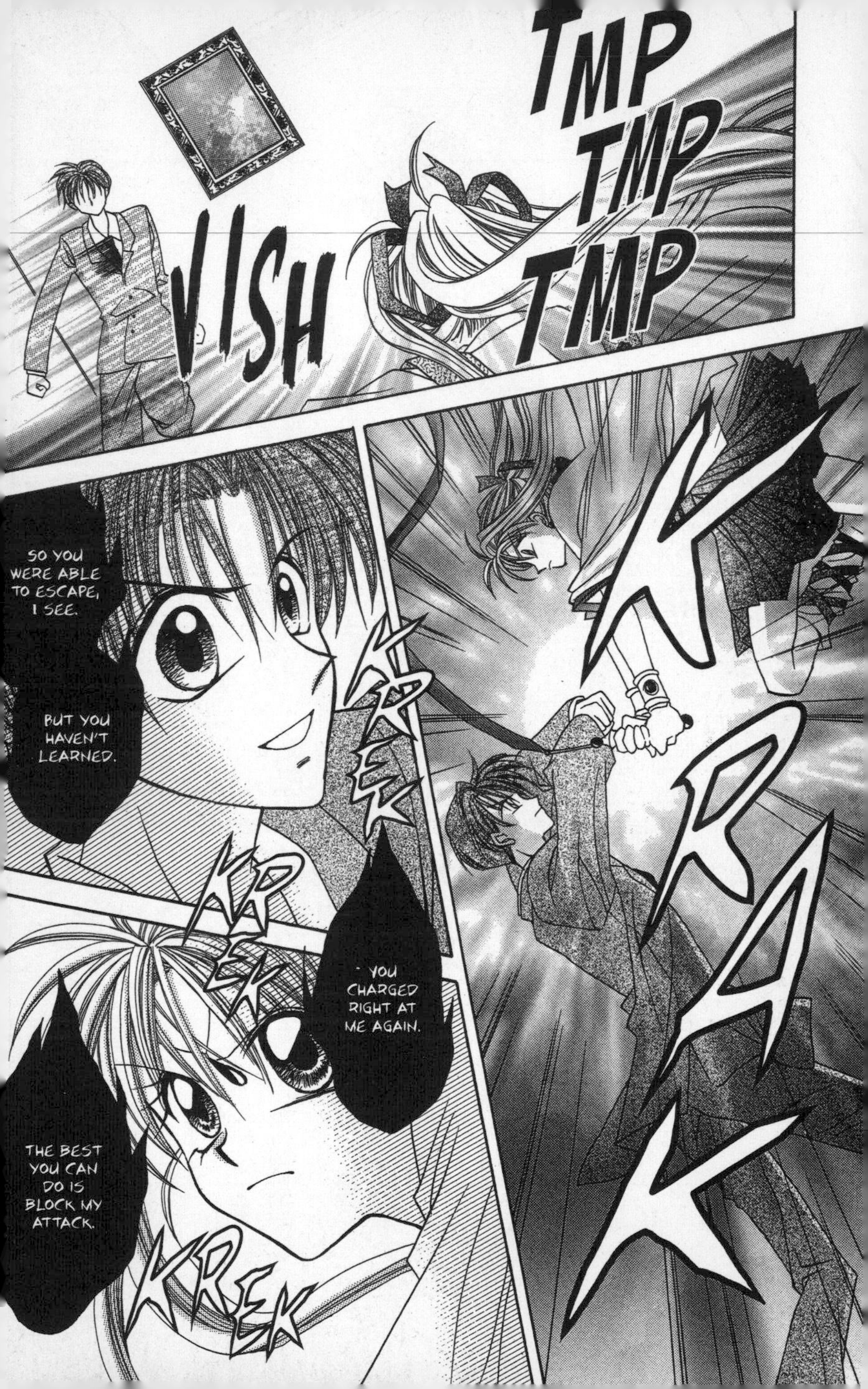

TMP
TMP
TMP
VISH
KRAK
SO YOU WERE ABLE TO ESCAPE, I SEE.
BUT YOU HAVEN'T LEARNED.
KREK
KREK
YOU CHARGED RIGHT AT ME AGAIN.
THE BEST YOU CAN DO IS BLOCK MY ATTACK.
KREK

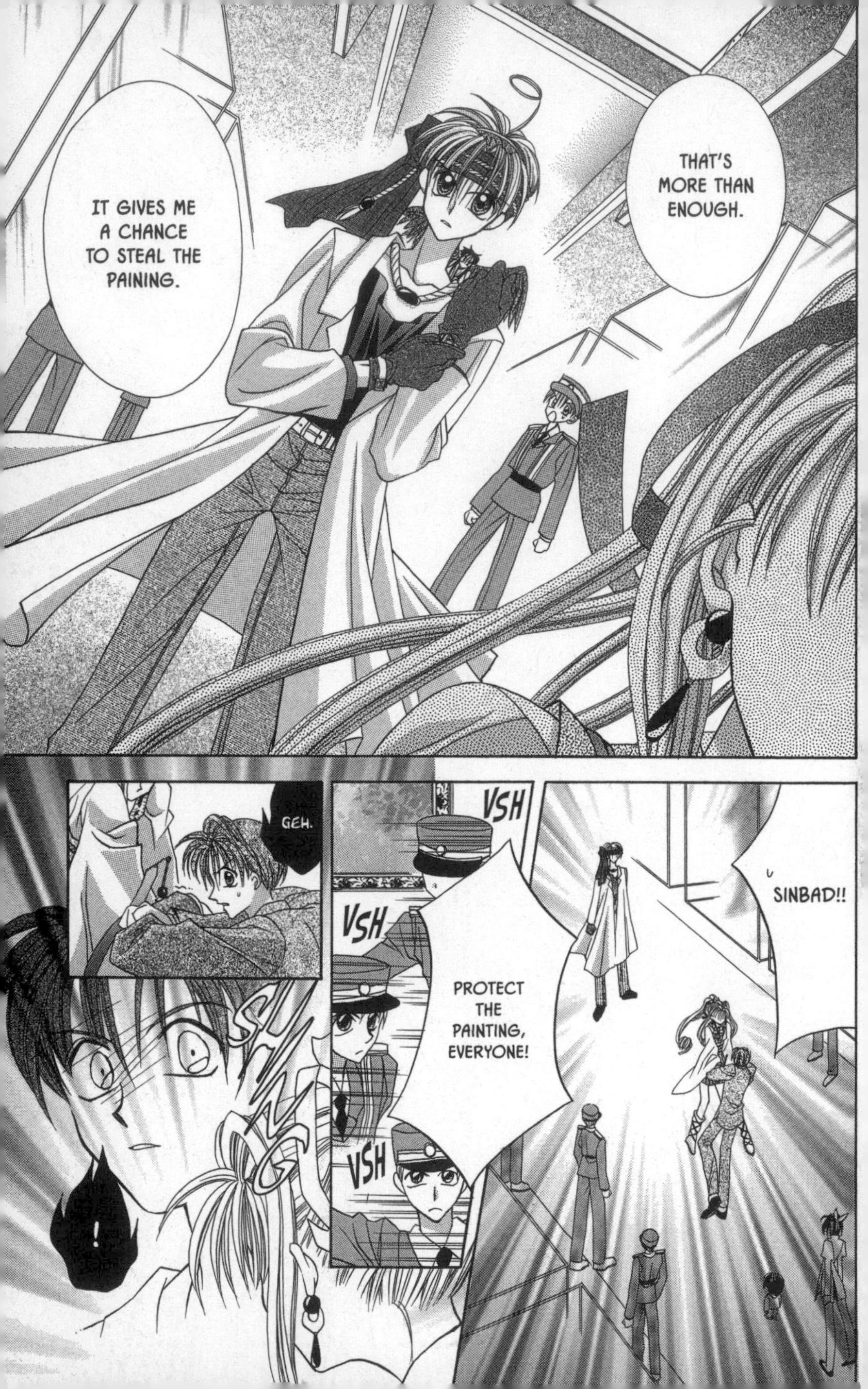
THAT'S MORE THAN ENOUGH.
IT GIVES ME A CHANCE TO STEAL THE PAINING.
SINBAD!!
VSH
VSH
PROTECT THE PAINTING, EVERYONE!
VSH
GEH.
!

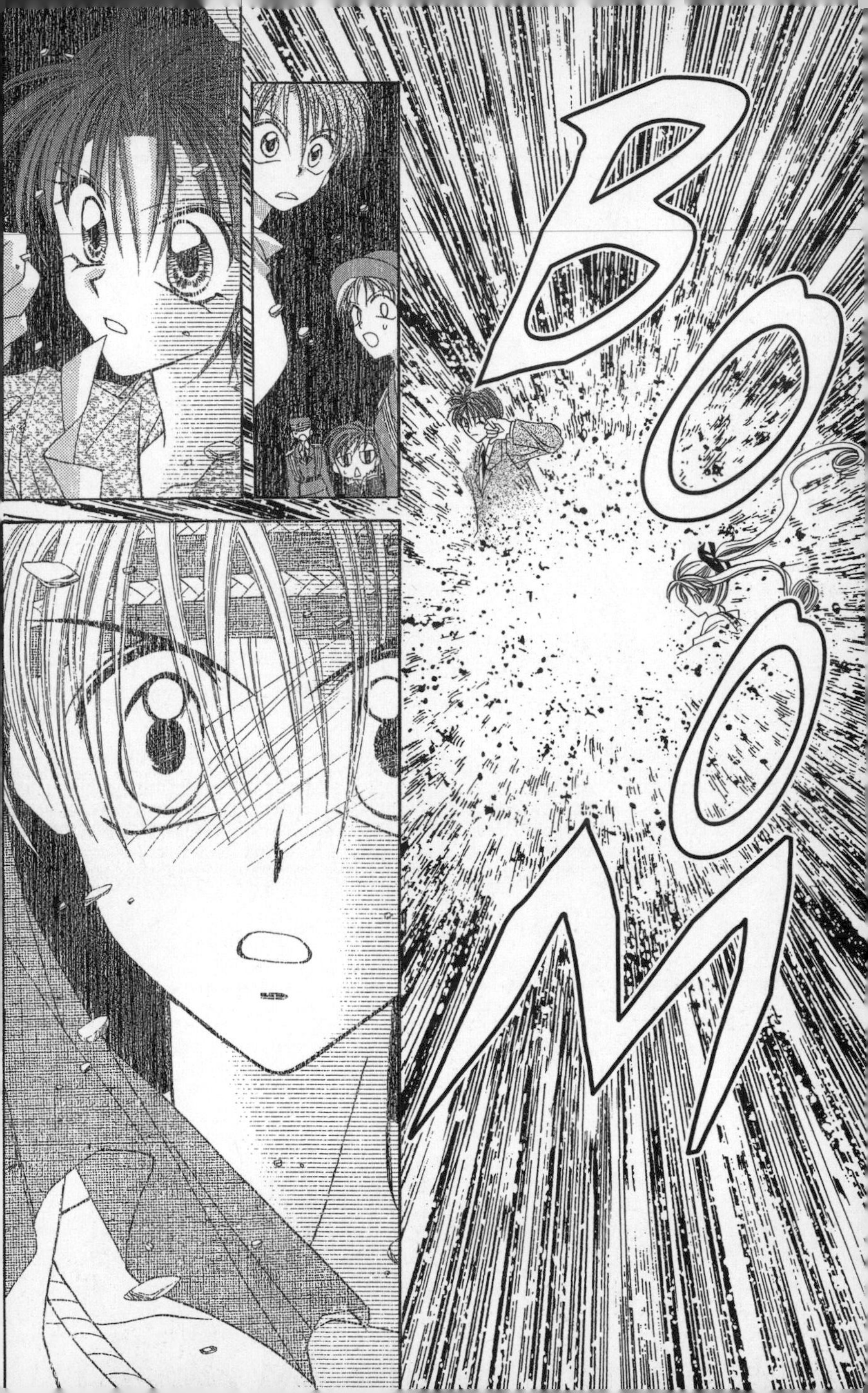
BOOM

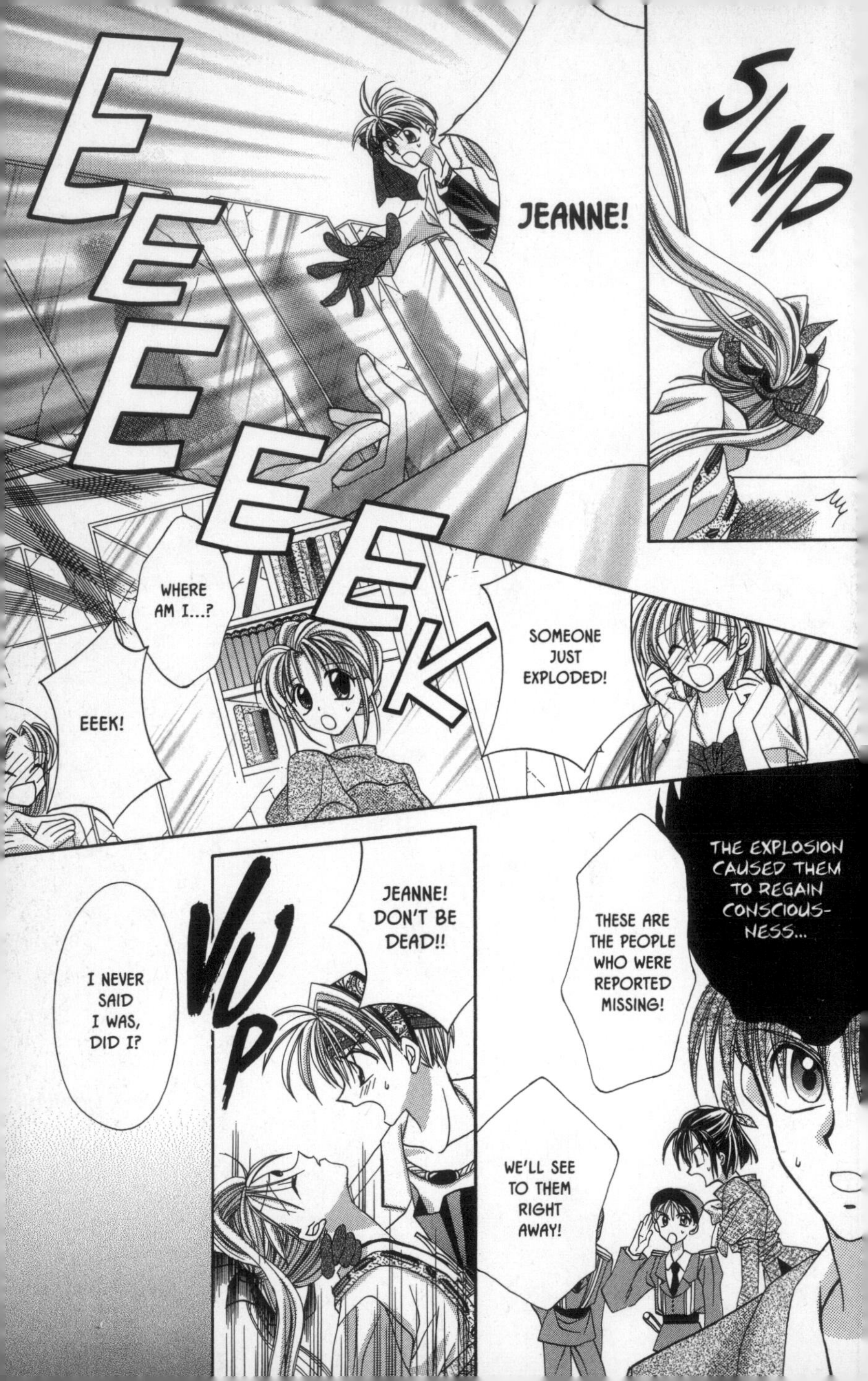
SLMP
JEANNE!
EEEEEEK
SOMEONE JUST EXPLODED!
WHERE AM I...?
EEEK!
THE EXPLOSION CAUSED THEM TO REGAIN CONSCIOUS-NESS...
THESE ARE THE PEOPLE WHO WERE REPORTED MISSING!
WE'LL SEE TO THEM RIGHT AWAY!
JEANNE! DON'T BE DEAD!!
VWP
I NEVER SAID I WAS, DID I?

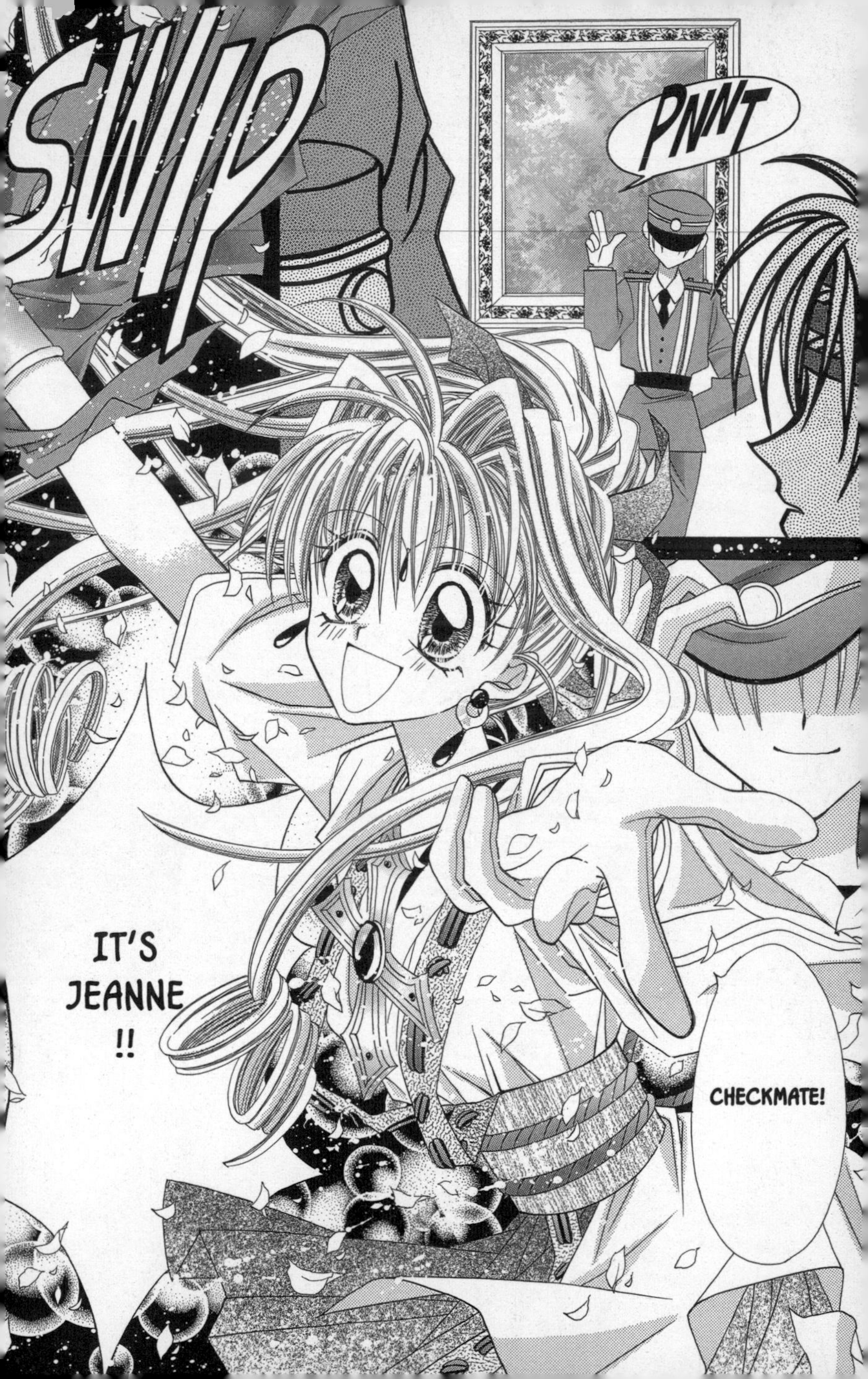
PNNT
SWIP
CHECKMATE!
IT'S JEANNE !!

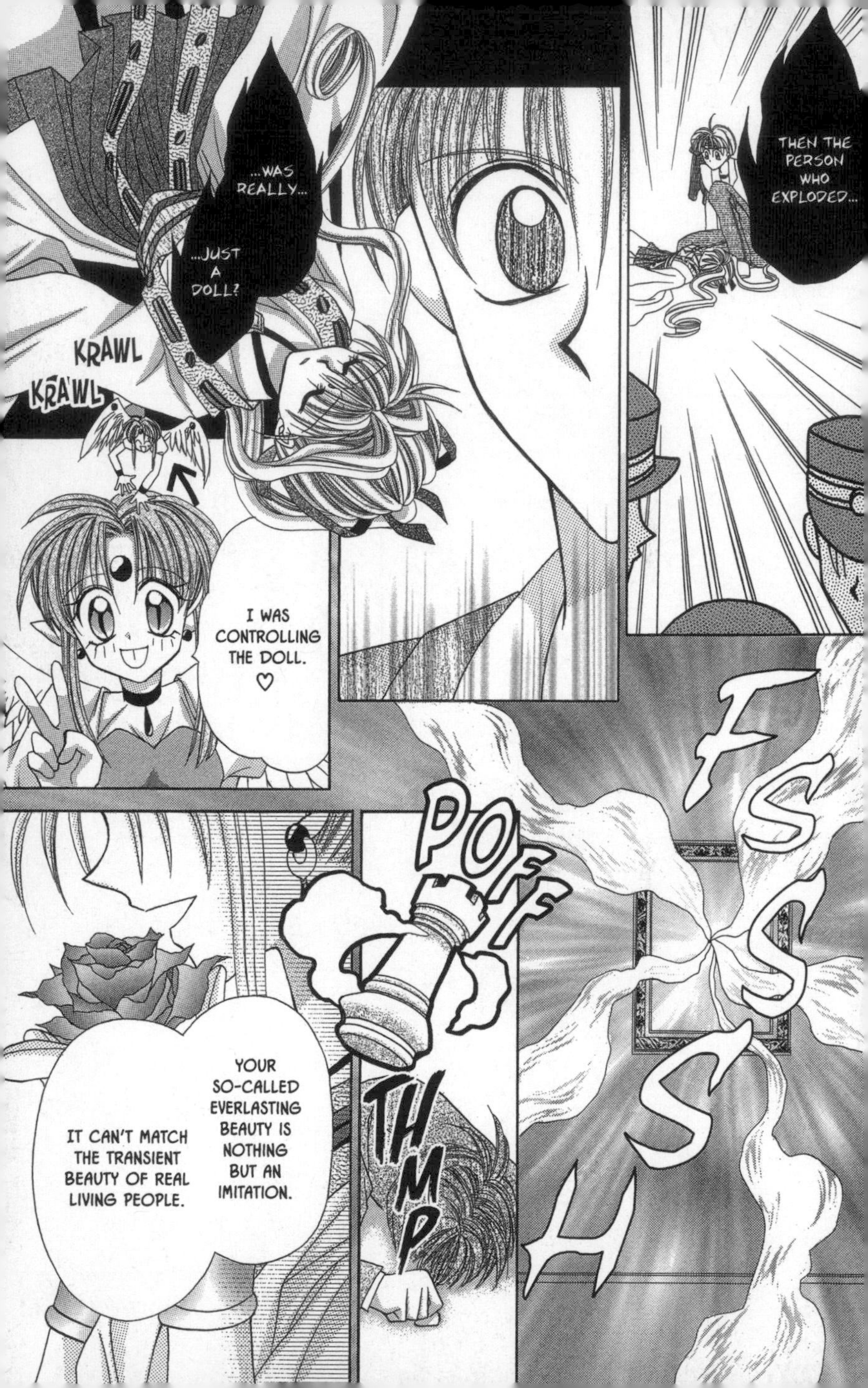
THEN THE PERSON WHO EXPLODED...
...WAS REALLY...
...JUST A DOLL?
KRAWL
KRAWL
I WAS CONTROLLING THE DOLL. ♡
FSSSH
POFF
THMP
YOUR SO-CALLED EVERLASTING BEAUTY IS NOTHING BUT AN IMITATION.
IT CAN'T MATCH THE TRANSIENT BEAUTY OF REAL LIVING PEOPLE.

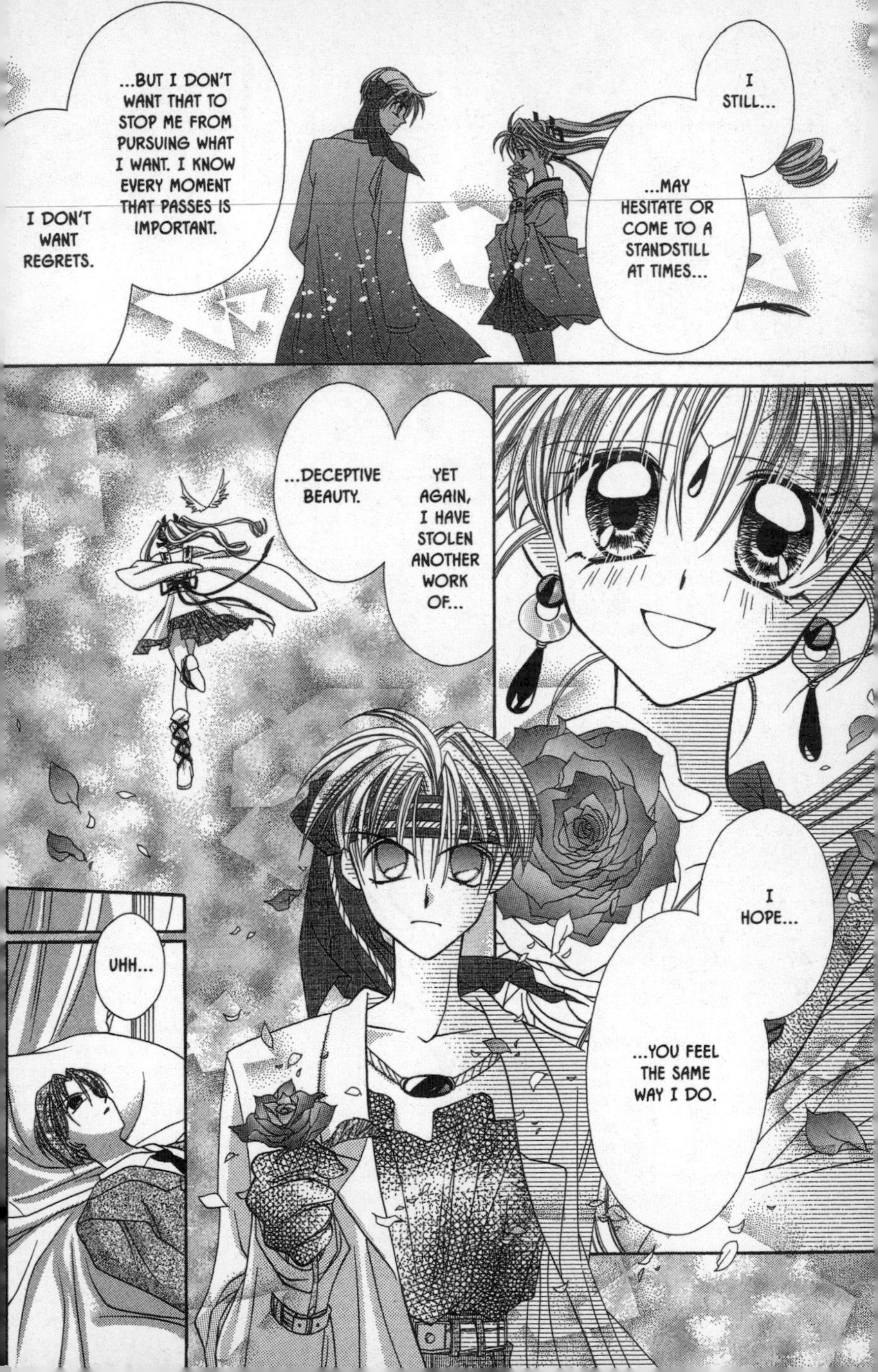
I STILL...
...MAY HESITATE OR COME TO A STANDSTILL AT TIMES...
...BUT I DON'T WANT THAT TO STOP ME FROM PURSUING WHAT I WANT. I KNOW EVERY MOMENT THAT PASSES IS IMPORTANT.
I DON'T WANT REGRETS.
I HOPE...
...YOU FEEL THE SAME WAY I DO.
YET AGAIN, I HAVE STOLEN ANOTHER WORK OF...
...DECEPTIVE BEAUTY.
UHH...

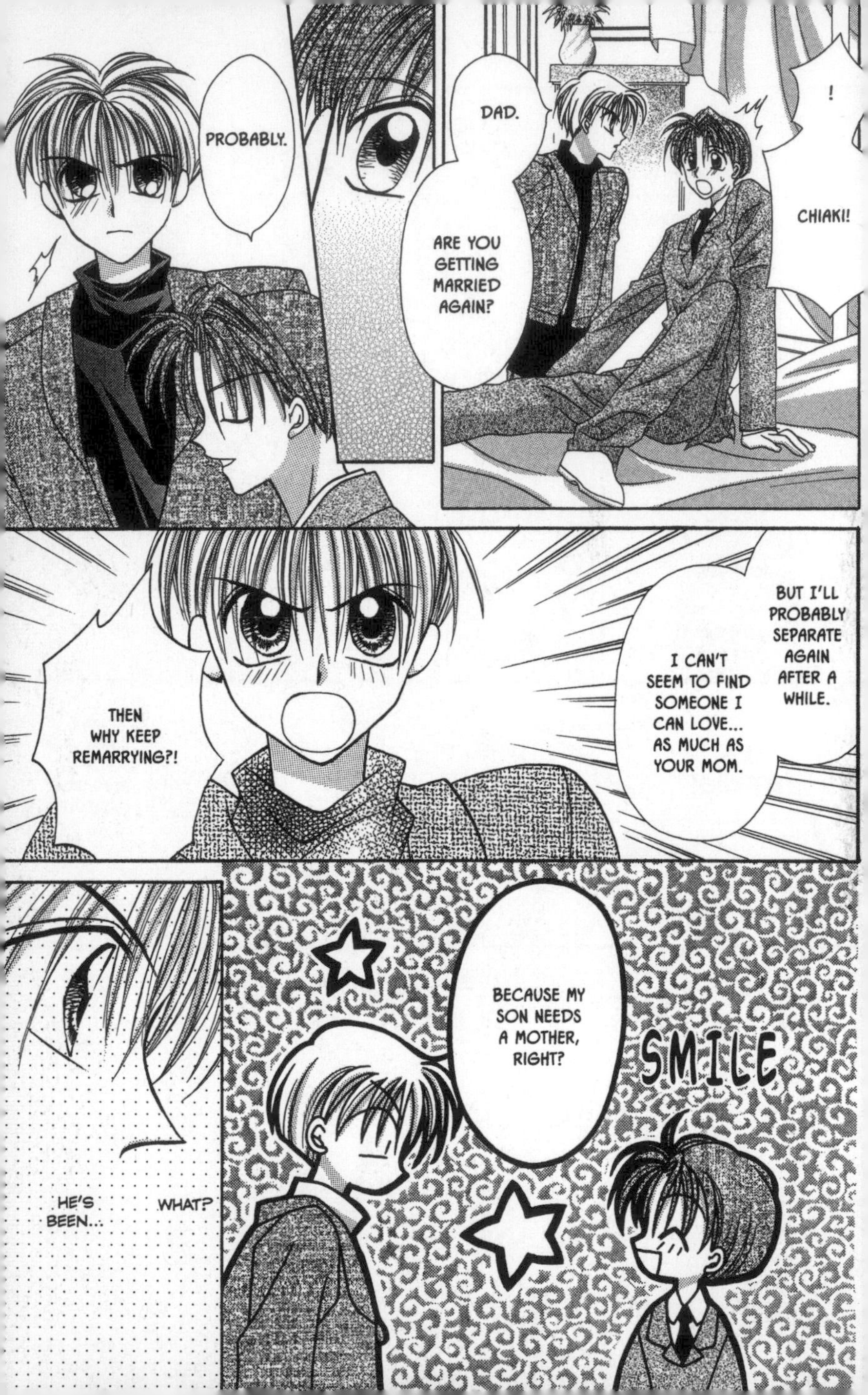
!
CHIAKI!
DAD.
ARE YOU GETTING MARRIED AGAIN?
PROBABLY.
BUT I'LL PROBABLY SEPARATE AGAIN AFTER A WHILE.
I CAN'T SEEM TO FIND SOMEONE I CAN LOVE... AS MUCH AS YOUR MOM.
THEN WHY KEEP REMARRYING?!
BECAUSE MY SON NEEDS A MOTHER, RIGHT?
SMILE
WHAT?
HE'S BEEN...

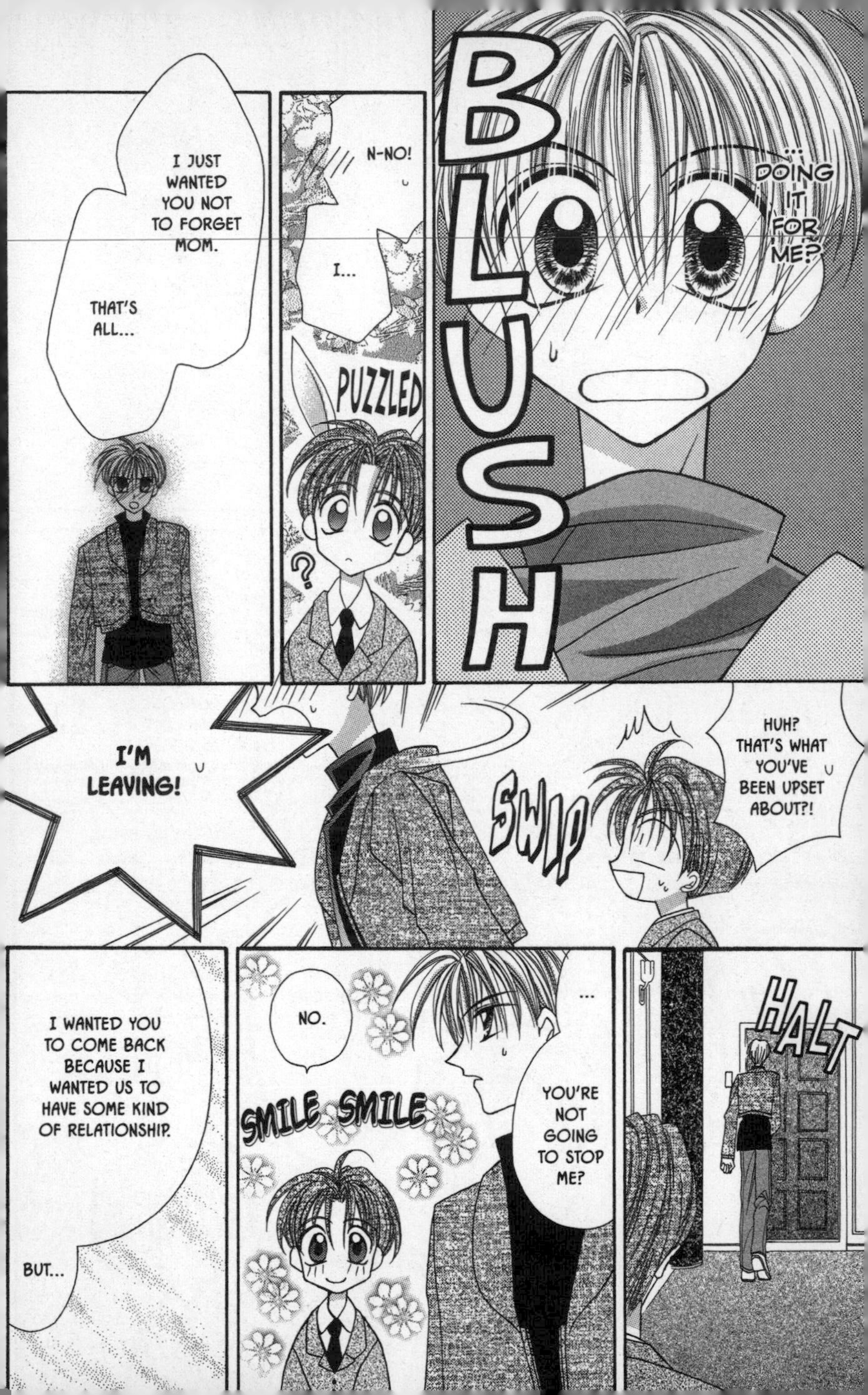
BLUSH
...DOING IT FOR ME?
N-NO!
I...
PUZZLED
?
I JUST WANTED YOU NOT TO FORGET MOM.
THAT'S ALL...
HUH? THAT'S WHAT YOU'VE BEEN UPSET ABOUT?!
SWIP
I'M LEAVING!
HALT
...
YOU'RE NOT GOING TO STOP ME?
NO.
SMILE SMILE
I WANTED YOU TO COME BACK BECAUSE I WANTED US TO HAVE SOME KIND OF RELATIONSHIP.
BUT...

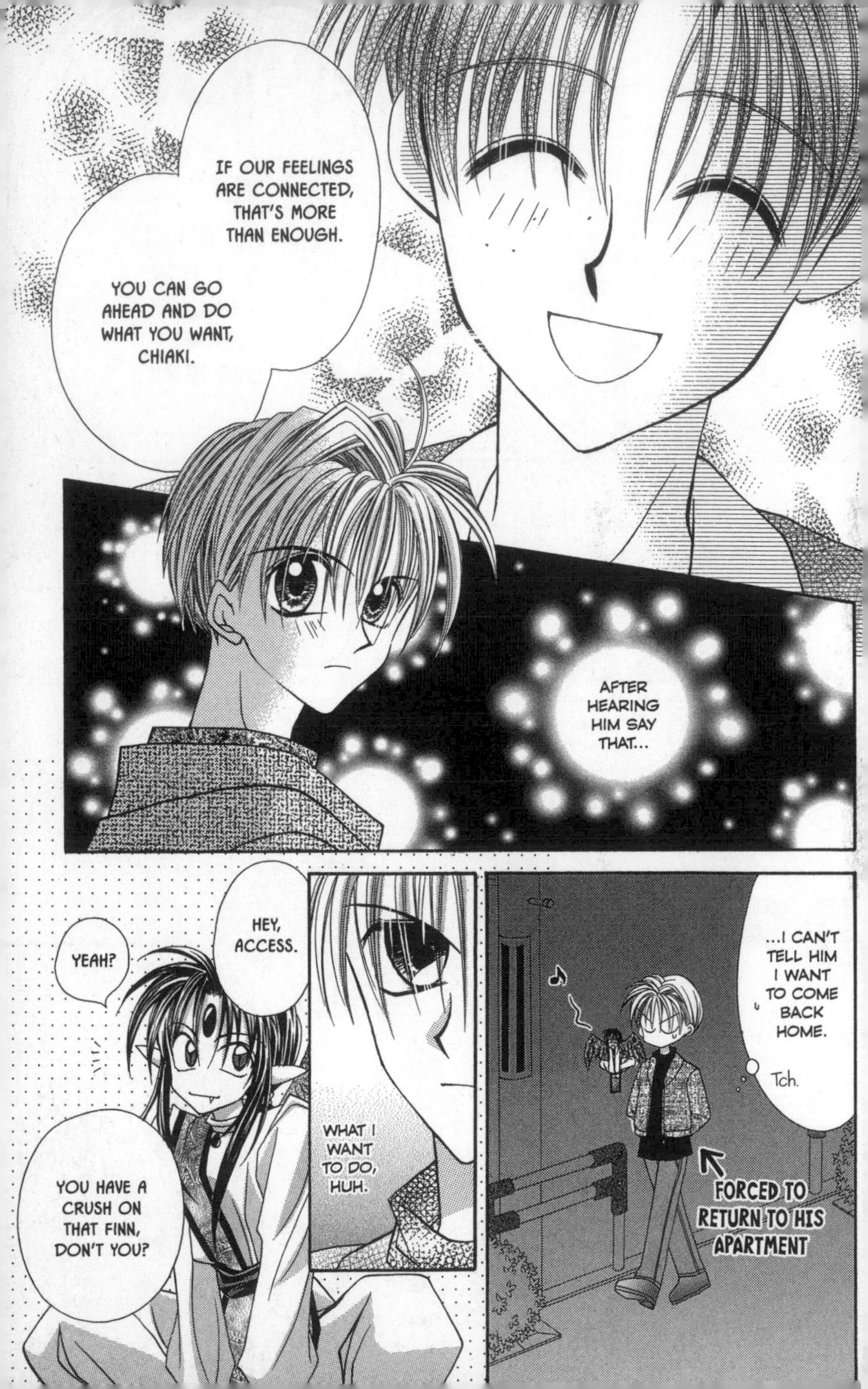
IF OUR FEELINGS ARE CONNECTED, THAT'S MORE THAN ENOUGH.
YOU CAN GO AHEAD AND DO WHAT YOU WANT, CHIAKI.
AFTER HEARING HIM SAY THAT...
...I CAN'T TELL HIM I WANT TO COME BACK HOME.
Tch.
FORCED TO RETURN TO HIS APARTMENT
HEY, ACCESS.
WHAT I WANT TO DO, HUH.
YEAH?
YOU HAVE A CRUSH ON THAT FINN, DON'T YOU?

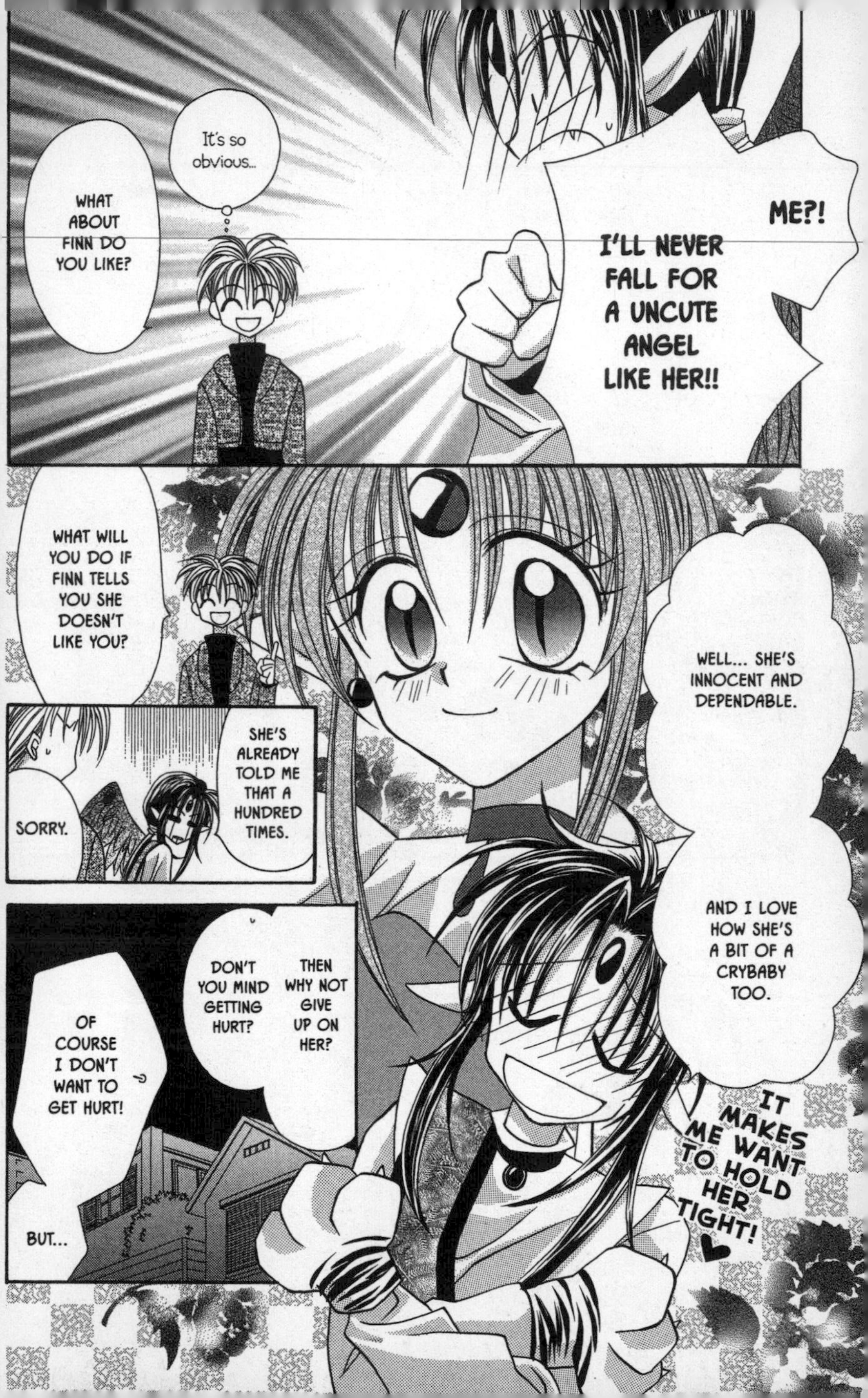
ME?!
I'LL NEVER FALL FOR A UNCUTE ANGEL LIKE HER!!
It's so obvious...
WHAT ABOUT FINN DO YOU LIKE?
WELL... SHE'S INNOCENT AND DEPENDABLE.
AND I LOVE HOW SHE'S A BIT OF A CRYBABY TOO.
IT MAKES ME WANT TO HOLD HER TIGHT!
WHAT WILL YOU DO IF FINN TELLS YOU SHE DOESN'T LIKE YOU?
SHE'S ALREADY TOLD ME THAT A HUNDRED TIMES.
SORRY.
THEN WHY NOT GIVE UP ON HER?
DON'T YOU MIND GETTING HURT?
OF COURSE I DON'T WANT TO GET HURT!
BUT...

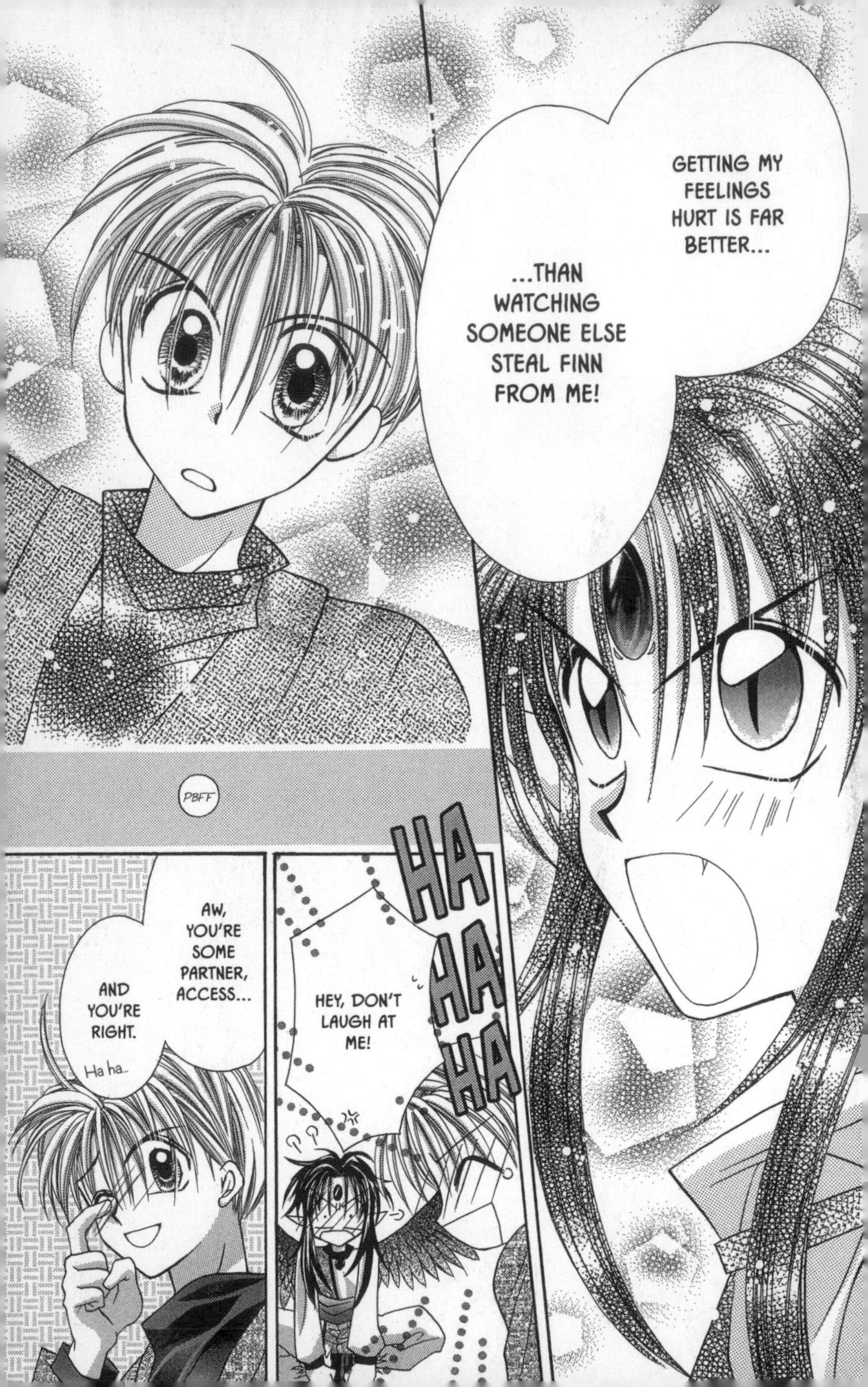
GETTING MY FEELINGS HURT IS FAR BETTER...
...THAN WATCHING SOMEONE ELSE STEAL FINN FROM ME!
PBFF
HA HA HA HA
HEY, DON'T LAUGH AT ME!
AW, YOU'RE SOME PARTNER, ACCESS...
AND YOU'RE RIGHT.
Ha ha...

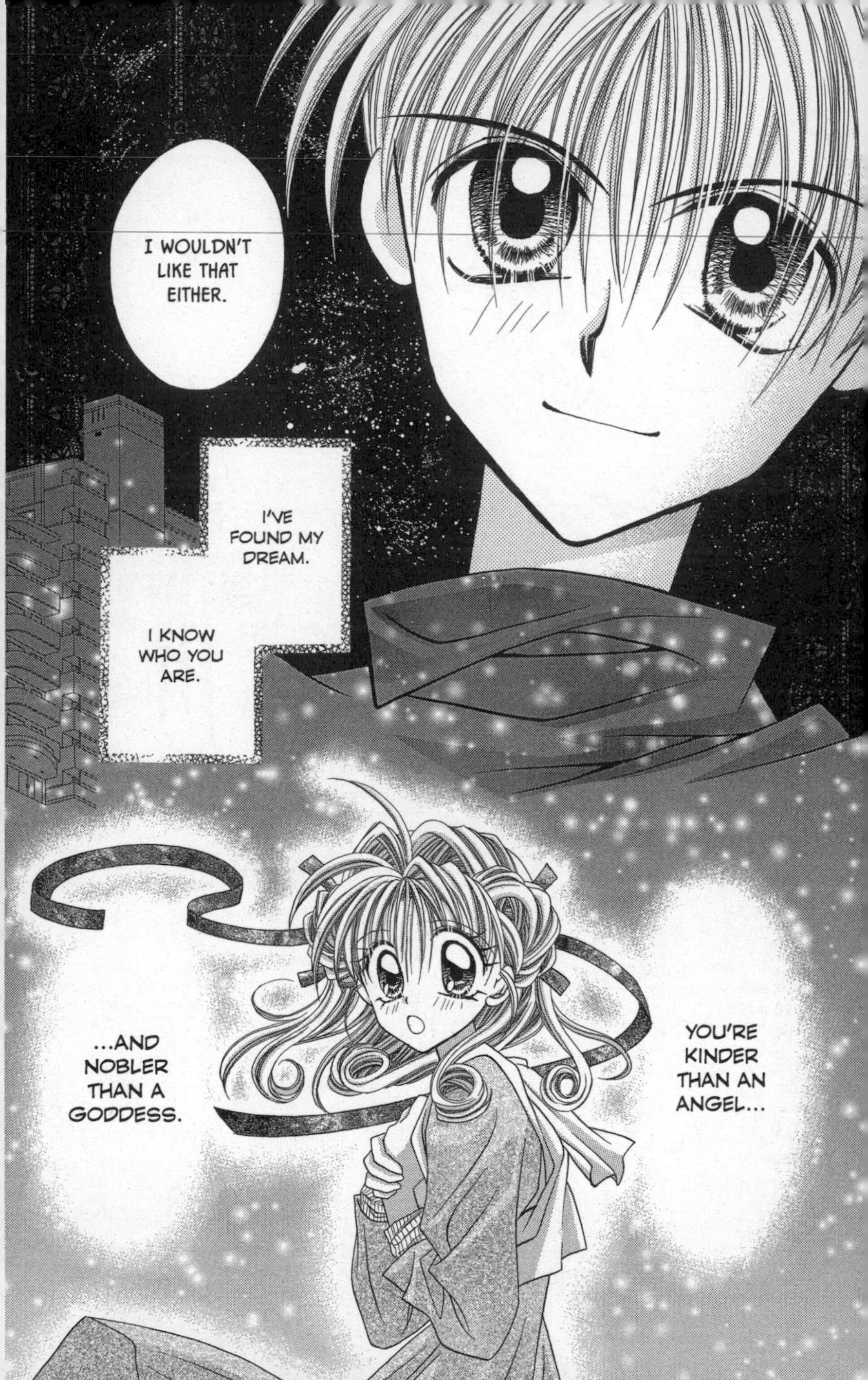
I WOULDN'T LIKE THAT EITHER.
I'VE FOUND MY DREAM.
I KNOW WHO YOU ARE.
YOU'RE KINDER THAN AN ANGEL...
...AND NOBLER THAN A GODDESS.

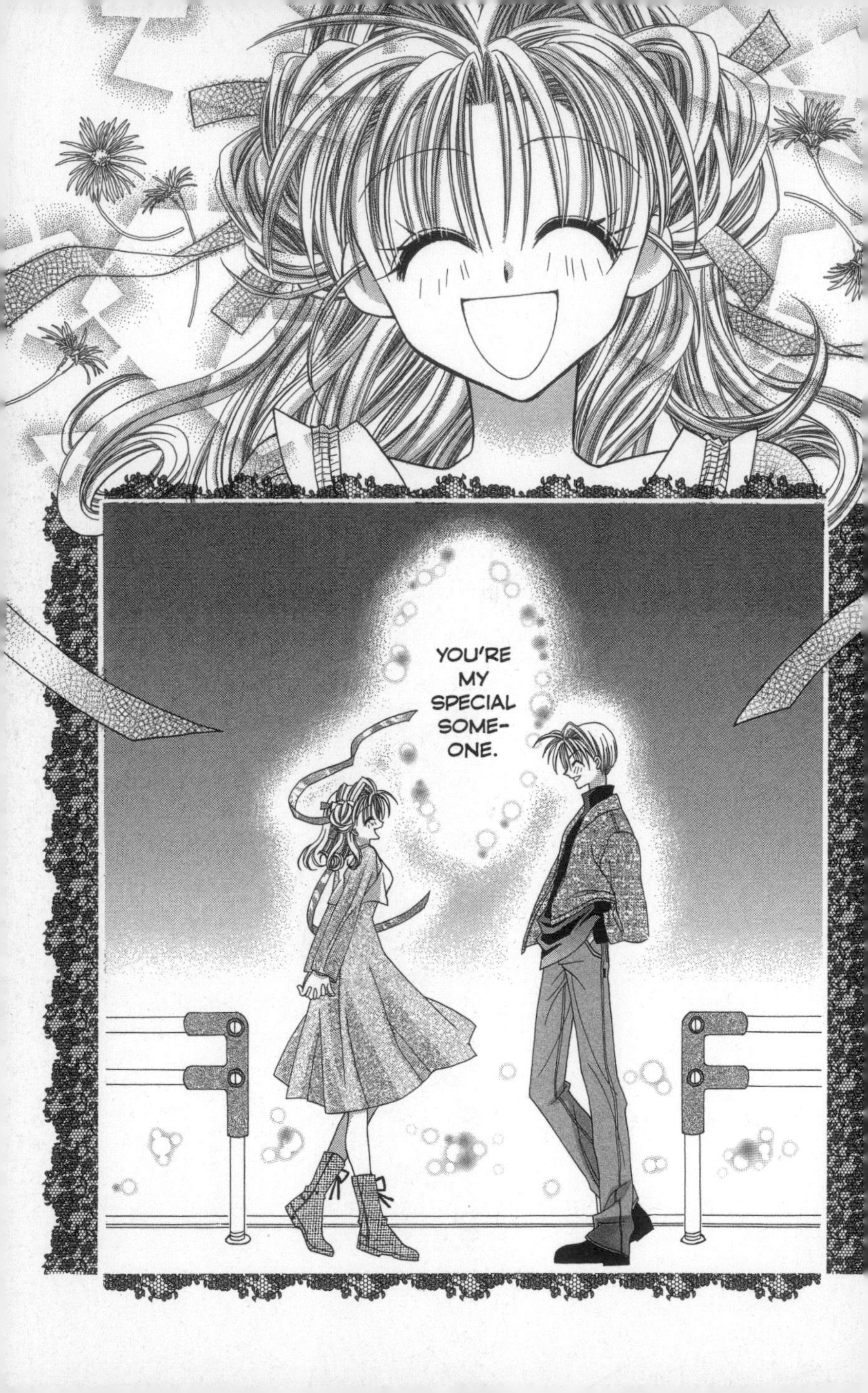
YOU'RE MY SPECIAL SOME-ONE.

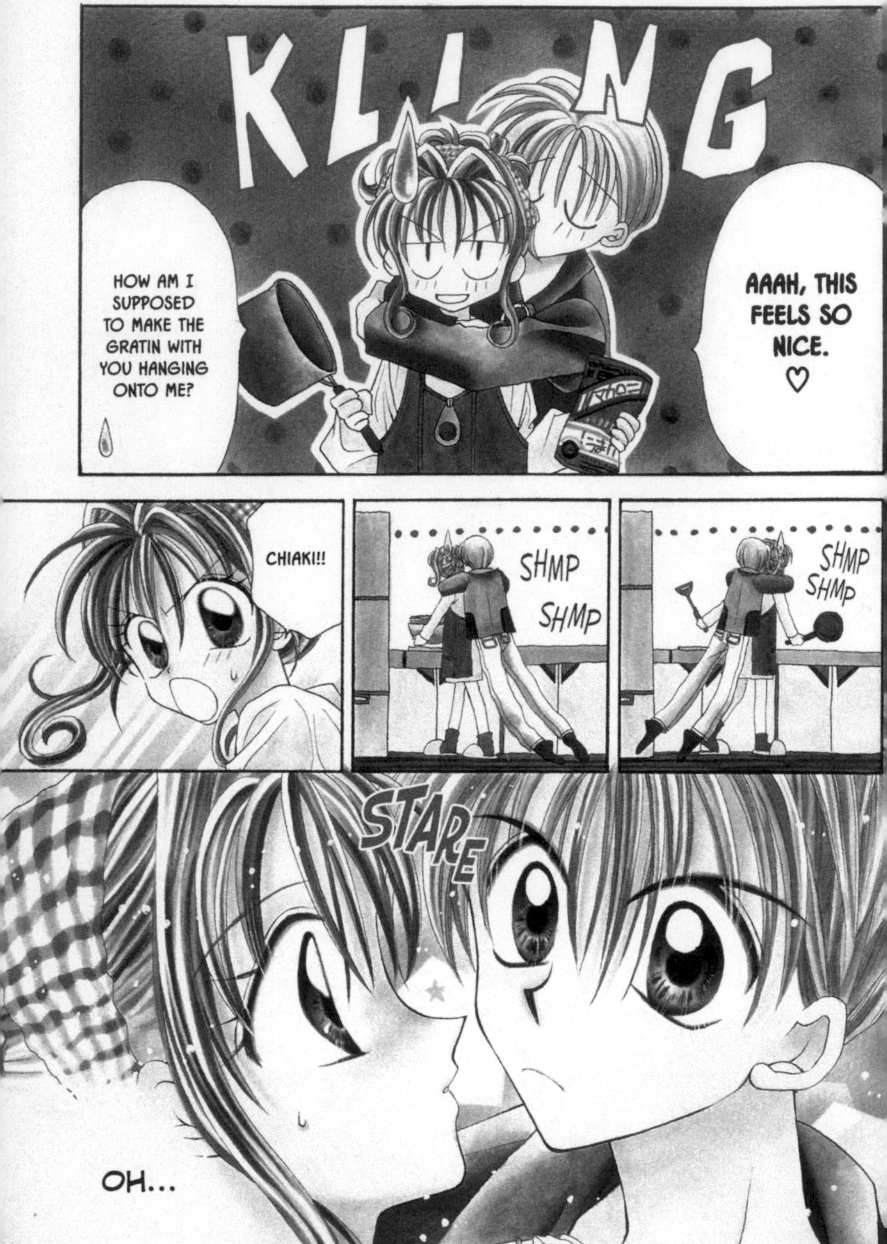
KLING
AAAH, THIS FEELS SO NICE. ♡
HOW AM I SUPPOSED TO MAKE THE GRATIN WITH YOU HANGING ONTO ME?
SHMP SHMP
SHMP SHMP
CHIAKI!!
STARE
OH...

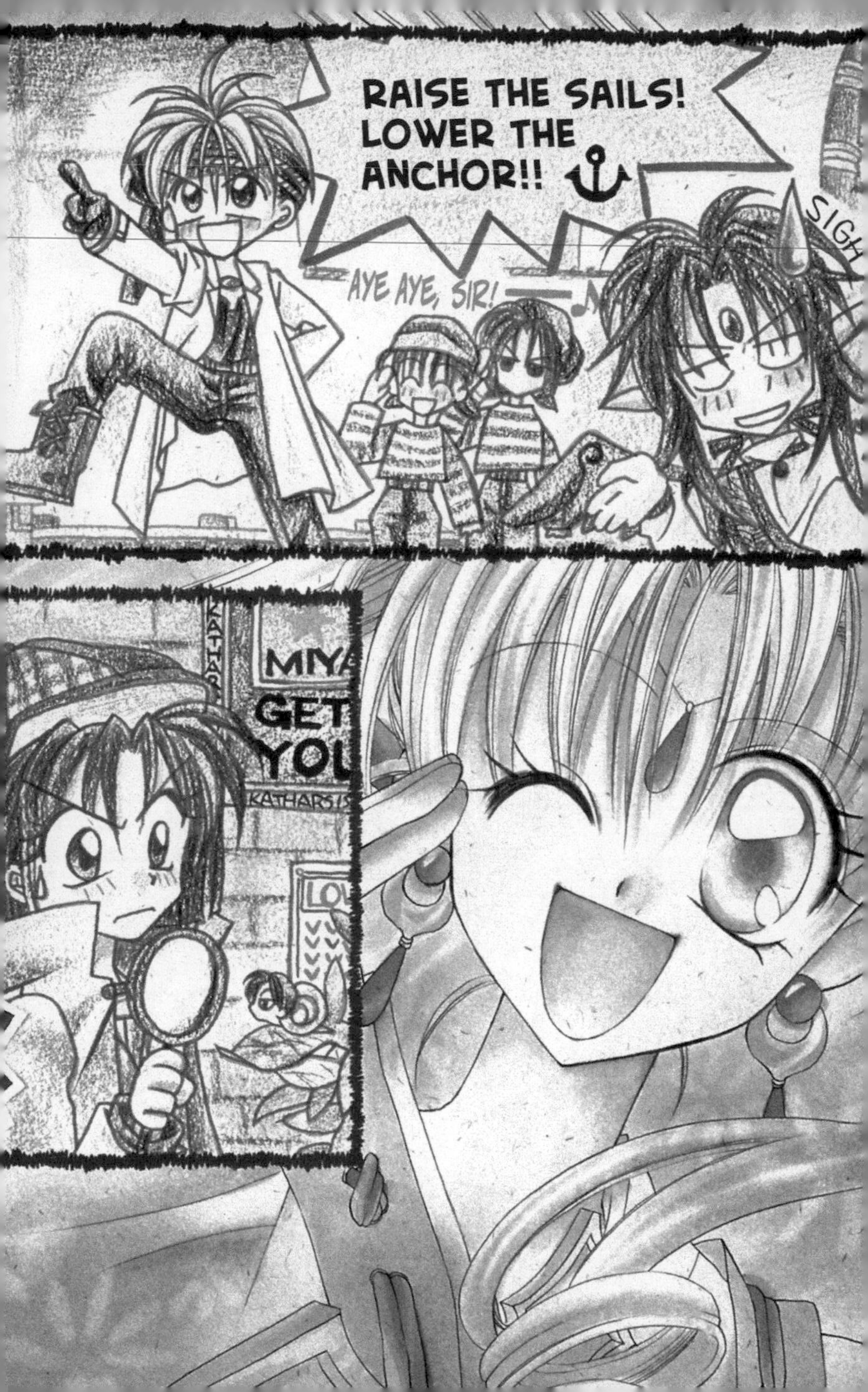
RAISE THE SAILS! LOWER THE ANCHOR!!
SIGH
AYE AYE, SIR!
MIYA
GET
YOU
KATHARSIS
KATHARSIS
LOV

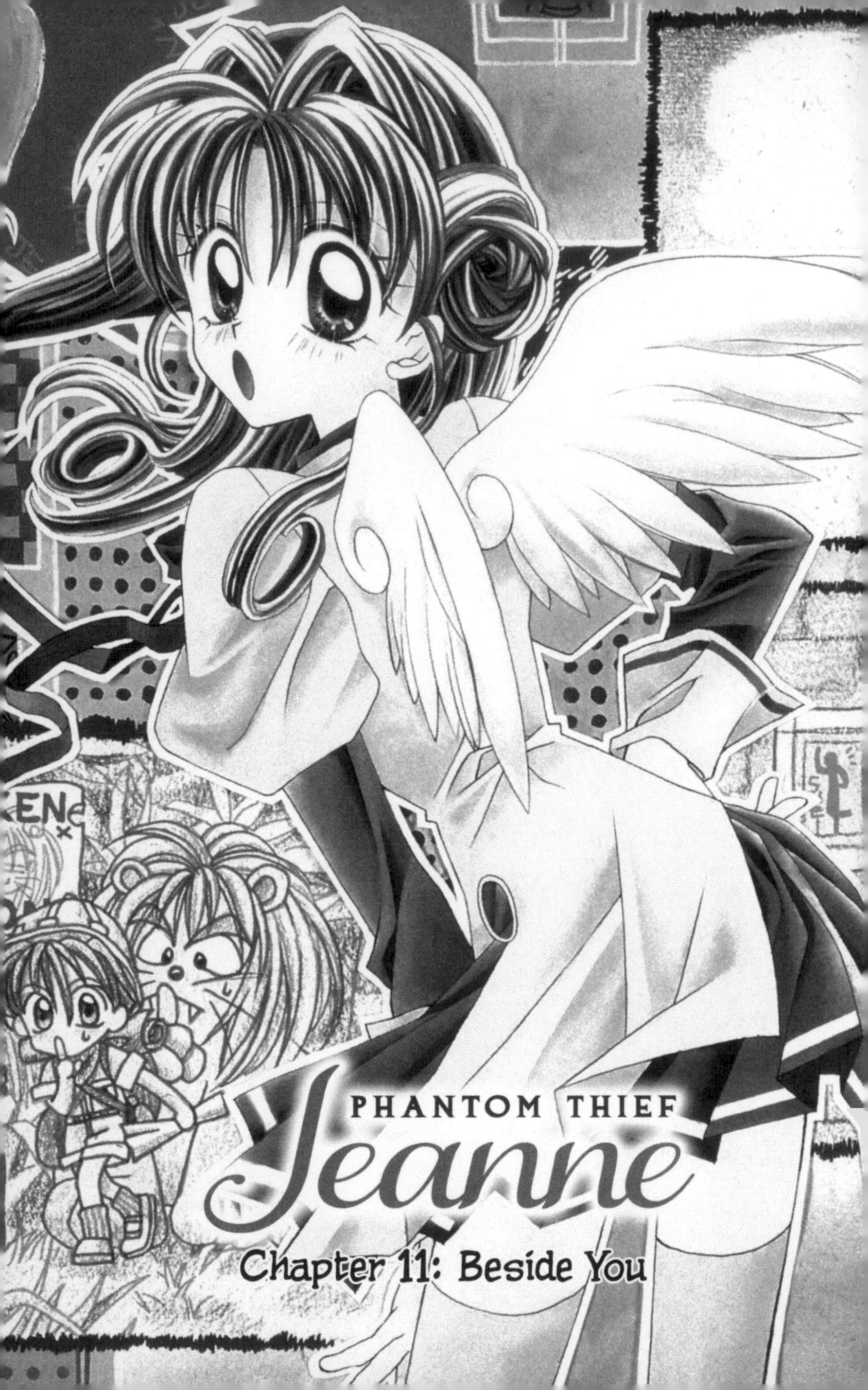
PHANTOM THIEF
Jeanne
Chapter 11: Beside You

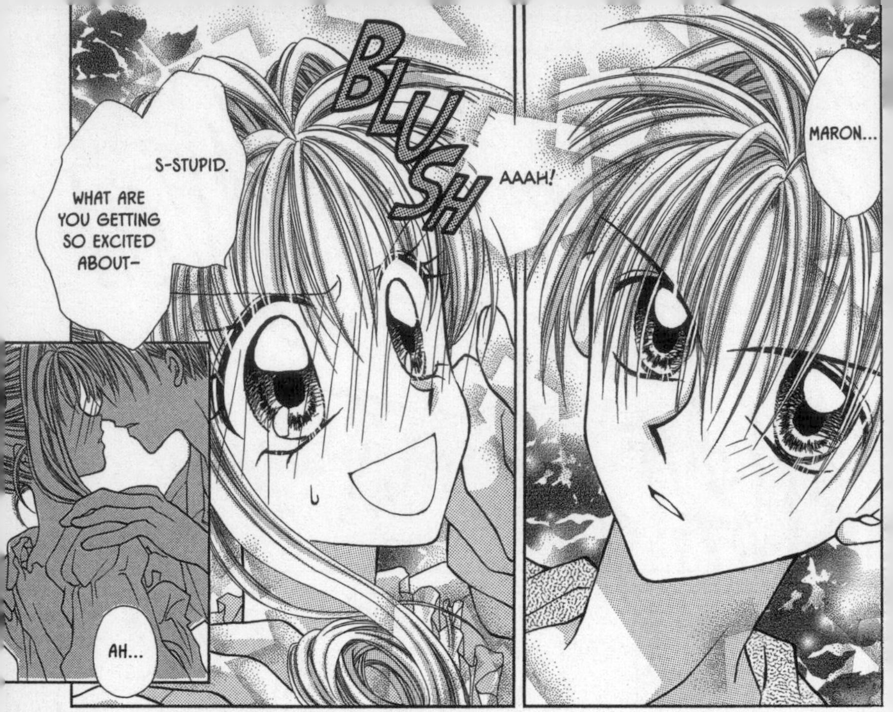
MARON...
AAAH!
BLUSH
S-STUPID.
WHAT ARE YOU GETTING SO EXCITED ABOUT-
AH...

PHANTOM
THIEF
JEANNE

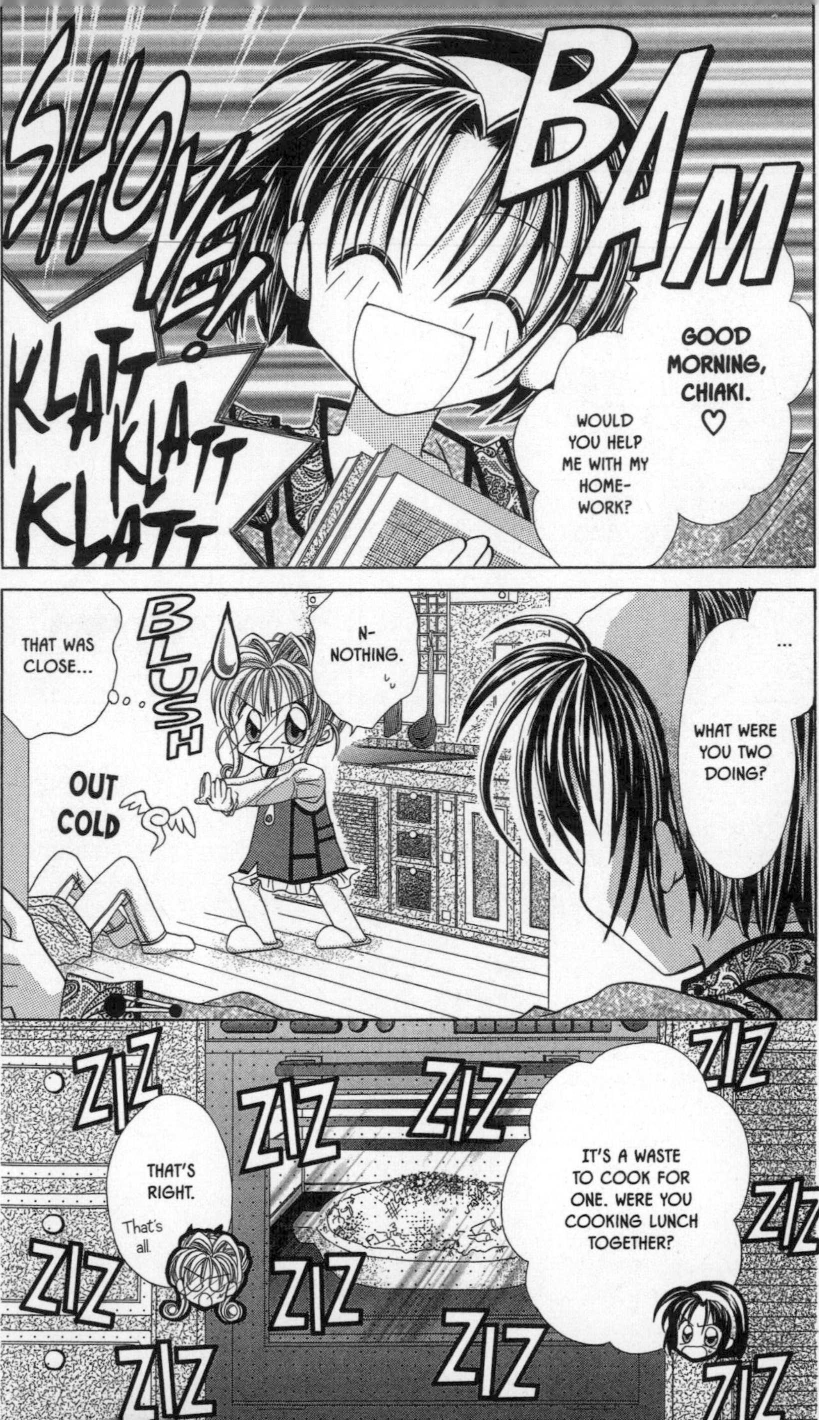
BAM
SHOVE!
KLATT KLATT KLATT KLATT
GOOD MORNING, CHIAKI. ♡
WOULD YOU HELP ME WITH MY HOME-WORK?
...
WHAT WERE YOU TWO DOING?
N-NOTHING.
BLUSH
THAT WAS CLOSE...
OUT COLD
IT'S A WASTE TO COOK FOR ONE. WERE YOU COOKING LUNCH TOGETHER?
THAT'S RIGHT.
That's all.
ZIZ ZIZ ZIZ ZIZ ZIZ ZIZ ZIZ ZIZ ZIZ ZIZ

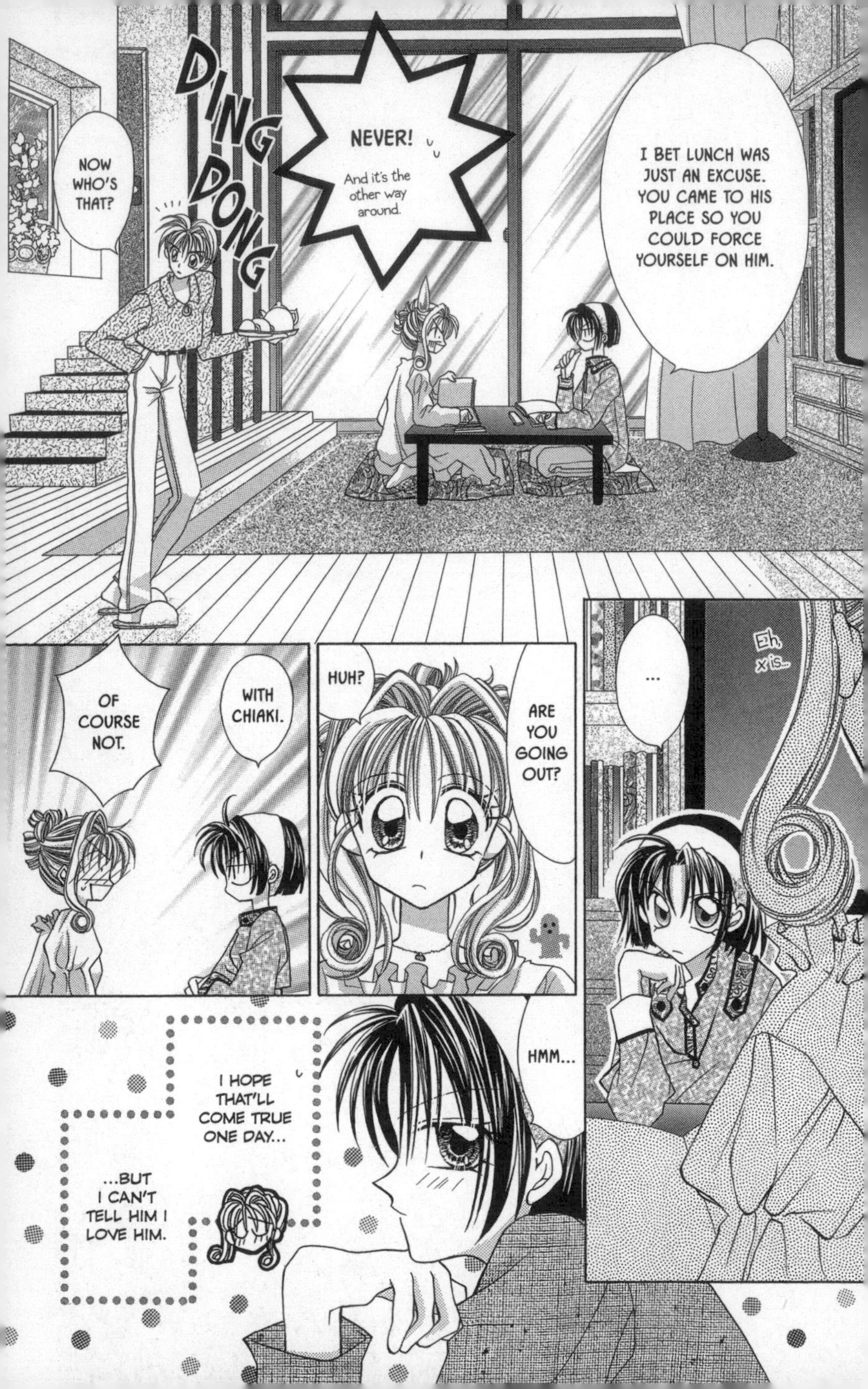
I BET LUNCH WAS JUST AN EXCUSE. YOU CAME TO HIS PLACE SO YOU COULD FORCE YOURSELF ON HIM.
NEVER!
And it's the other way around.
DING DONG
NOW WHO'S THAT?
Eh, x is...
...
ARE YOU GOING OUT?
HUH?
WITH CHIAKI.
OF COURSE NOT.
HMM...
I HOPE THAT'LL COME TRUE ONE DAY...
...BUT I CAN'T TELL HIM I LOVE HIM.

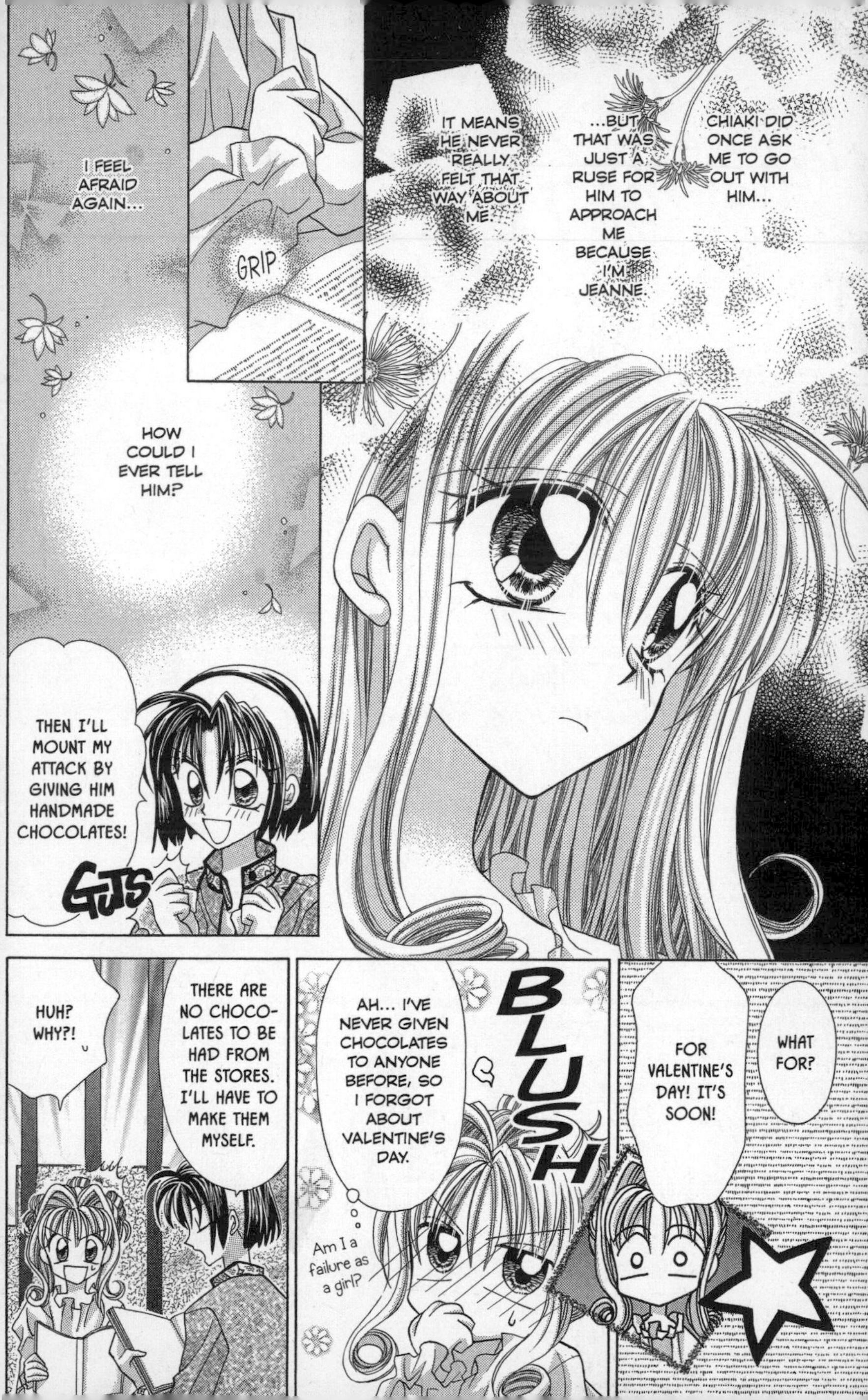
CHIAKI DID ONCE ASK ME TO GO OUT WITH HIM...
...BUT THAT WAS JUST A RUSE FOR HIM TO APPROACH ME BECAUSE I'M JEANNE.
IT MEANS HE NEVER REALLY FELT THAT WAY ABOUT ME.
GRIP
I FEEL AFRAID AGAIN...
HOW COULD I EVER TELL HIM?
THEN I'LL MOUNT MY ATTACK BY GIVING HIM HANDMADE CHOCOLATES!
GUTS
WHAT FOR?
FOR VALENTINE'S DAY! IT'S SOON!
BLUSH
AH... I'VE NEVER GIVEN CHOCOLATES TO ANYONE BEFORE, SO I FORGOT ABOUT VALENTINE'S DAY.
Am I a failure as a girl?
THERE ARE NO CHOCO-LATES TO BE HAD FROM THE STORES. I'LL HAVE TO MAKE THEM MYSELF.
HUH? WHY?!

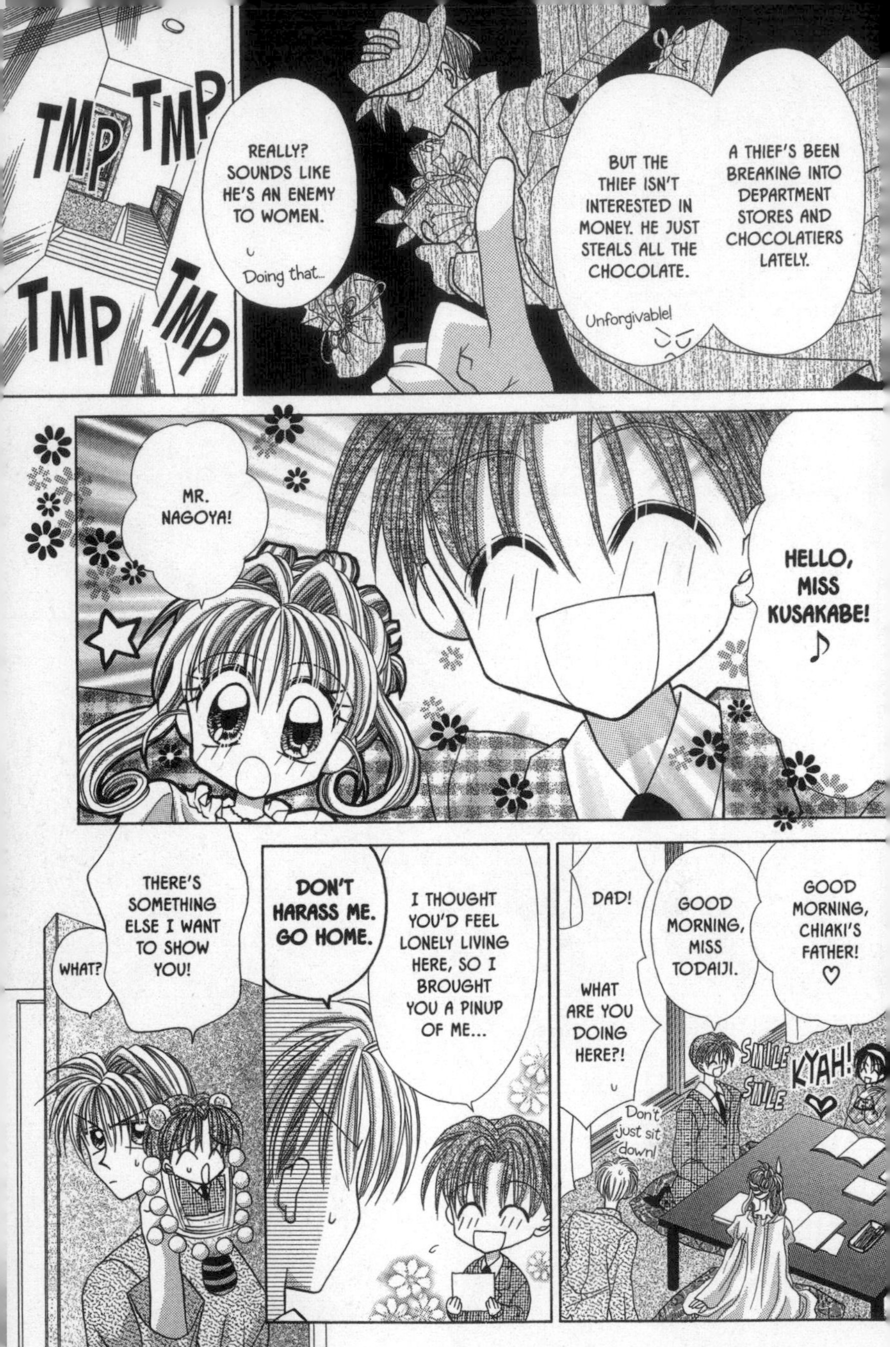
A THIEF'S BEEN BREAKING INTO DEPARTMENT STORES AND CHOCOLATIERS LATELY.
BUT THE THIEF ISN'T INTERESTED IN MONEY. HE JUST STEALS ALL THE CHOCOLATE.
Unforgivable!
REALLY? SOUNDS LIKE HE'S AN ENEMY TO WOMEN.
Doing that...
TMP TMP
TMP TMP
HELLO, MISS KUSAKABE! ♪
MR. NAGOYA!
GOOD MORNING, CHIAKI'S FATHER! ♡
GOOD MORNING, MISS TODAIJI.
SMILE SMILE
KYAH!
DAD!
WHAT ARE YOU DOING HERE?!
Don't just sit down!
I THOUGHT YOU'D FEEL LONELY LIVING HERE, SO I BROUGHT YOU A PINUP OF ME...
DON'T HARASS ME. GO HOME.
THERE'S SOMETHING ELSE I WANT TO SHOW YOU!
WHAT?

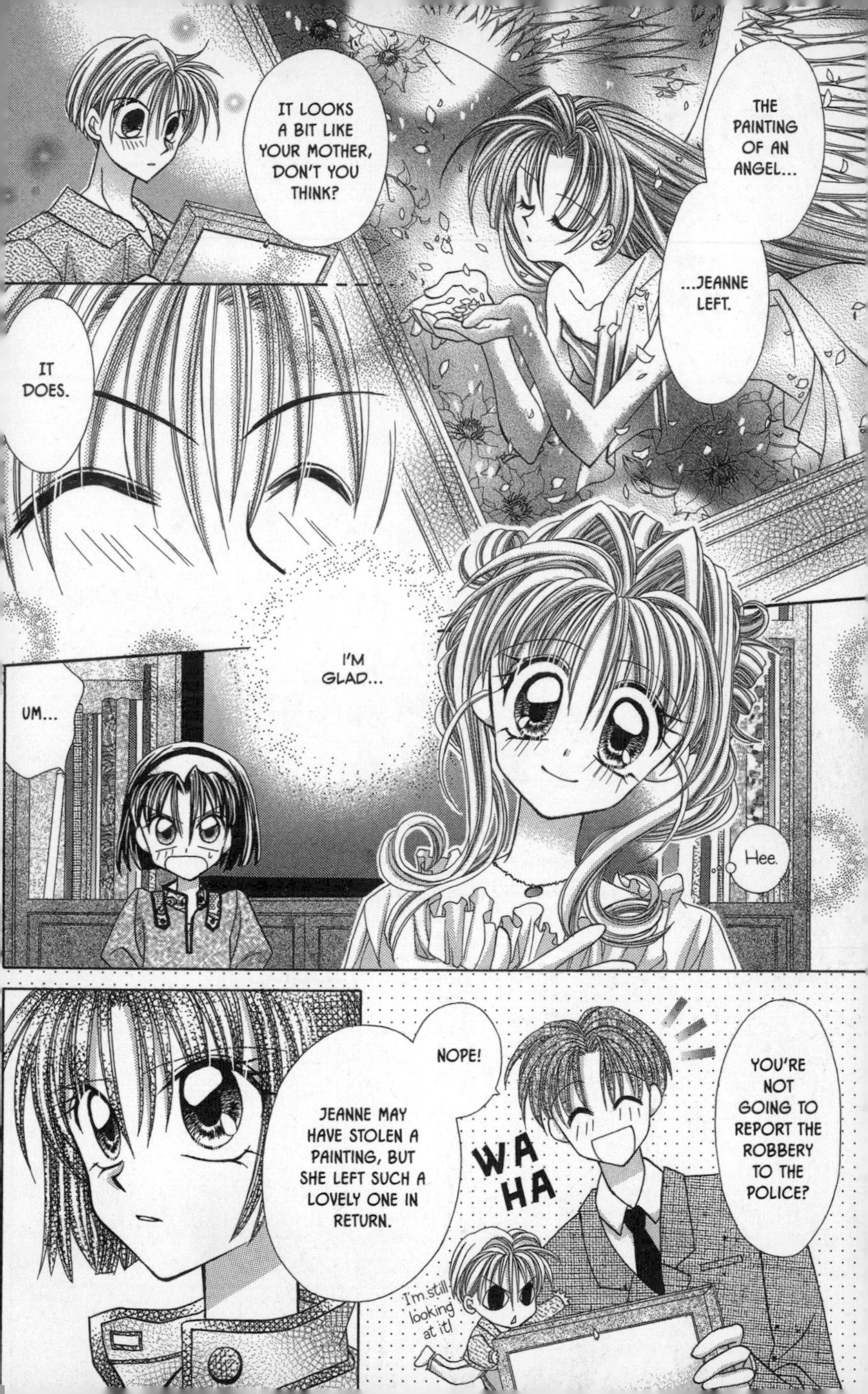
THE PAINTING OF AN ANGEL...
...JEANNE LEFT.
IT LOOKS A BIT LIKE YOUR MOTHER, DON'T YOU THINK?
IT DOES.
I'M GLAD...
Hee.
UM...
YOU'RE NOT GOING TO REPORT THE ROBBERY TO THE POLICE?
WA HA
NOPE!
JEANNE MAY HAVE STOLEN A PAINTING, BUT SHE LEFT SUCH A LOVELY ONE IN RETURN.
I'm still looking at it!

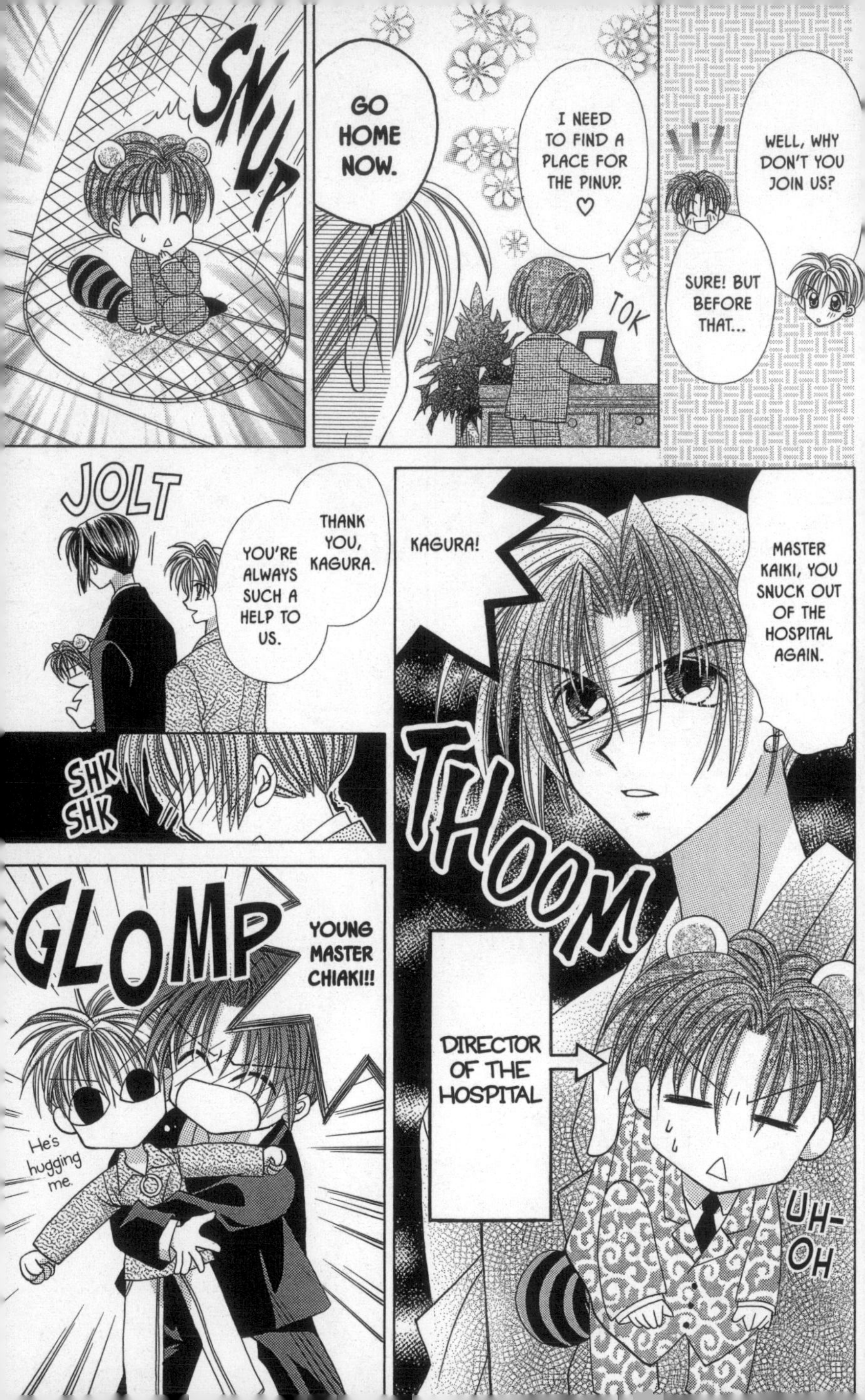
WELL, WHY DON'T YOU JOIN US?
SURE! BUT BEFORE THAT...
I NEED TO FIND A PLACE FOR THE PINUP. ♡
TOK
GO HOME NOW.
SNUP
MASTER KAIKI, YOU SNUCK OUT OF THE HOSPITAL AGAIN.
KAGURA!
THOOM
DIRECTOR OF THE HOSPITAL
UH-OH
THANK YOU, KAGURA.
YOU'RE ALWAYS SUCH A HELP TO US.
JOLT
SHK SHK
YOUNG MASTER CHIAKI!!
GLOMP
He's hugging me.

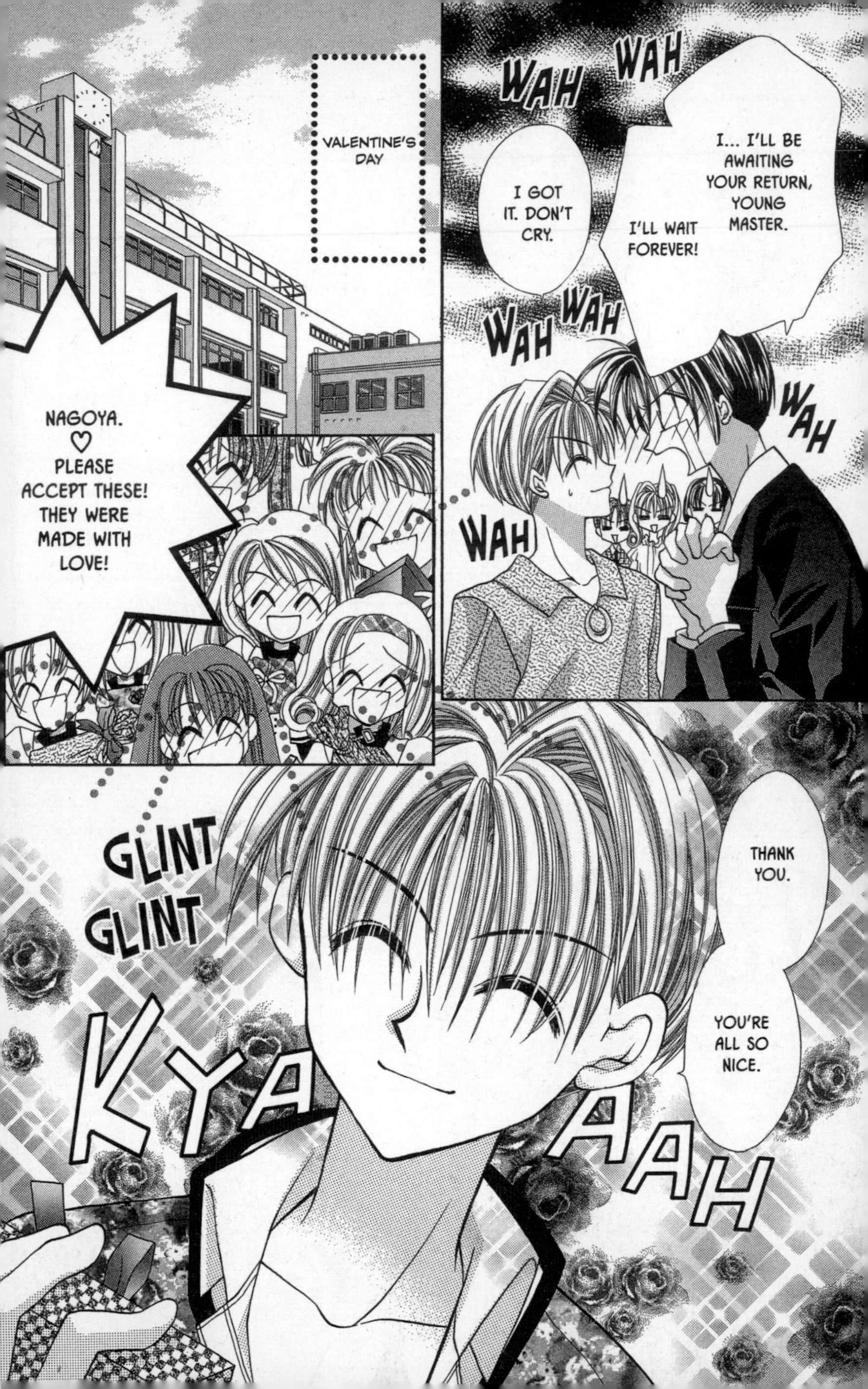
WAH WAH
I... I'LL BE AWAITING YOUR RETURN, YOUNG MASTER.
I'LL WAIT FOREVER!
I GOT IT. DON'T CRY.
WAH WAH
WAH
WAH
VALENTINE'S DAY
NAGOYA. ♡ PLEASE ACCEPT THESE! THEY WERE MADE WITH LOVE!
THANK YOU.
YOU'RE ALL SO NICE.
GLINT GLINT
KYAAAH

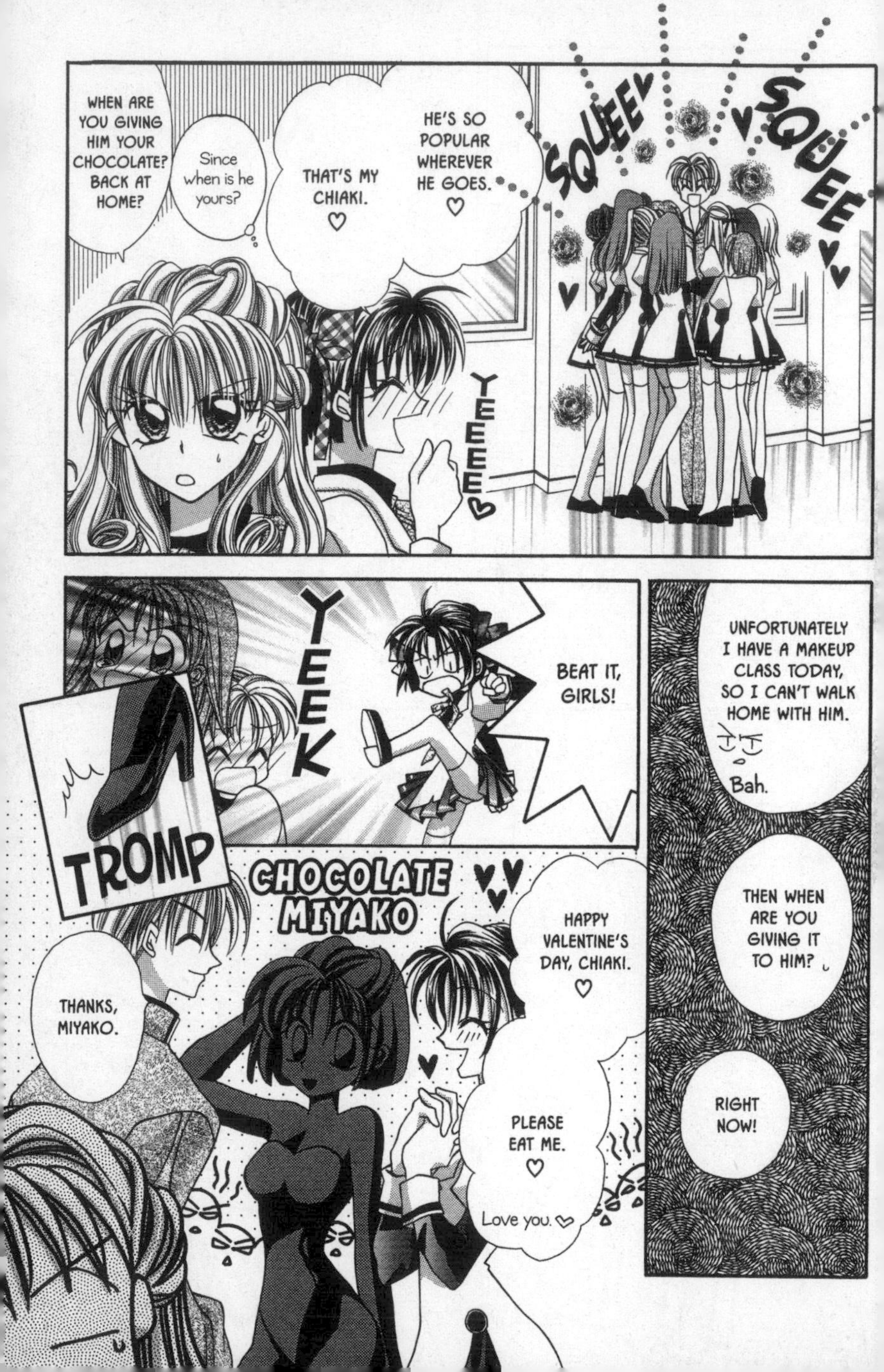
SQUEE
SQUEE
HE'S SO POPULAR WHEREVER HE GOES. ♡
THAT'S MY CHIAKI. ♡
Since when is he yours?
WHEN ARE YOU GIVING HIM YOUR CHOCOLATE? BACK AT HOME?
YEEEEE
UNFORTUNATELY I HAVE A MAKEUP CLASS TODAY, SO I CAN'T WALK HOME WITH HIM.
Bah.
THEN WHEN ARE YOU GIVING IT TO HIM?
RIGHT NOW!
BEAT IT, GIRLS!
YEEK
TROMP
CHOCOLATE MIYAKO
HAPPY VALENTINE'S DAY, CHIAKI. ♡
PLEASE EAT ME. ♡
Love you.
THANKS, MIYAKO.

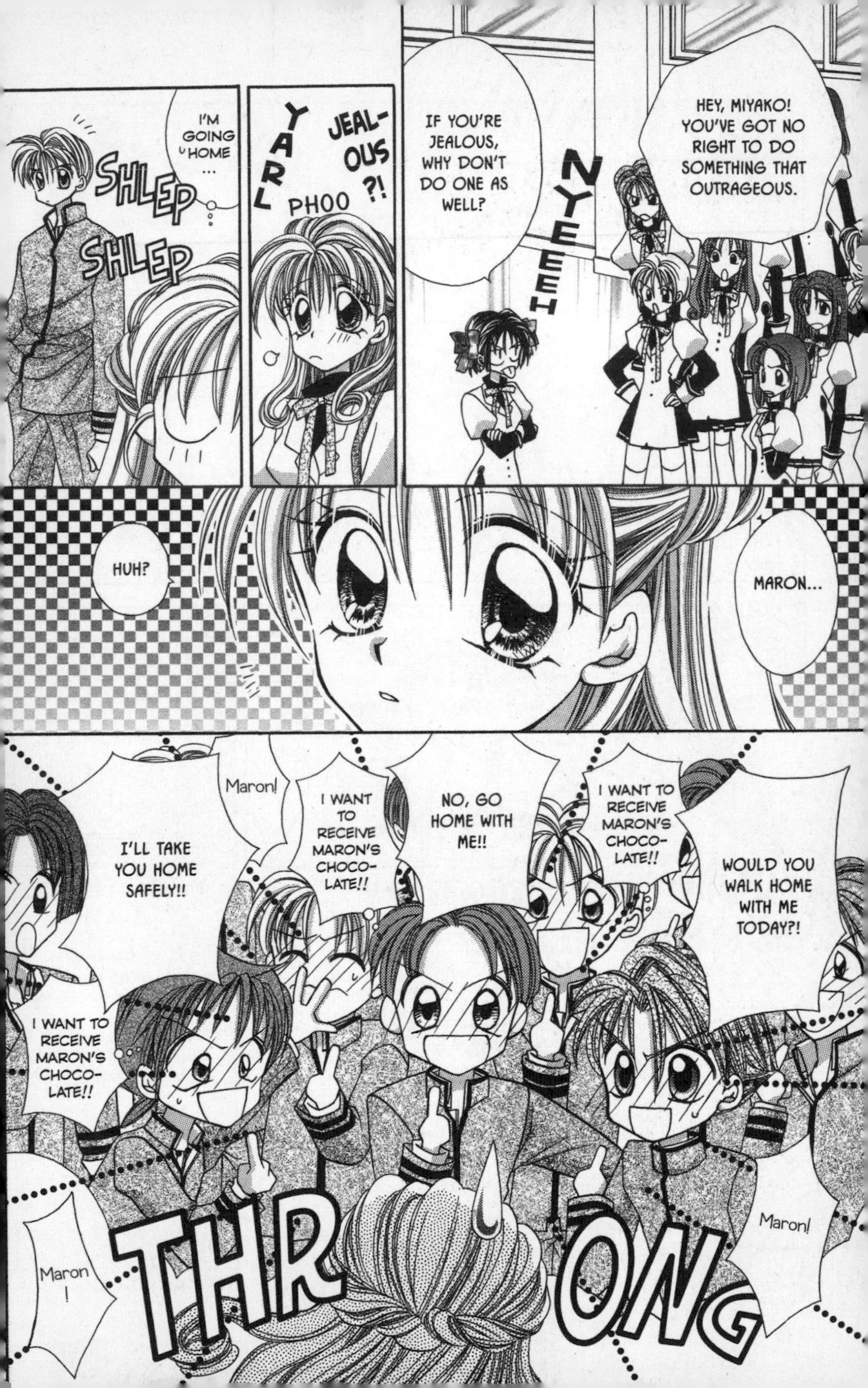
HEY, MIYAKO! YOU'VE GOT NO RIGHT TO DO SOMETHING THAT OUTRAGEOUS.
IF YOU'RE JEALOUS, WHY DON'T DO ONE AS WELL?
NYEEEEH
JEAL-OUS ?!
YARL
PHOO
I'M GOING HOME ...
SHLEP
SHLEP
MARON...
HUH?
WOULD YOU WALK HOME WITH ME TODAY?!
I WANT TO RECEIVE MARON'S CHOCO-LATE!!
NO, GO HOME WITH ME!!
I WANT TO RECEIVE MARON'S CHOCO-LATE!!
Maron!
I'LL TAKE YOU HOME SAFELY!!
Maron!
I WANT TO RECEIVE MARON'S CHOCO-LATE!!
Maron !
THRONG

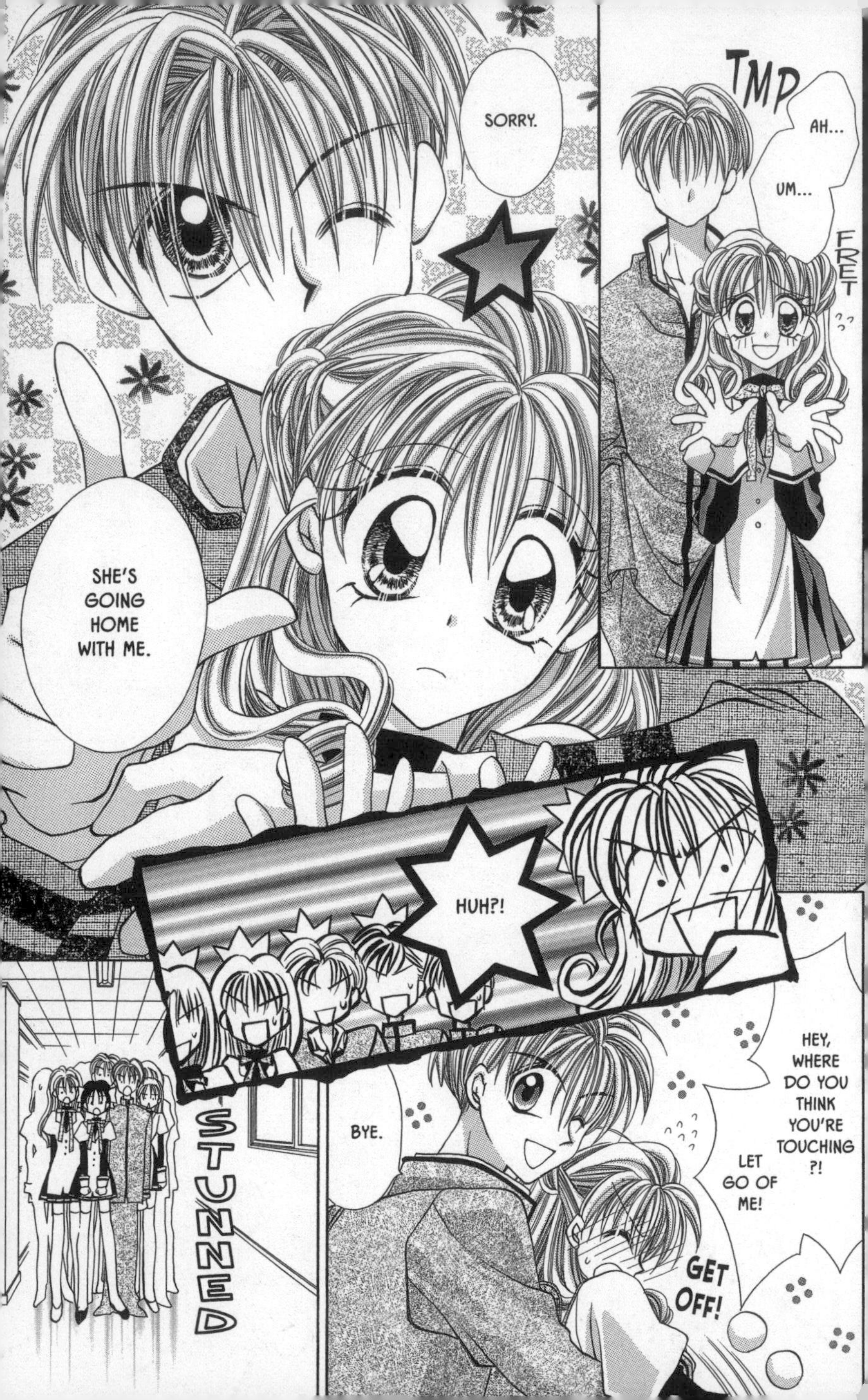
TMP
AH...
UM...
FRET
SORRY.
SHE'S GOING HOME WITH ME.
HUH?!
HEY, WHERE DO YOU THINK YOU'RE TOUCHING?!
LET GO OF ME!
BYE.
GET OFF!
STUNNED

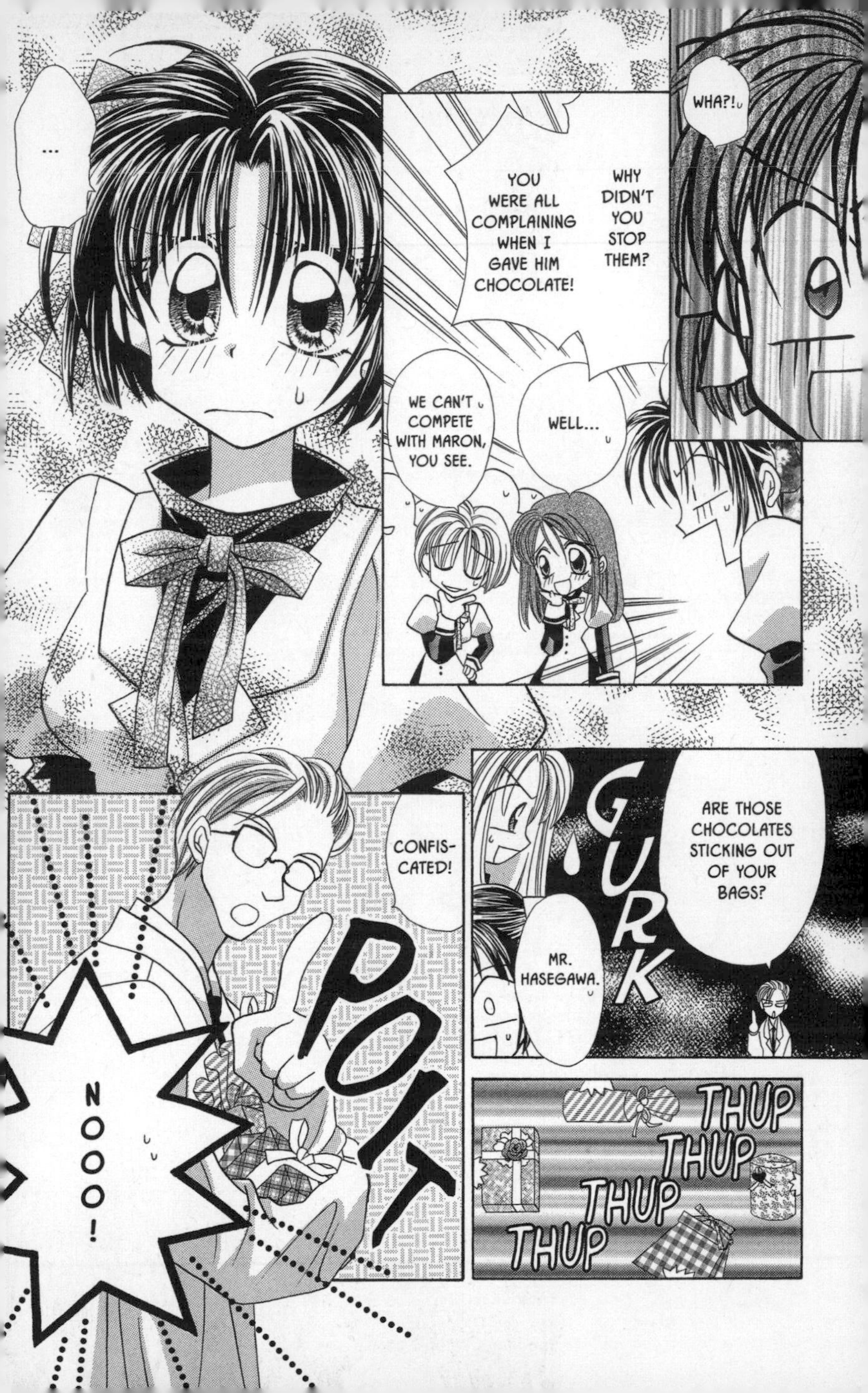
WHA?!
WHY DIDN'T YOU STOP THEM?
YOU WERE ALL COMPLAINING WHEN I GAVE HIM CHOCOLATE!
WELL...
WE CAN'T COMPETE WITH MARON, YOU SEE.
...
ARE THOSE CHOCOLATES STICKING OUT OF YOUR BAGS?
GURK
MR. HASEGAWA.
THUP THUP THUP THUP
CONFIS-CATED!
POI
NOOOO!

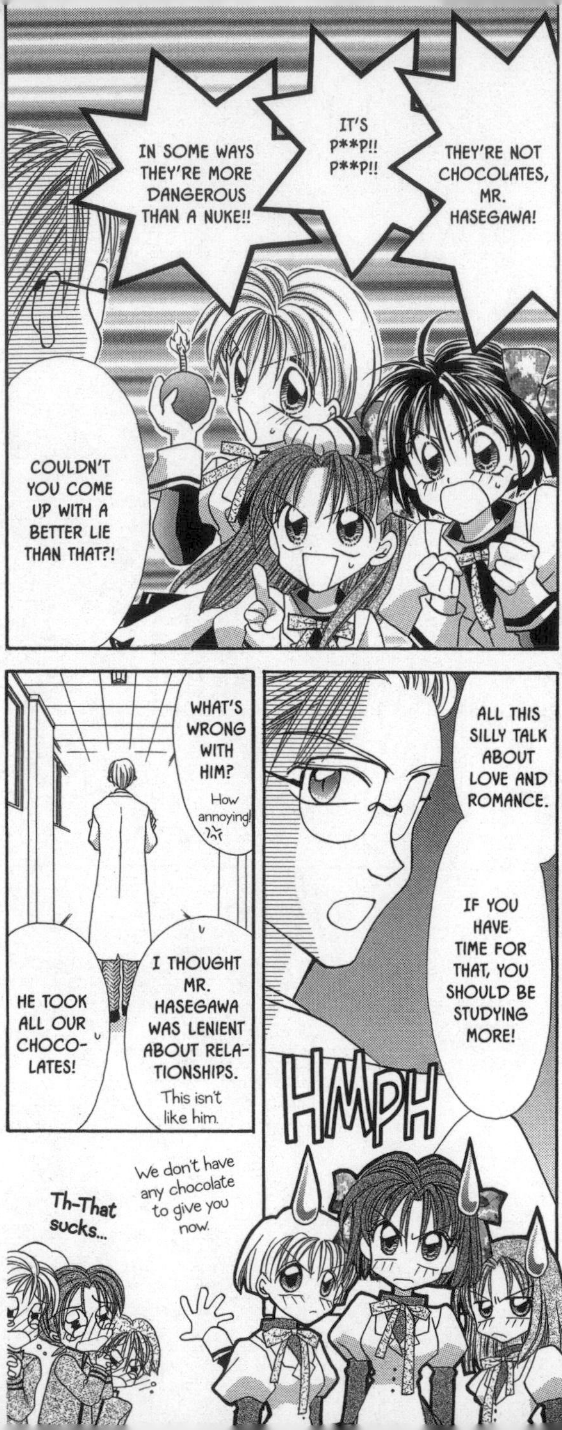
THEY'RE NOT CHOCOLATES, MR. HASEGAWA!
IT'S P**P!! P**P!!
IN SOME WAYS THEY'RE MORE DANGEROUS THAN A NUKE!!
COULDN'T YOU COME UP WITH A BETTER LIE THAN THAT?!
ALL THIS SILLY TALK ABOUT LOVE AND ROMANCE.
IF YOU HAVE TIME FOR THAT, YOU SHOULD BE STUDYING MORE!
HMPH
WHAT'S WRONG WITH HIM?
How annoying!
I THOUGHT MR. HASEGAWA WAS LENIENT ABOUT RELATIONSHIPS.
This isn't like him.
HE TOOK ALL OUR CHOCO-LATES!
We don't have any chocolate to give you now.
Th-That sucks...

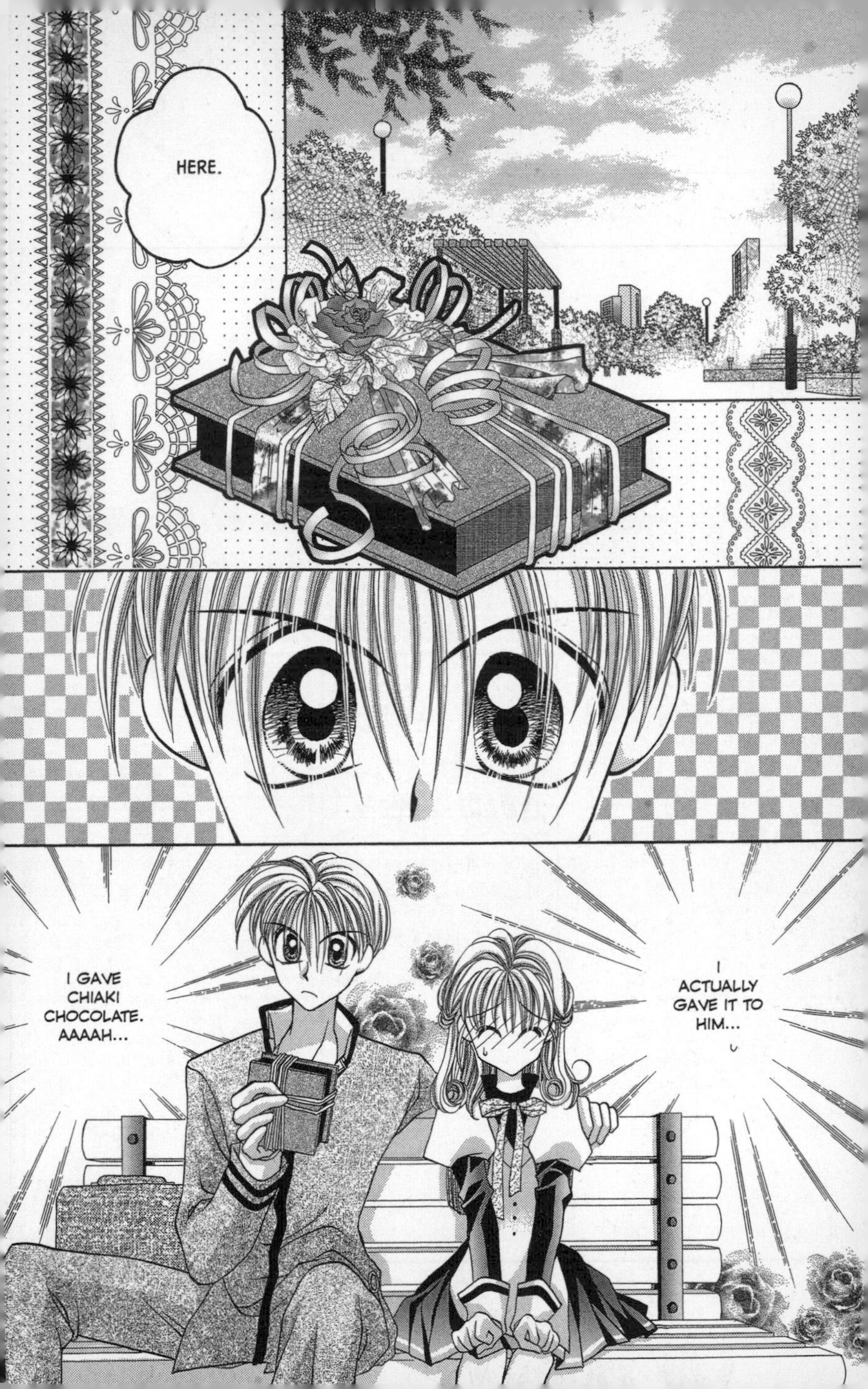
HERE.
I ACTUALLY GAVE IT TO HIM...
I GAVE CHIAKI CHOCOLATE. AAAAH...

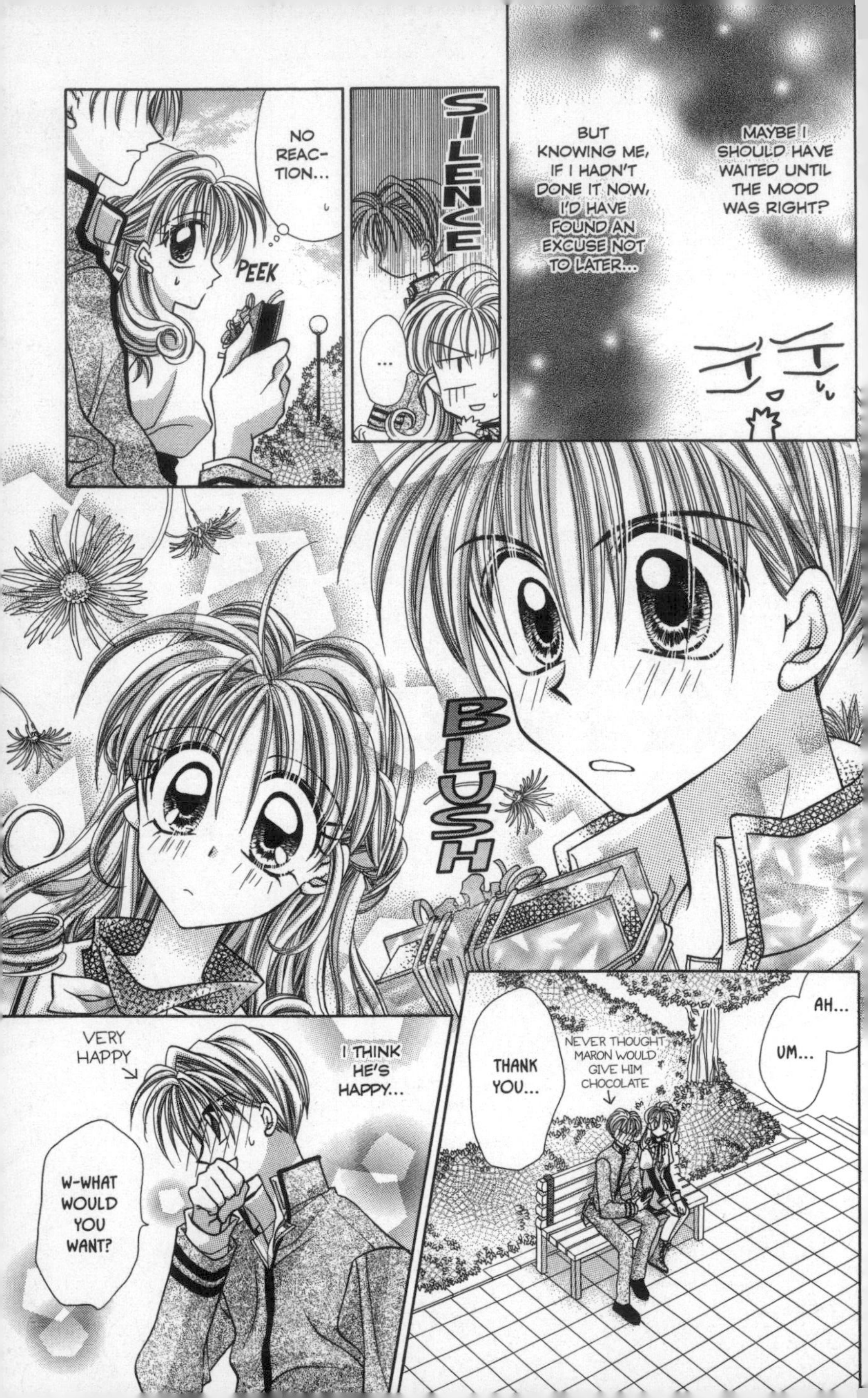

MAYBE I SHOULD HAVE WAITED UNTIL THE MOOD WAS RIGHT?
BUT KNOWING ME, IF I HADN'T DONE IT NOW, I'D HAVE FOUND AN EXCUSE NOT TO LATER...
SILENCE
...
NO REACTION...
PEEK
BLUSH
AH...
UM...
NEVER THOUGHT MARON WOULD GIVE HIM CHOCOLATE
THANK YOU...
I THINK HE'S HAPPY...
VERY HAPPY
W-WHAT WOULD YOU WANT?

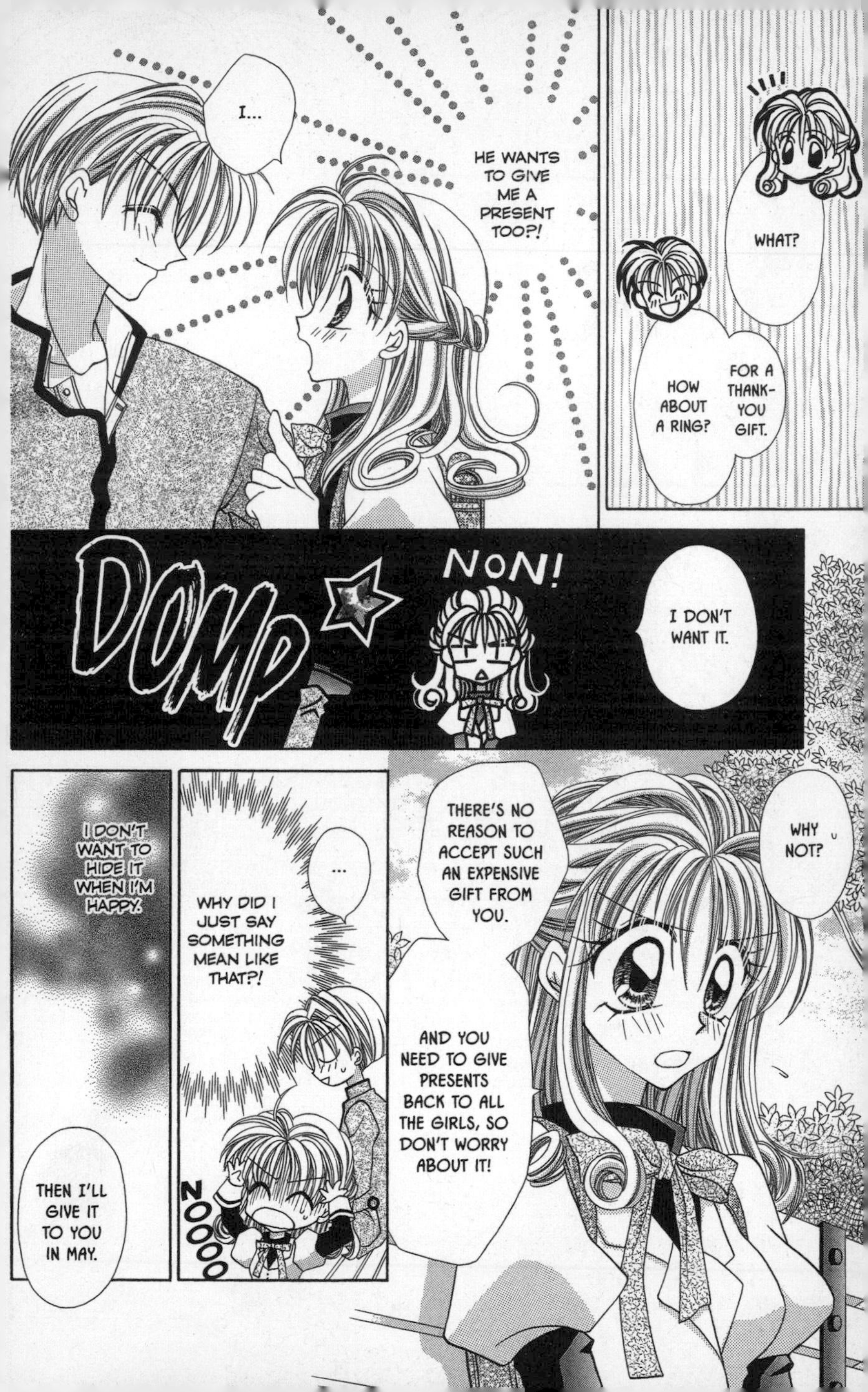
WHAT?
FOR A THANK-YOU GIFT.
HOW ABOUT A RING?
HE WANTS TO GIVE ME A PRESENT TOO?!
I...
I DON'T WANT IT.
NON!
DOMP
WHY NOT?
THERE'S NO REASON TO ACCEPT SUCH AN EXPENSIVE GIFT FROM YOU.
AND YOU NEED TO GIVE PRESENTS BACK TO ALL THE GIRLS, SO DON'T WORRY ABOUT IT!
...
WHY DID I JUST SAY SOMETHING MEAN LIKE THAT?!
NOOOO
I DON'T WANT TO HIDE IT WHEN I'M HAPPY.
THEN I'LL GIVE IT TO YOU IN MAY.

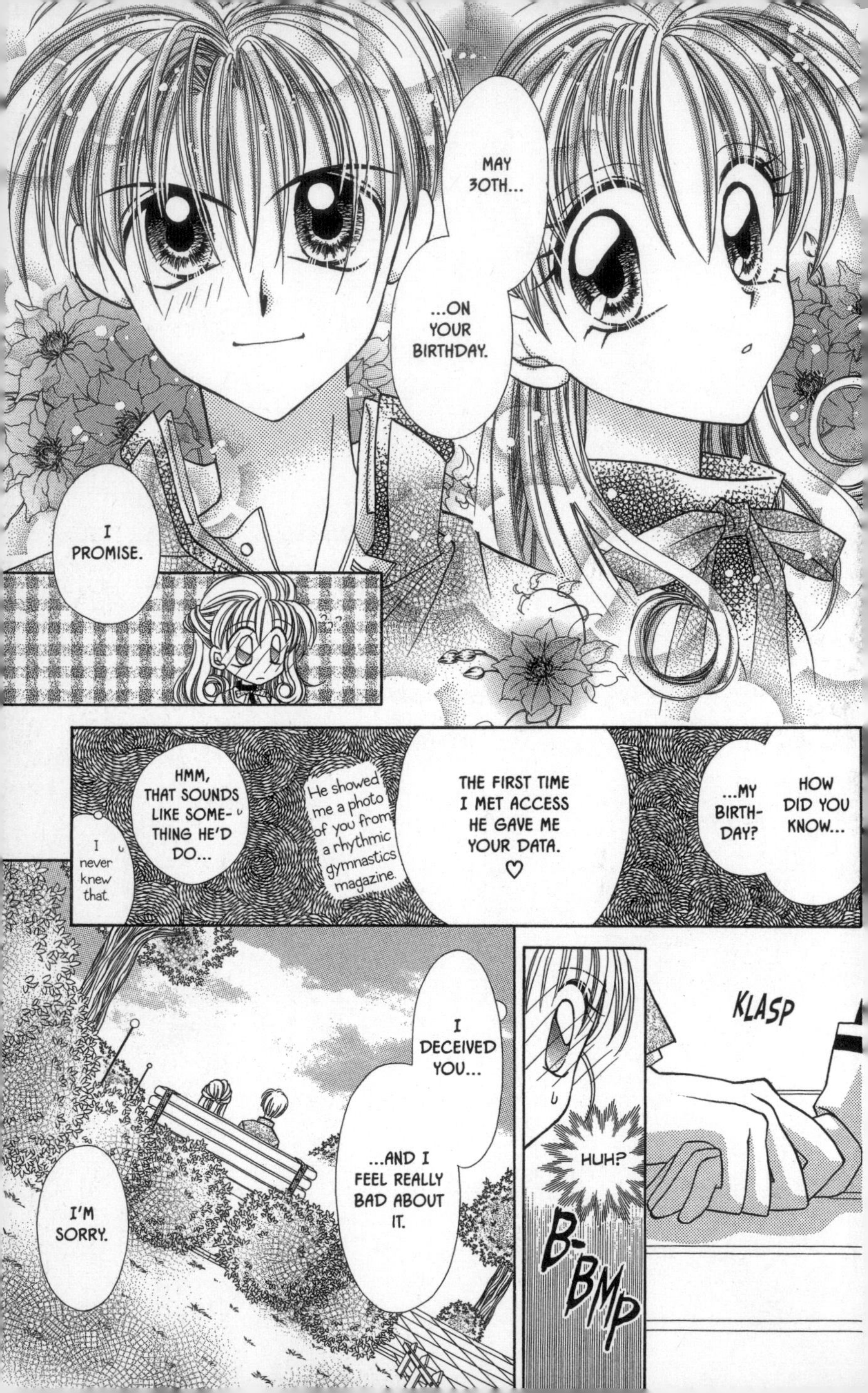
MAY 30TH...
...ON YOUR BIRTHDAY.
I PROMISE.
HOW DID YOU KNOW...
...MY BIRTH-DAY?
THE FIRST TIME I MET ACCESS HE GAVE ME YOUR DATA. ♡
He showed me a photo of you from a rhythmic gymnastics magazine.
HMM, THAT SOUNDS LIKE SOME-THING HE'D DO...
I never knew that.
KLASP
HUH?
B-BMP
I DECEIVED YOU...
...AND I FEEL REALLY BAD ABOUT IT.
I'M SORRY.

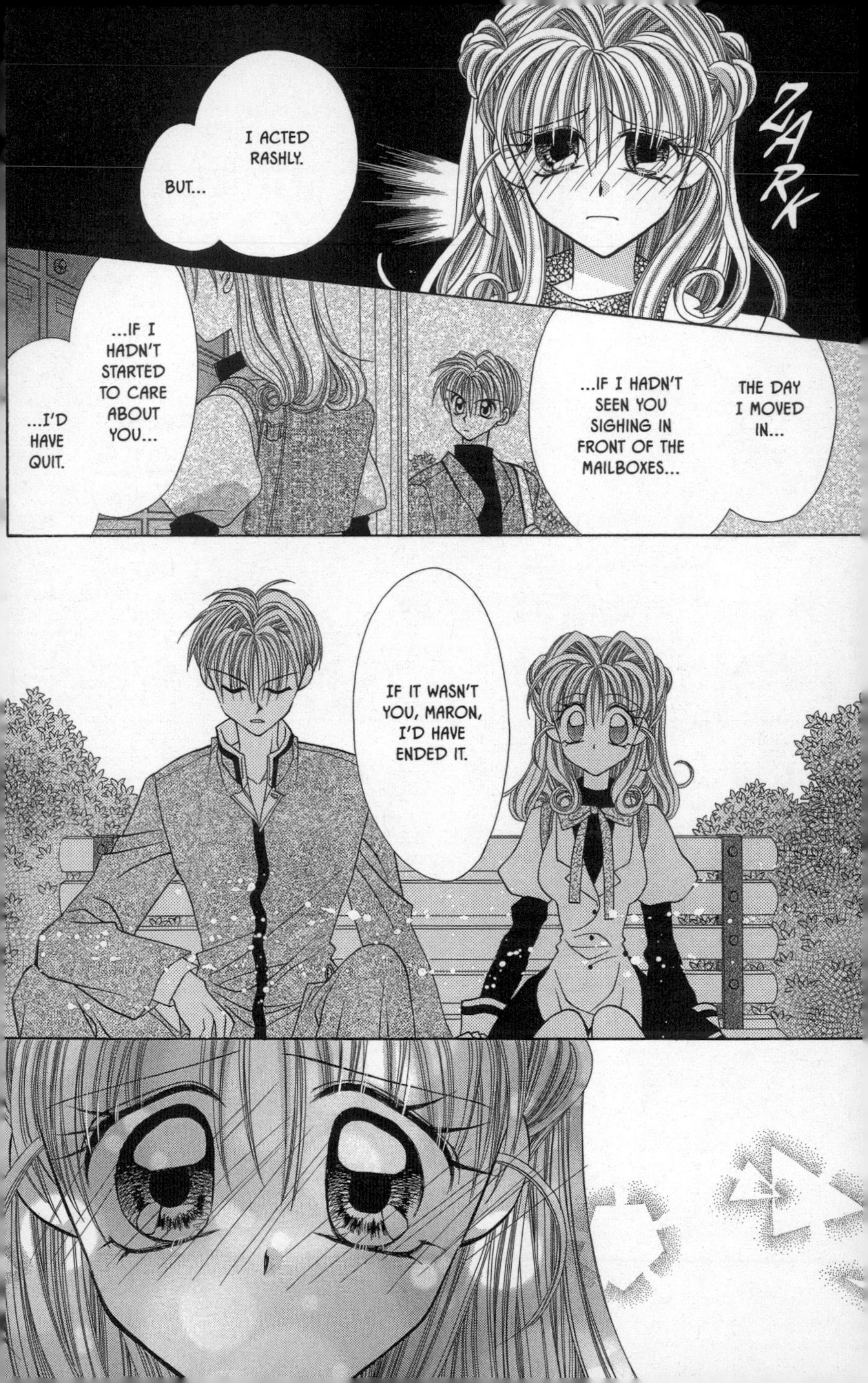
ZARK
I ACTED RASHLY.
BUT...
THE DAY I MOVED IN...
...IF I HADN'T SEEN YOU SIGHING IN FRONT OF THE MAILBOXES...
...IF I HADN'T STARTED TO CARE ABOUT YOU...
...I'D HAVE QUIT.
IF IT WASN'T YOU, MARON, I'D HAVE ENDED IT.

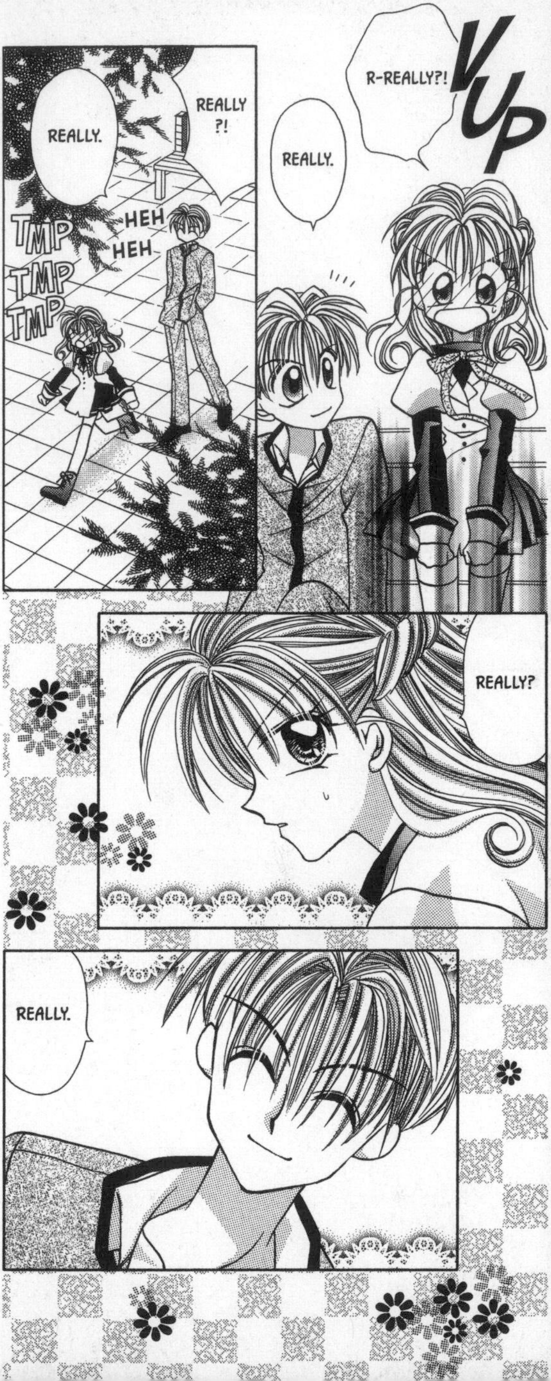
R-REALLY?!
VUP
REALLY.
REALLY ?!
REALLY.
HEH HEH
TMP
TMP
TMP
REALLY?
REALLY.

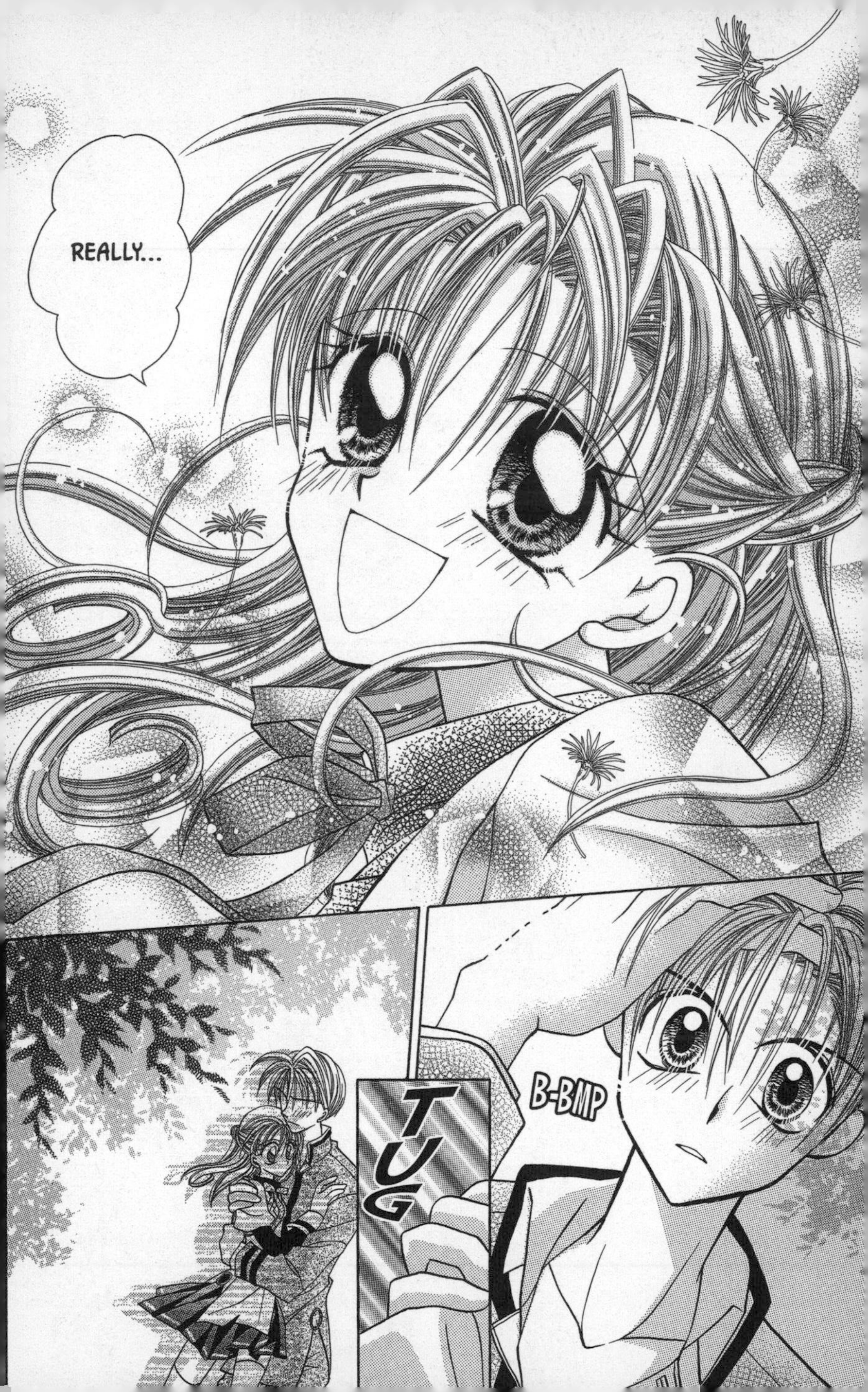
REALLY...
B-BMP
TUG

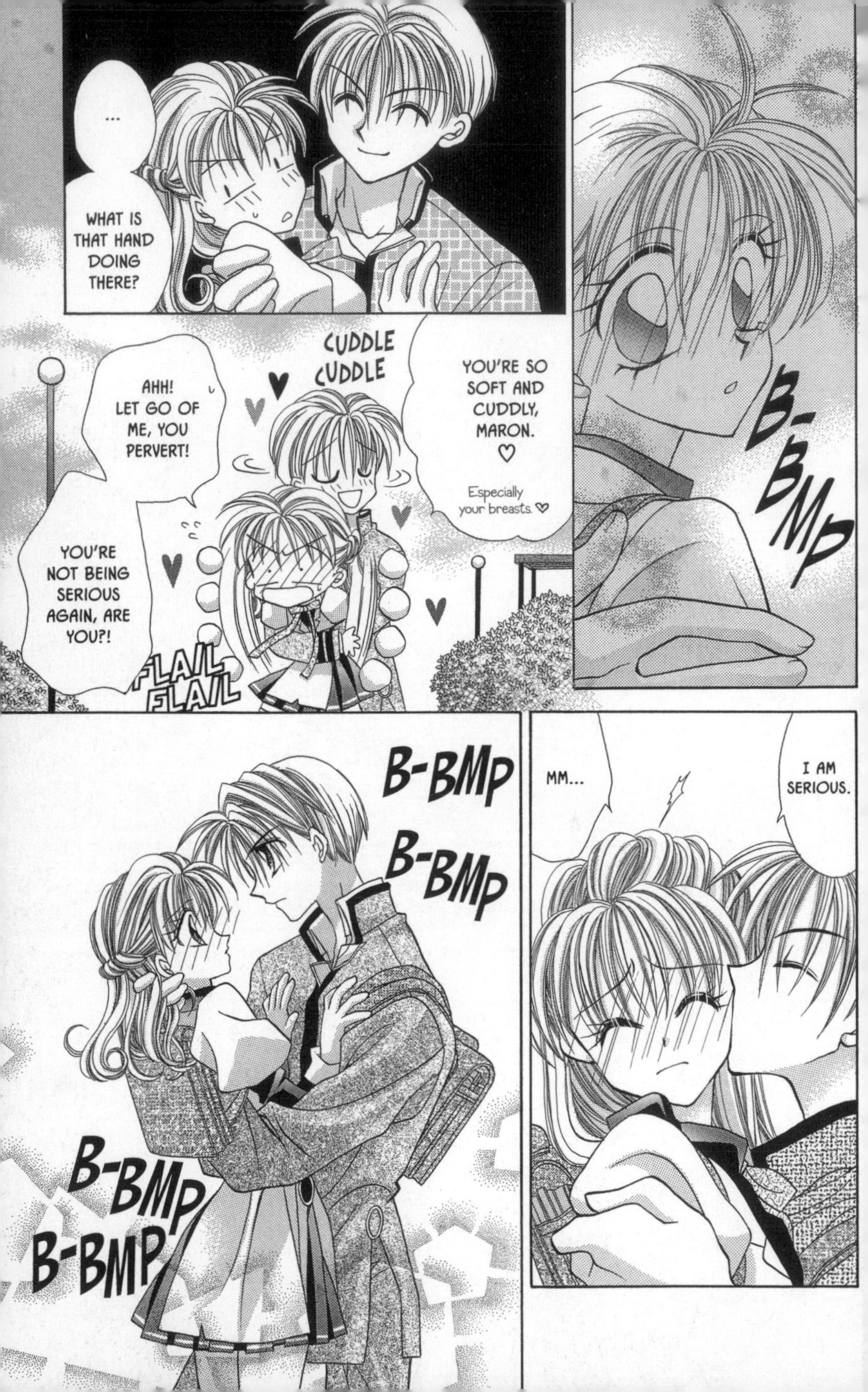
B-BMP
...
WHAT IS THAT HAND DOING THERE?
YOU'RE SO SOFT AND CUDDLY, MARON. ♡
Especially your breasts. ♡
CUDDLE CUDDLE
AHH! LET GO OF ME, YOU PERVERT!
YOU'RE NOT BEING SERIOUS AGAIN, ARE YOU?!
FLAIL FLAIL
I AM SERIOUS.
MM...
B-BMP
B-BMP
B-BMP
B-BMP

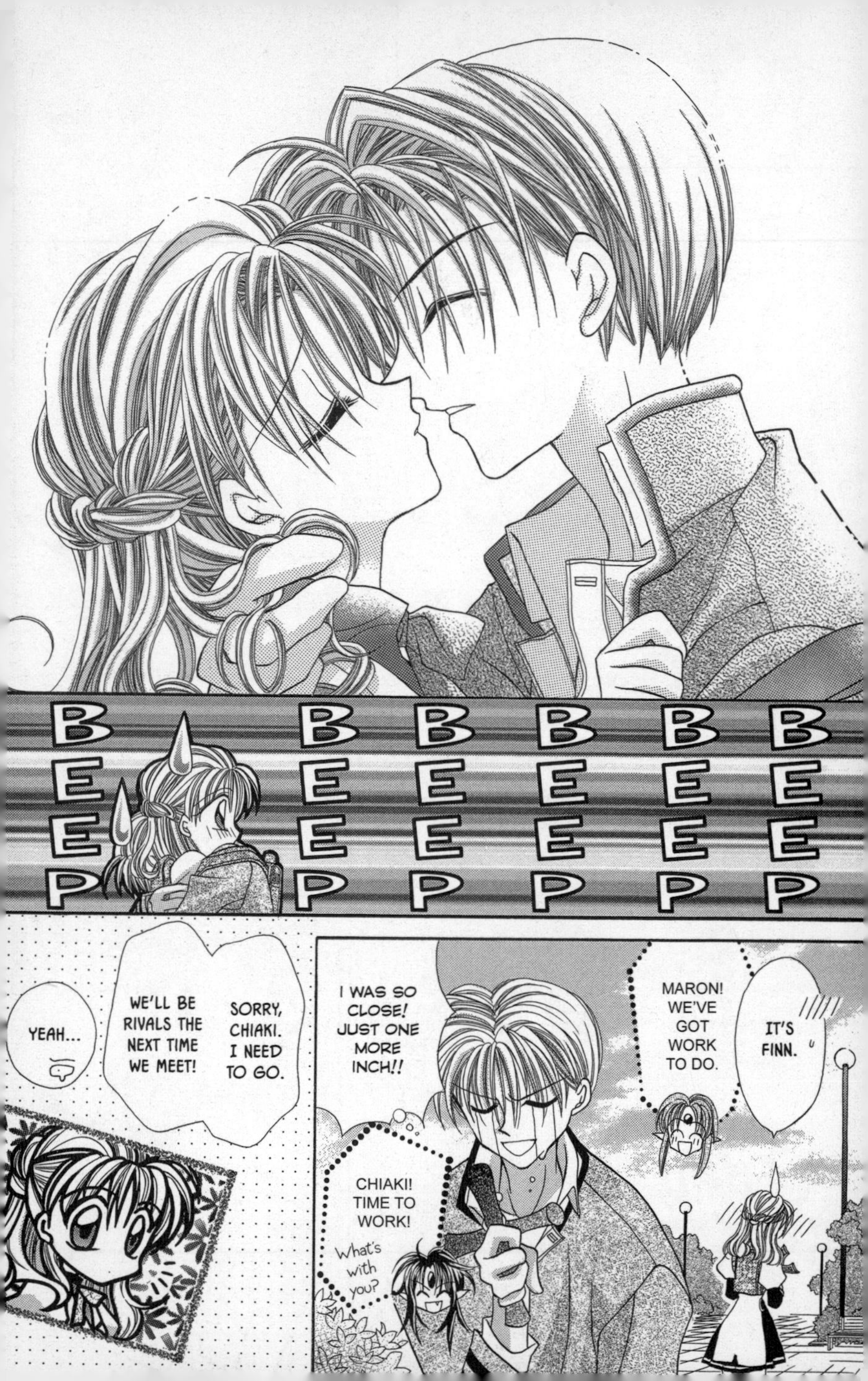
BEEP
BEEP
BEEP
BEEP
BEEP
BEEP
IT'S FINN.
MARON! WE'VE GOT WORK TO DO.
I WAS SO CLOSE! JUST ONE MORE INCH!!
CHIAKI! TIME TO WORK!
What's with you?
SORRY, CHIAKI. I NEED TO GO.
WE'LL BE RIVALS THE NEXT TIME WE MEET!
YEAH...

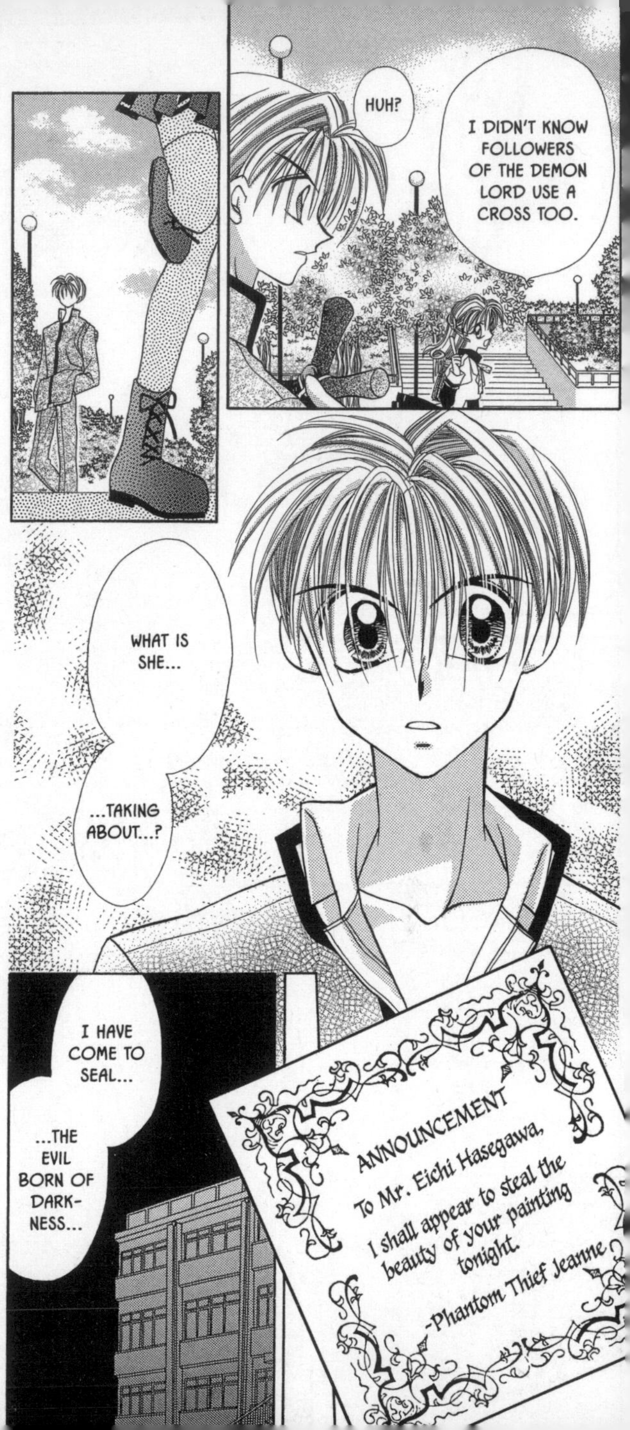
HUH?
I DIDN'T KNOW FOLLOWERS OF THE DEMON LORD USE A CROSS TOO.
WHAT IS SHE...
...TAKING ABOUT...?
ANNOUNCEMENT
To Mr. Eichi Hasegawa,
I shall appear to steal the beauty of your painting tonight.
-Phantom Thief Jeanne
I HAVE COME TO SEAL...
...THE EVIL BORN OF DARK-NESS...

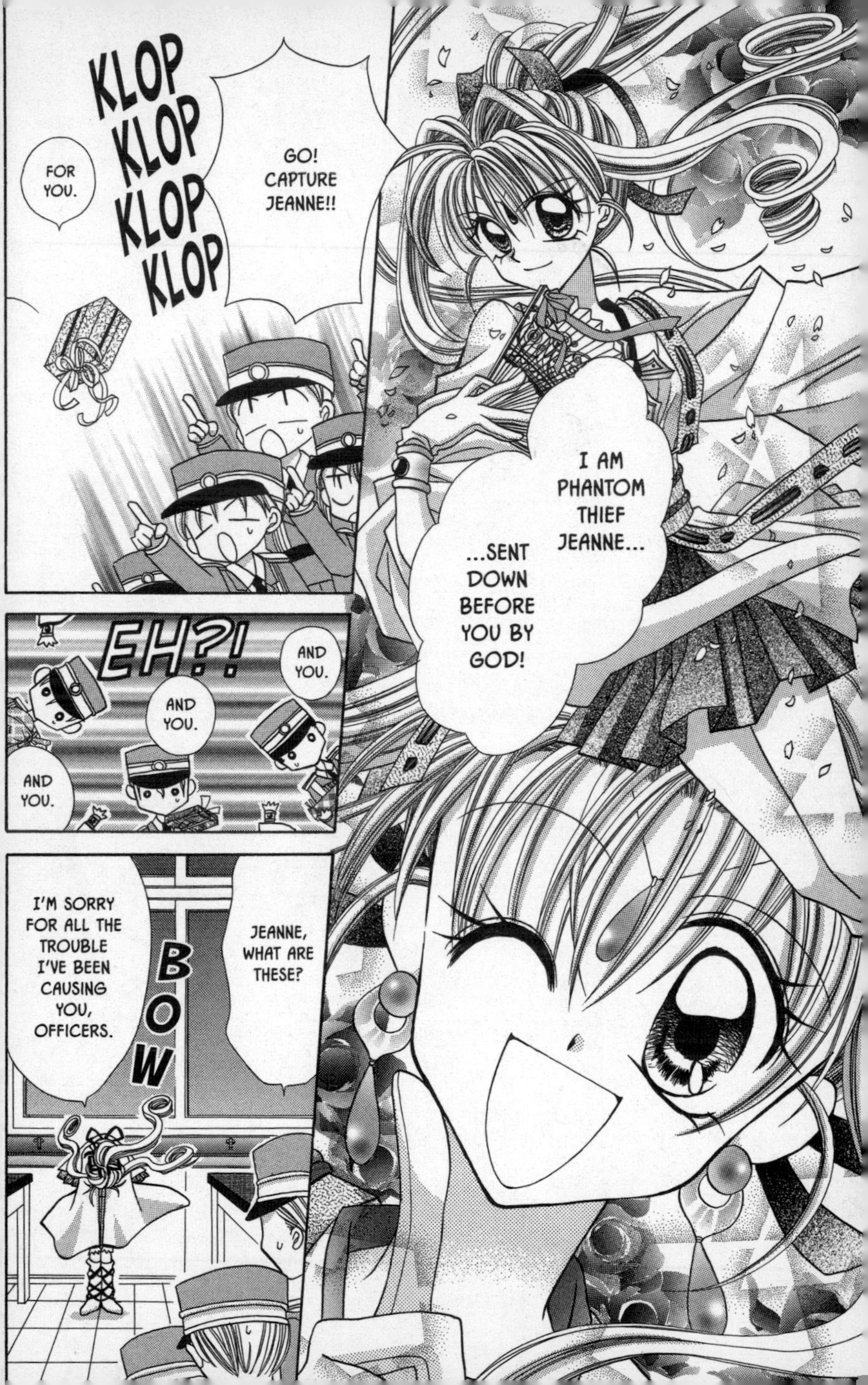
I AM PHANTOM THIEF JEANNE...
...SENT DOWN BEFORE YOU BY GOD!
GO! CAPTURE JEANNE!!
KLOP KLOP KLOP KLOP
FOR YOU.
AND YOU.
AND YOU.
EH?!
AND YOU.
JEANNE, WHAT ARE THESE?
BOW
I'M SORRY FOR ALL THE TROUBLE I'VE BEEN CAUSING YOU, OFFICERS.

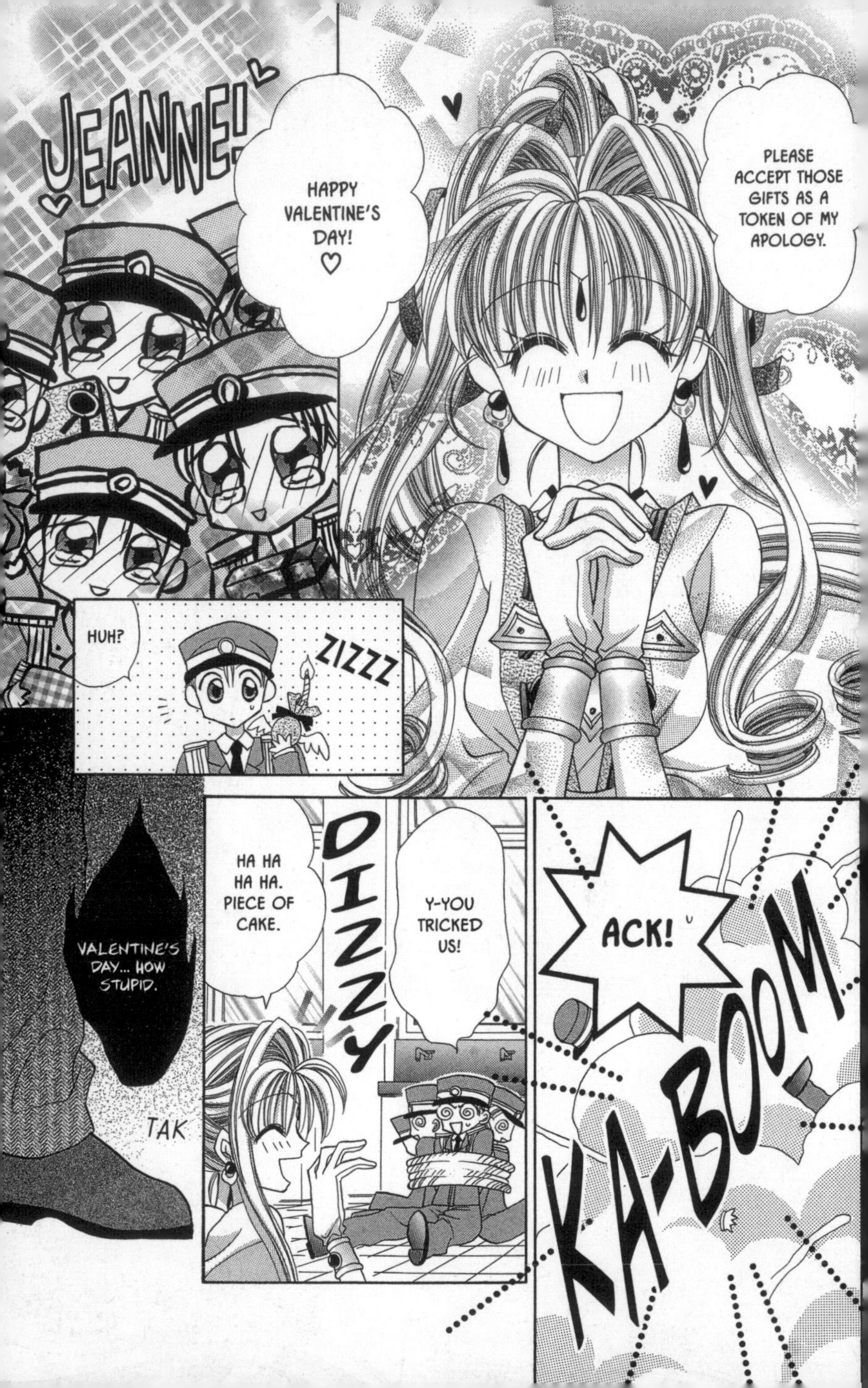
PLEASE ACCEPT THOSE GIFTS AS A TOKEN OF MY APOLOGY.
HAPPY VALENTINE'S DAY! ♡
JEANNE!
HUH?
ZIZZZ
ACK!
KA-BOOM
Y-YOU TRICKED US!
HA HA HA HA. PIECE OF CAKE.
DIZZY
VALENTINE'S DAY... HOW STUPID.
TAK

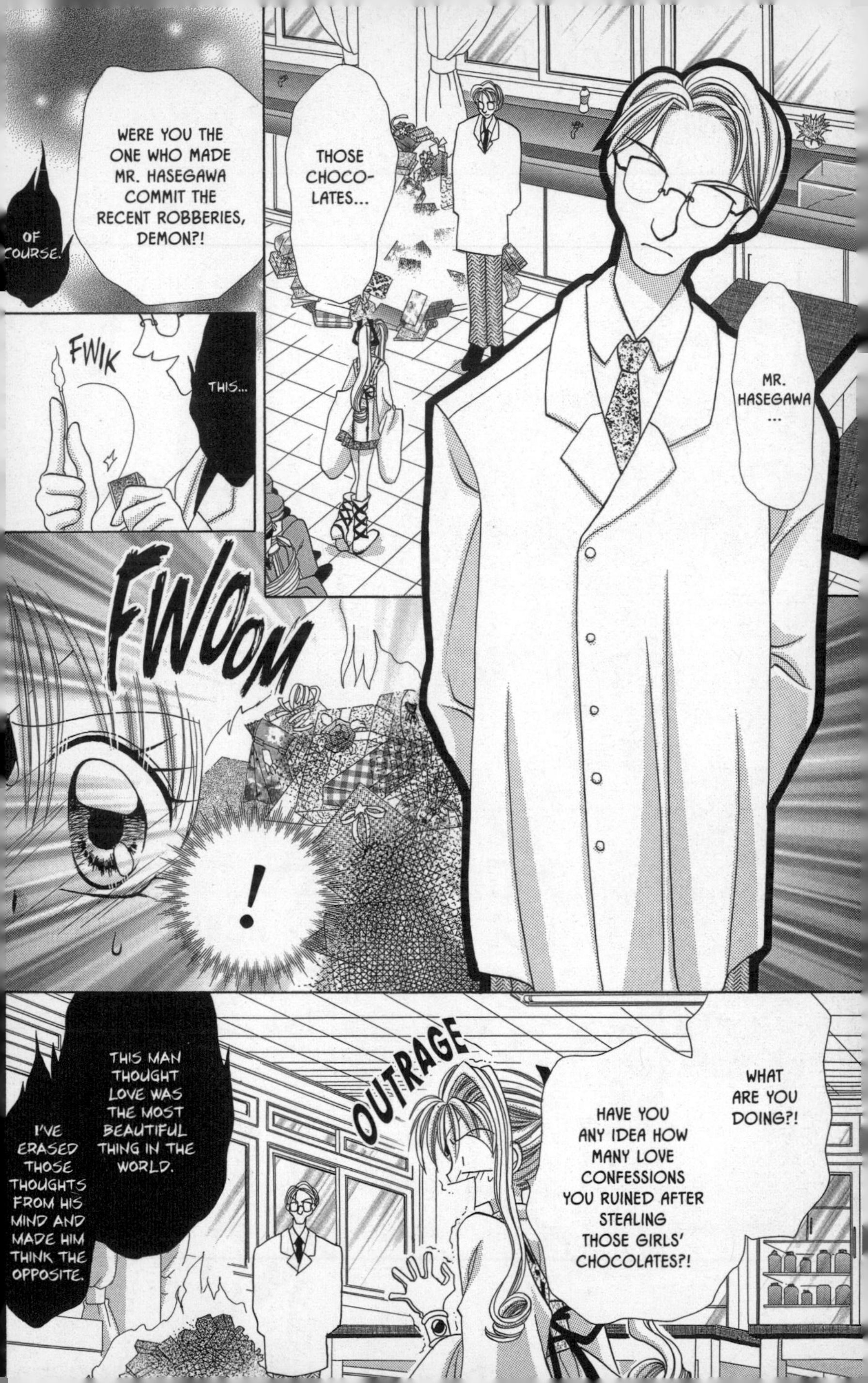
MR. HASEGAWA ...
THOSE CHOCO-LATES...
WERE YOU THE ONE WHO MADE MR. HASEGAWA COMMIT THE RECENT ROBBERIES, DEMON?!
OF COURSE.
FWIK
THIS...
FWOOM
!
WHAT ARE YOU DOING?!
HAVE YOU ANY IDEA HOW MANY LOVE CONFESSIONS YOU RUINED AFTER STEALING THOSE GIRLS' CHOCOLATES?!
OUTRAGE
THIS MAN THOUGHT LOVE WAS THE MOST BEAUTIFUL THING IN THE WORLD.
I'VE ERASED THOSE THOUGHTS FROM HIS MIND AND MADE HIM THINK THE OPPOSITE.

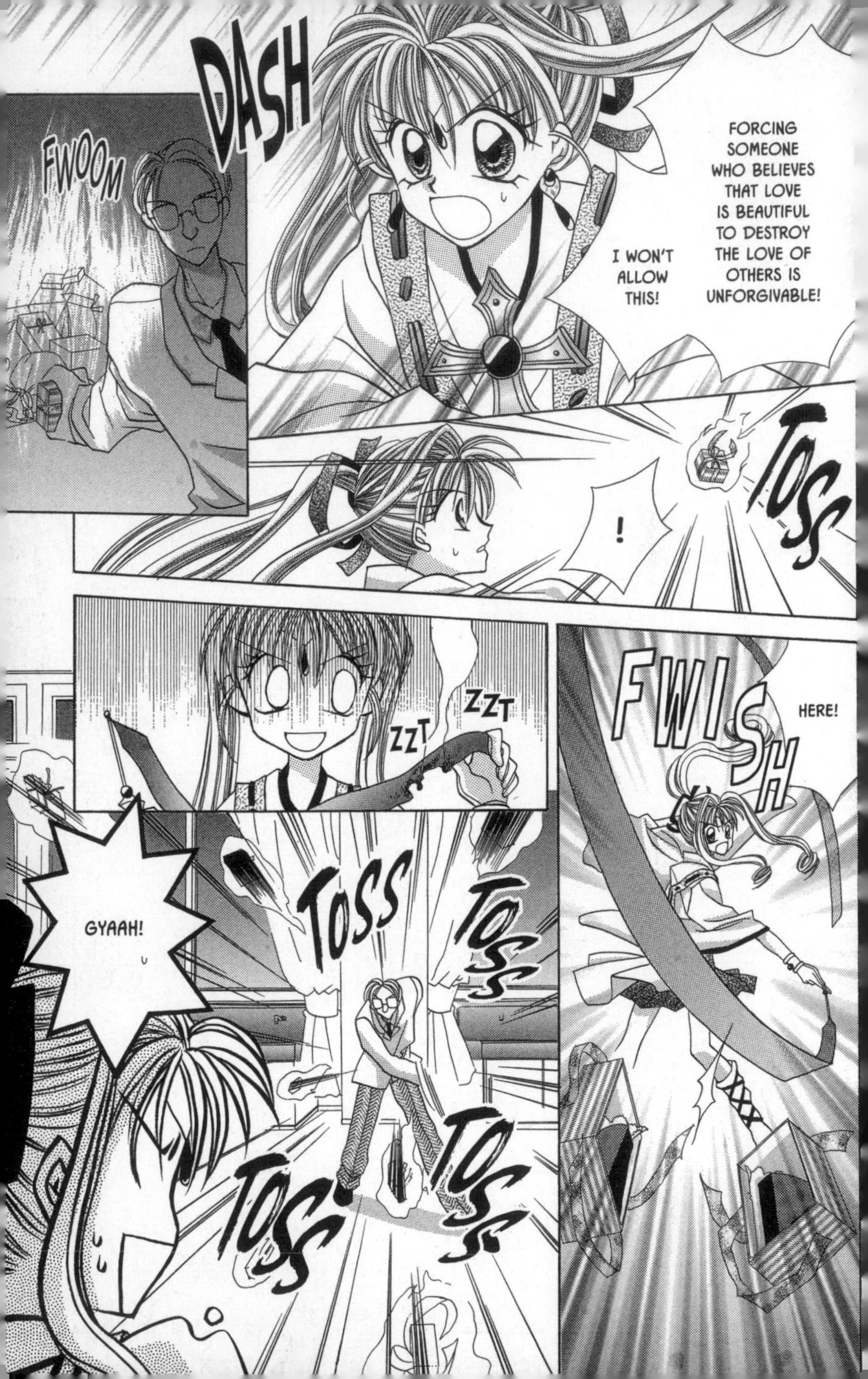
DASH
FORCING SOMEONE WHO BELIEVES THAT LOVE IS BEAUTIFUL TO DESTROY THE LOVE OF OTHERS IS UNFORGIVABLE!
I WON'T ALLOW THIS!
FWOOM
TOSS
!
FWISH
HERE!
ZZT
ZZT
TOSS
TOSS
GYAAH!
TOSS
TOSS

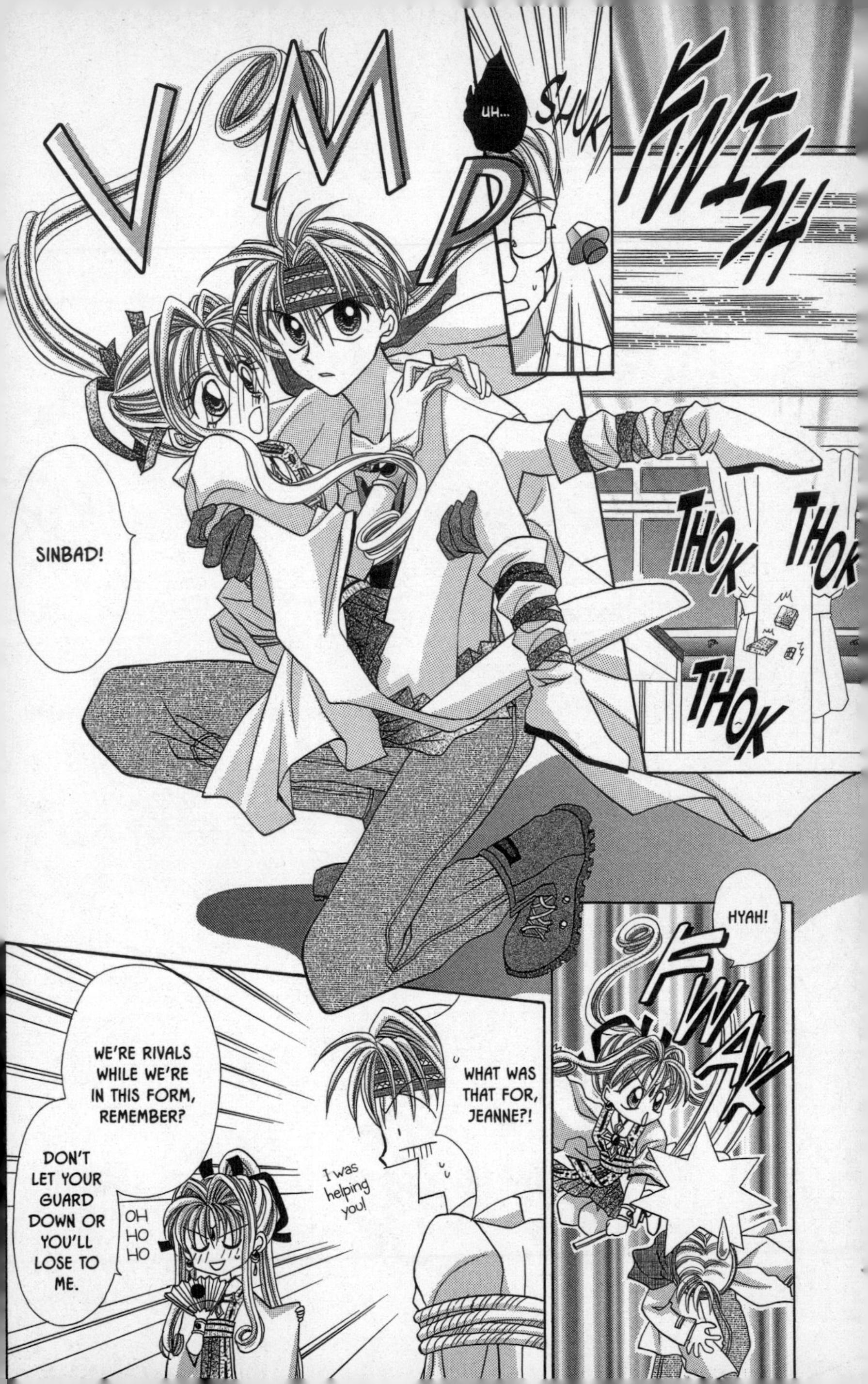
FWISH
SHUK
UH...
VMP
THOK THOK
THOK
SINBAD!
HYAH!
FWAK
WHAT WAS THAT FOR, JEANNE?!
I was helping you!
WE'RE RIVALS WHILE WE'RE IN THIS FORM, REMEMBER?
DON'T LET YOUR GUARD DOWN OR YOU'LL LOSE TO ME.
OH HO HO

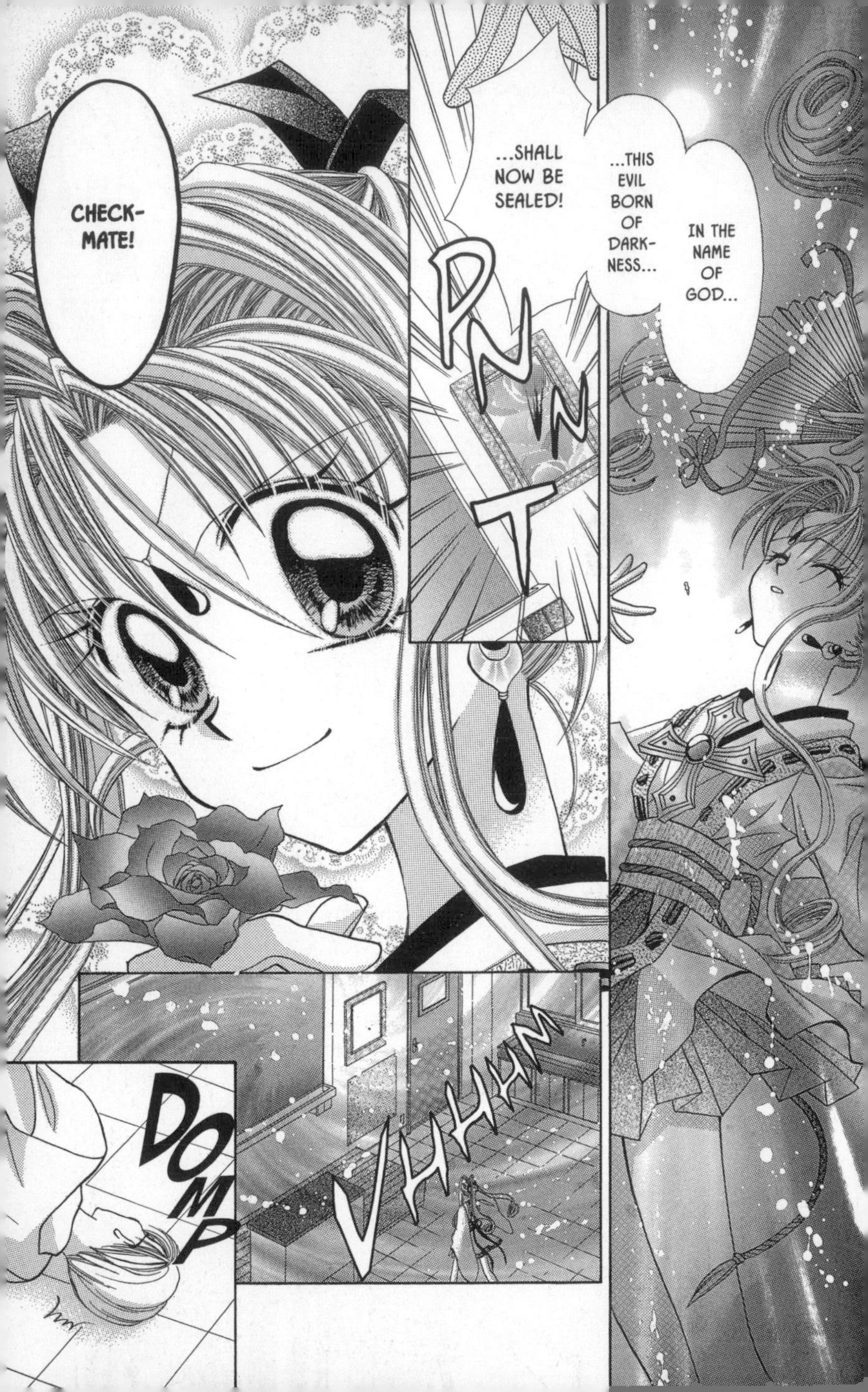
IN THE NAME OF GOD...
...THIS EVIL BORN OF DARKNESS...
...SHALL NOW BE SEALED!
PNNT
CHECK-MATE!
VHHHM
DOMP

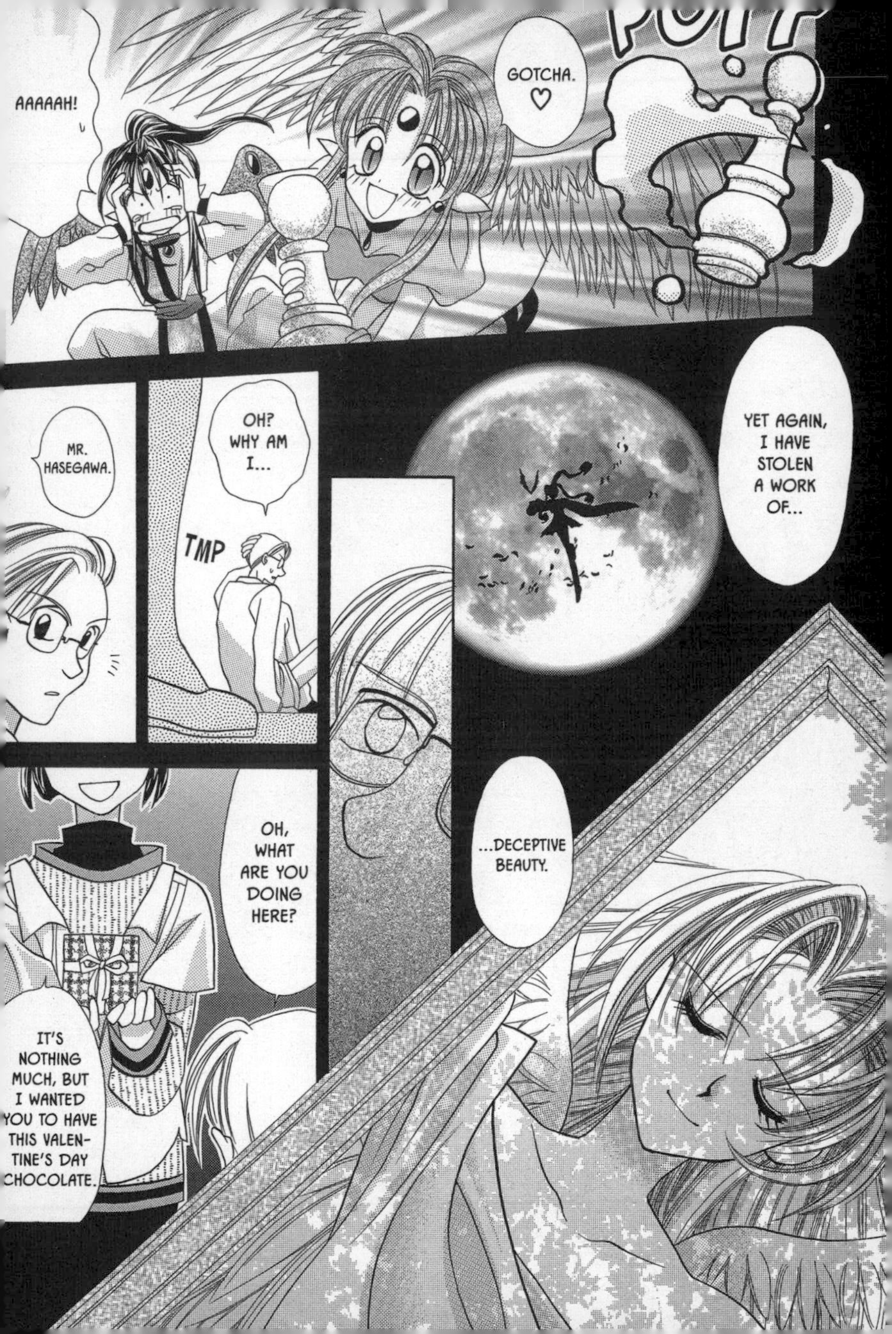
GOTCHA. ♡
AAAAAH!
YET AGAIN, I HAVE STOLEN A WORK OF...
...DECEPTIVE BEAUTY.
OH? WHY AM I...
TMP
MR. HASEGAWA.
OH, WHAT ARE YOU DOING HERE?
IT'S NOTHING MUCH, BUT I WANTED YOU TO HAVE THIS VALENTINE'S DAY CHOCOLATE.

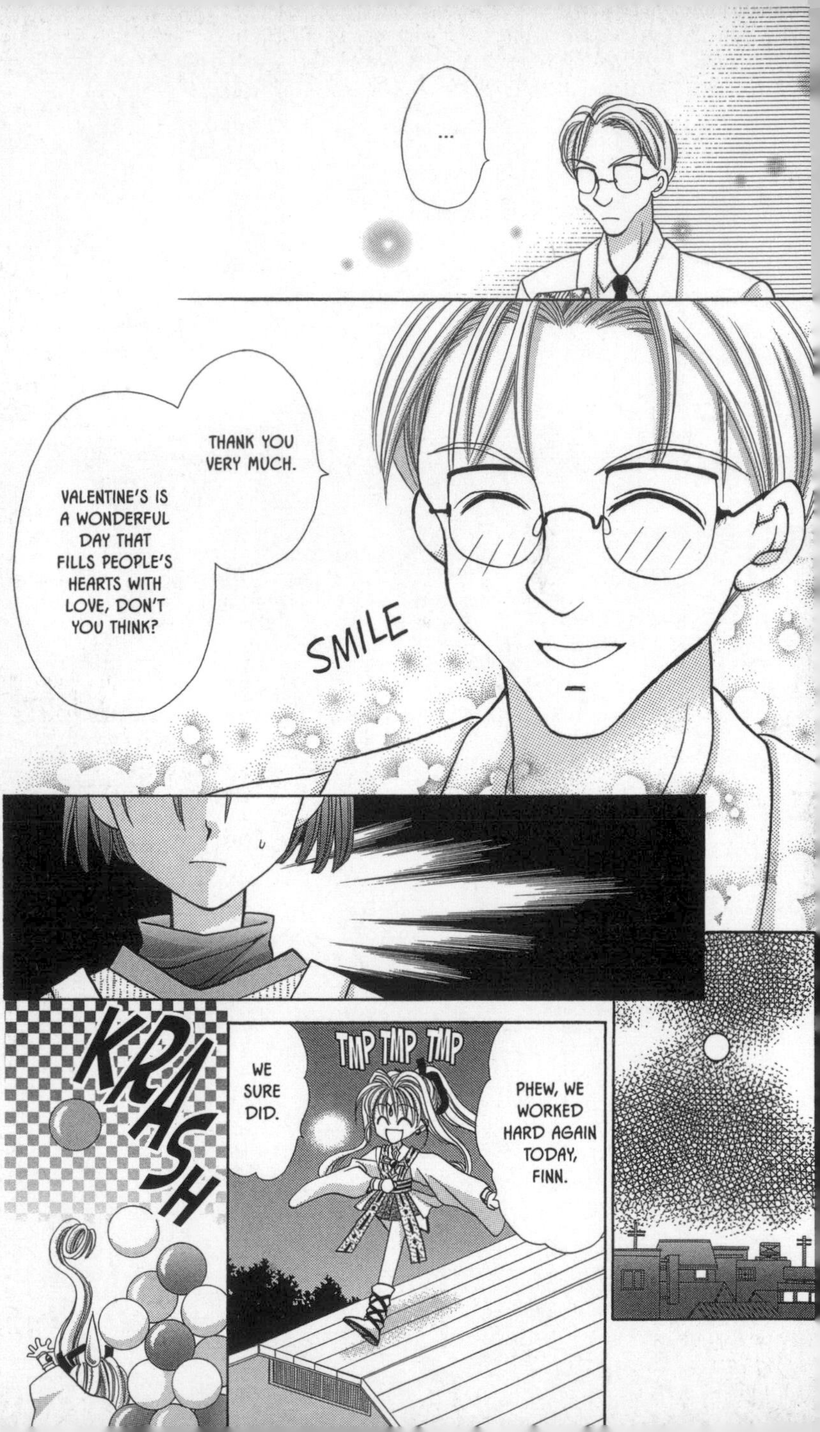
...
THANK YOU VERY MUCH.
VALENTINE'S IS A WONDERFUL DAY THAT FILLS PEOPLE'S HEARTS WITH LOVE, DON'T YOU THINK?
SMILE
PHEW, WE WORKED HARD AGAIN TODAY, FINN.
TMP TMP TMP
WE SURE DID.
KRASH

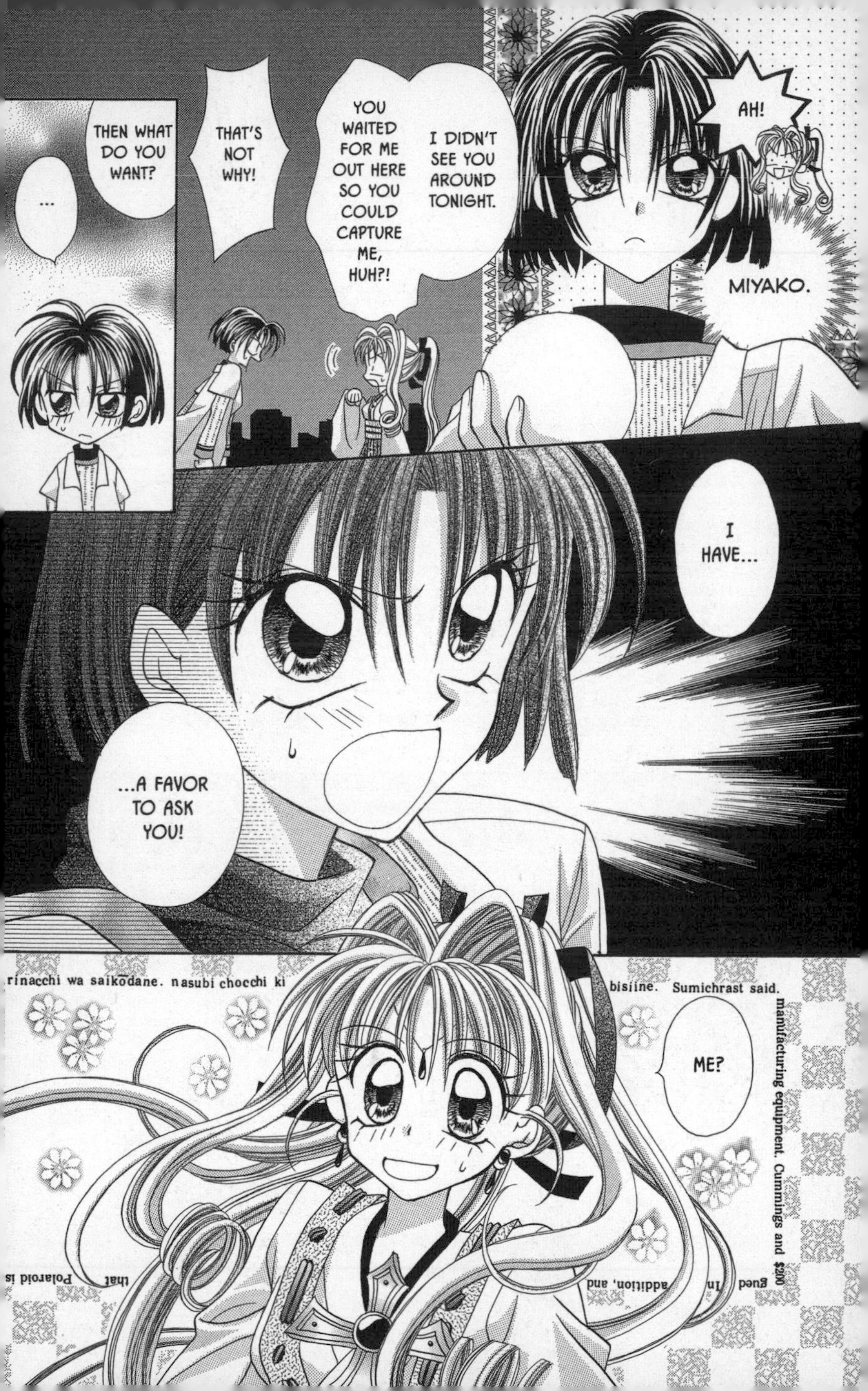
AH!
MIYAKO.
I DIDN'T SEE YOU AROUND TONIGHT.
YOU WAITED FOR ME OUT HERE SO YOU COULD CAPTURE ME, HUH?!
THAT'S NOT WHY!
THEN WHAT DO YOU WANT?
...
I HAVE...
...A FAVOR TO ASK YOU!
rinacchi wa saikodane. nasubi chocchi ki
bisiine. Sumichrast said.
manufacturing equipment. Cummings and $200
ME?

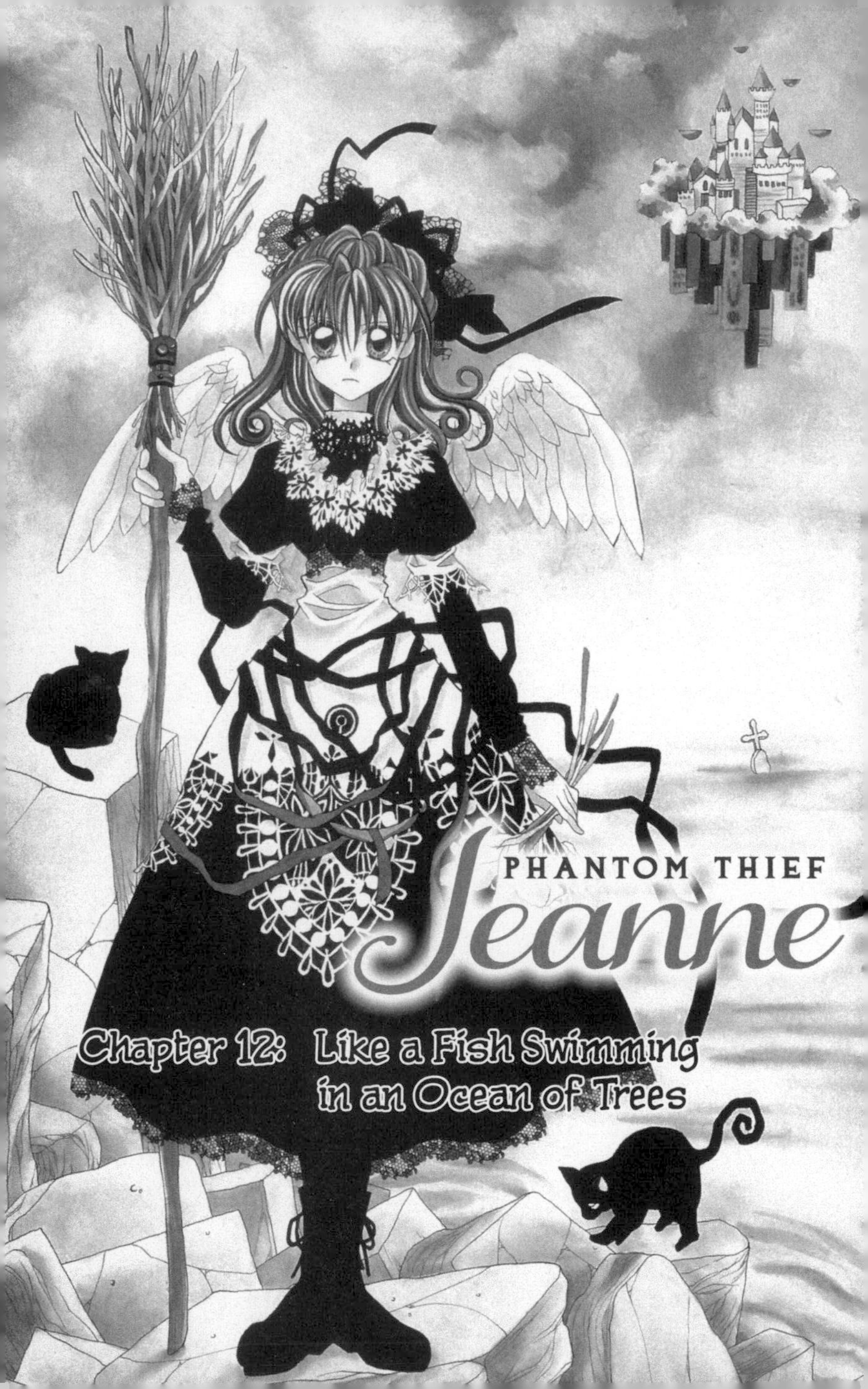
PHANTOM THIEF
Jeanne
Chapter 12: Like a Fish Swimming in an Ocean of Trees

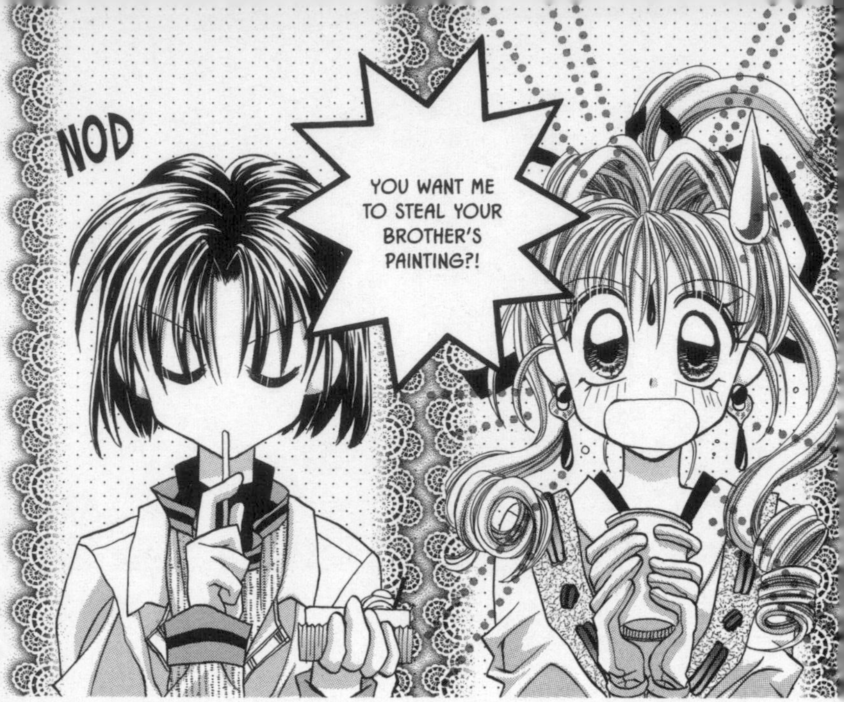
YOU WANT ME TO STEAL YOUR BROTHER'S PAINTING?!
NOD

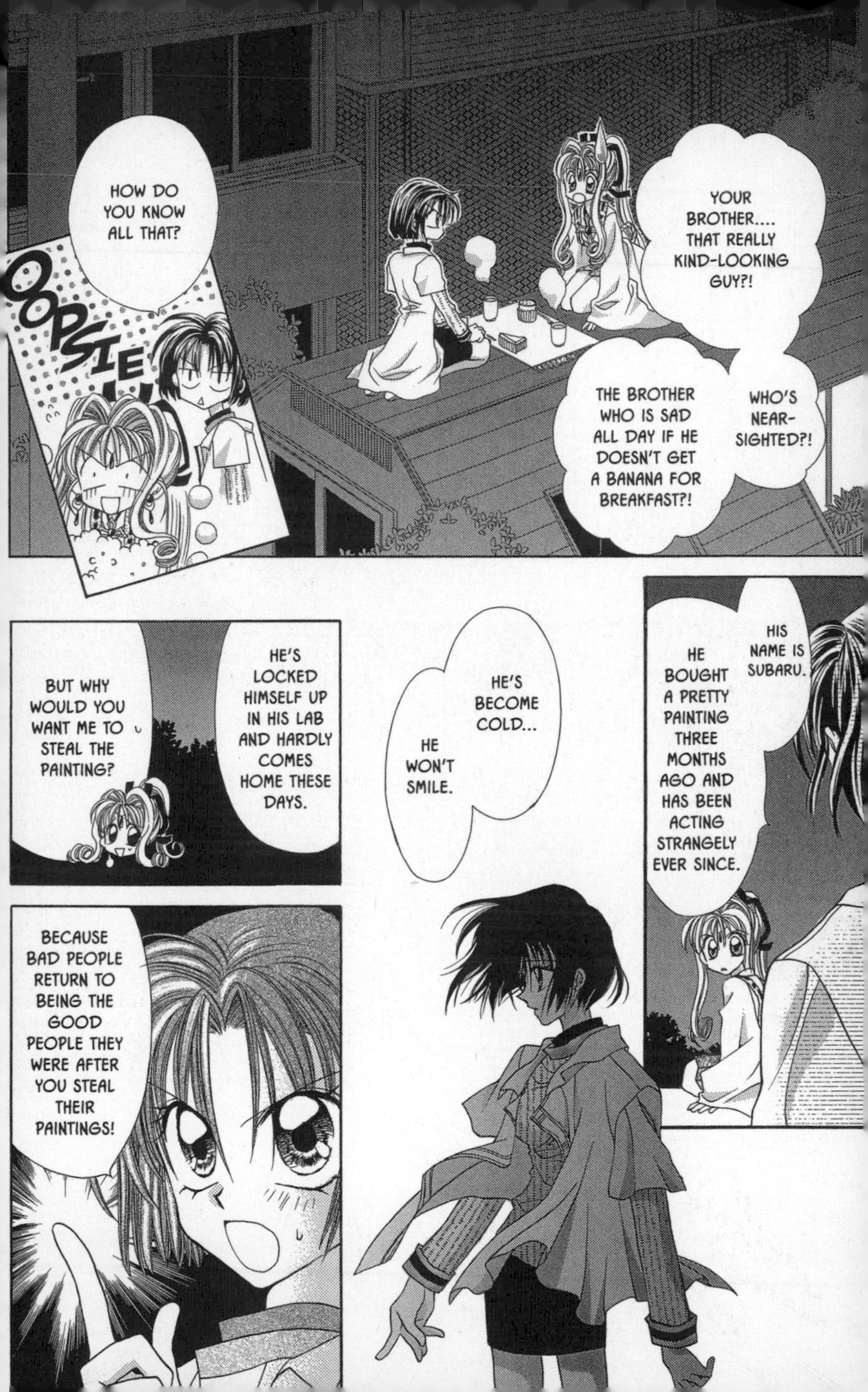
YOUR BROTHER.... THAT REALLY KIND-LOOKING GUY?!
WHO'S NEAR-SIGHTED?!
THE BROTHER WHO IS SAD ALL DAY IF HE DOESN'T GET A BANANA FOR BREAKFAST?!
HOW DO YOU KNOW ALL THAT?
OOPSIE
HIS NAME IS SUBARU.
HE BOUGHT A PRETTY PAINTING THREE MONTHS AGO AND HAS BEEN ACTING STRANGELY EVER SINCE.
HE'S BECOME COLD...
HE WON'T SMILE.
HE'S LOCKED HIMSELF UP IN HIS LAB AND HARDLY COMES HOME THESE DAYS.
BUT WHY WOULD YOU WANT ME TO STEAL THE PAINTING?
BECAUSE BAD PEOPLE RETURN TO BEING THE GOOD PEOPLE THEY WERE AFTER YOU STEAL THEIR PAINTINGS!

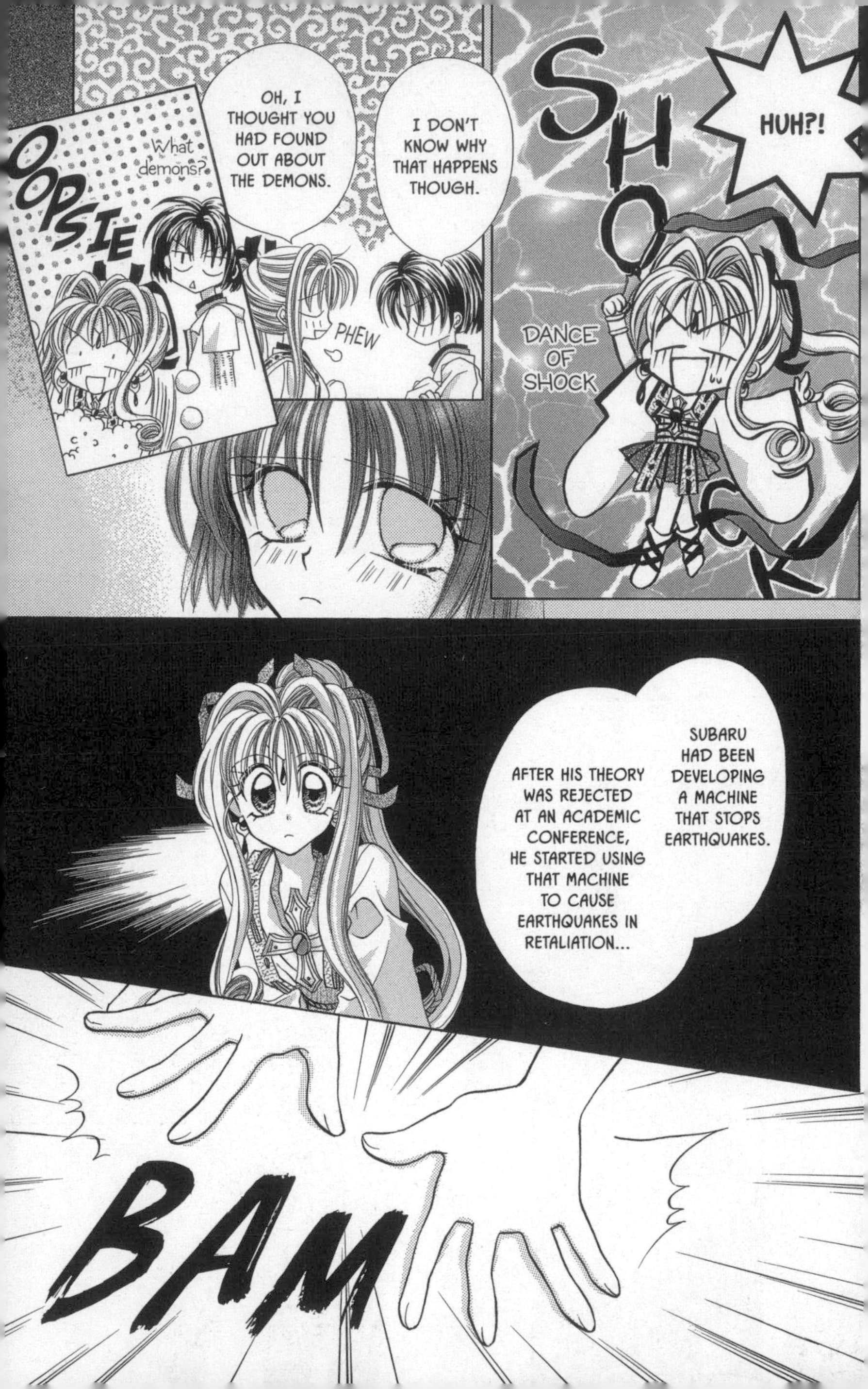
SHOCK
HUH?!
DANCE OF SHOCK
I DON'T KNOW WHY THAT HAPPENS THOUGH.
OH, I THOUGHT YOU HAD FOUND OUT ABOUT THE DEMONS.
PHEW
OOPSIE
What demons?
SUBARU HAD BEEN DEVELOPING A MACHINE THAT STOPS EARTHQUAKES.
AFTER HIS THEORY WAS REJECTED AT AN ACADEMIC CONFERENCE, HE STARTED USING THAT MACHINE TO CAUSE EARTHQUAKES IN RETALIATION...
BAM

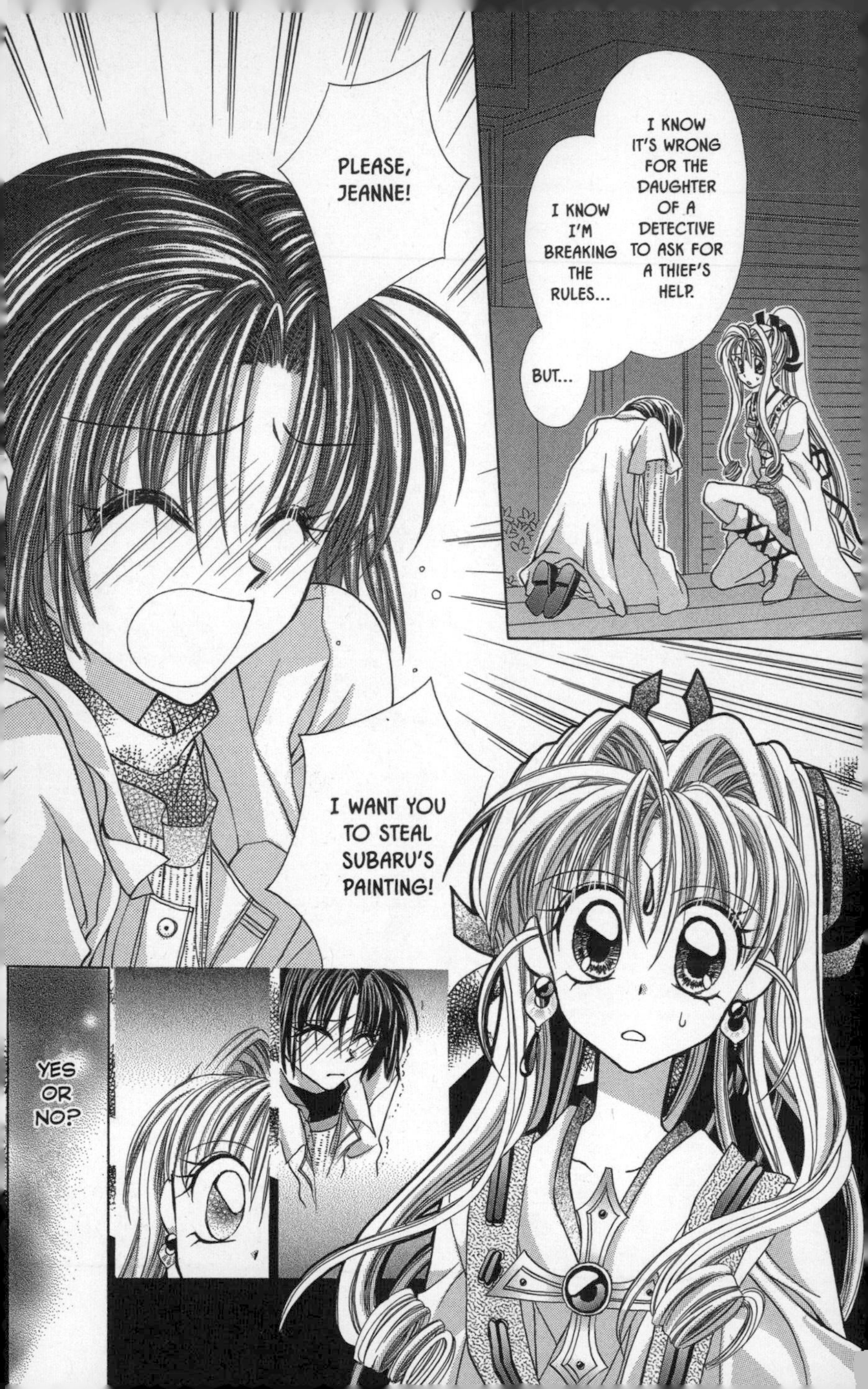
I KNOW IT'S WRONG FOR THE DAUGHTER OF A DETECTIVE TO ASK FOR A THIEF'S HELP.
I KNOW I'M BREAKING THE RULES...
BUT...
PLEASE, JEANNE!
I WANT YOU TO STEAL SUBARU'S PAINTING!
YES OR NO?

THE ANSWER IS OBVIOUS.

OF COURSE I WILL.

PHANTOM
THIEF
JEANNE

I DECIDED LONG AGO TO HELP HER WITH ANYTHING SHE NEEDS...

YAY!

...BECAUSE IT'S SO RARE FOR A SELFISH PERSON LIKE HER TO ASK FOR HELP.

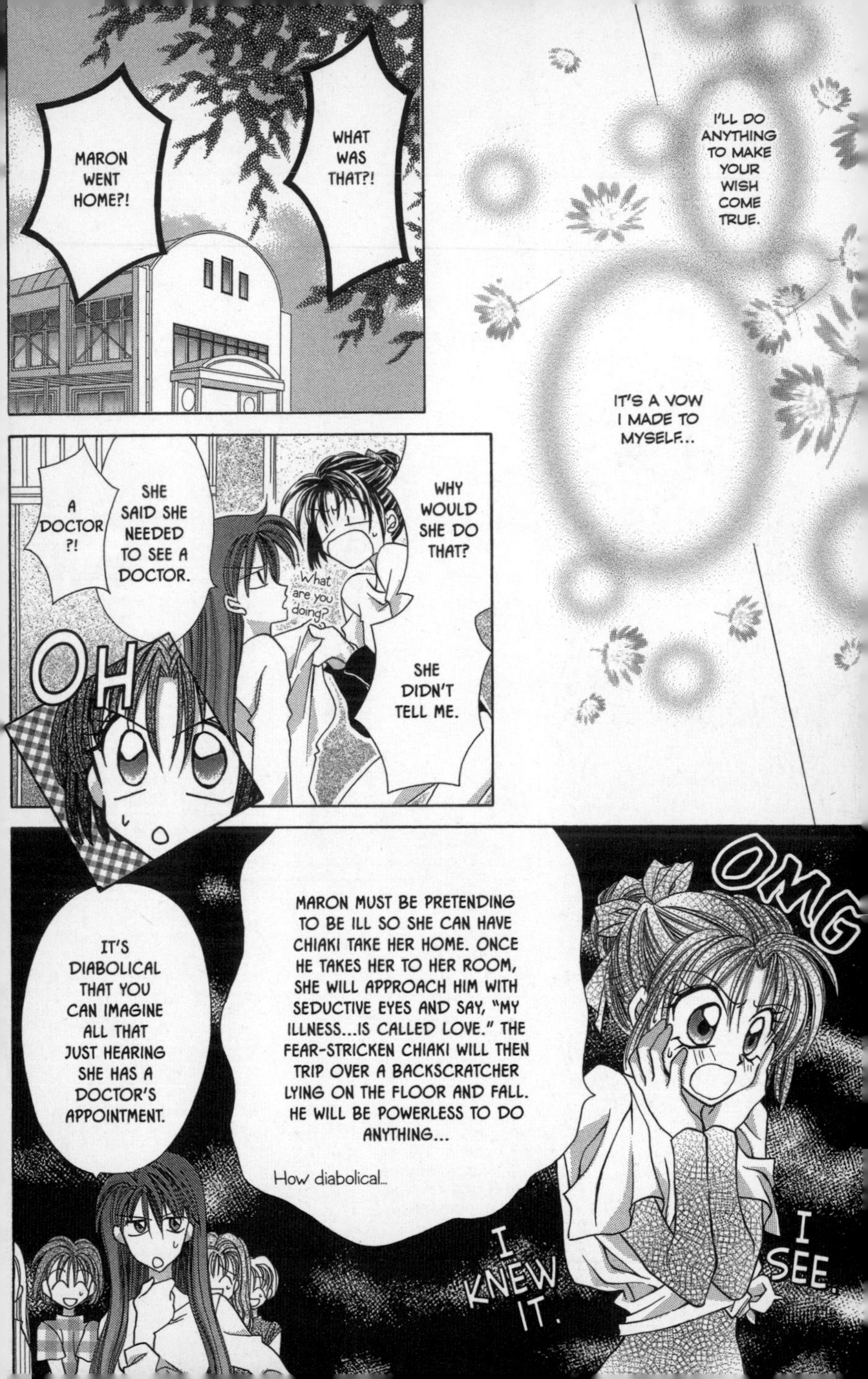

I'LL DO ANYTHING TO MAKE YOUR WISH COME TRUE.
IT'S A VOW I MADE TO MYSELF...
WHAT WAS THAT?!
MARON WENT HOME?!
WHY WOULD SHE DO THAT?
What are you doing?
SHE SAID SHE NEEDED TO SEE A DOCTOR.
A DOCTOR?!
SHE DIDN'T TELL ME.
OH
OMG
I SEE.
I KNEW IT.
MARON MUST BE PRETENDING TO BE ILL SO SHE CAN HAVE CHIAKI TAKE HER HOME. ONCE HE TAKES HER TO HER ROOM, SHE WILL APPROACH HIM WITH SEDUCTIVE EYES AND SAY, "MY ILLNESS...IS CALLED LOVE." THE FEAR-STRICKEN CHIAKI WILL THEN TRIP OVER A BACKSCRATCHER LYING ON THE FLOOR AND FALL. HE WILL BE POWERLESS TO DO ANYTHING...
How diabolical...
IT'S DIABOLICAL THAT YOU CAN IMAGINE ALL THAT JUST HEARING SHE HAS A DOCTOR'S APPOINTMENT.

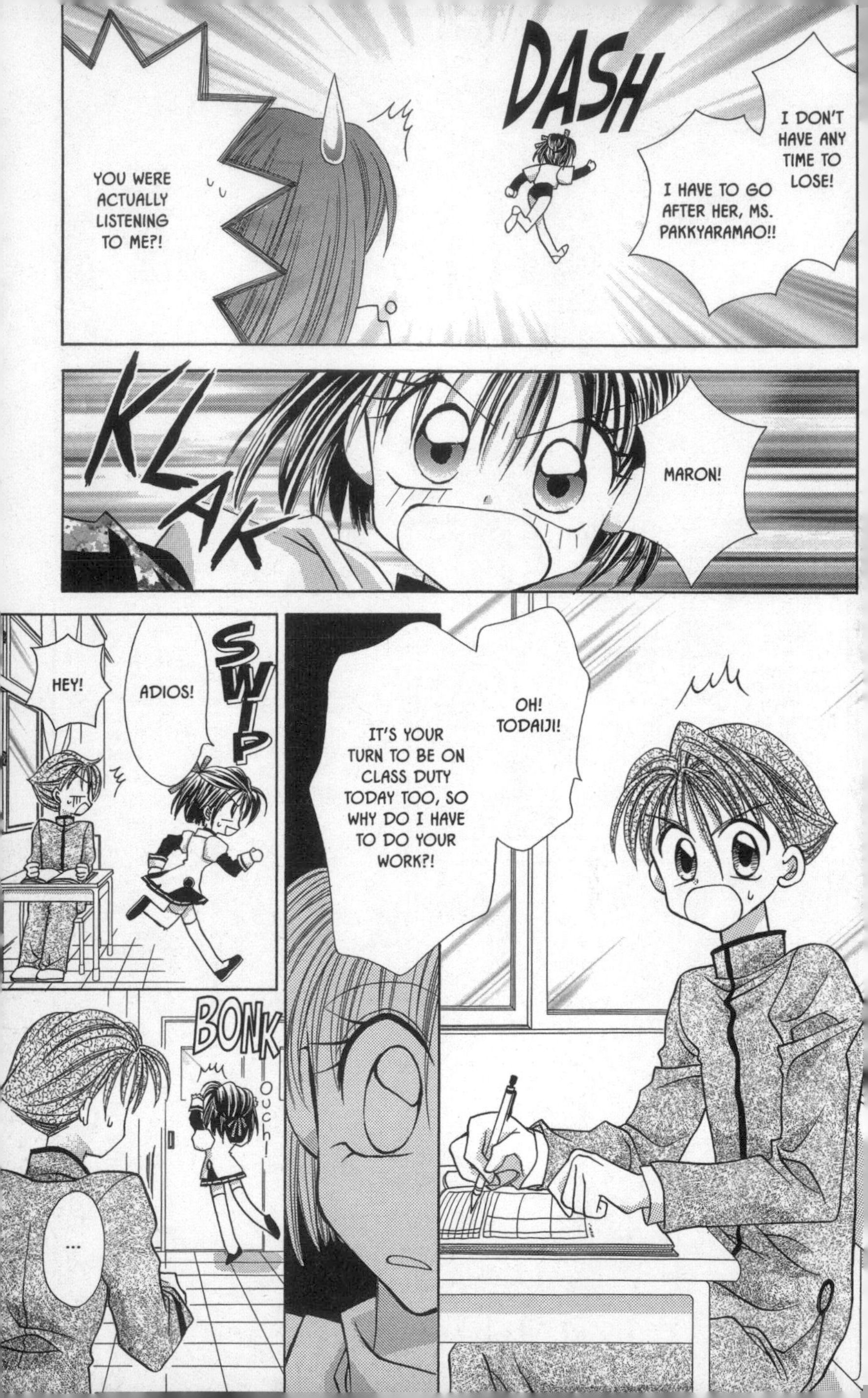
DASH
I DON'T HAVE ANY TIME TO LOSE!
I HAVE TO GO AFTER HER, MS. PAKKYARAMAO!!
YOU WERE ACTUALLY LISTENING TO ME?!
MARON!
KLAK
OH! TODAIJI!
IT'S YOUR TURN TO BE ON CLASS DUTY TODAY TOO, SO WHY DO I HAVE TO DO YOUR WORK?!
SWIP
ADIOS!
HEY!
BONK
Ouch!
...

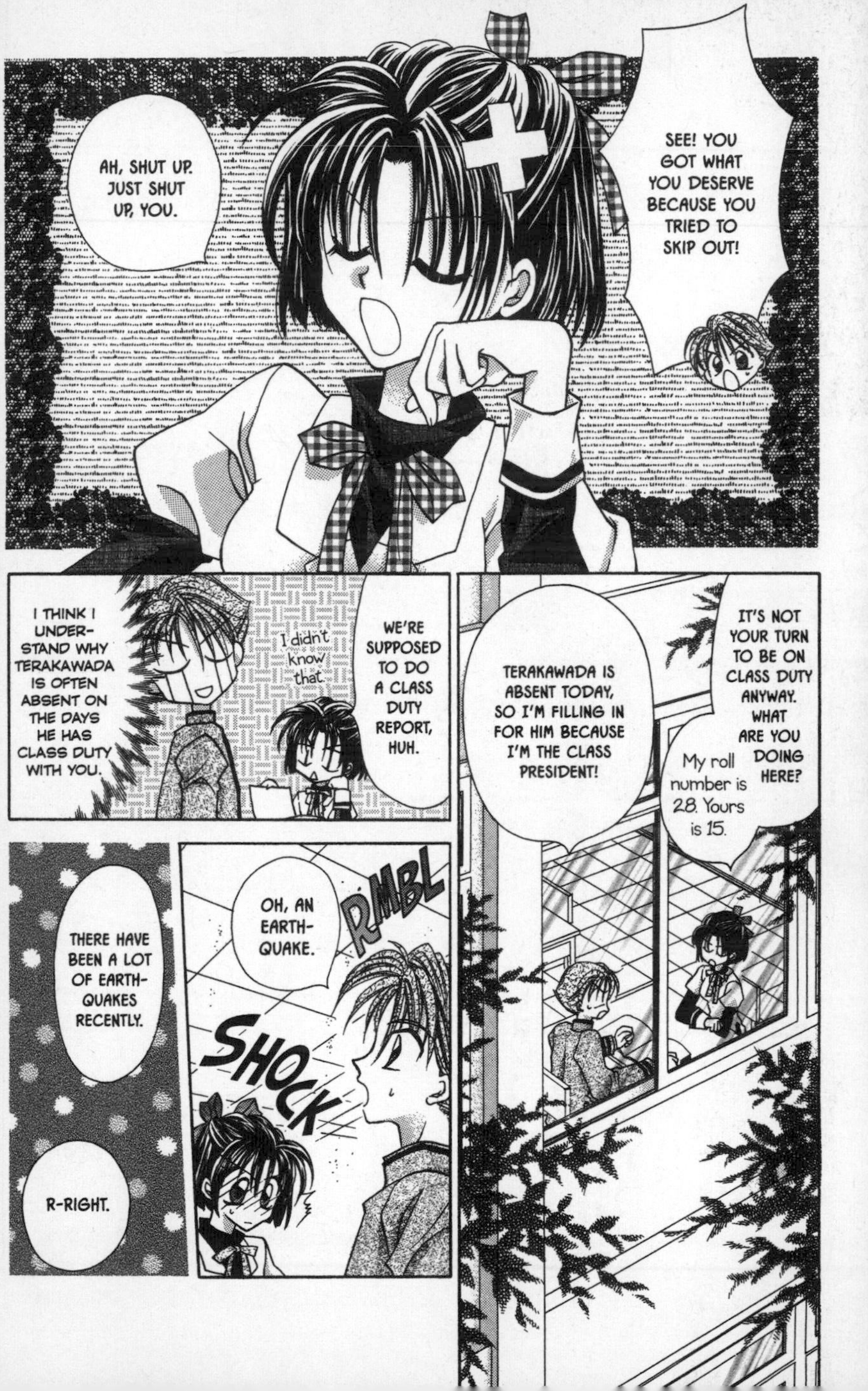
SEE! YOU GOT WHAT YOU DESERVE BECAUSE YOU TRIED TO SKIP OUT!
AH, SHUT UP. JUST SHUT UP, YOU.
IT'S NOT YOUR TURN TO BE ON CLASS DUTY ANYWAY. WHAT ARE YOU DOING HERE?
My roll number is 28. Yours is 15.
TERAKAWADA IS ABSENT TODAY, SO I'M FILLING IN FOR HIM BECAUSE I'M THE CLASS PRESIDENT!
WE'RE SUPPOSED TO DO A CLASS DUTY REPORT, HUH.
I didn't know that.
I THINK I UNDERSTAND WHY TERAKAWADA IS OFTEN ABSENT ON THE DAYS HE HAS CLASS DUTY WITH YOU.
RMBL
OH, AN EARTHQUAKE.
SHOCK
THERE HAVE BEEN A LOT OF EARTHQUAKES RECENTLY.
R-RIGHT.

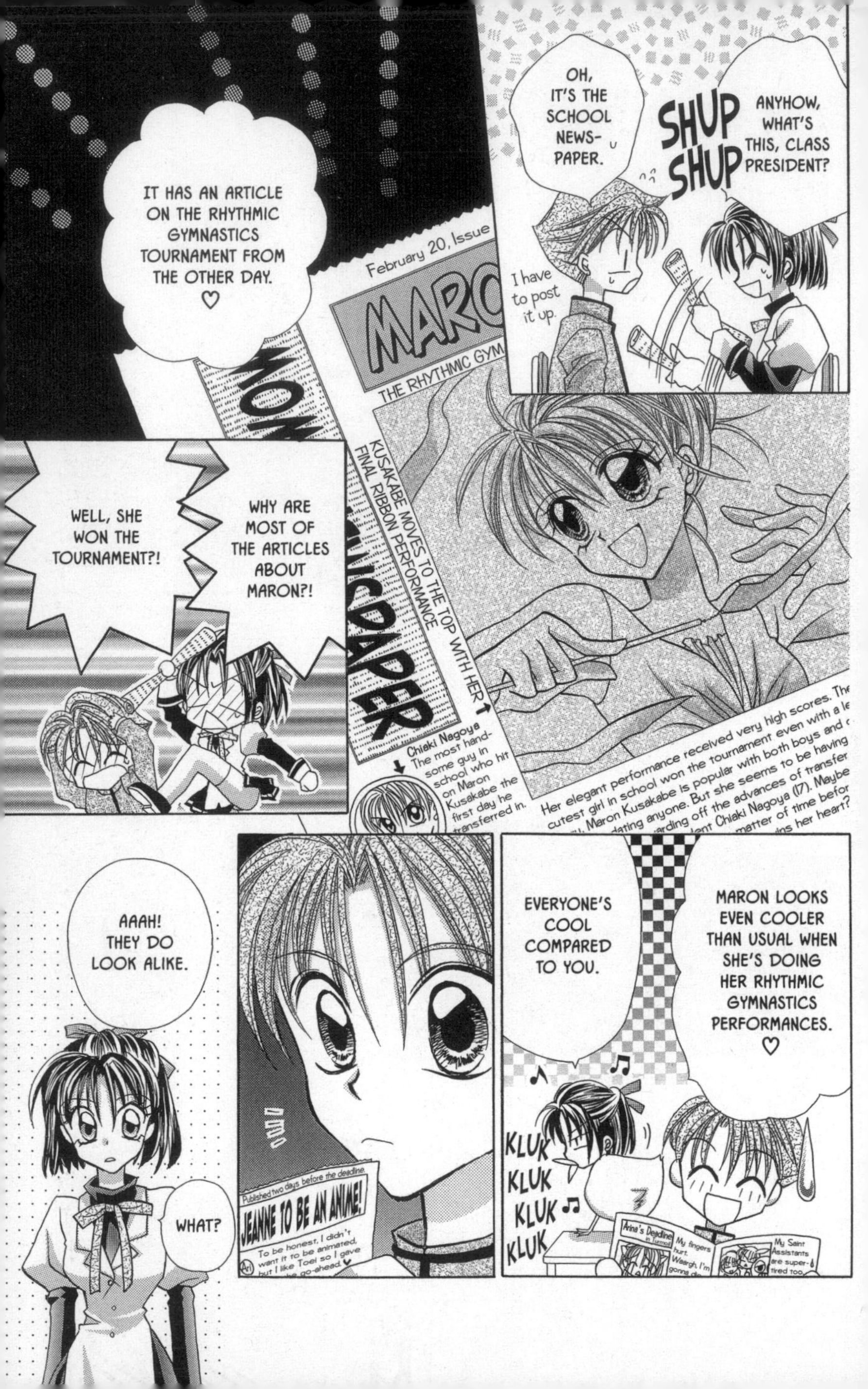
ANYHOW, WHAT'S THIS, CLASS PRESIDENT?
SHUP SHUP
OH, IT'S THE SCHOOL NEWS-PAPER.
I have to post it up.
IT HAS AN ARTICLE ON THE RHYTHMIC GYMNASTICS TOURNAMENT FROM THE OTHER DAY. ♡
February 20, Issue
MARO
THE RHYTHMIC GYM
MOMO
NEWSPAPER
KUSAKABE MOVES TO THE TOP WITH HER FINAL RIBBON PERFORMANCE
Chiaki Nagoya The most hand-some guy in school who hit on Maron Kusakabe the first day he transferred in.
Her elegant performance received very high scores. The cutest girl in school won the tournament even with a le
WHY ARE MOST OF THE ARTICLES ABOUT MARON?!
WELL, SHE WON THE TOURNAMENT?!
MARON LOOKS EVEN COOLER THAN USUAL WHEN SHE'S DOING HER RHYTHMIC GYMNASTICS PERFORMANCES. ♡
EVERYONE'S COOL COMPARED TO YOU.
KLUK KLUK KLUK KLUK
Arina's Deadline
My fingers hurt. Waargh, I'm
My Saint Assistants are super-tired too.
Published two days before the deadline.
JEANNE TO BE AN ANIME!
To be honest, I didn't want it to be animated, but I like Toei so I gave
AAAH! THEY DO LOOK ALIKE.
WHAT?

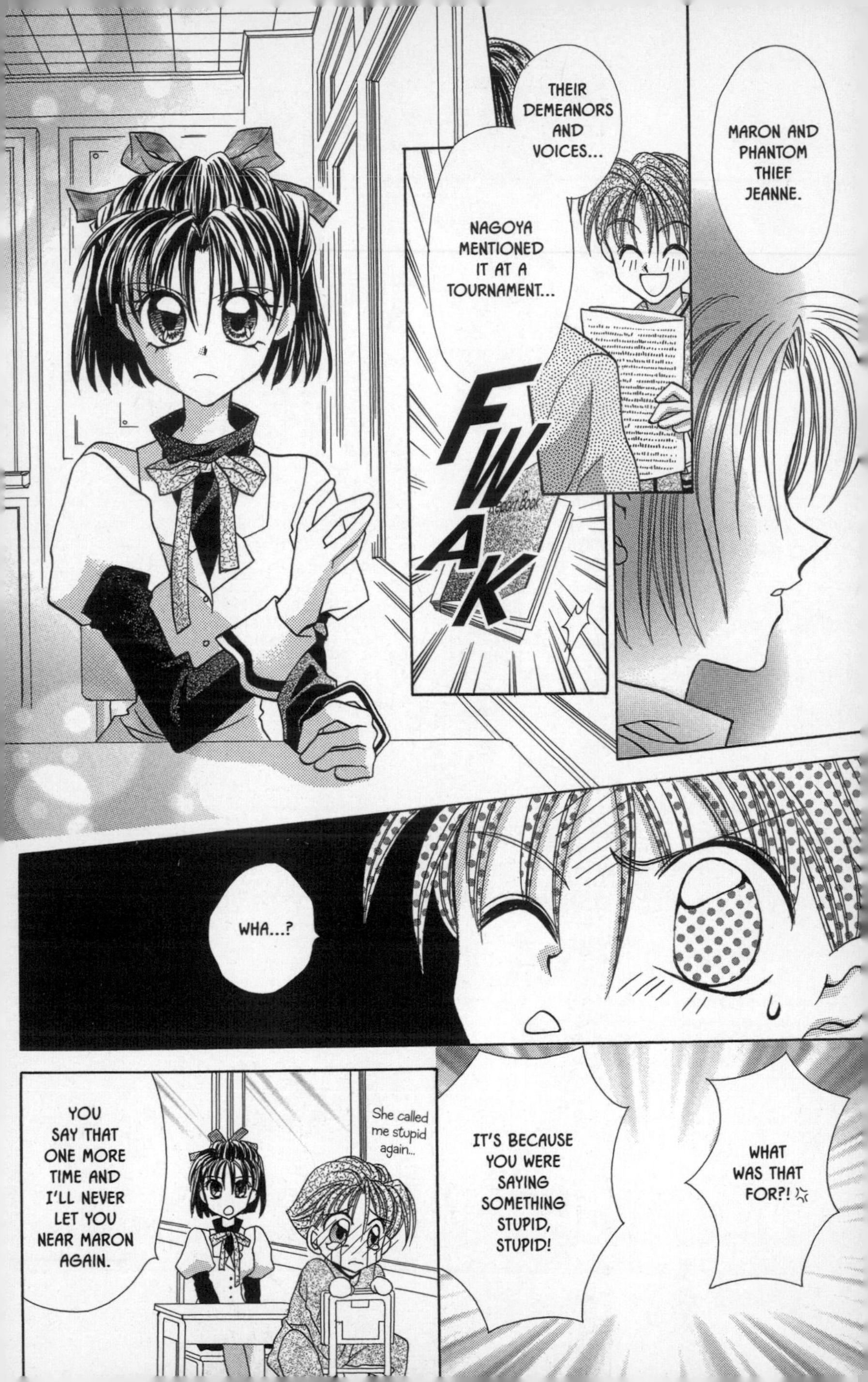
MARON AND PHANTOM THIEF JEANNE.
THEIR DEMEANORS AND VOICES...
NAGOYA MENTIONED IT AT A TOURNAMENT...
FWAK
WHA...?
WHAT WAS THAT FOR?!
IT'S BECAUSE YOU WERE SAYING SOMETHING STUPID, STUPID!
She called me stupid again...
YOU SAY THAT ONE MORE TIME AND I'LL NEVER LET YOU NEAR MARON AGAIN.

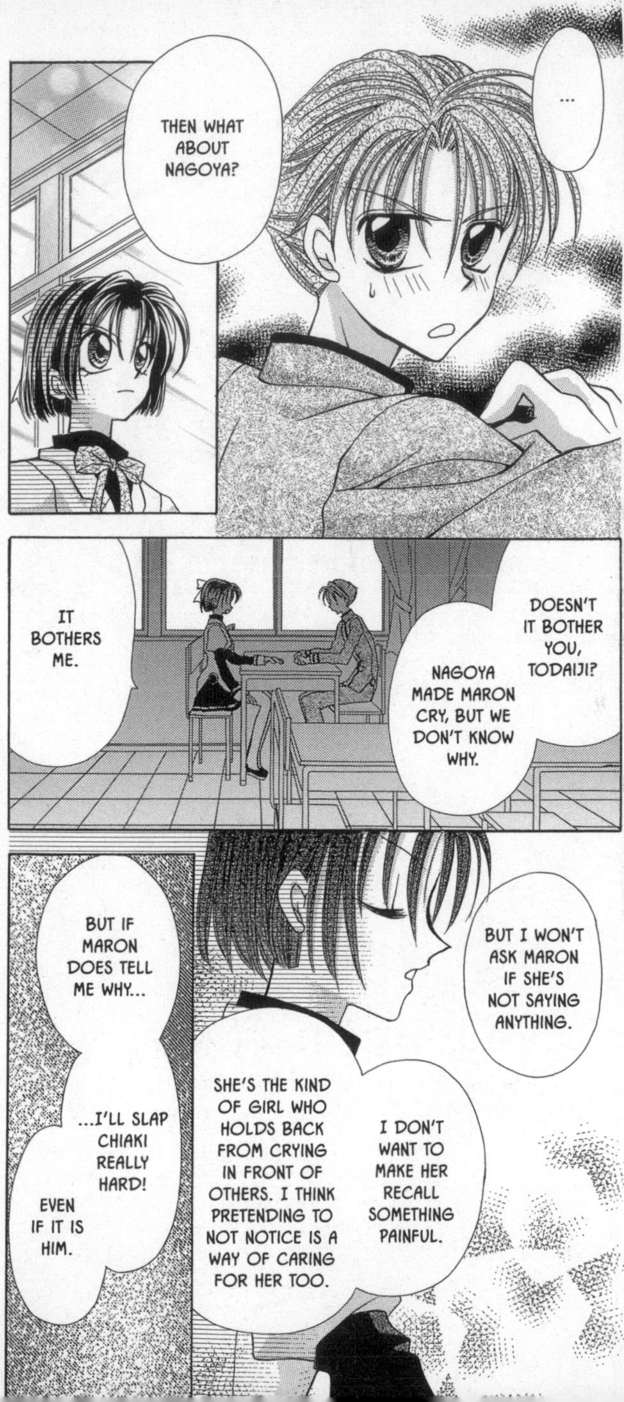
...
THEN WHAT ABOUT NAGOYA?
DOESN'T IT BOTHER YOU, TODAIJI?
NAGOYA MADE MARON CRY, BUT WE DON'T KNOW WHY.
IT BOTHERS ME.
BUT I WON'T ASK MARON IF SHE'S NOT SAYING ANYTHING.
I DON'T WANT TO MAKE HER RECALL SOMETHING PAINFUL.
SHE'S THE KIND OF GIRL WHO HOLDS BACK FROM CRYING IN FRONT OF OTHERS. I THINK PRETENDING TO NOT NOTICE IS A WAY OF CARING FOR HER TOO.
BUT IF MARON DOES TELL ME WHY...
...I'LL SLAP CHIAKI REALLY HARD!
EVEN IF IT IS HIM.

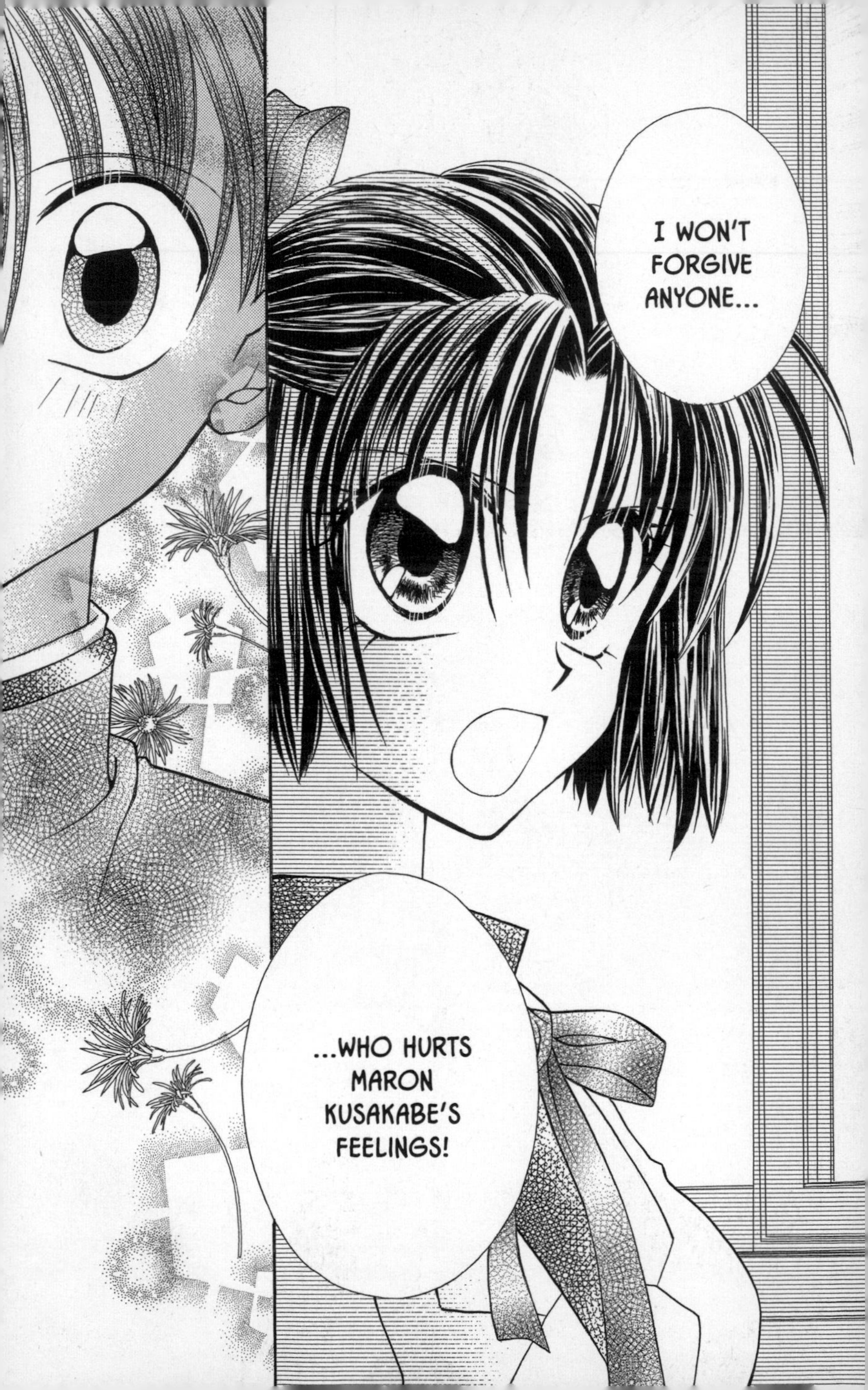
I WON'T FORGIVE ANYONE...
...WHO HURTS MARON KUSAKABE'S FEELINGS!

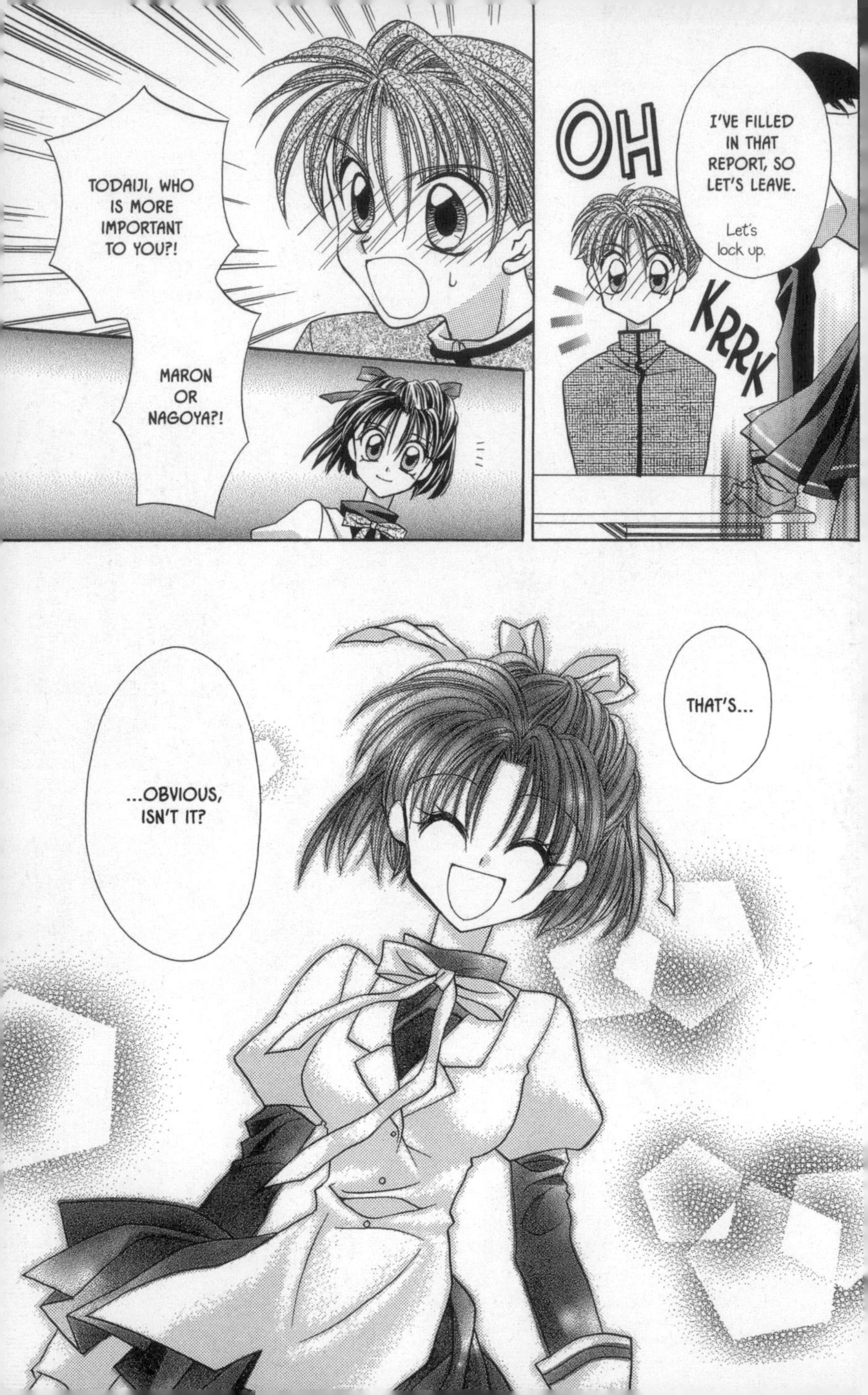
I'VE FILLED IN THAT REPORT, SO LET'S LEAVE.
OH
Let's lock up.
KRRK
TODAIJI, WHO IS MORE IMPORTANT TO YOU?!
MARON OR NAGOYA?!
THAT'S...
...OBVIOUS, ISN'T IT?

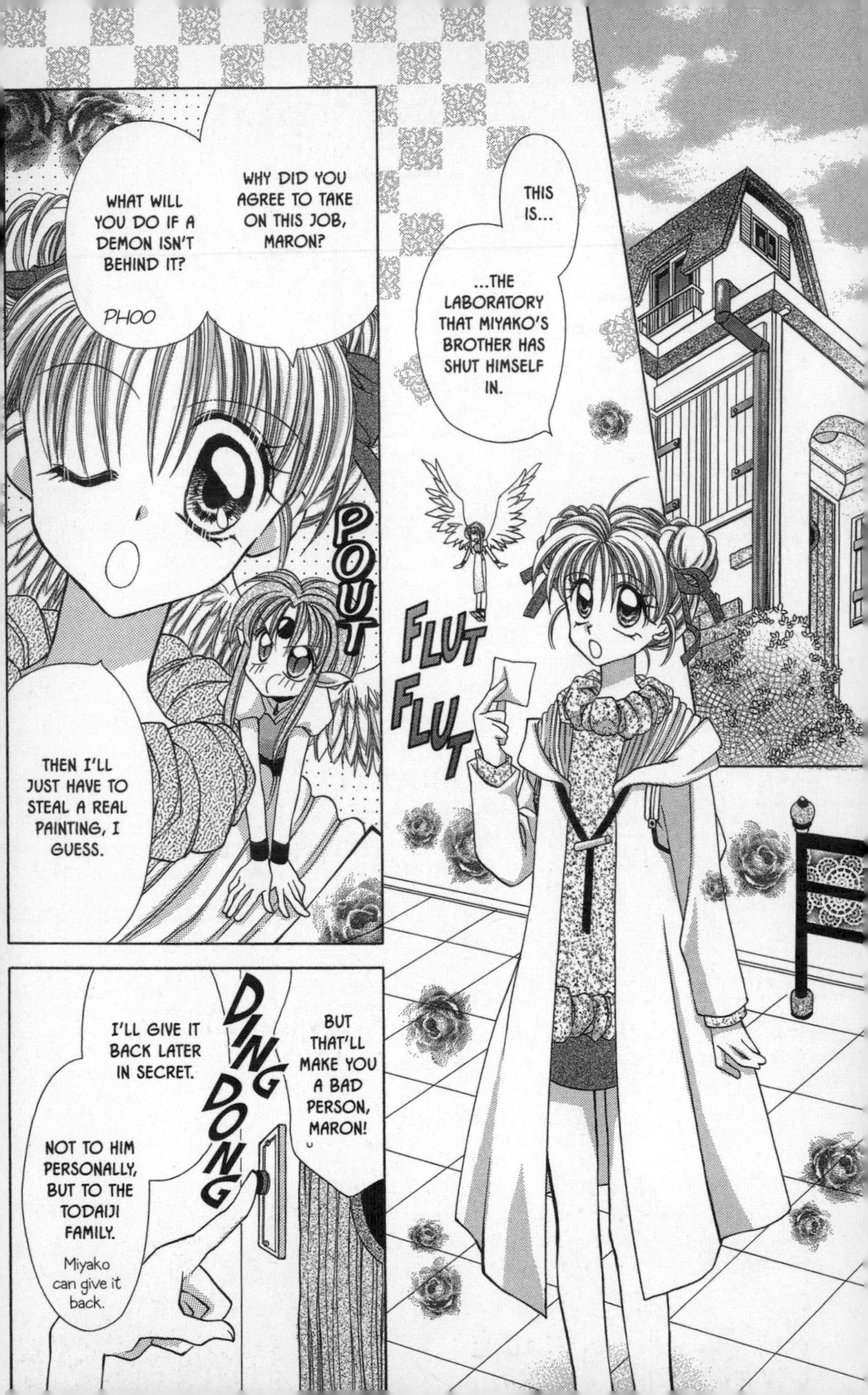
THIS IS...
...THE LABORATORY THAT MIYAKO'S BROTHER HAS SHUT HIMSELF IN.
FLUT FLUT
WHY DID YOU AGREE TO TAKE ON THIS JOB, MARON?
WHAT WILL YOU DO IF A DEMON ISN'T BEHIND IT?
PHOO
POUT
THEN I'LL JUST HAVE TO STEAL A REAL PAINTING, I GUESS.
BUT THAT'LL MAKE YOU A BAD PERSON, MARON!
DING DONG
I'LL GIVE IT BACK LATER IN SECRET.
NOT TO HIM PERSONALLY, BUT TO THE TODAIJI FAMILY.
Miyako can give it back.

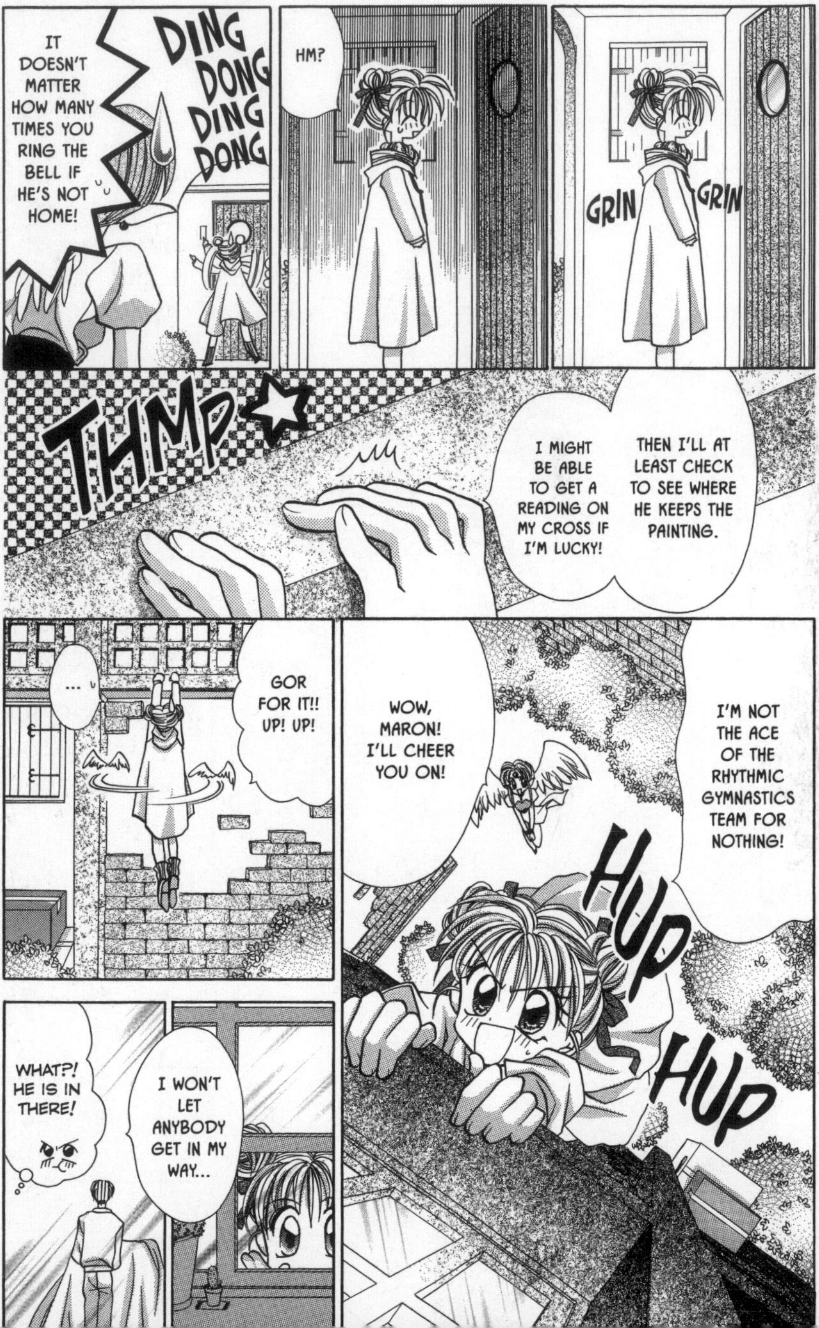
GRIN
GRIN
HM?
DING DONG DING DONG
IT DOESN'T MATTER HOW MANY TIMES YOU RING THE BELL IF HE'S NOT HOME!
THEN I'LL AT LEAST CHECK TO SEE WHERE HE KEEPS THE PAINTING.
I MIGHT BE ABLE TO GET A READING ON MY CROSS IF I'M LUCKY!
THMP
I'M NOT THE ACE OF THE RHYTHMIC GYMNASTICS TEAM FOR NOTHING!
WOW, MARON! I'LL CHEER YOU ON!
HUP
HUP
HUP
GOR FOR IT!! UP! UP!
...
I WON'T LET ANYBODY GET IN MY WAY...
WHAT?! HE IS IN THERE!

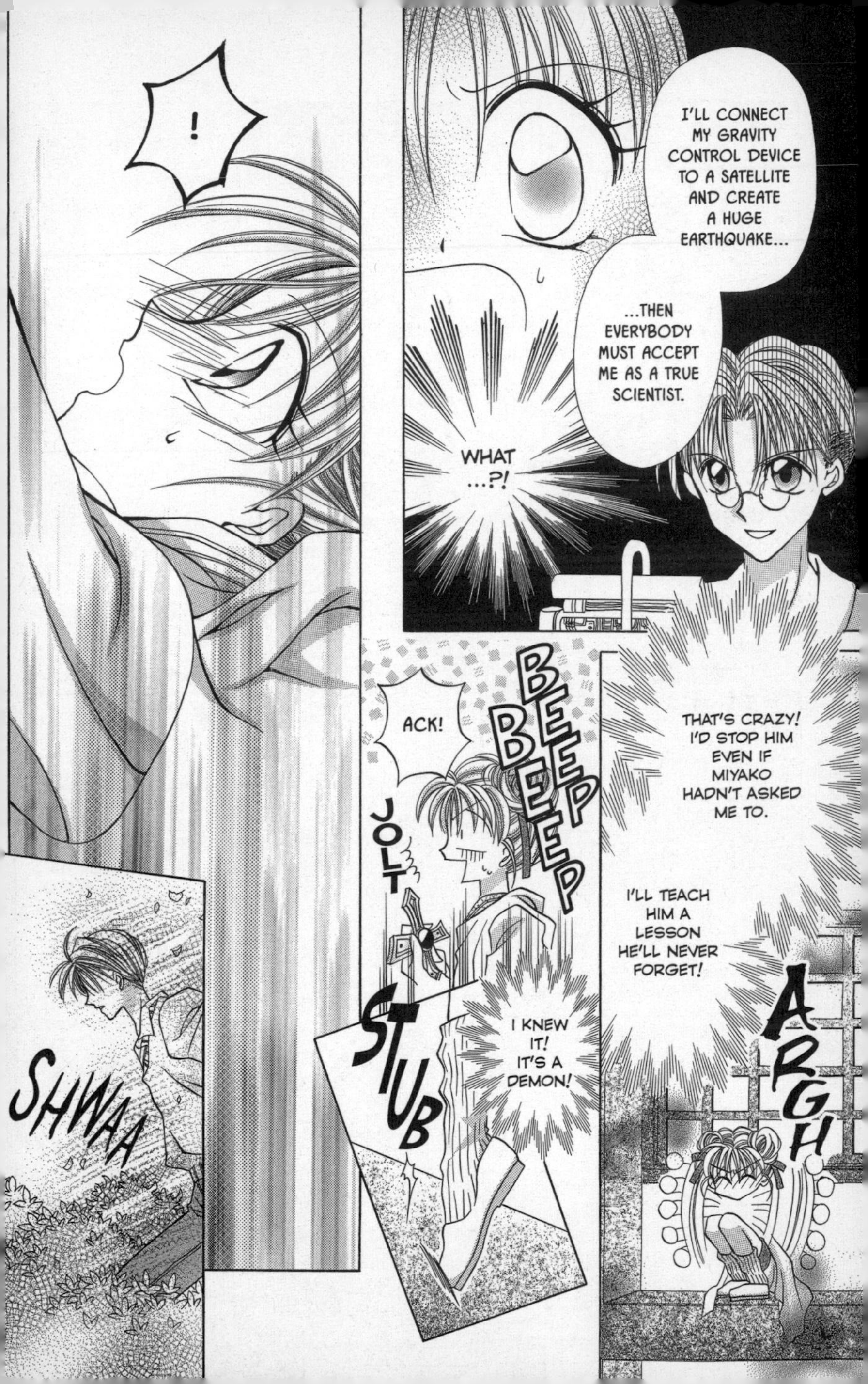
I'LL CONNECT MY GRAVITY CONTROL DEVICE TO A SATELLITE AND CREATE A HUGE EARTHQUAKE...
...THEN EVERYBODY MUST ACCEPT ME AS A TRUE SCIENTIST.
WHAT ...?!
THAT'S CRAZY! I'D STOP HIM EVEN IF MIYAKO HADN'T ASKED ME TO.
I'LL TEACH HIM A LESSON HE'LL NEVER FORGET!
ARGH
BEEEP BEEEP
ACK!
JOLT
STUB
I KNEW IT! IT'S A DEMON!
!
SHWAA

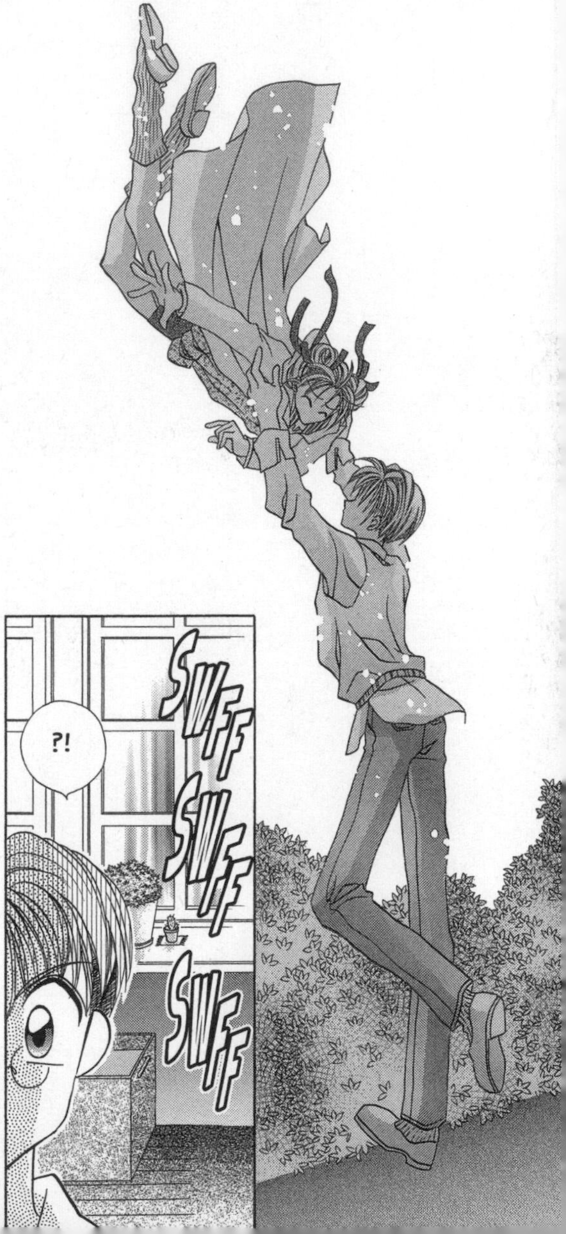
SWFF
SWFF
SWFF
SWFF
?!

PHANTOM
THIEF
JEANNE

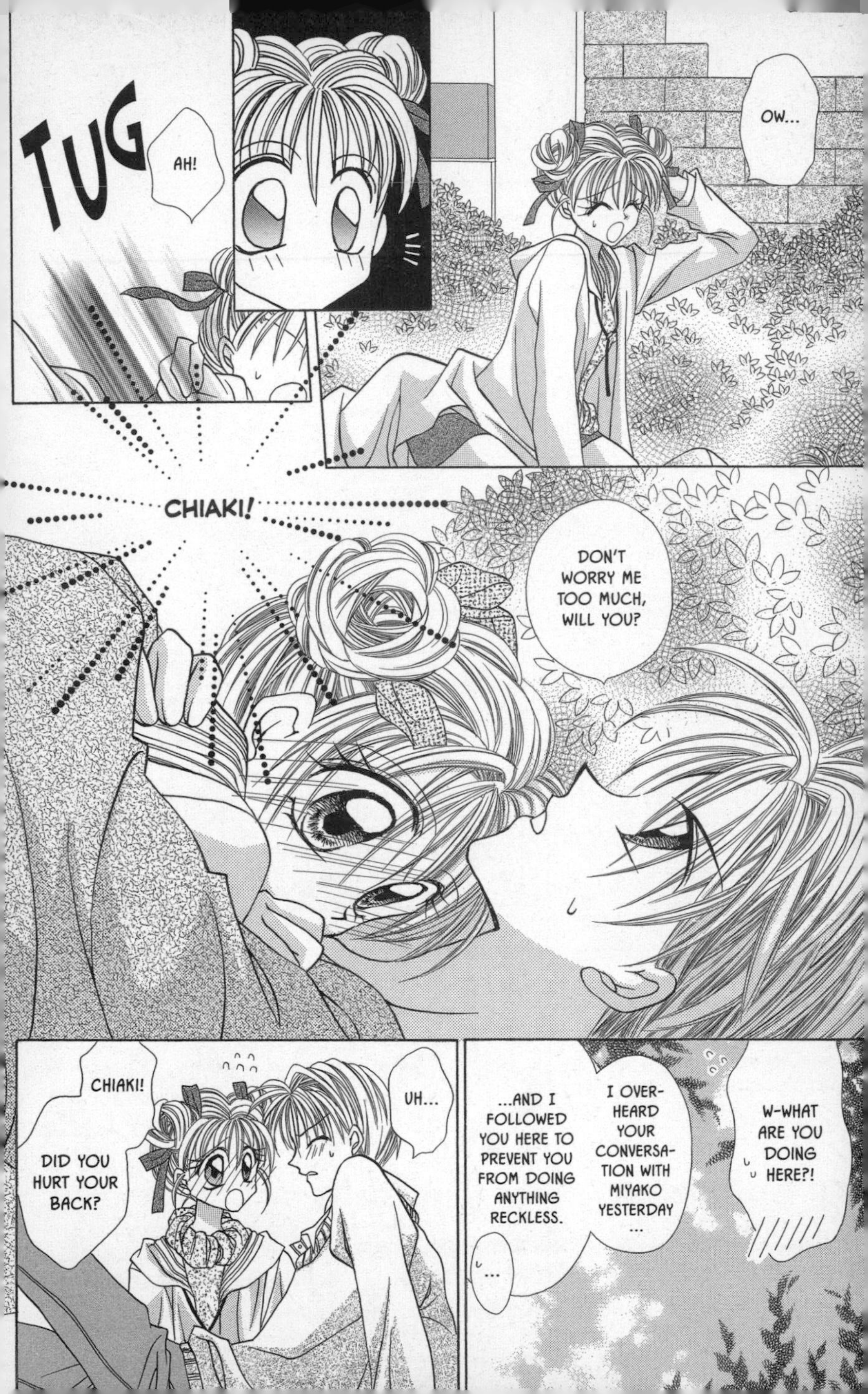
OW...
AH!
TUG
CHIAKI!
DON'T WORRY ME TOO MUCH, WILL YOU?
W-WHAT ARE YOU DOING HERE?!
I OVERHEARD YOUR CONVERSATION WITH MIYAKO YESTERDAY...
...AND I FOLLOWED YOU HERE TO PREVENT YOU FROM DOING ANYTHING RECKLESS.
...
UH...
CHIAKI!
DID YOU HURT YOUR BACK?

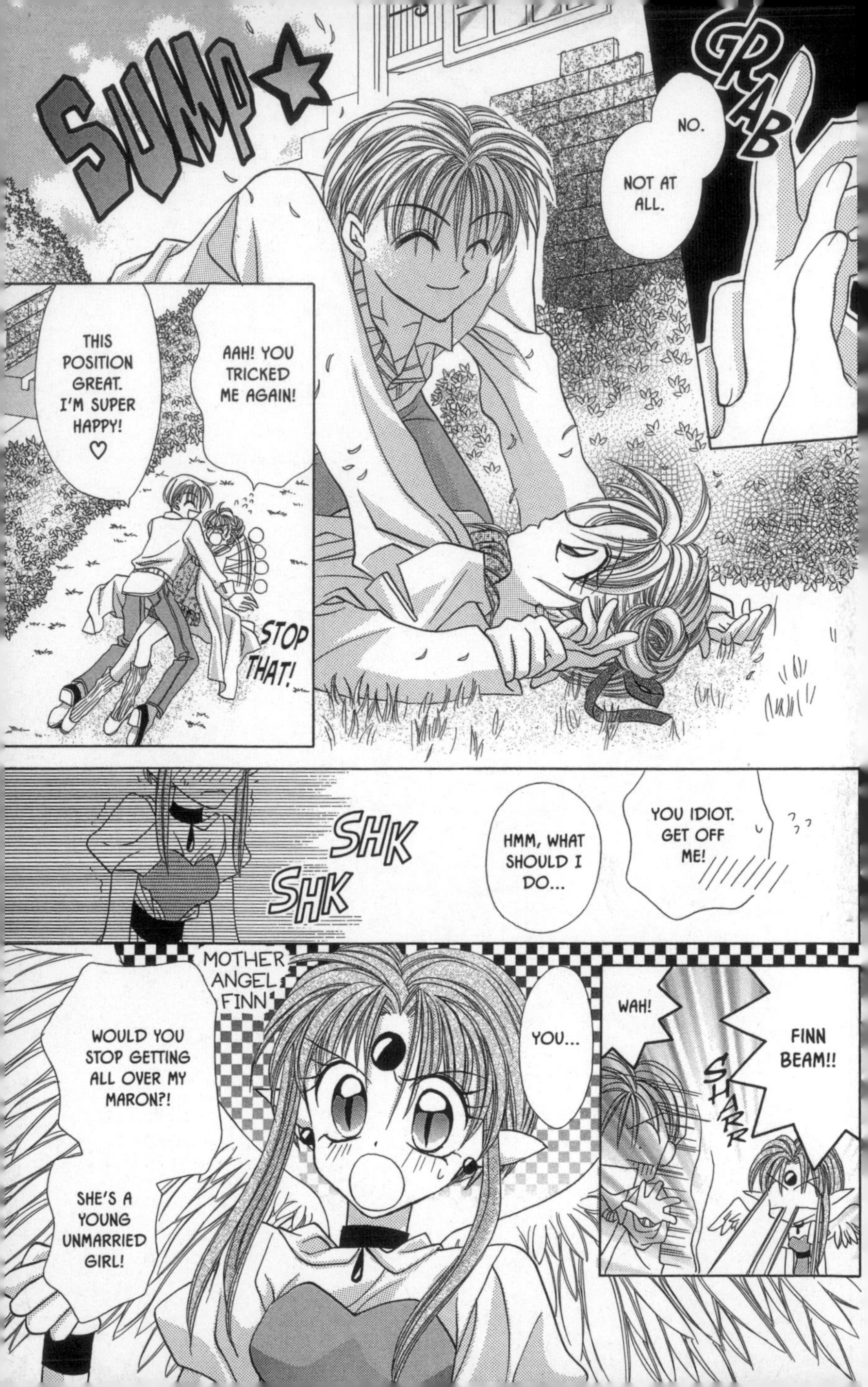
GRAB
NO.
NOT AT ALL.
SUMP
AAH! YOU TRICKED ME AGAIN!
THIS POSITION GREAT. I'M SUPER HAPPY! ♡
STOP THAT!
YOU IDIOT. GET OFF ME!
HMM, WHAT SHOULD I DO...
SHK
SHK
FINN BEAM!!
WAH!
SHARR
YOU...
MOTHER ANGEL FINN
WOULD YOU STOP GETTING ALL OVER MY MARON?!
SHE'S A YOUNG UNMARRIED GIRL!

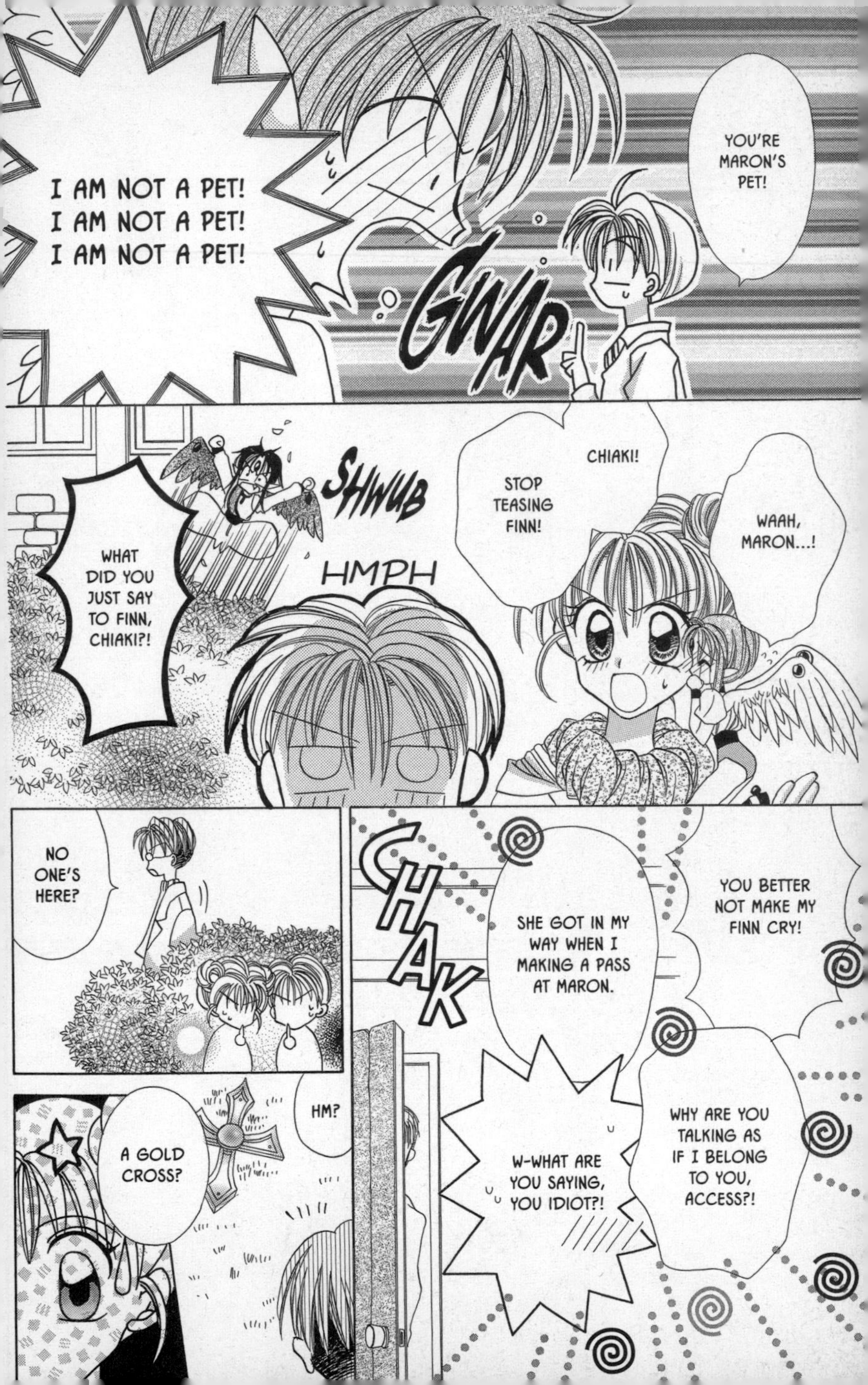
YOU'RE MARON'S PET!
GWAR
I AM NOT A PET! I AM NOT A PET! I AM NOT A PET!
WAAH, MARON...!
CHIAKI! STOP TEASING FINN!
SHWUB
HMPH
WHAT DID YOU JUST SAY TO FINN, CHIAKI?!
YOU BETTER NOT MAKE MY FINN CRY!
SHE GOT IN MY WAY WHEN I MAKING A PASS AT MARON.
CHAK
WHY ARE YOU TALKING AS IF I BELONG TO YOU, ACCESS?!
W-WHAT ARE YOU SAYING, YOU IDIOT?!
NO ONE'S HERE?
HM?
A GOLD CROSS?

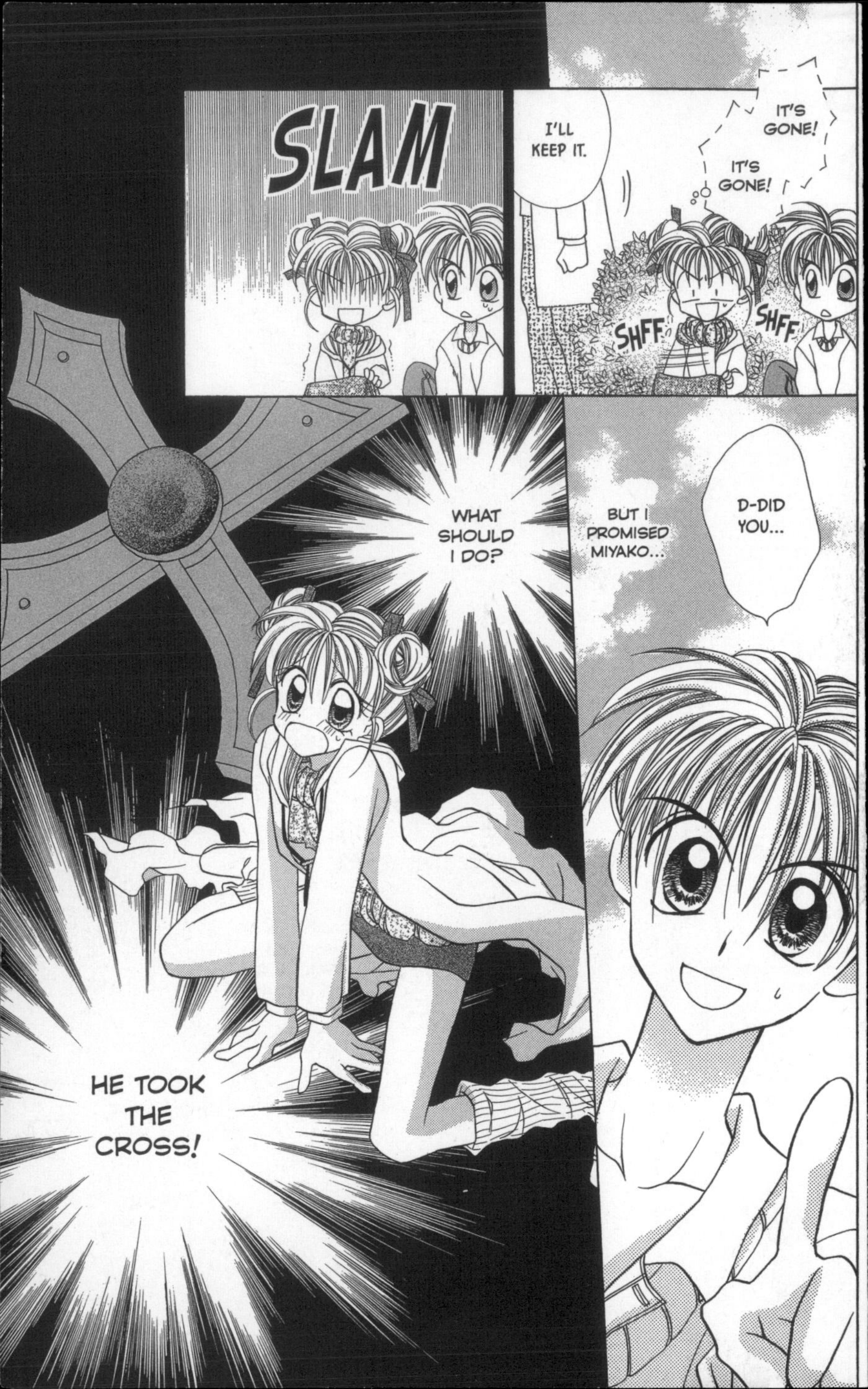
I'LL KEEP IT.
IT'S GONE!
IT'S GONE!
SHFF
SHFF
SLAM
D-DID YOU...
BUT I PROMISED MIYAKO...
WHAT SHOULD I DO?
HE TOOK THE CROSS!

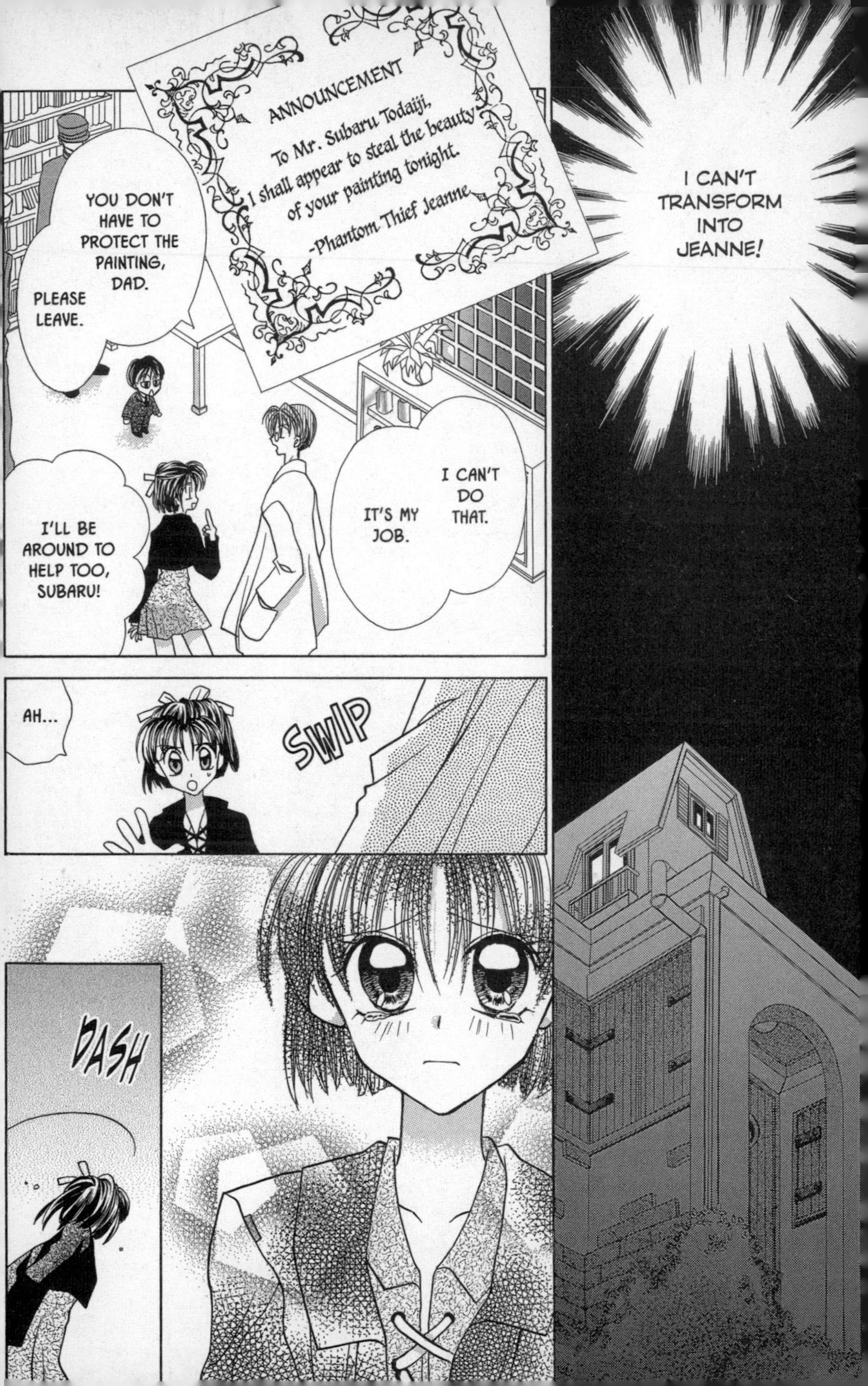
I CAN'T TRANSFORM INTO JEANNE!
ANNOUNCEMENT
To Mr. Subaru Todaiji, I shall appear to steal the beauty of your painting tonight.
-Phantom Thief Jeanne
YOU DON'T HAVE TO PROTECT THE PAINTING, DAD.
PLEASE LEAVE.
I CAN'T DO THAT.
IT'S MY JOB.
I'LL BE AROUND TO HELP TOO, SUBARU!
SWIP
AH...
DASH

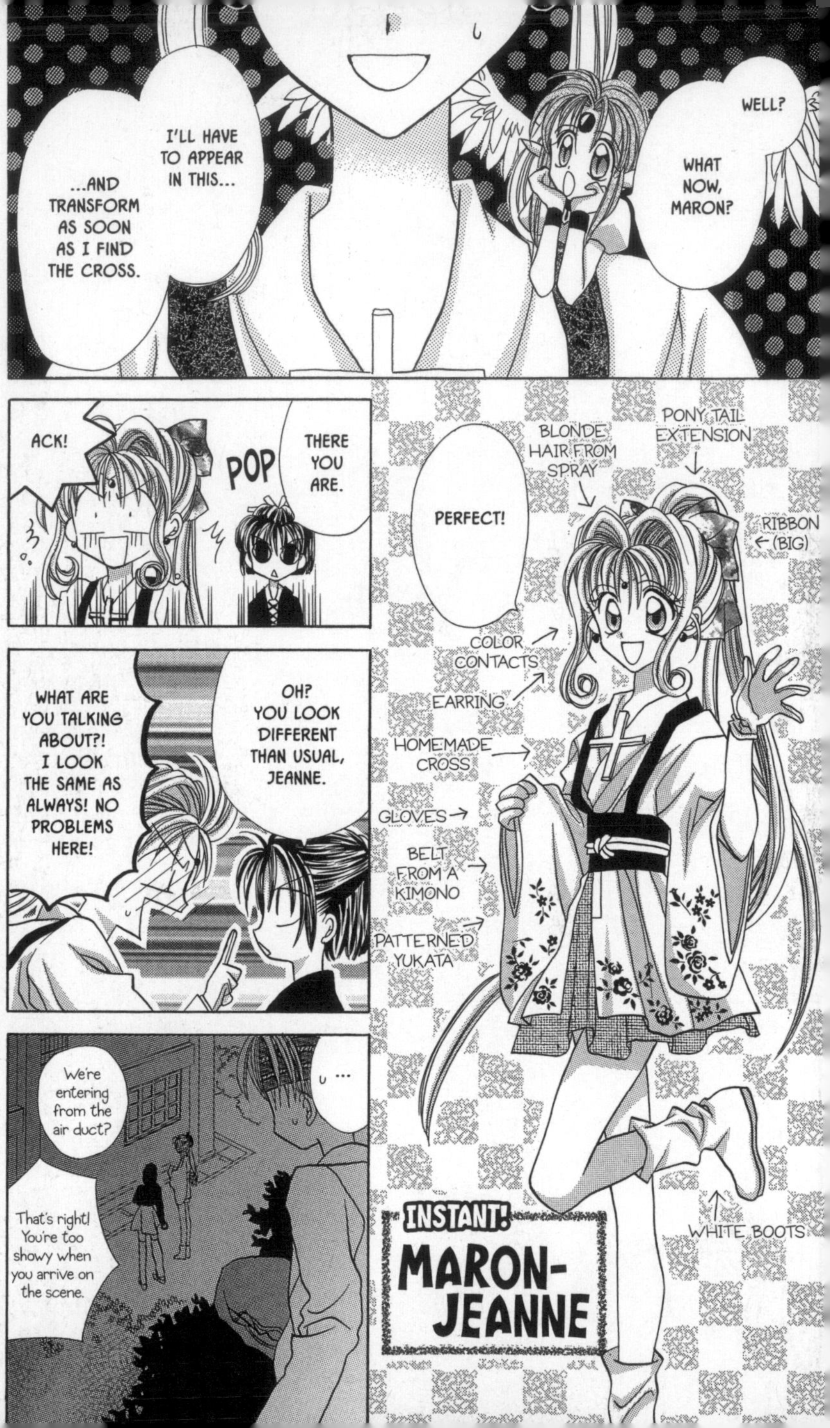

WELL?
WHAT NOW, MARON?
I'LL HAVE TO APPEAR IN THIS...
...AND TRANSFORM AS SOON AS I FIND THE CROSS.
PERFECT!
PONY TAIL EXTENSION
BLONDE HAIR FROM SPRAY
RIBBON ←(BIG)
COLOR CONTACTS
EARRING
HOMEMADE CROSS
GLOVES
BELT FROM A KIMONO
PATTERNED YUKATA
WHITE BOOTS
INSTANT!
MARON-JEANNE
THERE YOU ARE.
POP
ACK!
OH? YOU LOOK DIFFERENT THAN USUAL, JEANNE.
WHAT ARE YOU TALKING ABOUT?! I LOOK THE SAME AS ALWAYS! NO PROBLEMS HERE!
...
We're entering from the air duct?
That's right! You're too showy when you arrive on the scene.

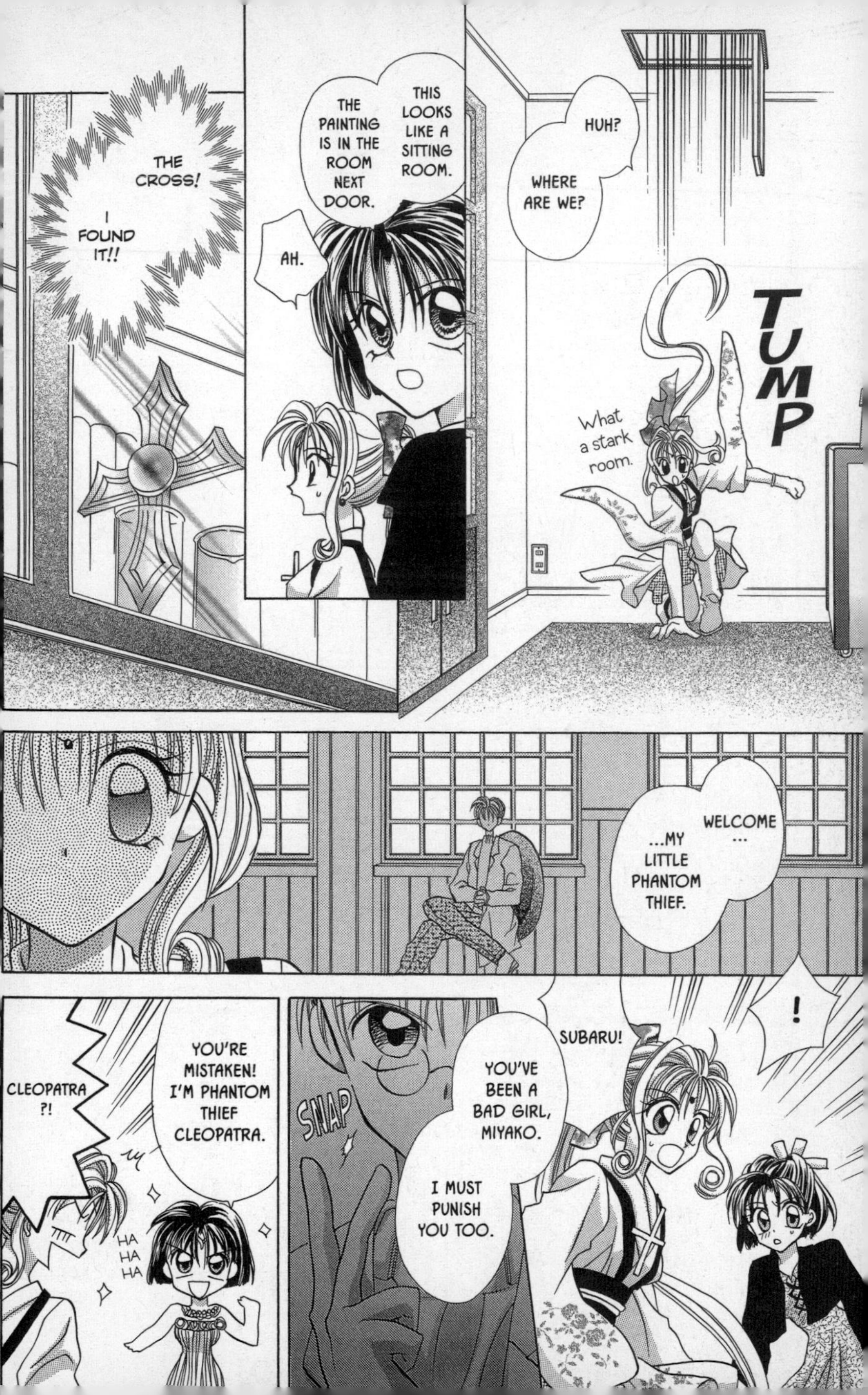
HUH?
WHERE ARE WE?
TUMP
What a stark room.
THIS LOOKS LIKE A SITTING ROOM.
THE PAINTING IS IN THE ROOM NEXT DOOR.
AH.
THE CROSS!
I FOUND IT!!
WELCOME...
...MY LITTLE PHANTOM THIEF.
!
SUBARU!
YOU'VE BEEN A BAD GIRL, MIYAKO.
I MUST PUNISH YOU TOO.
SNAP
YOU'RE MISTAKEN! I'M PHANTOM THIEF CLEOPATRA.
CLEOPATRA?!
HA HA HA

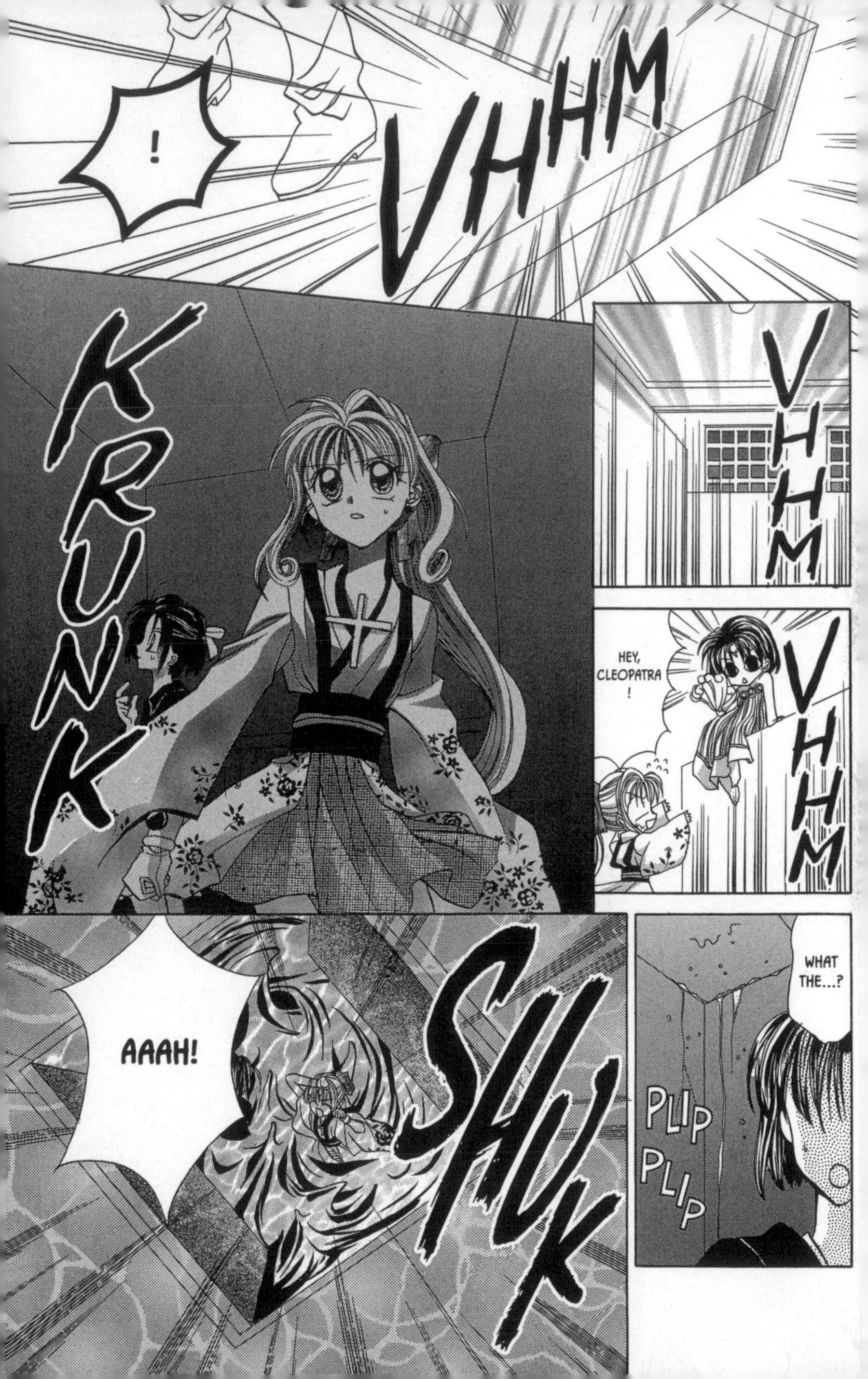
VHHM
!
VHHM
HEY, CLEOPATRA!
VHHM
KRUNK
WHAT THE...?
PLIP PLIP
AAAH!
SHUK

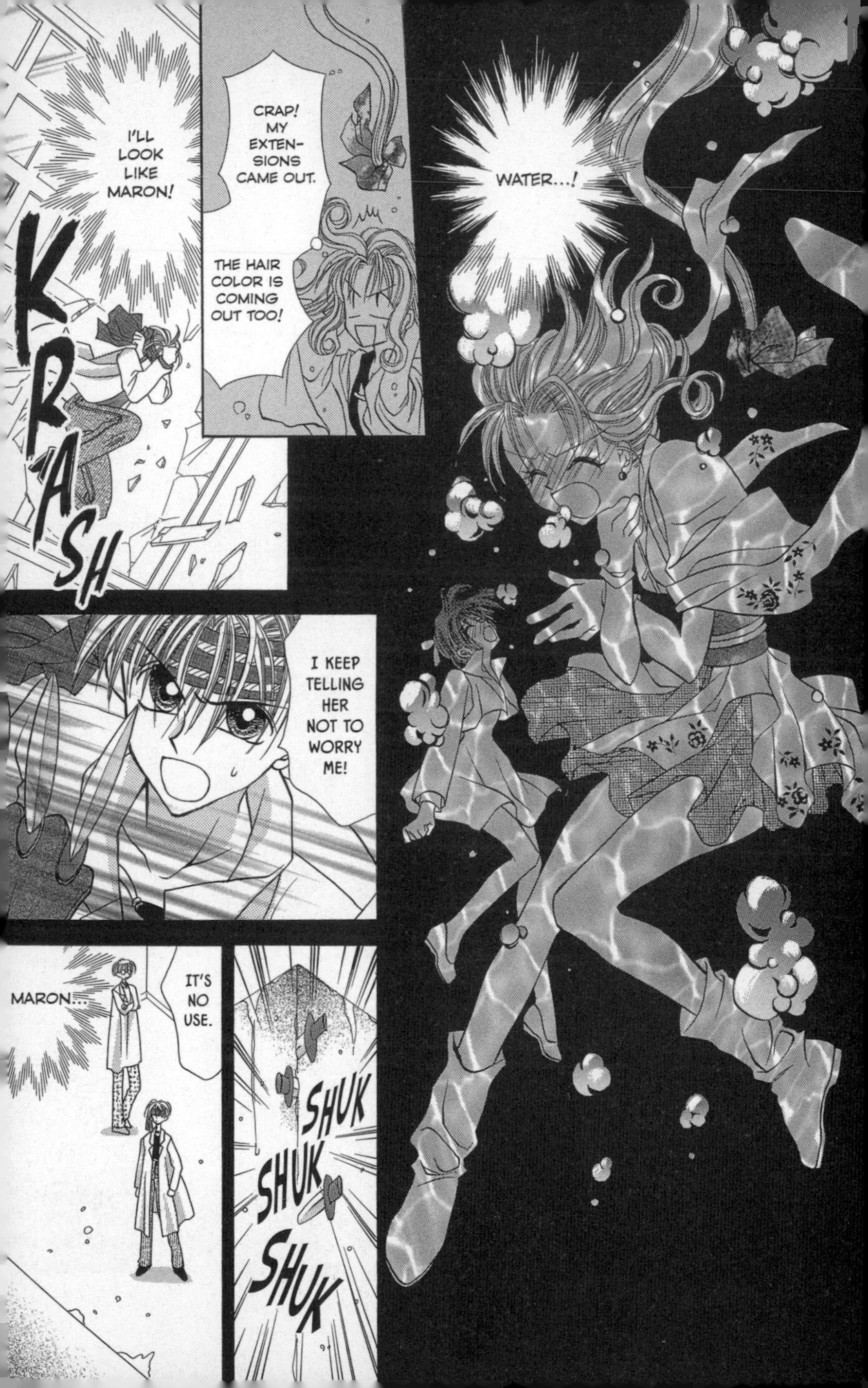
WATER...!
CRAP! MY EXTEN-SIONS CAME OUT.
THE HAIR COLOR IS COMING OUT TOO!
I'LL LOOK LIKE MARON!
KRASH
I KEEP TELLING HER NOT TO WORRY ME!
SHUK SHUK SHUK
IT'S NO USE.
MARON...

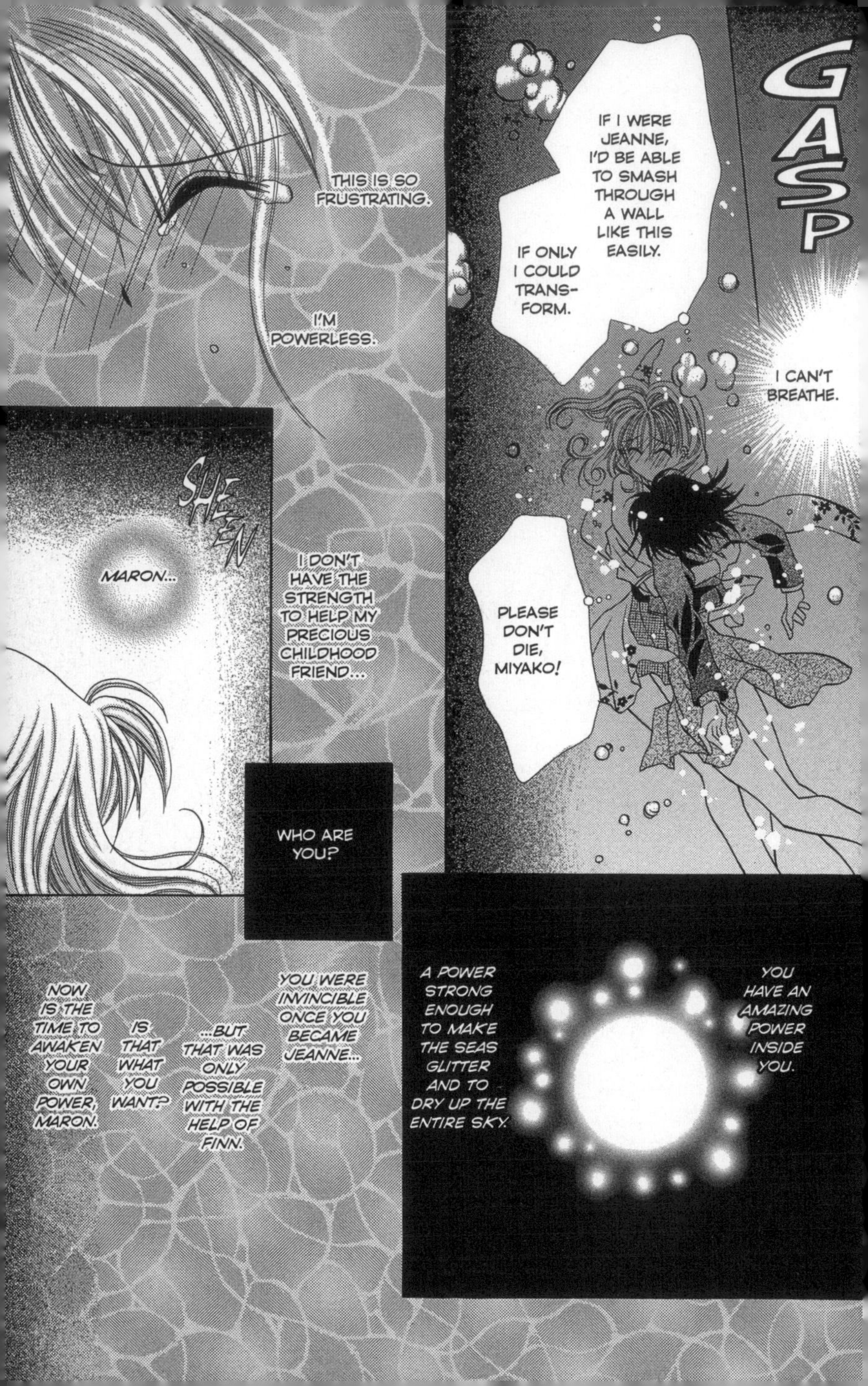
GASP
IF I WERE JEANNE, I'D BE ABLE TO SMASH THROUGH A WALL LIKE THIS EASILY.
IF ONLY I COULD TRANS-FORM.
I CAN'T BREATHE.
PLEASE DON'T DIE, MIYAKO!
THIS IS SO FRUSTRATING.
I'M POWERLESS.
SHEEN
MARON...
I DON'T HAVE THE STRENGTH TO HELP MY PRECIOUS CHILDHOOD FRIEND...
WHO ARE YOU?
YOU HAVE AN AMAZING POWER INSIDE YOU.
A POWER STRONG ENOUGH TO MAKE THE SEAS GLITTER AND TO DRY UP THE ENTIRE SKY.
YOU WERE INVINCIBLE ONCE YOU BECAME JEANNE...
...BUT THAT WAS ONLY POSSIBLE WITH THE HELP OF FINN.
IS THAT WHAT YOU WANT?
NOW IS THE TIME TO AWAKEN YOUR OWN POWER, MARON.

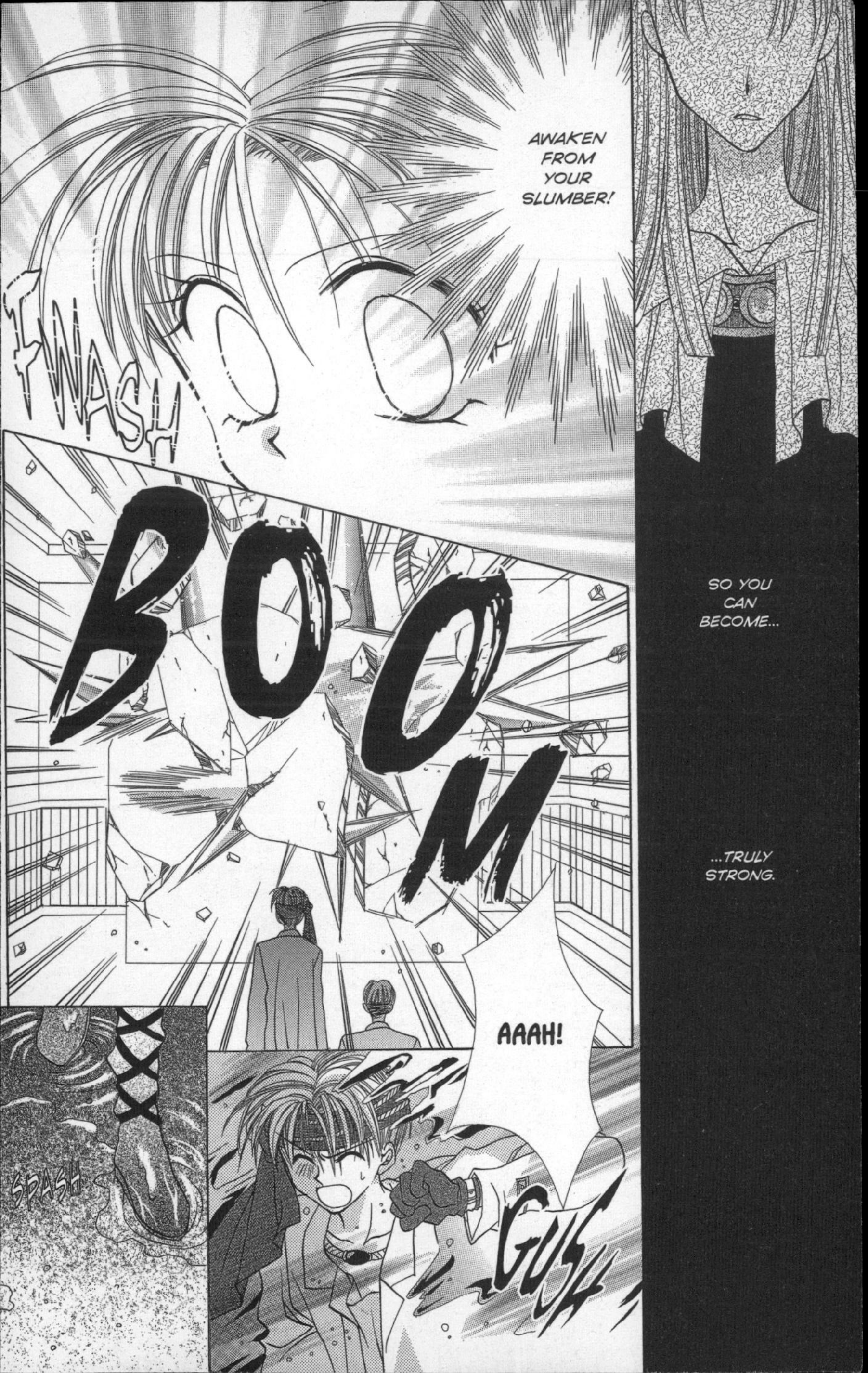
AWAKEN FROM YOUR SLUMBER!
SO YOU CAN BECOME...
...TRULY STRONG.
FWASH
BOOM
AAAH!
GUSH
SPASH

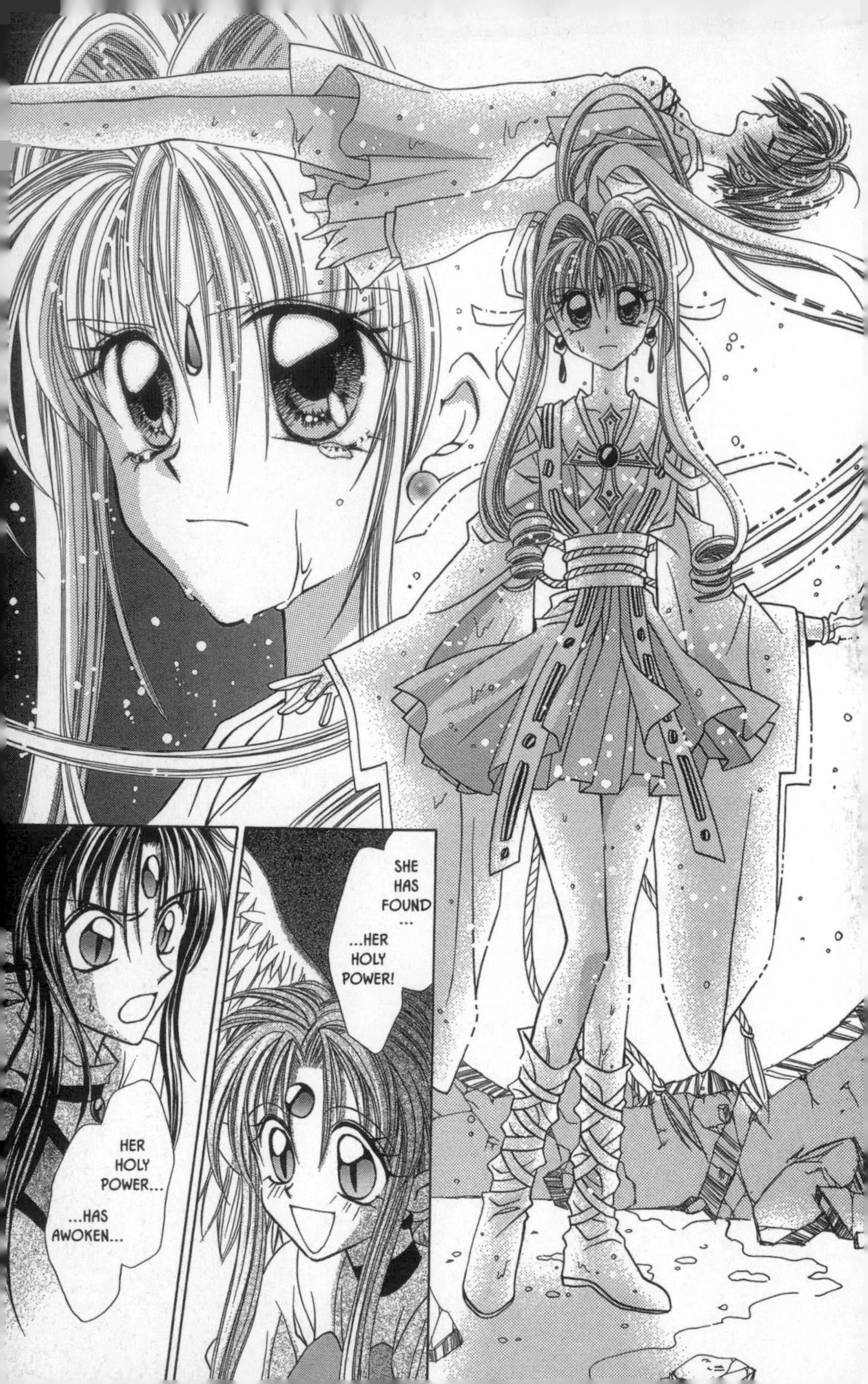
SHE HAS FOUND ...
...HER HOLY POWER!
HER HOLY POWER...
...HAS AWOKEN...

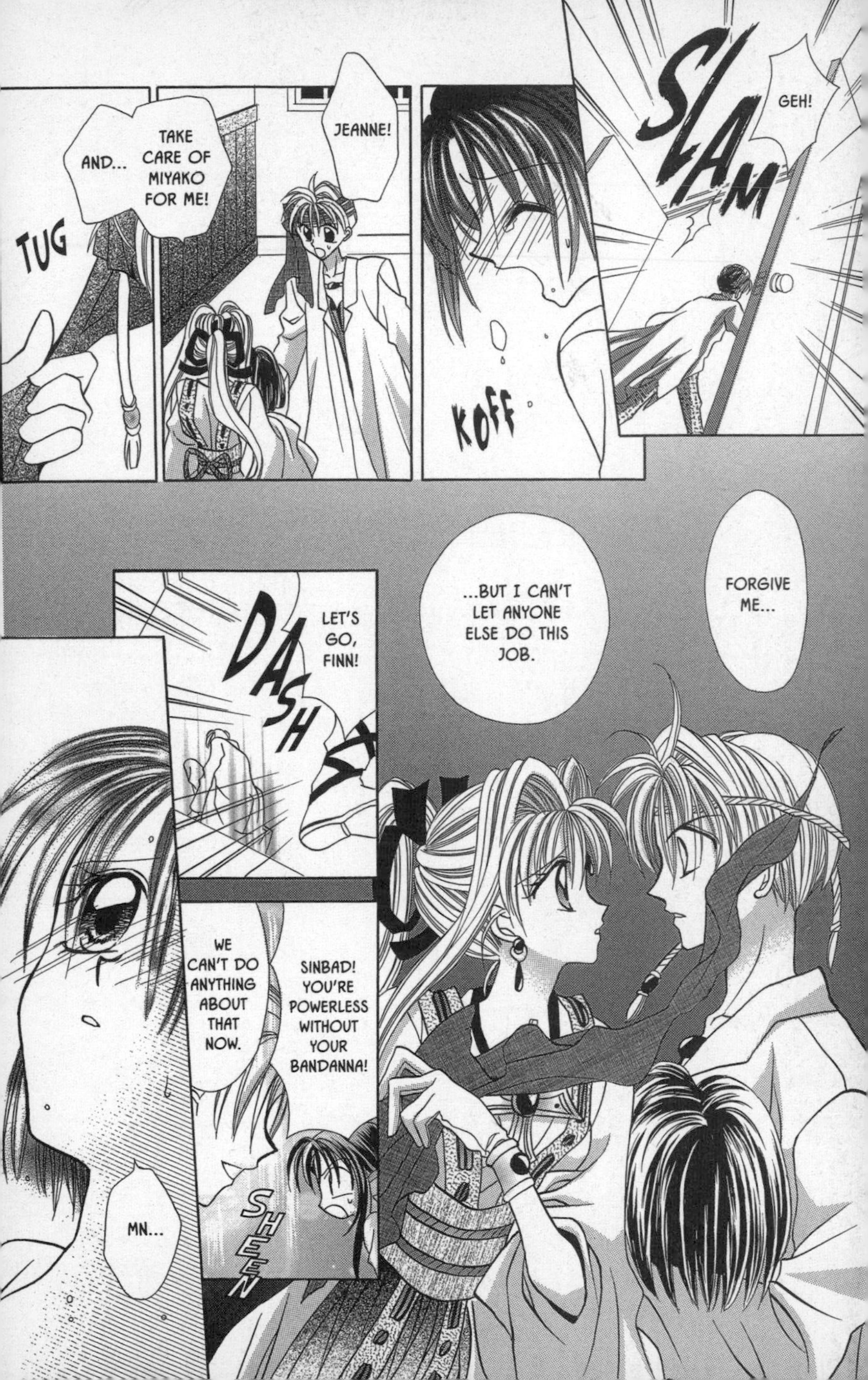
SLAM
GEH!
KOFF
JEANNE!
TUG
AND...
TAKE CARE OF MIYAKO FOR ME!
FORGIVE ME...
...BUT I CAN'T LET ANYONE ELSE DO THIS JOB.
DASH
LET'S GO, FINN!
SINBAD! YOU'RE POWERLESS WITHOUT YOUR BANDANNA!
WE CAN'T DO ANYTHING ABOUT THAT NOW.
SHEEN
MN...

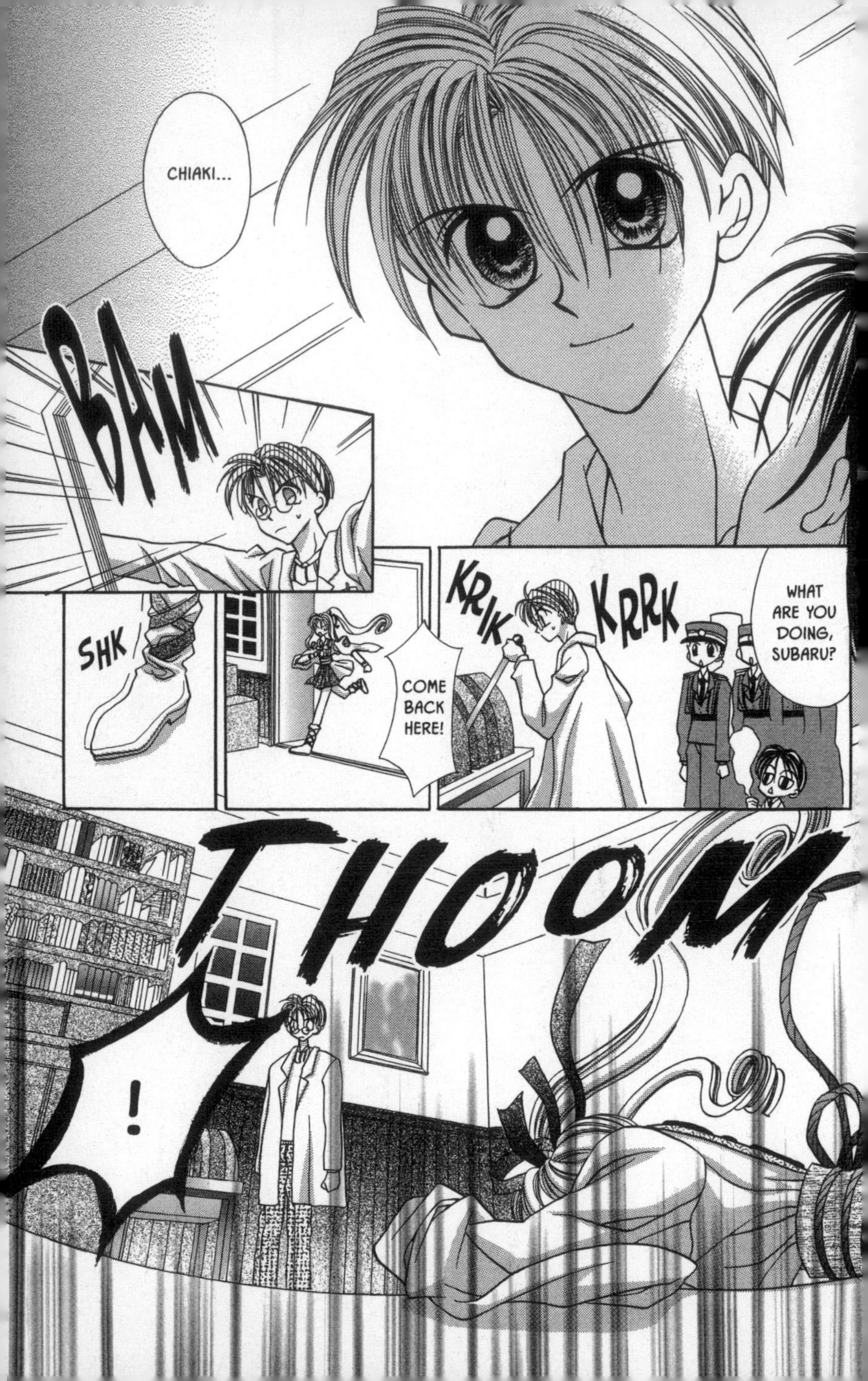
CHIAKI...
BAM
WHAT ARE YOU DOING, SUBARU?
KRRK
KRIK
COME BACK HERE!
SHK
THOOM
!

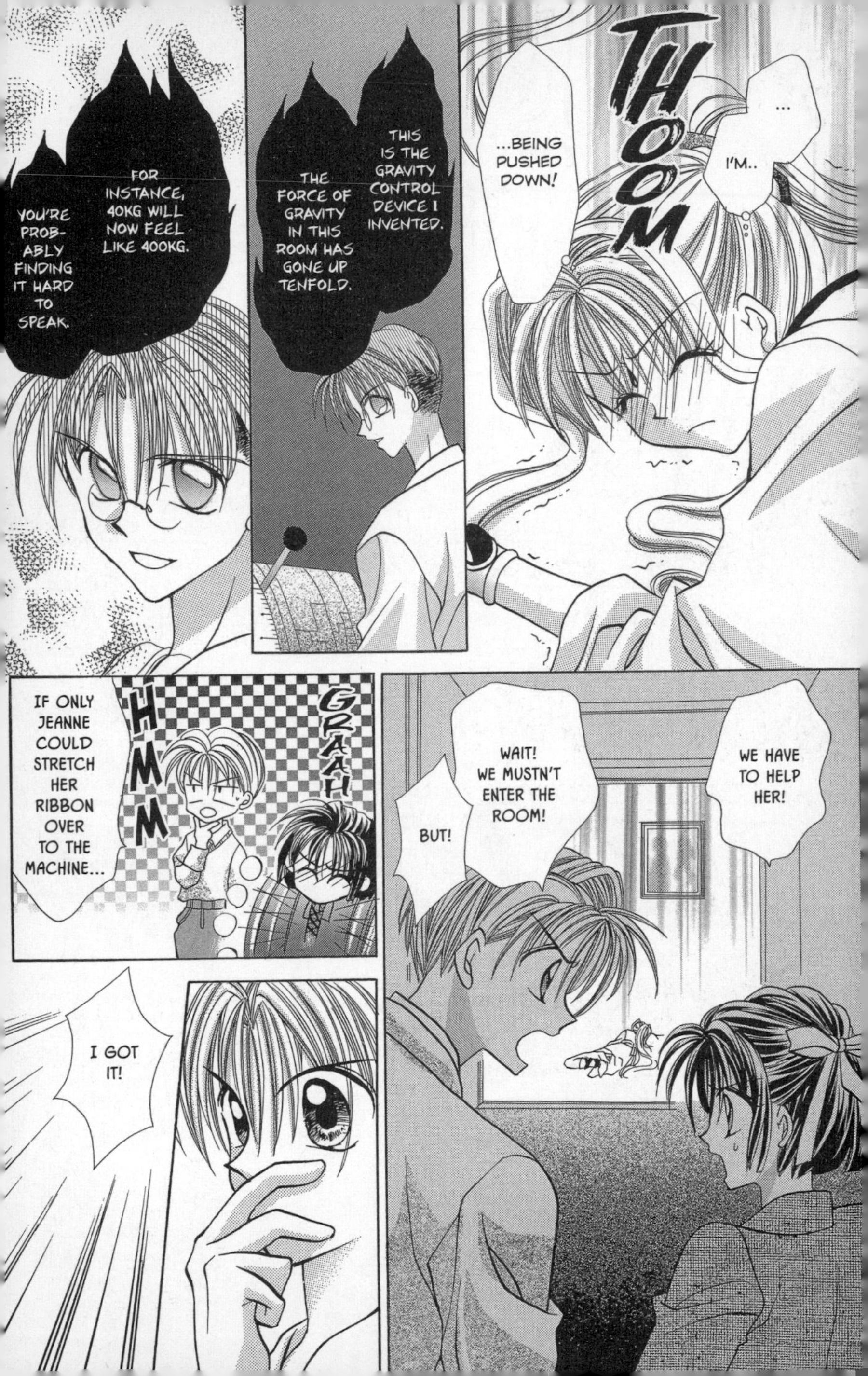
...
I'M..
THOOM
...BEING PUSHED DOWN!
THIS IS THE GRAVITY CONTROL DEVICE I INVENTED.
THE FORCE OF GRAVITY IN THIS ROOM HAS GONE UP TENFOLD.
FOR INSTANCE, 40KG WILL NOW FEEL LIKE 400KG.
YOU'RE PROB-ABLY FINDING IT HARD TO SPEAK.
WE HAVE TO HELP HER!
WAIT! WE MUSTN'T ENTER THE ROOM!
BUT!
GRAAH!
HMM
IF ONLY JEANNE COULD STRETCH HER RIBBON OVER TO THE MACHINE...
I GOT IT!

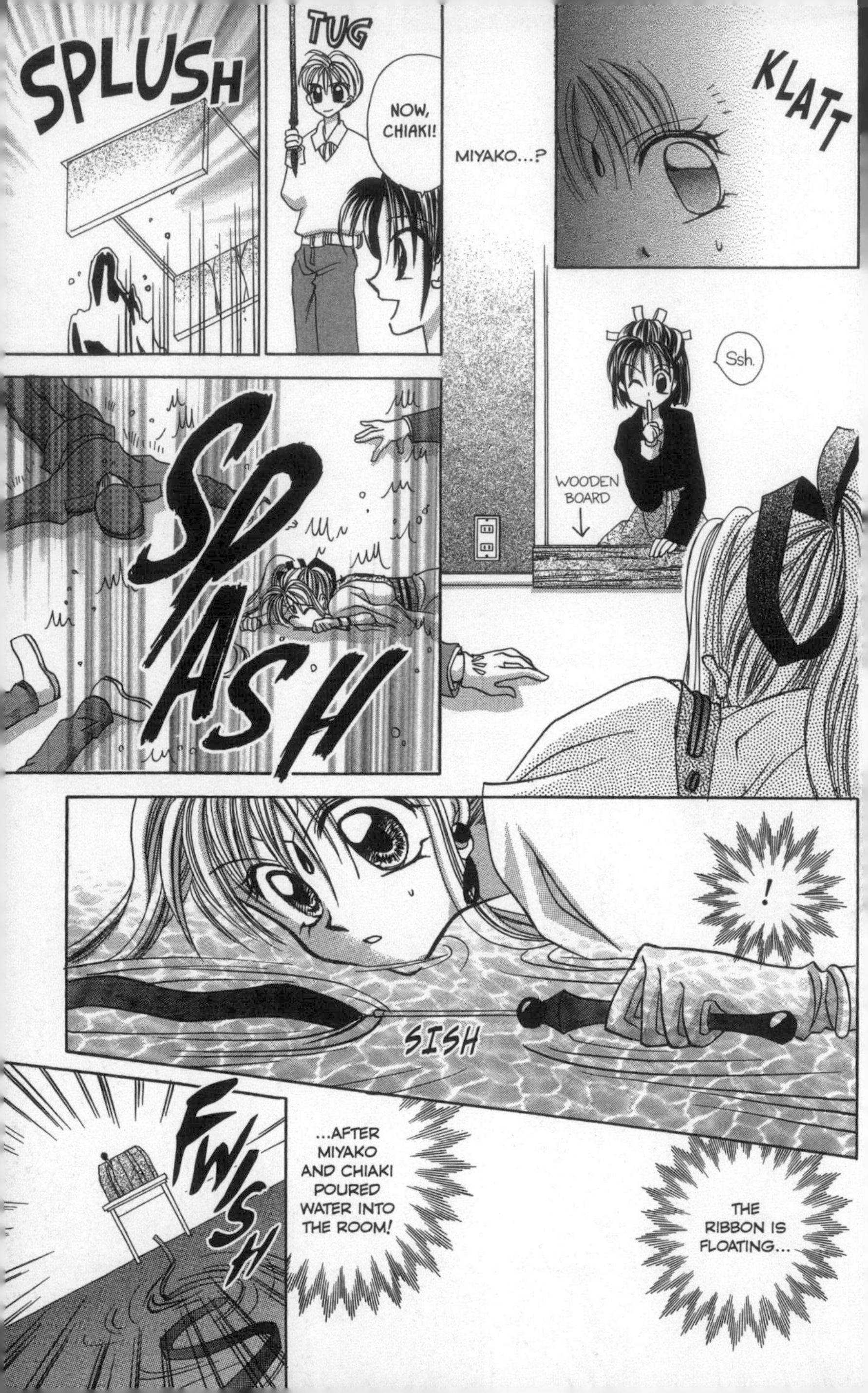
KLATT
MIYAKO...?
TUG
NOW, CHIAKI!
SPLUSH
Ssh.
WOODEN BOARD
SPASH
!
SISH
THE RIBBON IS FLOATING...
...AFTER MIYAKO AND CHIAKI POURED WATER INTO THE ROOM!
FWISH

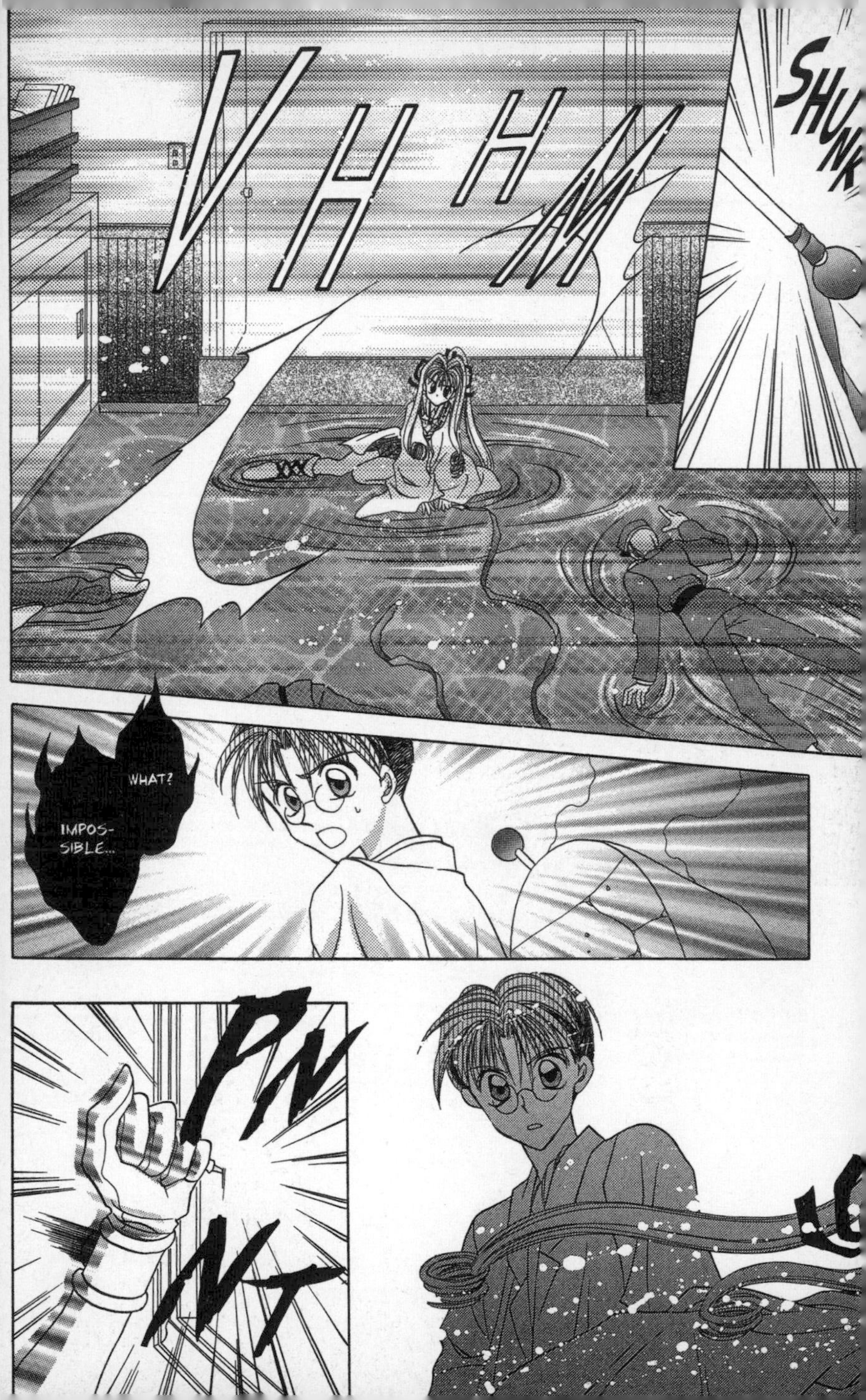
SHUNK
VHHM
WHAT?
IMPOSSIBLE...
PNNT

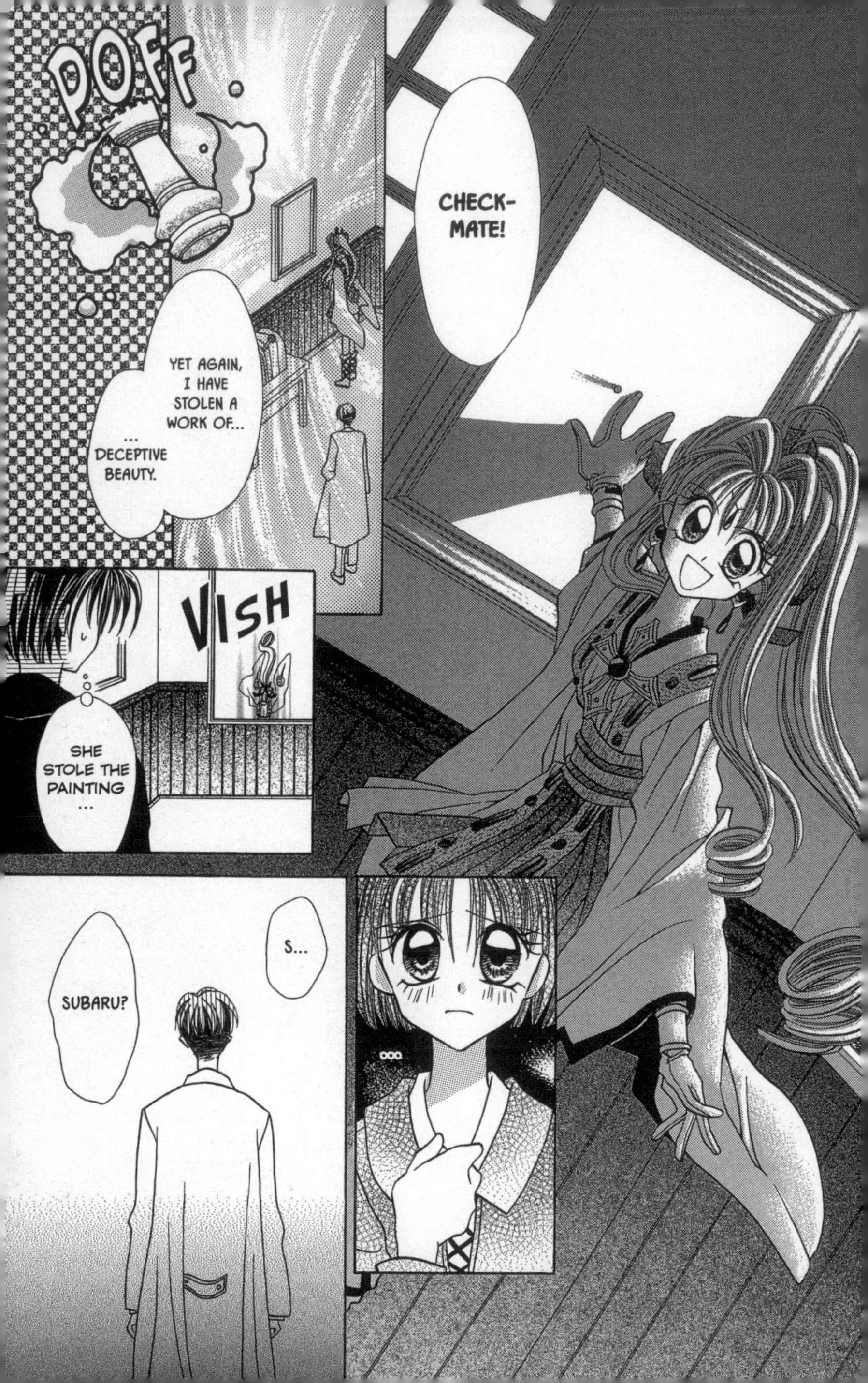
CHECK-MATE!
POFF
YET AGAIN, I HAVE STOLEN A WORK OF... ...DECEPTIVE BEAUTY.
VISH
SHE STOLE THE PAINTING ...
S...
SUBARU?

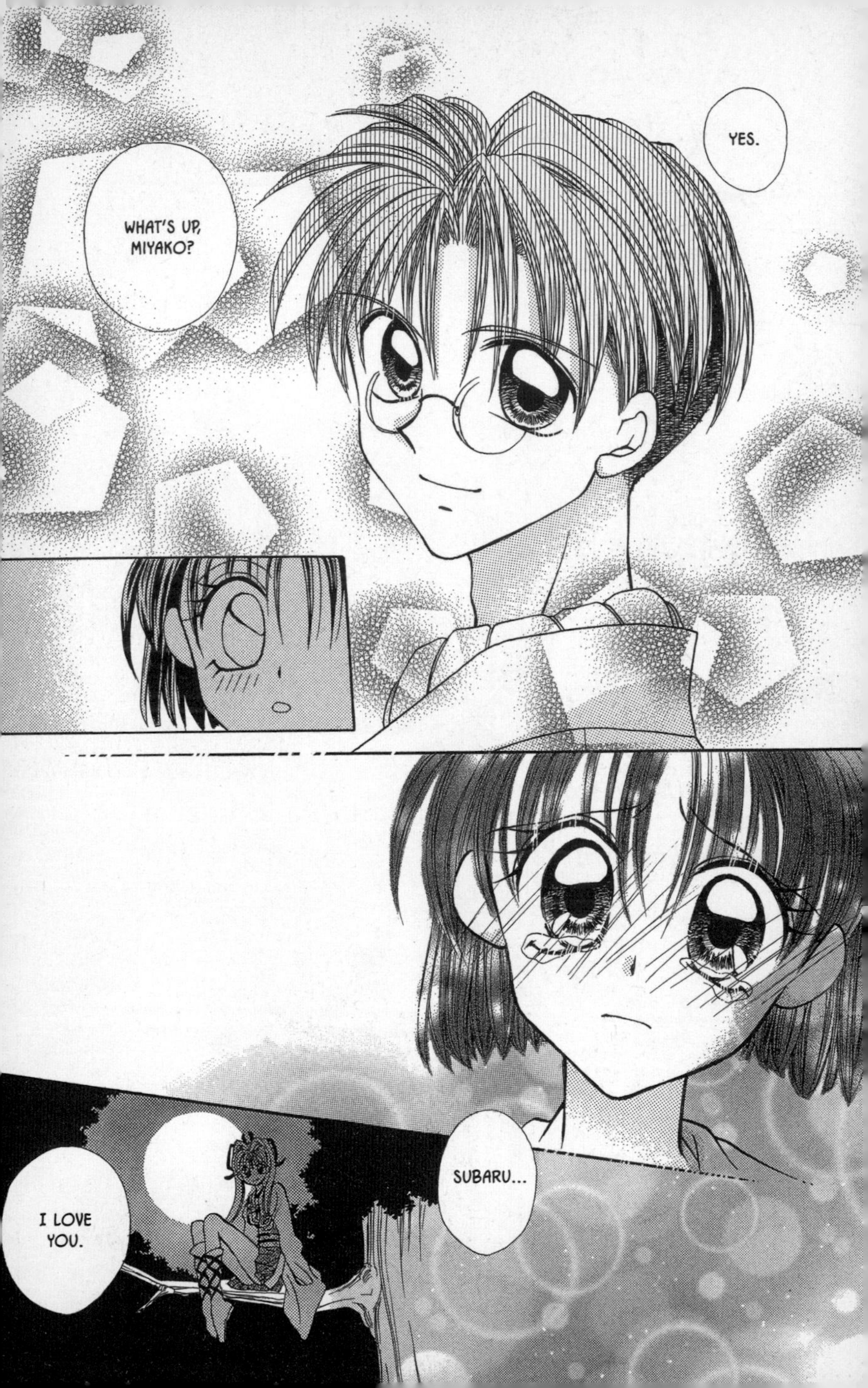
YES.
WHAT'S UP, MIYAKO?
SUBARU...
I LOVE YOU.

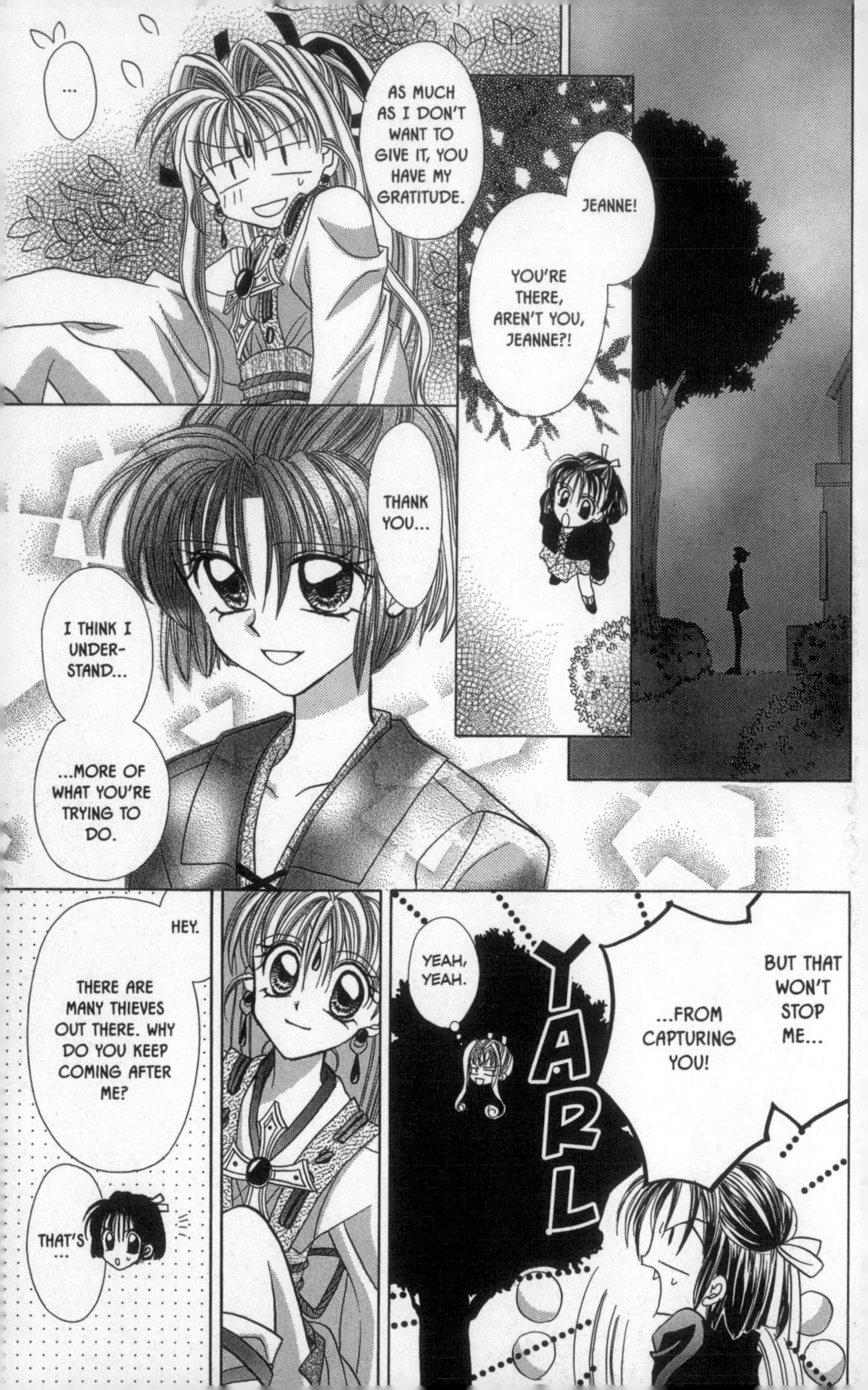
JEANNE!
YOU'RE THERE, AREN'T YOU, JEANNE?!
AS MUCH AS I DON'T WANT TO GIVE IT, YOU HAVE MY GRATITUDE.
...
THANK YOU...
I THINK I UNDERSTAND...
...MORE OF WHAT YOU'RE TRYING TO DO.
BUT THAT WON'T STOP ME...
...FROM CAPTURING YOU!
YARL
YEAH, YEAH.
HEY.
THERE ARE MANY THIEVES OUT THERE. WHY DO YOU KEEP COMING AFTER ME?
THAT'S ...

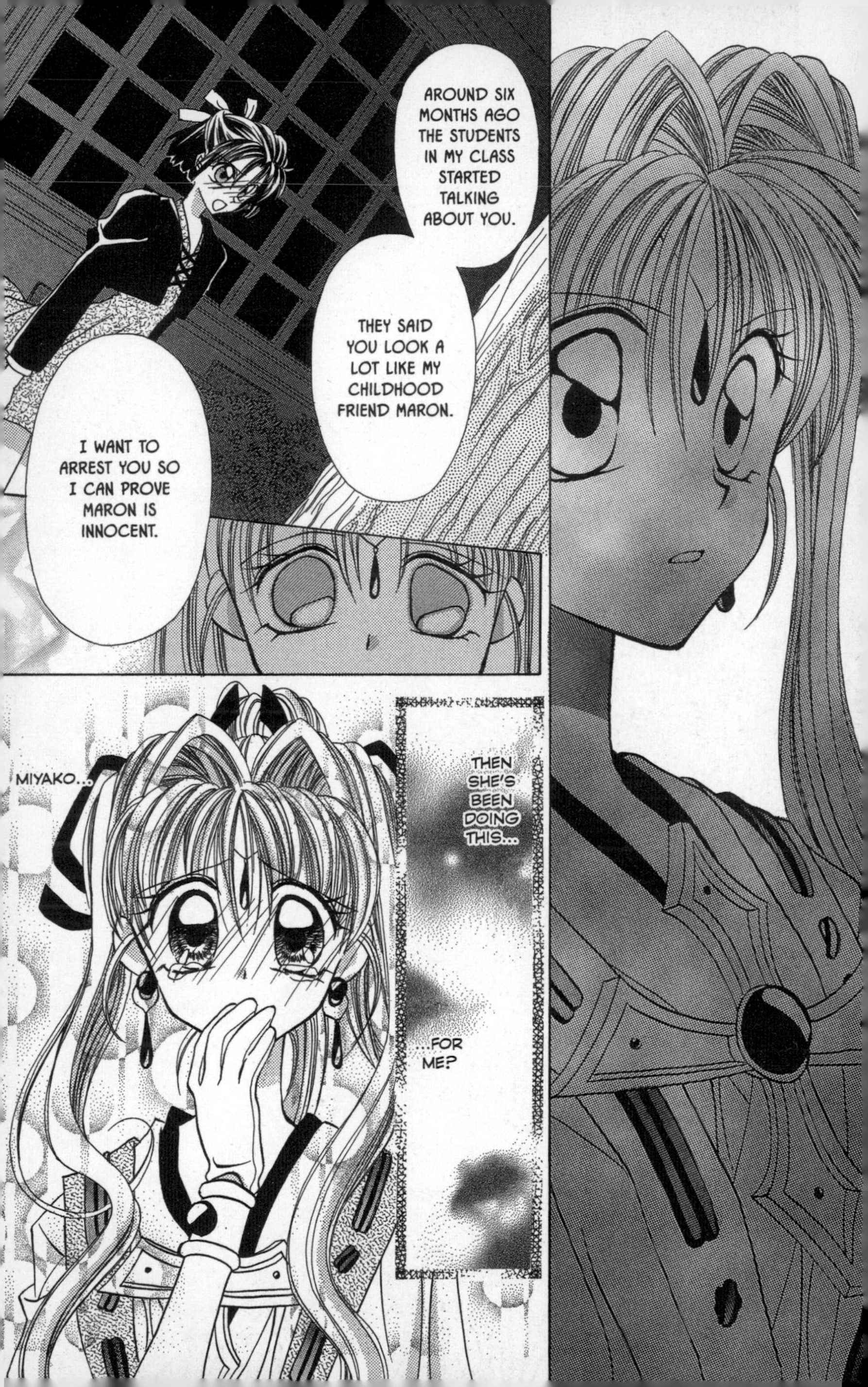
AROUND SIX MONTHS AGO THE STUDENTS IN MY CLASS STARTED TALKING ABOUT YOU.
THEY SAID YOU LOOK A LOT LIKE MY CHILDHOOD FRIEND MARON.
I WANT TO ARREST YOU SO I CAN PROVE MARON IS INNOCENT.
THEN SHE'S BEEN DOING THIS...
...FOR ME?
MIYAKO...

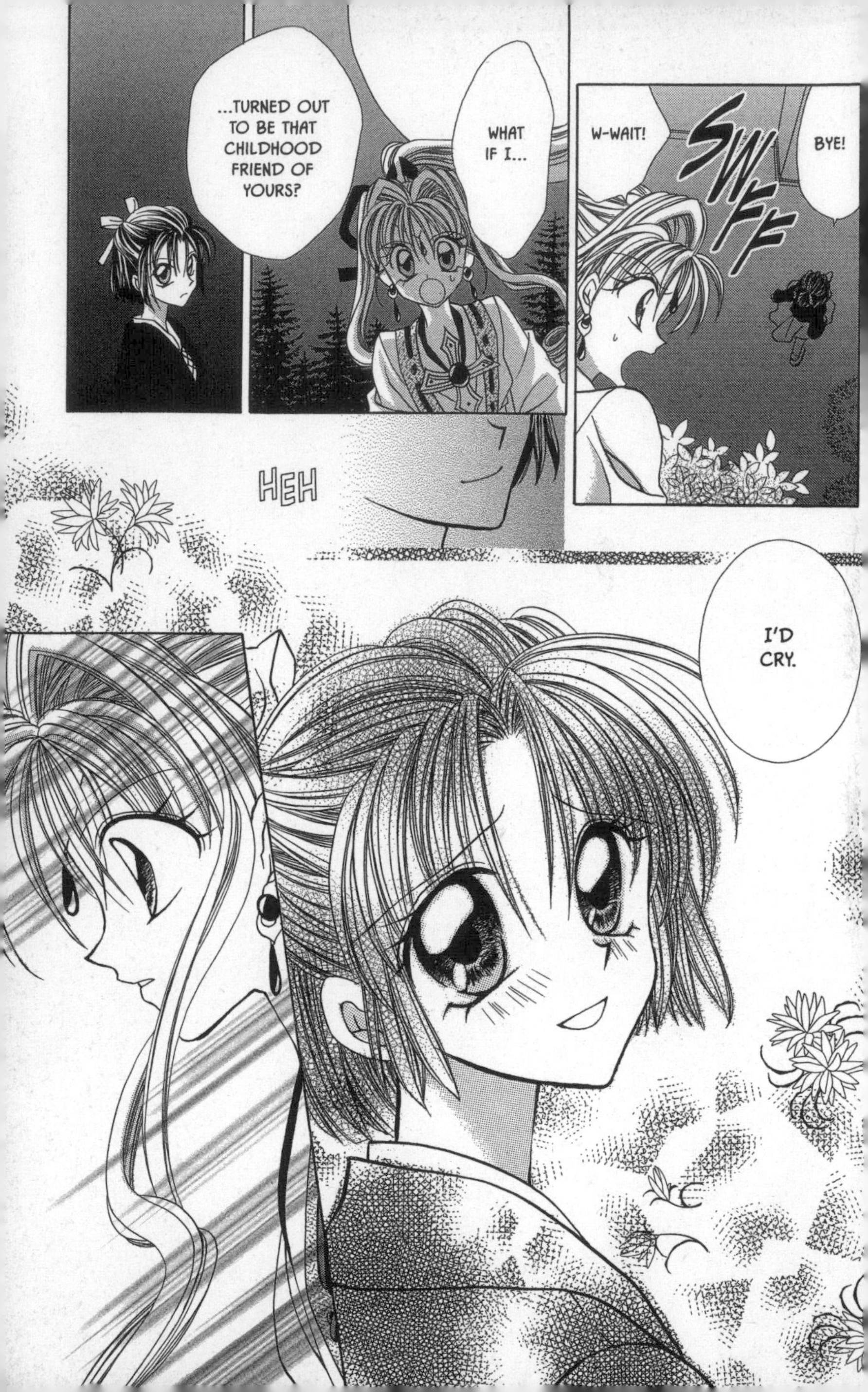
BYE!
SWFF
W-WAIT!
WHAT IF I...
...TURNED OUT TO BE THAT CHILDHOOD FRIEND OF YOURS?
HEH
I'D CRY.

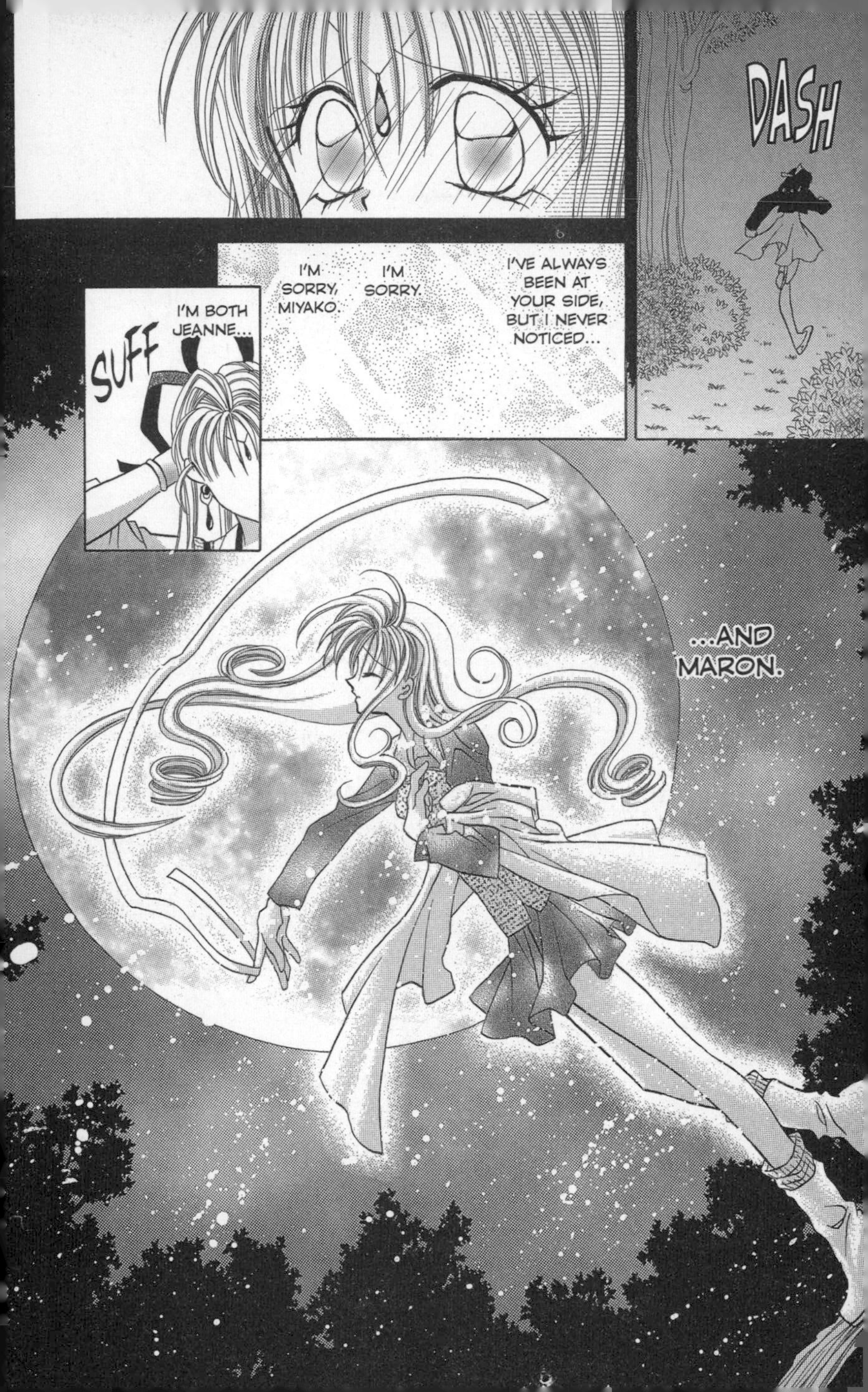
DASH
I'VE ALWAYS BEEN AT YOUR SIDE, BUT I NEVER NOTICED...
I'M SORRY.
I'M SORRY, MIYAKO.
I'M BOTH JEANNE...
SUFF
...AND MARON.

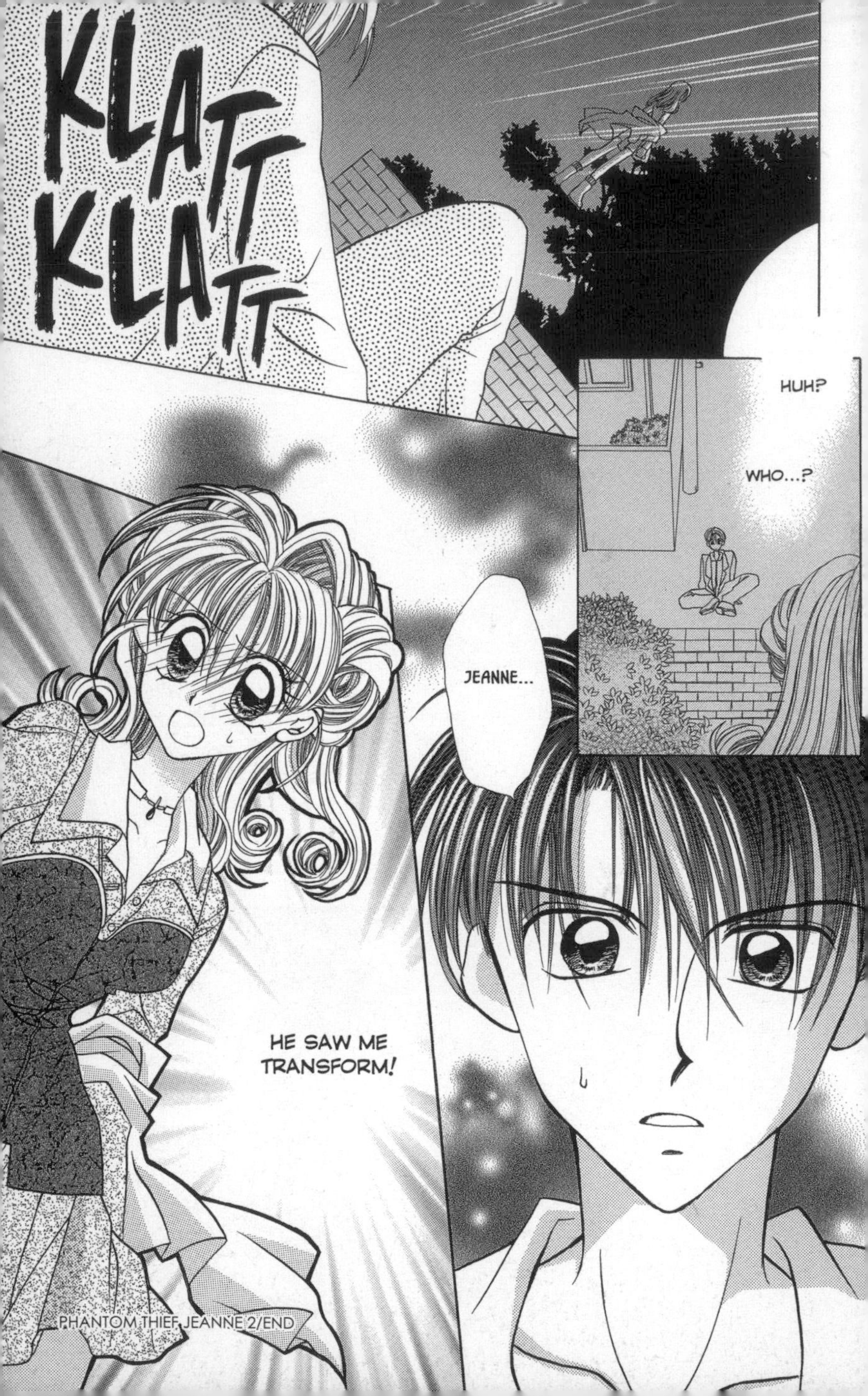
KLATT KLATT
HUH?
WHO...?
JEANNE...
HE SAW ME TRANSFORM!
PHANTOM THIEF JEANNE 2/END

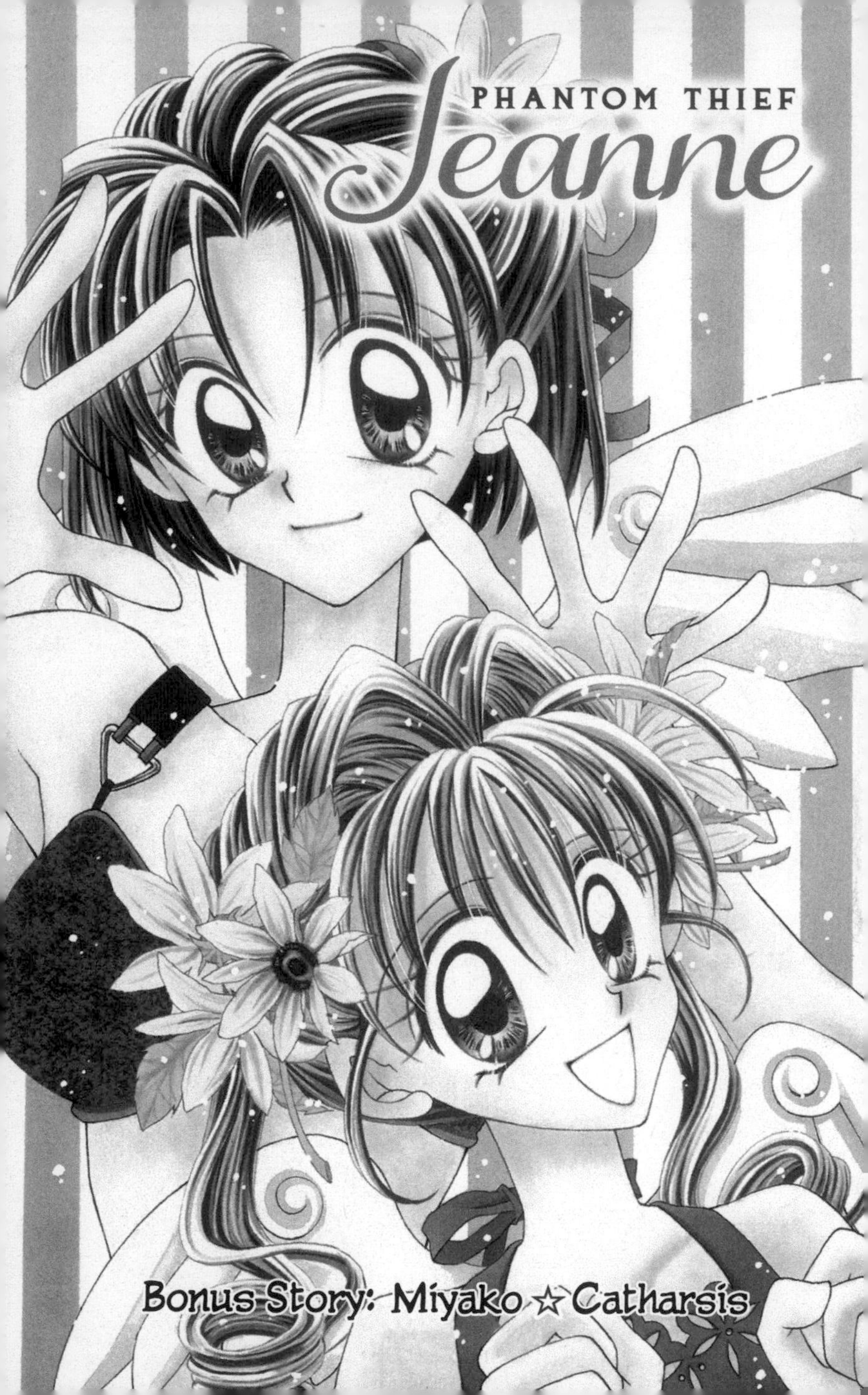
PHANTOM THIEF
Jeanne
Bonus Story: Miyako ☆ Catharsis

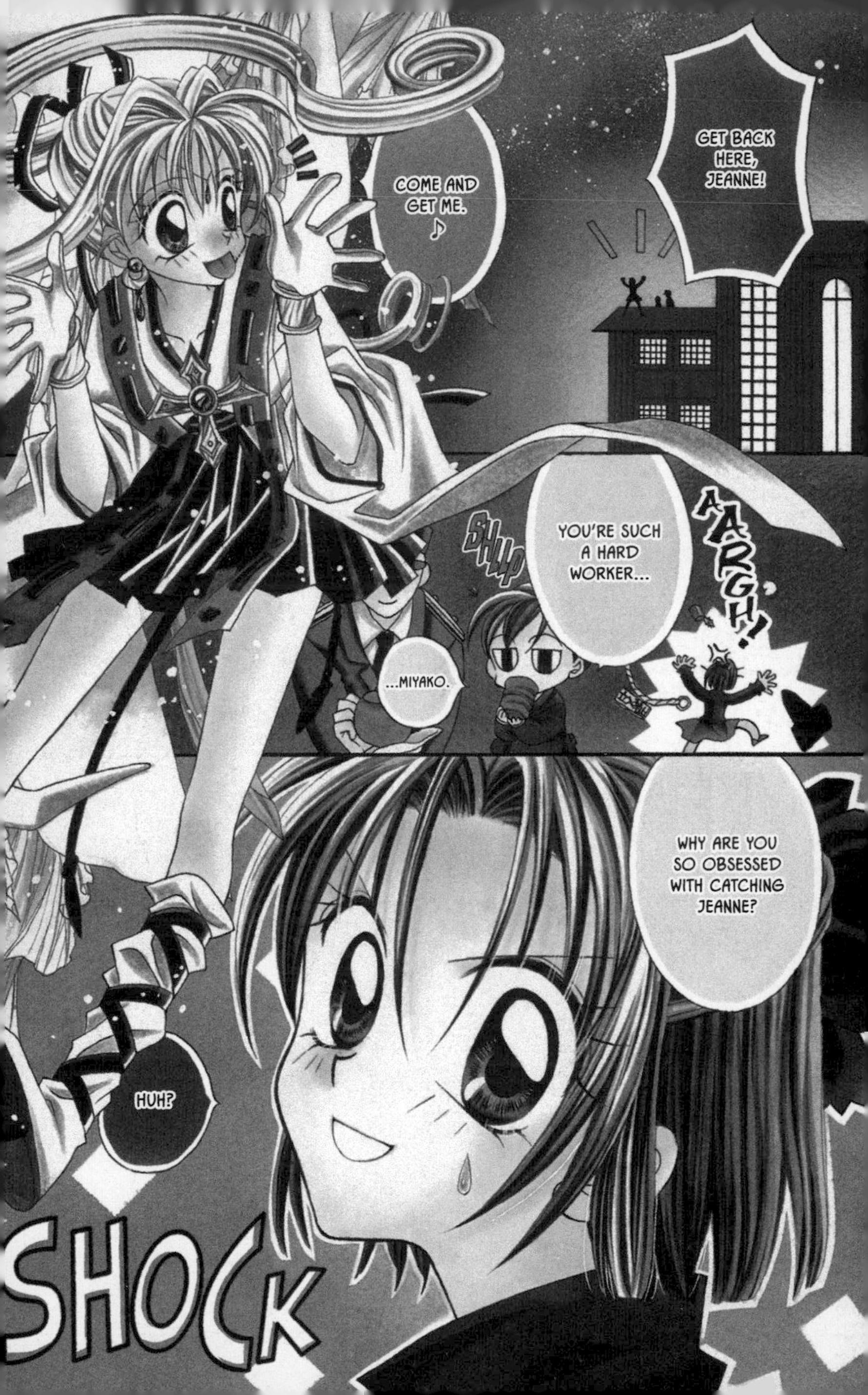
GET BACK HERE, JEANNE!
COME AND GET ME. ♪
AARGH!
YOU'RE SUCH A HARD WORKER...
SHLLP
...MIYAKO.
WHY ARE YOU SO OBSESSED WITH CATCHING JEANNE?
HUH?
SHOCK

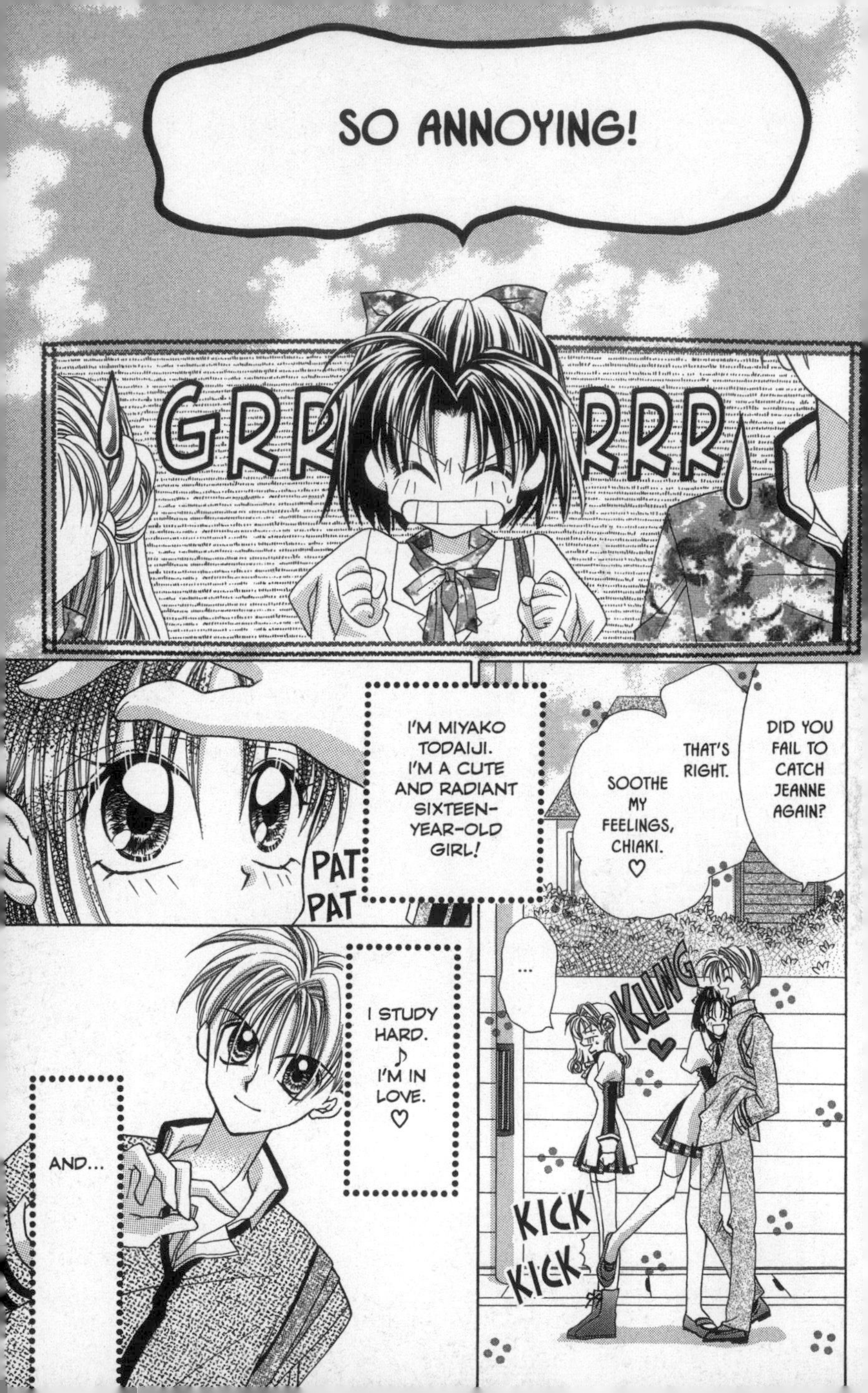
SO ANNOYING!
GRRRRRR
DID YOU FAIL TO CATCH JEANNE AGAIN?
THAT'S RIGHT.
SOOTHE MY FEELINGS, CHIAKI. ♡
I'M MIYAKO TODAIJI. I'M A CUTE AND RADIANT SIXTEEN-YEAR-OLD GIRL!
PAT PAT
...
KLING ♥
KICK KICK
I STUDY HARD. ♪ I'M IN LOVE. ♡
AND...

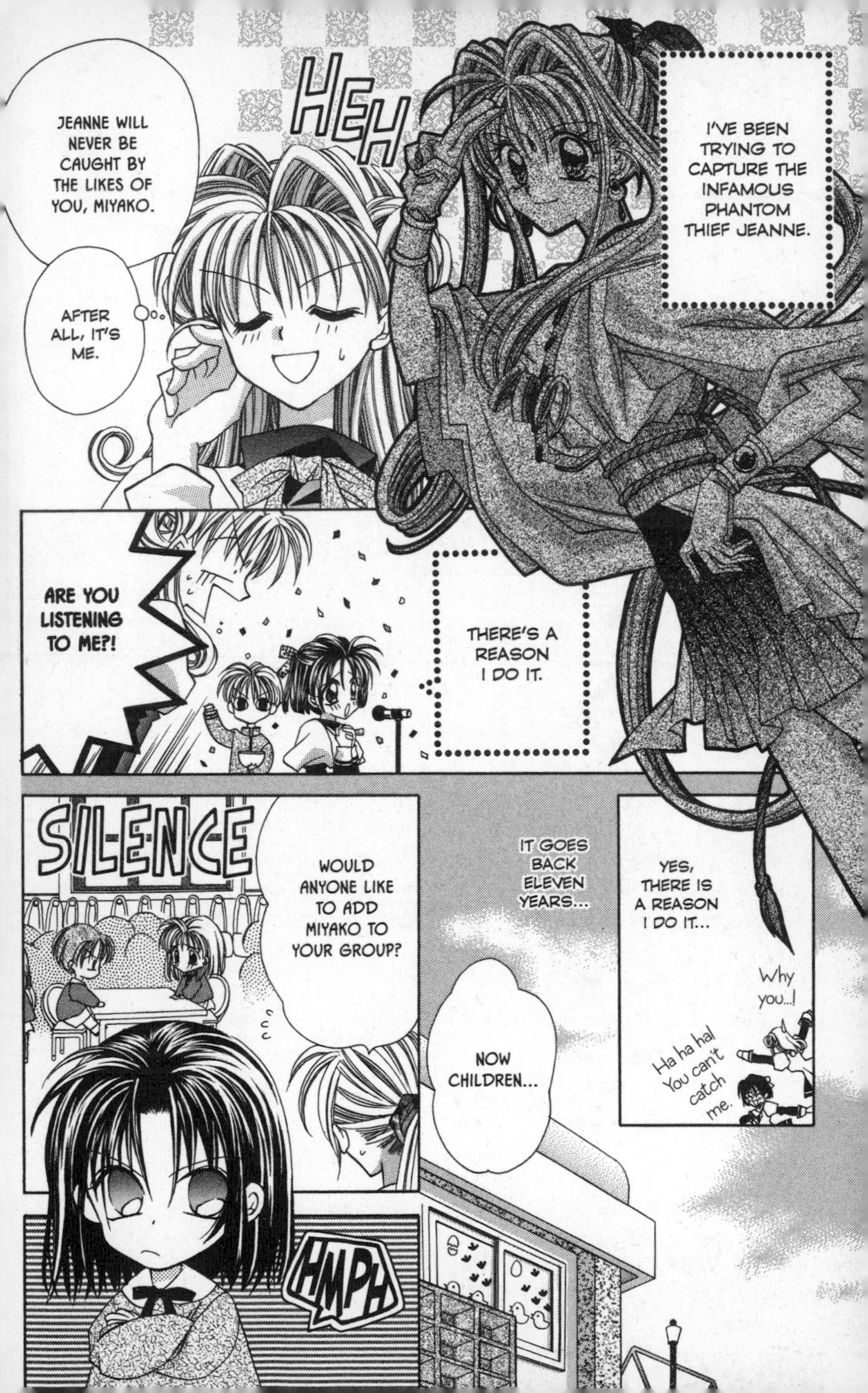
I'VE BEEN TRYING TO CAPTURE THE INFAMOUS PHANTOM THIEF JEANNE.
HEH
JEANNE WILL NEVER BE CAUGHT BY THE LIKES OF YOU, MIYAKO.
AFTER ALL, IT'S ME.
THERE'S A REASON I DO IT.
ARE YOU LISTENING TO ME?!
YES, THERE IS A REASON I DO IT...
Why you...!
Ha ha ha! You can't catch me.
IT GOES BACK ELEVEN YEARS...
NOW CHILDREN...
WOULD ANYONE LIKE TO ADD MIYAKO TO YOUR GROUP?
SILENCE
HMPH

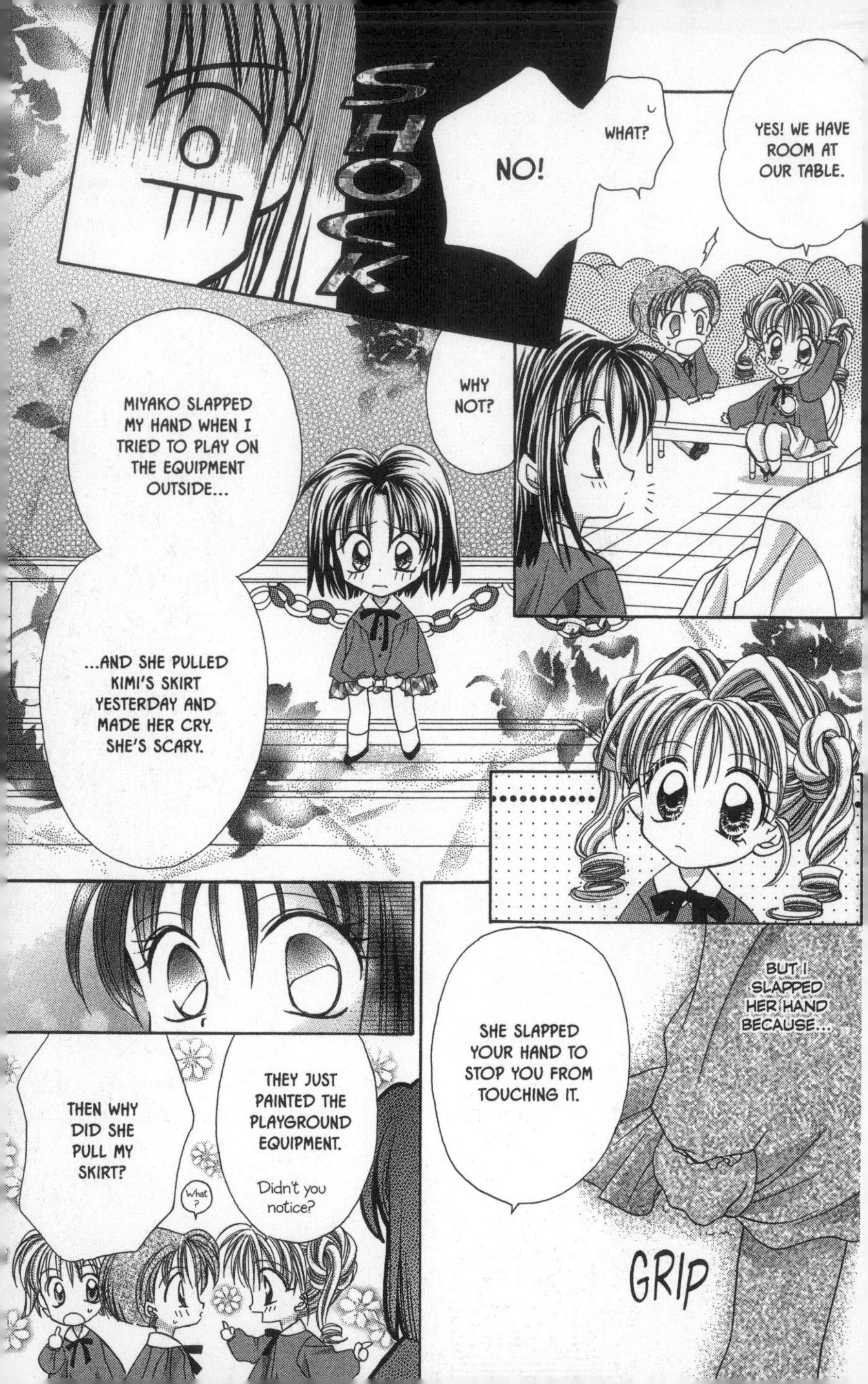
YES! WE HAVE ROOM AT OUR TABLE.
WHAT?
NO!
SHOCK
WHY NOT?
MIYAKO SLAPPED MY HAND WHEN I TRIED TO PLAY ON THE EQUIPMENT OUTSIDE...
...AND SHE PULLED KIMI'S SKIRT YESTERDAY AND MADE HER CRY. SHE'S SCARY.
....
BUT I SLAPPED HER HAND BECAUSE...
SHE SLAPPED YOUR HAND TO STOP YOU FROM TOUCHING IT.
GRIP
THEY JUST PAINTED THE PLAYGROUND EQUIPMENT.
Didn't you notice?
What?
THEN WHY DID SHE PULL MY SKIRT?

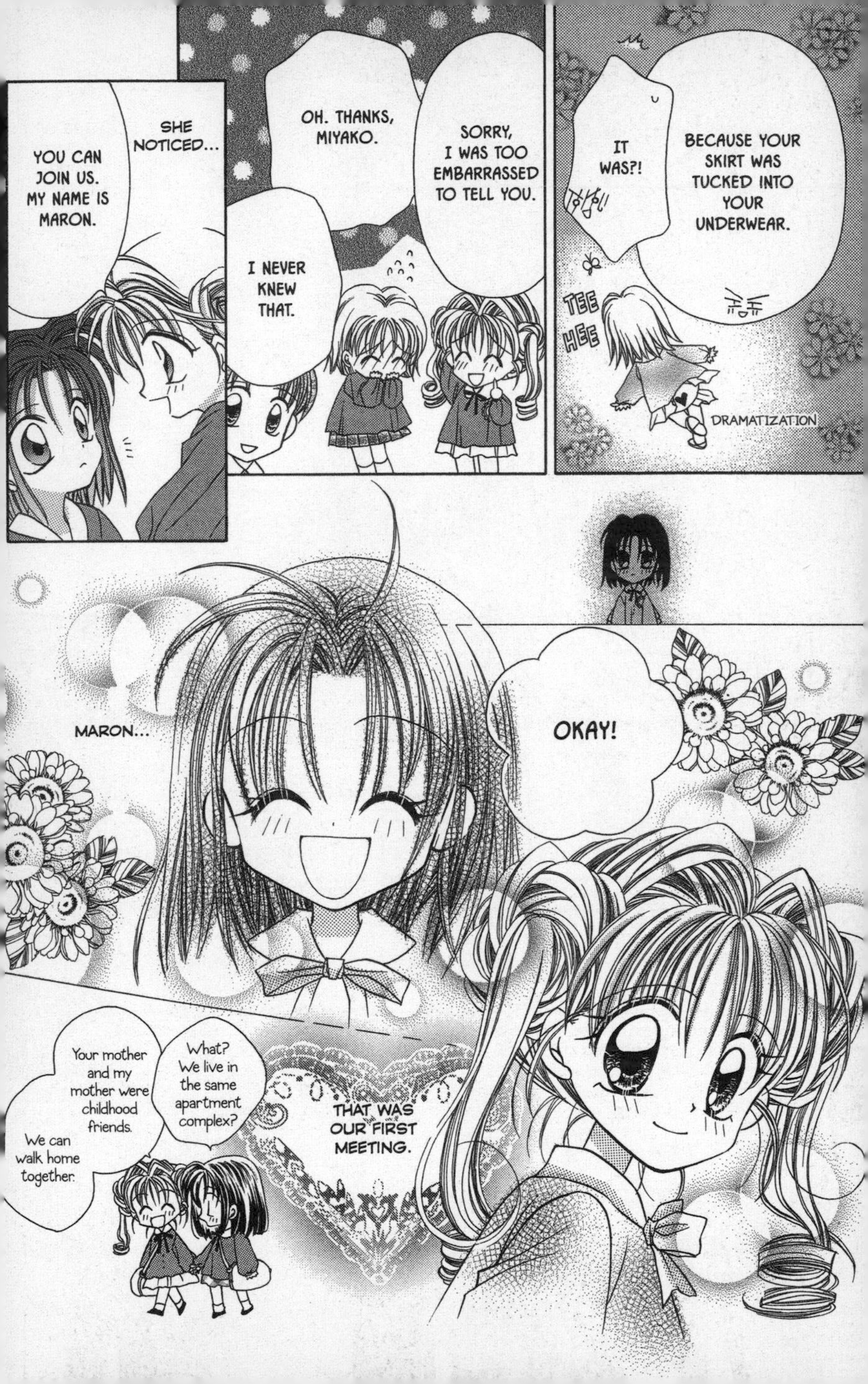
BECAUSE YOUR SKIRT WAS TUCKED INTO YOUR UNDERWEAR.
IT WAS?!
TEE HEE
DRAMATIZATION
SORRY, I WAS TOO EMBARRASSED TO TELL YOU.
OH. THANKS, MIYAKO.
I NEVER KNEW THAT.
SHE NOTICED...
YOU CAN JOIN US. MY NAME IS MARON.
OKAY!
MARON...
THAT WAS OUR FIRST MEETING.
What? We live in the same apartment complex?
Your mother and my mother were childhood friends.
We can walk home together.

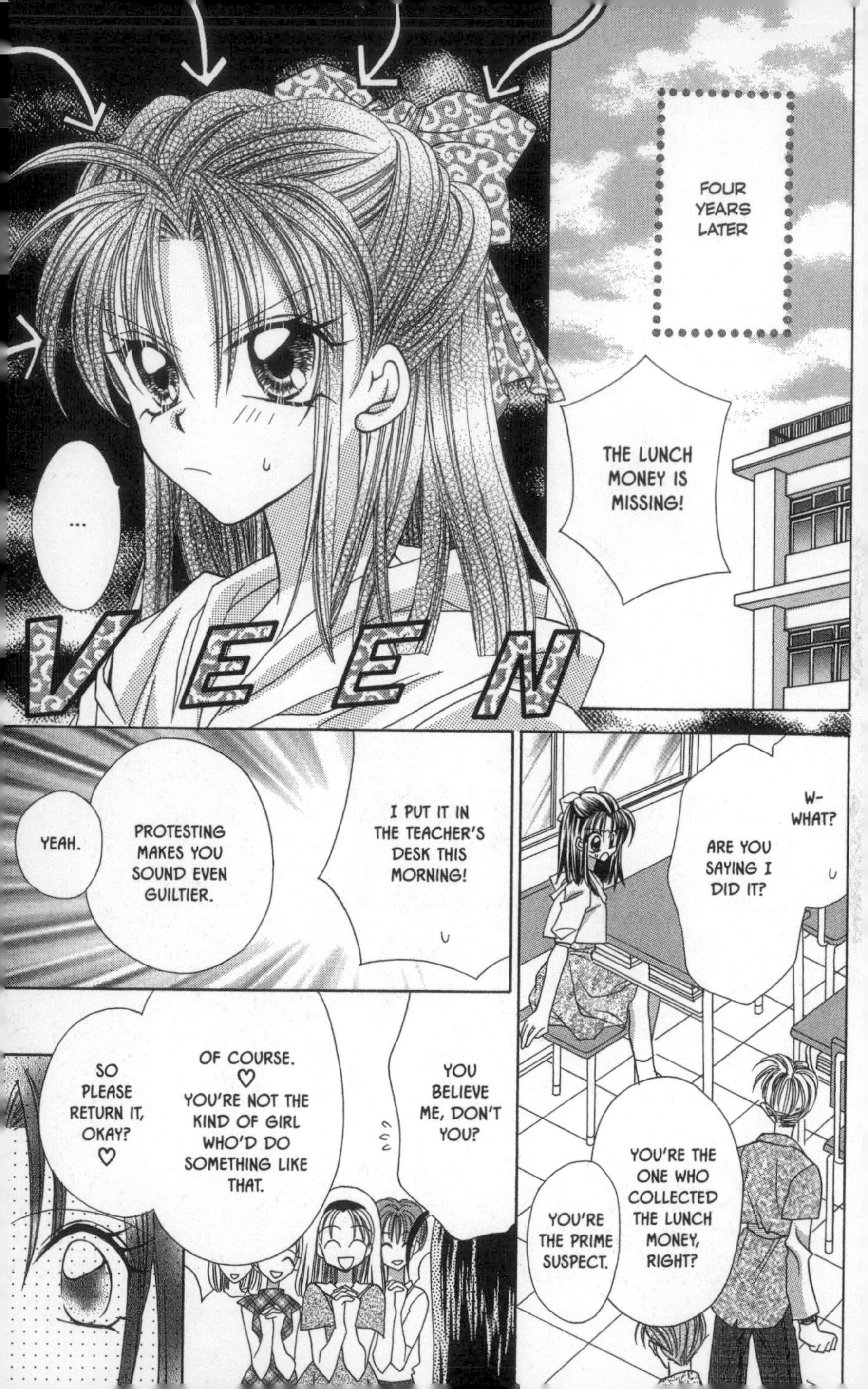
FOUR YEARS LATER
THE LUNCH MONEY IS MISSING!
...
VEEN
W- WHAT?
ARE YOU SAYING I DID IT?
YOU'RE THE ONE WHO COLLECTED THE LUNCH MONEY, RIGHT?
YOU'RE THE PRIME SUSPECT.
I PUT IT IN THE TEACHER'S DESK THIS MORNING!
PROTESTING MAKES YOU SOUND EVEN GUILTIER.
YEAH.
YOU BELIEVE ME, DON'T YOU?
OF COURSE. ♡ YOU'RE NOT THE KIND OF GIRL WHO'D DO SOMETHING LIKE THAT.
SO PLEASE RETURN IT, OKAY? ♡

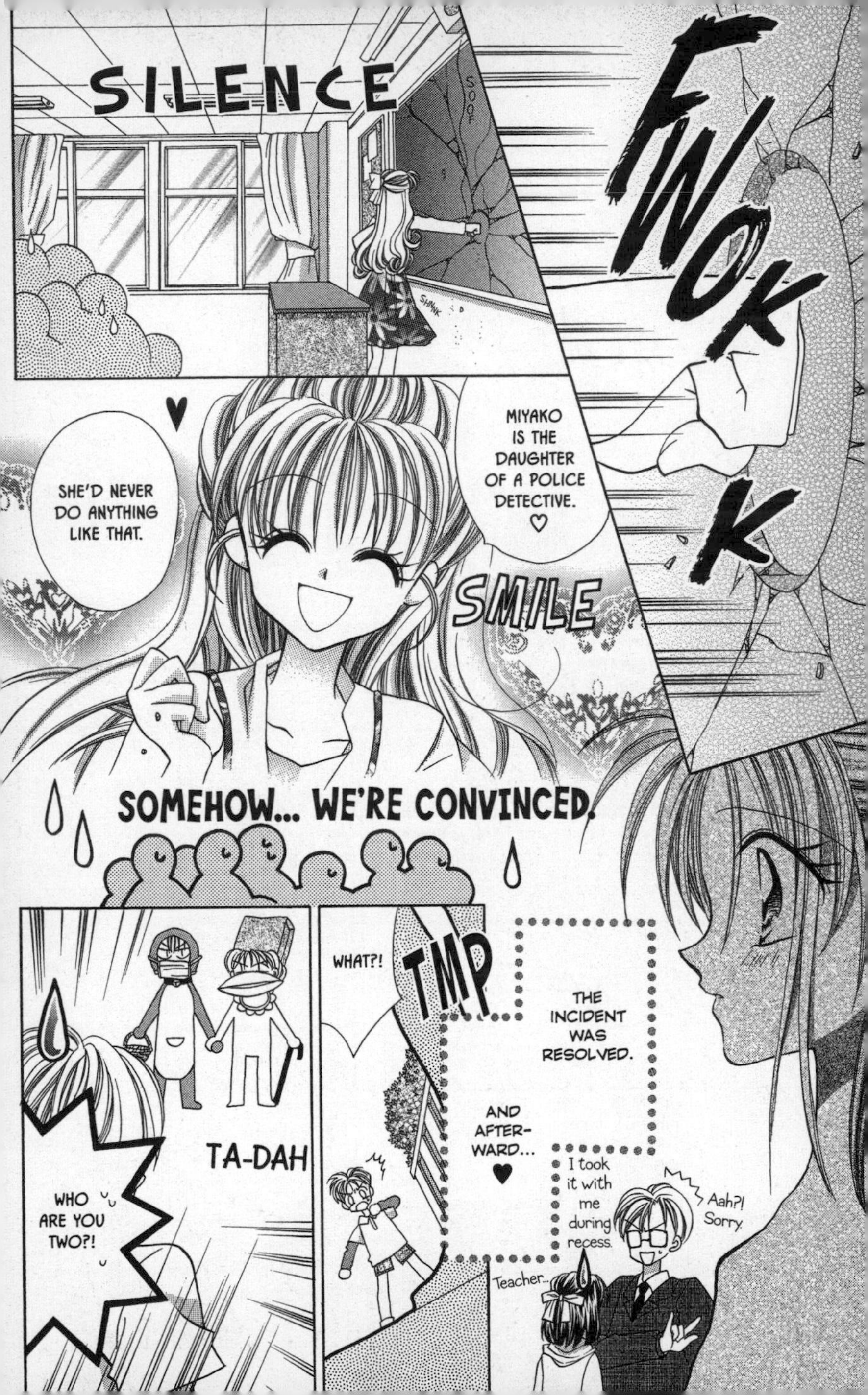
FWOK
SILENCE
SOOF
SHNK
MIYAKO IS THE DAUGHTER OF A POLICE DETECTIVE. ♡
SHE'D NEVER DO ANYTHING LIKE THAT.
SMILE
SOMEHOW... WE'RE CONVINCED.
THE INCIDENT WAS RESOLVED.
AND AFTER-WARD... ♥
I took it with me during recess.
Aah?! Sorry.
Teacher...
TMP
WHAT?!
TA-DAH
WHO ARE YOU TWO?!

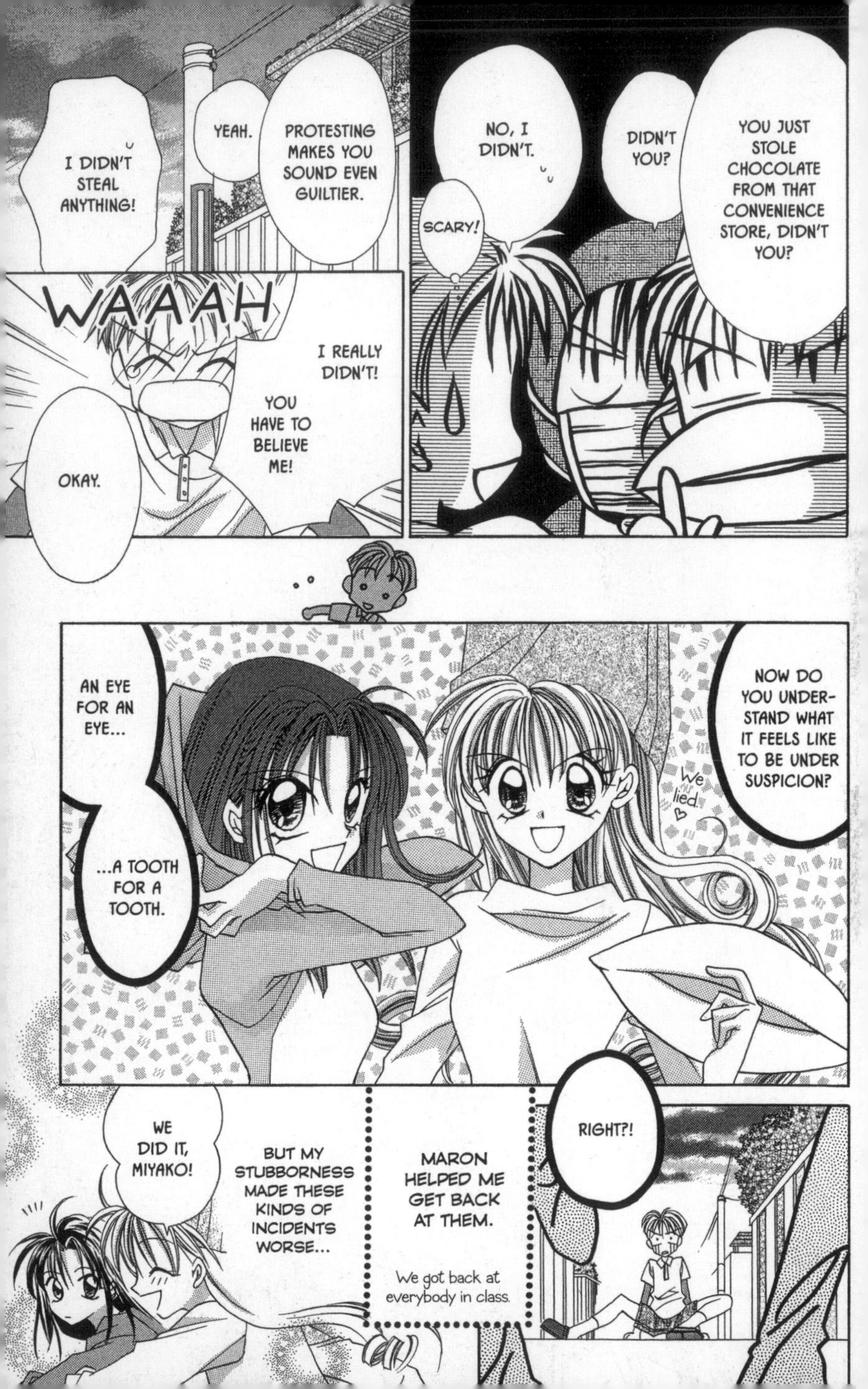
YOU JUST STOLE CHOCOLATE FROM THAT CONVENIENCE STORE, DIDN'T YOU?
DIDN'T YOU?
NO, I DIDN'T.
SCARY!
PROTESTING MAKES YOU SOUND EVEN GUILTIER.
YEAH.
I DIDN'T STEAL ANYTHING!
WAAAH
I REALLY DIDN'T!
YOU HAVE TO BELIEVE ME!
OKAY.
NOW DO YOU UNDER-STAND WHAT IT FEELS LIKE TO BE UNDER SUSPICION?
We lied. ♥
AN EYE FOR AN EYE...
...A TOOTH FOR A TOOTH.
RIGHT?!
MARON HELPED ME GET BACK AT THEM.
We got back at everybody in class.
BUT MY STUBBORNESS MADE THESE KINDS OF INCIDENTS WORSE...
WE DID IT, MIYAKO!

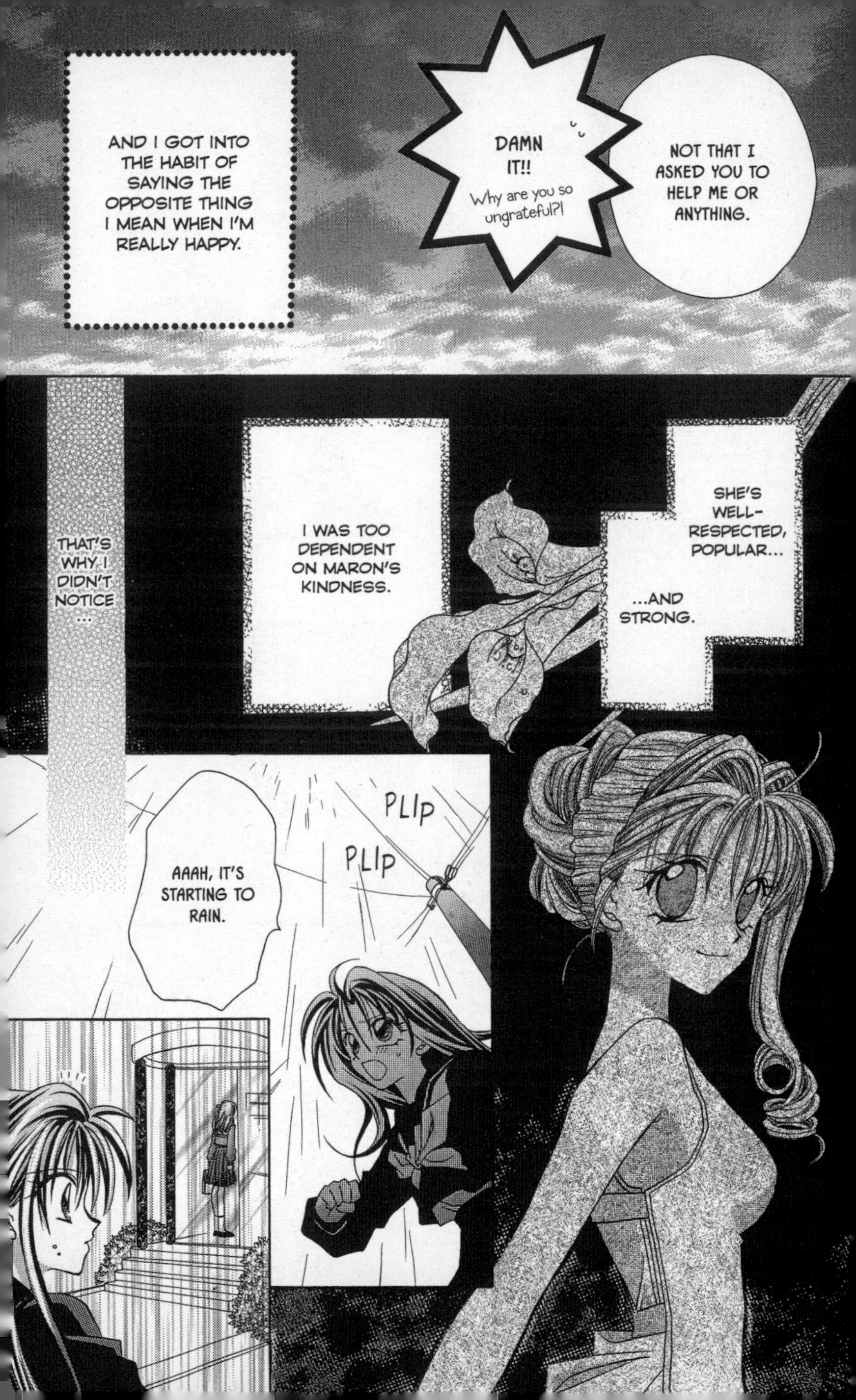
NOT THAT I ASKED YOU TO HELP ME OR ANYTHING.
DAMN IT!!
Why are you so ungrateful?!
AND I GOT INTO THE HABIT OF SAYING THE OPPOSITE THING I MEAN WHEN I'M REALLY HAPPY.
SHE'S WELL-RESPECTED, POPULAR...
...AND STRONG.
I WAS TOO DEPENDENT ON MARON'S KINDNESS.
THAT'S WHY I DIDN'T NOTICE...
PLIP
PLIP
AAAH, IT'S STARTING TO RAIN.

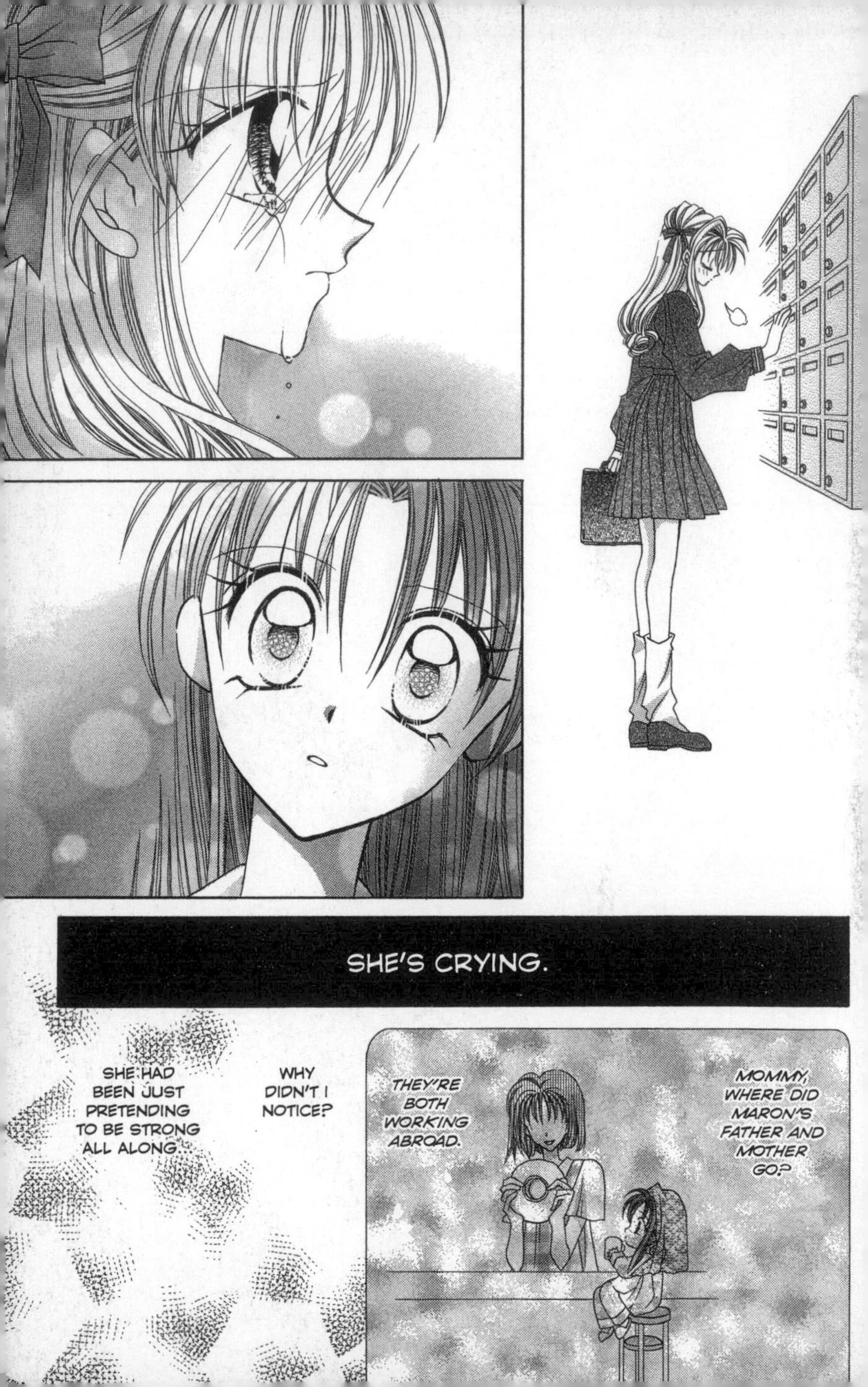
SHE'S CRYING.
MOMMY, WHERE DID MARON'S FATHER AND MOTHER GO?
THEY'RE BOTH WORKING ABROAD.
WHY DIDN'T I NOTICE?
SHE HAD BEEN JUST PRETENDING TO BE STRONG ALL ALONG...

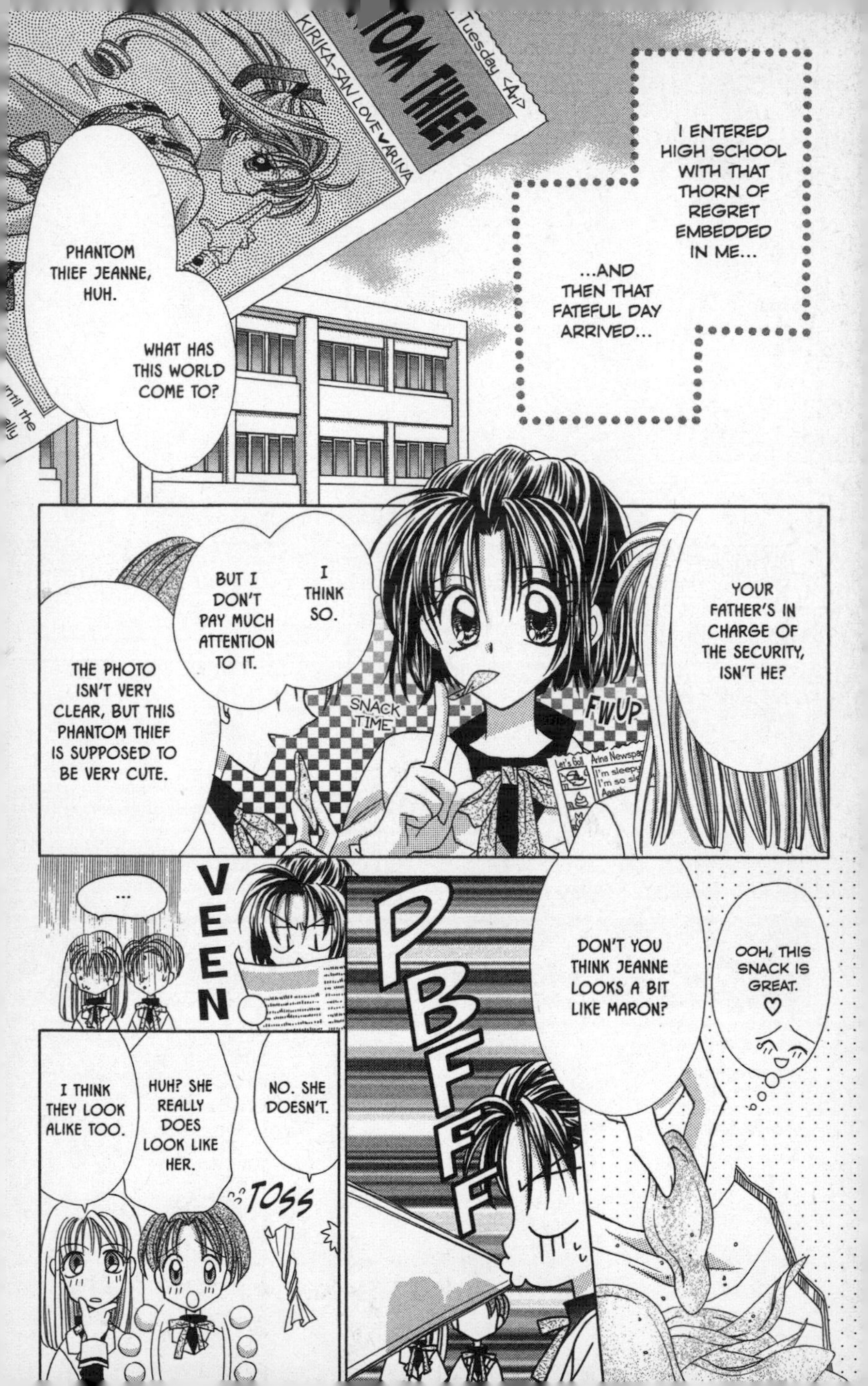
I ENTERED HIGH SCHOOL WITH THAT THORN OF REGRET EMBEDDED IN ME...
...AND THEN THAT FATEFUL DAY ARRIVED...
Tuesday <Ari>
TOM THIEF
KIRIKA-SAN LOVE♥ARINA
PHANTOM THIEF JEANNE, HUH.
WHAT HAS THIS WORLD COME TO?
YOUR FATHER'S IN CHARGE OF THE SECURITY, ISN'T HE?
FWUP
I THINK SO.
BUT I DON'T PAY MUCH ATTENTION TO IT.
SNACK TIME
THE PHOTO ISN'T VERY CLEAR, BUT THIS PHANTOM THIEF IS SUPPOSED TO BE VERY CUTE.
OOH, THIS SNACK IS GREAT. ♡
DON'T YOU THINK JEANNE LOOKS A BIT LIKE MARON?
PBFFF
VEEN
...
NO. SHE DOESN'T.
HUH? SHE REALLY DOES LOOK LIKE HER.
I THINK THEY LOOK ALIKE TOO.
TOSS

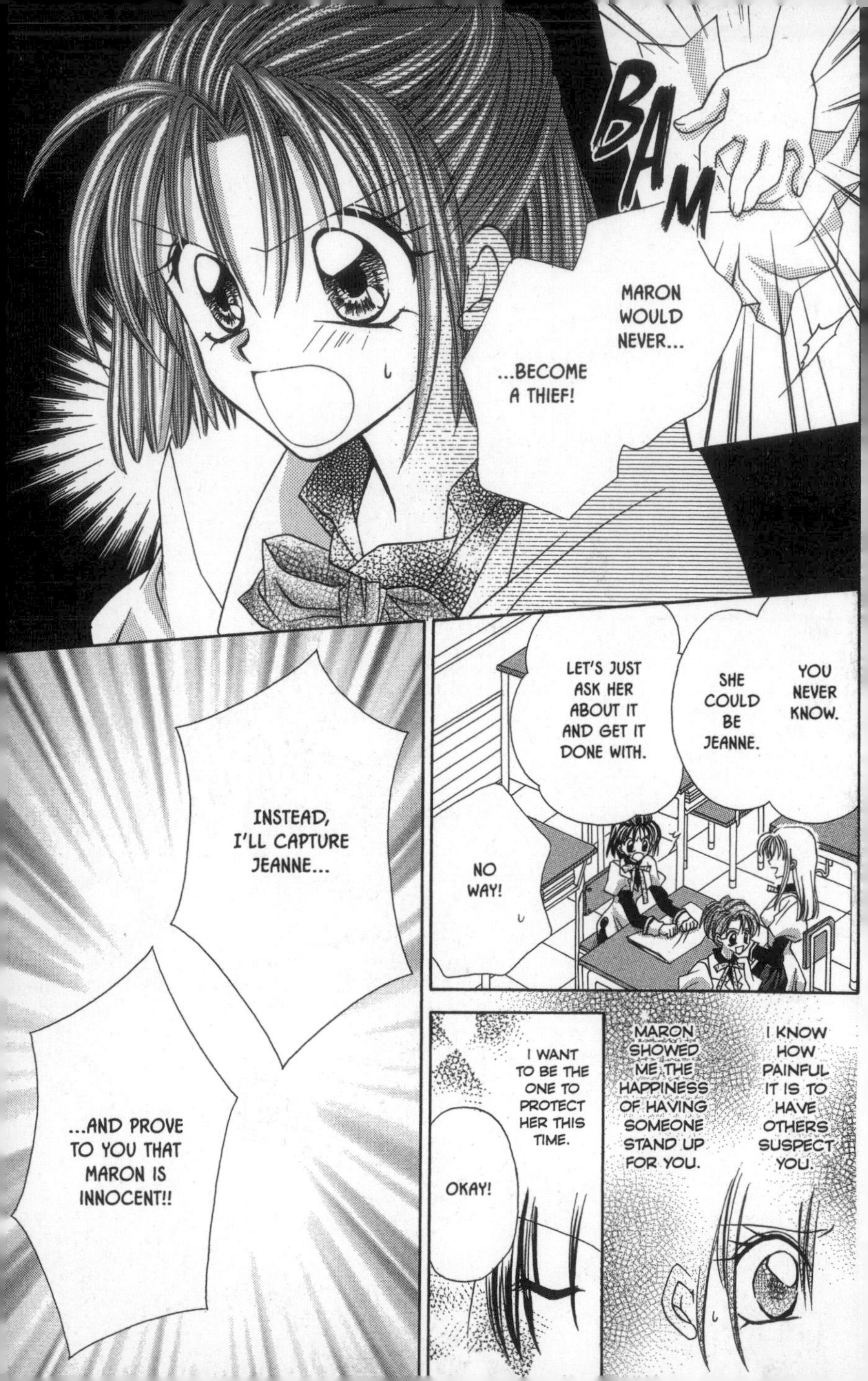
BAM
MARON WOULD NEVER...
...BECOME A THIEF!
YOU NEVER KNOW.
SHE COULD BE JEANNE.
LET'S JUST ASK HER ABOUT IT AND GET IT DONE WITH.
NO WAY!
I KNOW HOW PAINFUL IT IS TO HAVE OTHERS SUSPECT YOU.
MARON SHOWED ME THE HAPPINESS OF HAVING SOMEONE STAND UP FOR YOU.
I WANT TO BE THE ONE TO PROTECT HER THIS TIME.
OKAY!
INSTEAD, I'LL CAPTURE JEANNE...
...AND PROVE TO YOU THAT MARON IS INNOCENT!!

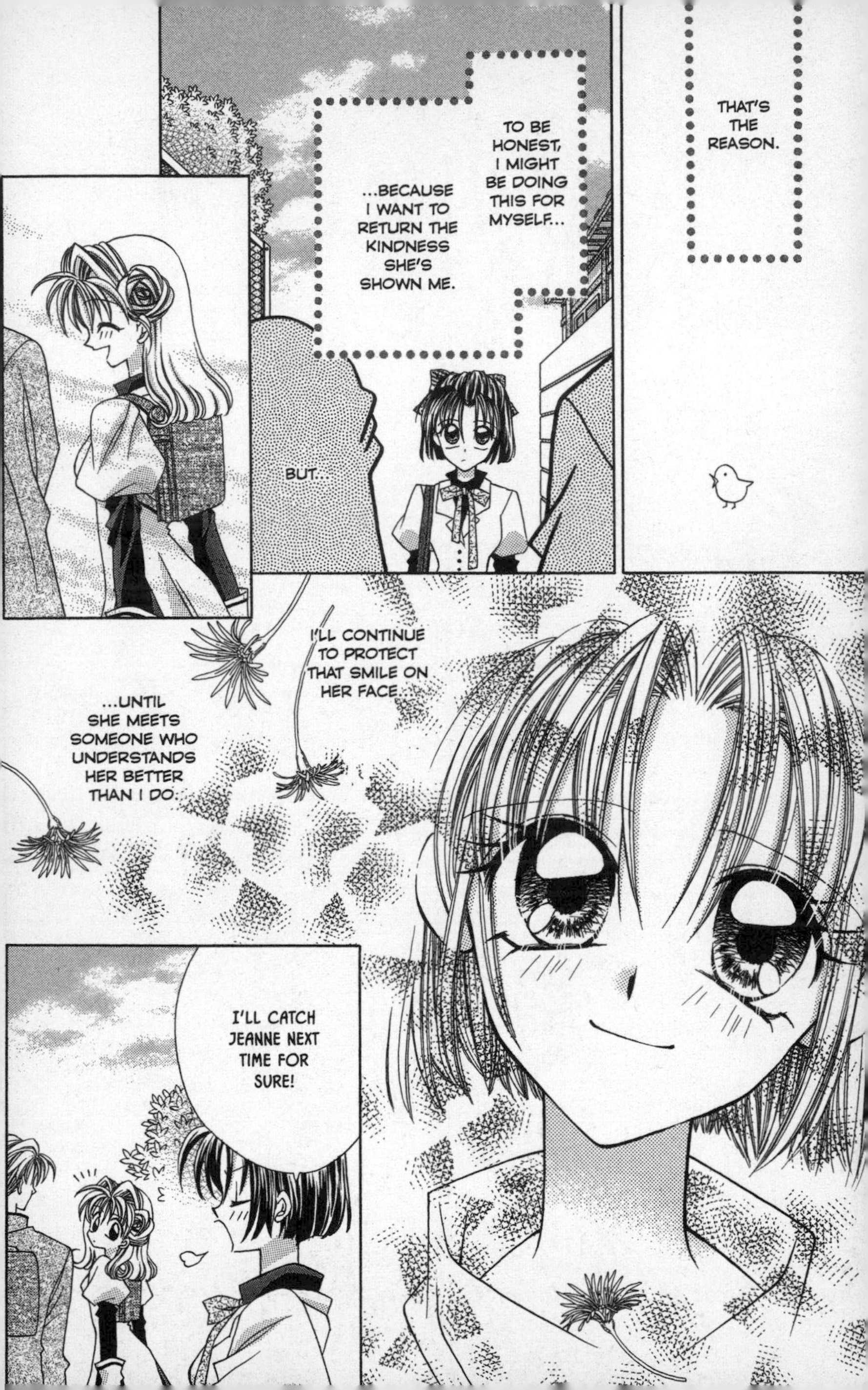
THAT'S THE REASON.
TO BE HONEST, I MIGHT BE DOING THIS FOR MYSELF...
...BECAUSE I WANT TO RETURN THE KINDNESS SHE'S SHOWN ME.
BUT...
I'LL CONTINUE TO PROTECT THAT SMILE ON HER FACE...
...UNTIL SHE MEETS SOMEONE WHO UNDERSTANDS HER BETTER THAN I DO.
I'LL CATCH JEANNE NEXT TIME FOR SURE!

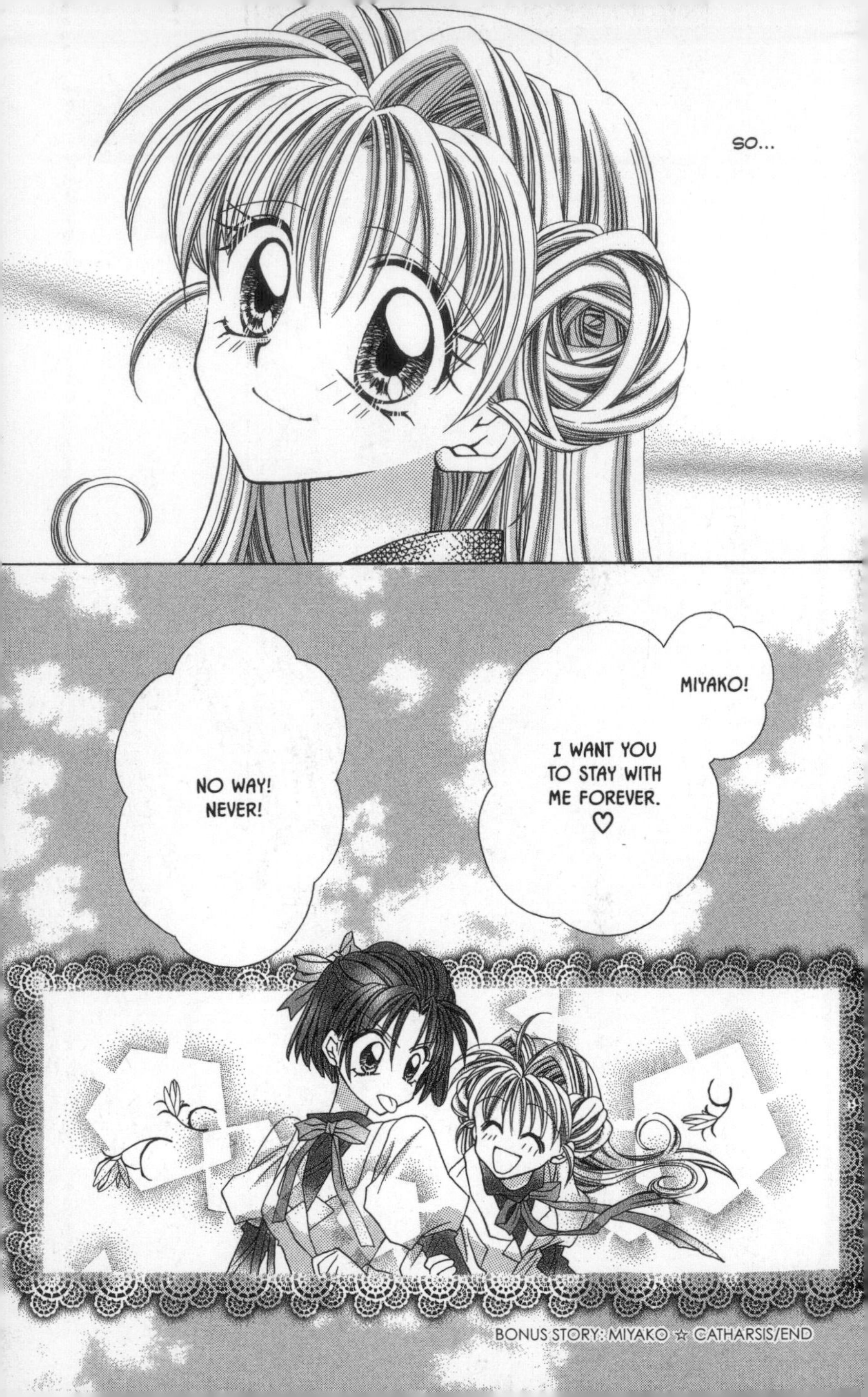
SO...
MIYAKO!
I WANT YOU TO STAY WITH ME FOREVER. ♡
NO WAY! NEVER!
BONUS STORY: MIYAKO ☆ CATHARSIS/END

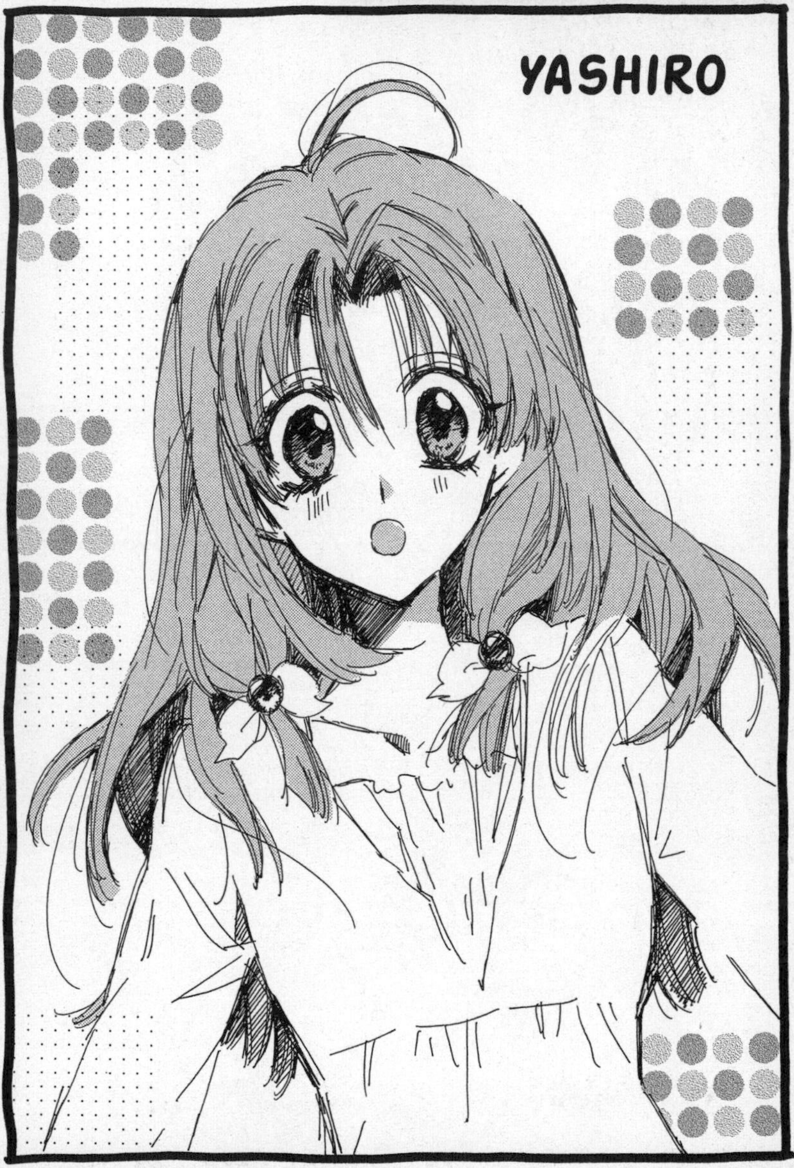
YASHIRO

Jeanne Special Illustrations

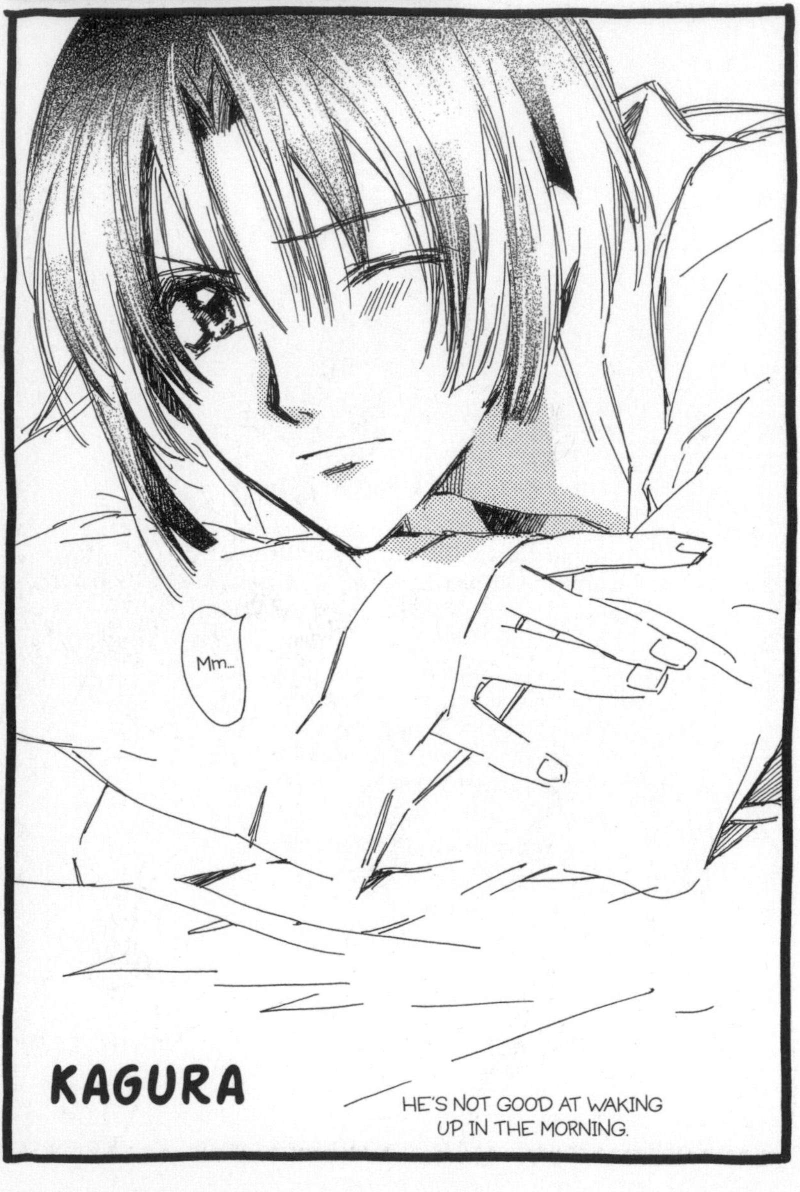
Mm...
KAGURA
HE'S NOT GOOD AT WAKING UP IN THE MORNING.

ARINA TANEMURA

Arina Tanemura began her manga
career in 1996 when her short stories
debuted in *Ribon* magazine. She gained
fame with the 1997 publication of *I·O·N*,
and ever since her debut Tanemura
has been a major force in shojo manga
with popular series *Phantom Thief
Jeanne, Time Stranger Kyoko, Full Moon,*
and *The Gentlemen's Alliance †*. Both
Phantom Thief Jeanne and *Full Moon*
have been adapted into
animated TV series.

PHANTOM THIEF *Jeanne*

VOLUME 2
SHOJO BEAT EDITION

STORY AND ART BY Arina Tanemura

TRANSLATION Tetsuichiro Miyaki
TOUCH-UP ART & LETTERING Inori Fukuda Trant
DESIGN Shawn Carrico
EDITOR Nancy Thistlethwaite

KAMIKAZE KAITO JEANNE © 1998 by Arina Tanemura
All rights reserved.
First published in Japan in 1998 by SHUEISHA Inc., Tokyo.
English translation rights arranged by SHUEISHA Inc.

The stories, characters and incidents mentioned
in this publication are entirely fictional.

No portion of this book may be reproduced or
transmitted in any form or by any means without
written permission from the copyright holders.

Printed in the U.S.A.

Published by VIZ Media, LLC
P.O. Box 77010
San Francisco, CA 94107

10 9 8 7 6 5 4 3 2 1
First printing, May 2014

PARENTAL ADVISORY
PHANTOM THIEF JEANNE is rated
T for Teen and is recommended for
ages 13 and up.
ratings.viz.com

www.viz.com

www.shojobeat.com

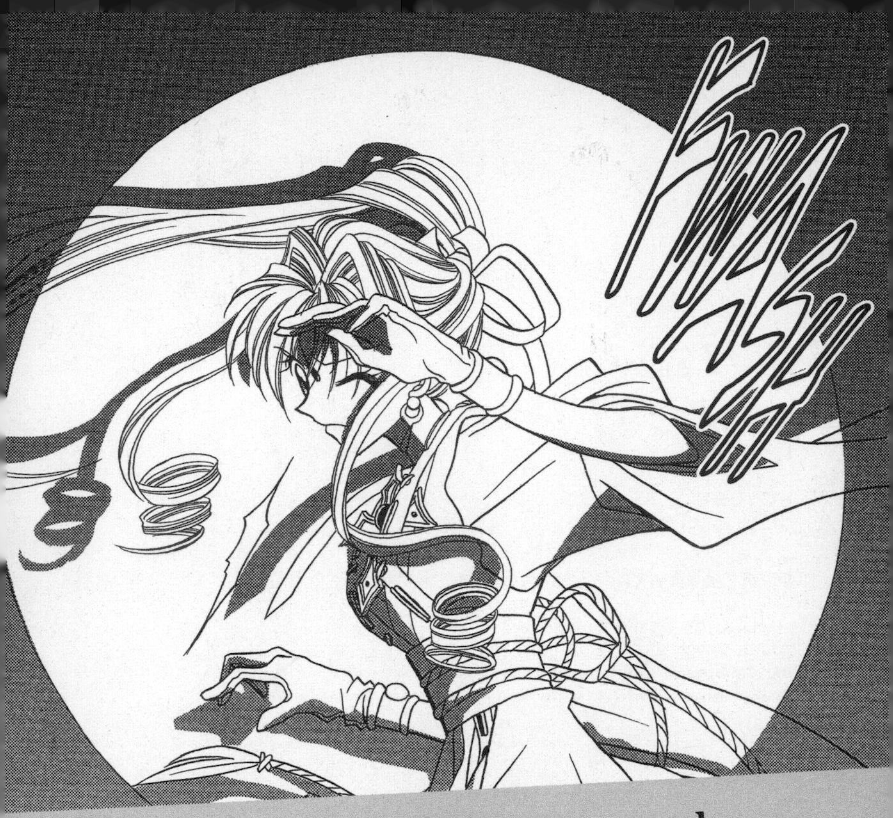

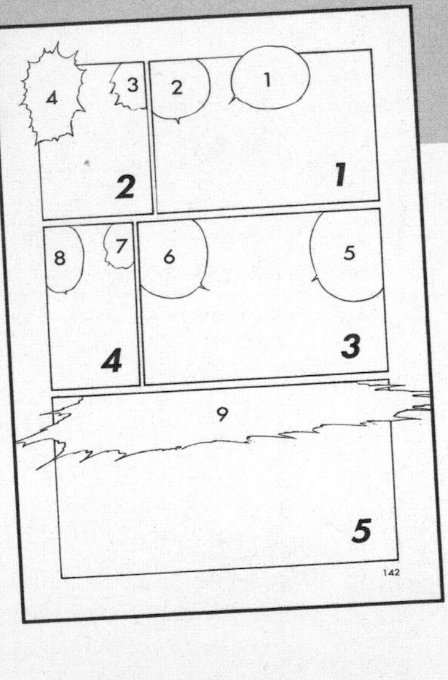

STOP! You may be reading the wrong way!

It's true: In keeping with the original Japanese comic format, this book reads from right to left—so action, sound effects, and word balloons are completely reversed. This preserves the orientation of the original artwork—plus, it's fun! Check out the diagram shown here to get the hang of things, and then turn to the other side of the book to get started!